A·N·N·U·A·L E·D·I·T·I·O·N·S

Human Sexuality 99/00

Twenty-Fourth Edition

EDITOR

Susan J. Bunting
Lincoln College

Susan Bunting is the coordinator of curriculum and instruction at Chestnut Health Systems, a therapist for Employment Development Associates, and an instructor in sociology and psychology at Lincoln College in Illinois. Dr. Bunting received her B.S. and M.S. in sociology and her Ed.D. in curriculum and instruction from Illinois State University. She has taught, counseled, trained, and developed curriculum in human sexuality, sexual abuse, substance abuse, self-esteem, child and human development, learning disabilities, marriage, family, and intimate relationships. Dr. Bunting publishes pamphlets, instructional materials, articles, and books in these areas.

Dushkin/McGraw-Hill
Sluice Dock, Guilford, Connecticut 06437

Visit us on the Internet
http://www.dushkin.com/annualeditions/

Credits

1. Sexuality and Society
Facing overview—© 1999 by PhotoDisc, Inc.
2. Sexual Biology, Behavior, and Orientation
Facing overview—AP/Wide World photo by Darcy Padilla. 43—Illustration by Andres Wenngren.
3. Interpersonal Relationships
Facing overview—United Nations photo by Bedrich Grunzweig.
4. Reproduction
Facing overview—Dushkin/McGraw-Hill illustration by Mike Eagle.
5. Sexuality through the Life Cycle
Facing overview—Photo courtesy of Louis Raucci Jr.
6. Old/New Sexual Concerns
Facing overview—EPA Documerica photo. 215—Illustration by Tom Chalkley.

Copyright

Cataloging in Publication Data
Main entry under title: Annual Editions: Human sexuality. 1999/2000.
      1. Sexual behavior—Periodicals. 2. Sexual Hygiene—Periodicals. 3. Sex education—Periodicals.
4. Human relations—Periodicals. I. Bunting, Susan J., *comp.* II. Title: Human sexuality.
ISBN 0–07–041171–9   155.3'05   75–20756   ISSN 1091-9961

© 1999 by Dushkin/McGraw-Hill, Guilford, CT 06437, A Division of The McGraw-Hill Companies.

Twenty-Fourth Edition

Cover image © 1999 PhotoDisc, Inc.

Printed in the United States of America   1234567890BAHBAH54321098   Printed on Recycled Paper

WITHDRAWN

FEB 2000

To the Reader

In publishing ANNUAL EDITIONS we recognize the enormous role played by the magazines, newspapers, and journals of the public press in providing current, first-rate educational information in a broad spectrum of interest areas. Many of these articles are appropriate for students, researchers, and professionals seeking accurate, current material to help bridge the gap between principles and theories and the real world. These articles, however, become more useful for study when those of lasting value are carefully collected, organized, indexed, and reproduced in a low-cost format, which provides easy and permanent access when the material is needed. That is the role played by ANNUAL EDITIONS.

New to ANNUAL EDITIONS is the inclusion of related World Wide Web sites. These sites have been selected by our editorial staff to represent some of the best resources found on the World Wide Web today. Through our carefully developed topic guide, we have linked these Web resources to the articles covered in this ANNUAL EDITIONS reader. We think that you will find this volume useful, and we hope that you will take a moment to visit us on the Web at *http://www.dushkin.com* to tell us what you think.

Sex lies at the root of life, and we can never learn to reverence life until we know how to understand sex.
—Havelock Ellis

A century ago Havelock Ellis, one of the first sexologists, uttered the objective printed above. Since then, generations of sexologists, sex educators, and books like this one have worked toward that goal. Readers of this edition of *Annual Editions: Human Sexuality 99/00* might wonder if this goal has been accomplished, and they would not be alone. Today many sexuality specialists, as well as others who study sociocultural trends, note that how sexuality is approached, understood, and experienced seems to have changed in some noteworthy ways. Yet in other important ways, sexuality and people's perceptions and experiences have not changed.

While we are all born with basic sexual interests, drives, and desires, human sexuality is a dynamic and complex force that involves psychological and sociocultural dimensions in addition to the physiological ones. Sexuality includes an individual's whole body and personality. We are not born with a fully developed body or mind, but instead we grow and learn; so it is with respect to our sexuality. A great deal of our sexuality is learned. We learn what "appropriate" sexual behavior is, how to express it, when to do so, and under what circumstances. We also learn sexual feelings—positive feelings such as joy and the acceptance of sexuality, or negative and repressive feelings such as guilt and shame.

For much of the past, sexuality received little attention in scientific research and even less within higher education communities. Sex education was perceived as unnecessary, dangerous, or a kind of education inappropriate for the public education setting. The last century has seen changes in these areas. Prime examples include marked changes in the don't-talk-about-it dictum and the resultant explosion of books and articles on sexuality topics available to the public. In addition, the last 35 years have ushered in changes with respect to the traditional double standard, including greater sexual freedom for women with reverberations in gender roles, and more acknowledgement, understanding, and acceptance of the sexuality of people who deviate in some way from the traditional sexual images—those who are handicapped, the young, the aged, the nonmarried, and those who make or are born into less common sexual or relationship choices. However, without the proper understanding referred to in our initial Ellis quote, this expansion in sexual freedom can lead to new forms of sexual bondage rather than to the increased joy and pleasure of healthy sexuality.

Annual Editions: Human Sexuality 99/00 is organized into six sections. *Sexuality and Society* notes historical and cross-cultural views and analyzes our constantly changing society and sexuality. *Sexual Biology, Behavior, and Orientation* explains the functioning and responses of the human body and contains expanded sections on sexual hygiene, diseases and conditions affecting sexuality and functioning, and guides to preventive and ongoing sexual health care. *Interpersonal Relationships* provides suggestions for establishing and maintaining intimate, responsible, quality relationships. *Reproduction* discusses some recent trends related to pregnancy and childbearing and deals with reproductive topics, including conception, contraception, and abortion. *Sexuality through the Life Cycle* looks at what happens sexually throughout one's lifetime—from childhood to the later years. Finally, *Old/New Sexual Concerns* deals with such topics as sexual abuse, rape, sexual harassment, and legal and ethical issues regarding sexual behavior. It closes with a focus on the future of sex, questioning whether changes that have occurred so far (and those to come) will make sexuality and life in the new century better or worse.

Also, in this edition of *Annual Editions: Human Sexuality 99/00* are selected *World Wide Web* sites that can be used to further explore the topics. These sites will be cross-referenced by number in the *topic guide*.

The articles in this anthology have been carefully reviewed and selected for their quality, currency, and interest. They present a variety of viewpoints. Some you will agree with, some you will not, but we hope you will learn from all of them.

Appreciation and thanks go to Loree Adams for her suggestions and expertise; to Bruce Boeck, Mychele Kenney, and Sue LeSeure for their willingness to act as two-way sounding boards; to Monica Shutt for her organization and assistance, to Ollie Pocs for inspiration, and to those who have submitted articles and reviewed previous editions. We feel that *Annual Editions: Human Sexuality 99/00* is one of the most useful and up-to-date books available. Please let us know what you think. Return the postage-paid article rating form on the last page of this book with your suggestions and comments. Any book can be improved. This one will continue to be—annually.

Susan J. Bunting
Editor

Contents

A. HISTORICAL AND CROSS-CULTURAL PERSPECTIVES

B. CHANGING SOCIETY/CHANGING SEXUALITY

UNIT 1

Sexuality and Society

Seven selections consider sexuality from historical and cross-cultural perspectives and examine today's changing attitudes toward human sexual interaction.

The concepts in bold italics are developed in the article. For further expansion please refer to the Topic Guide, the Glossary, and the Index.

UNIT 2

Sexual Biology, Behavior, and Orientation

Ten selections examine the biological aspects of human sexuality, sexual attitudes, hygiene and sexual health care, and sexual orientation.

The concepts in bold italics are developed in the article. For further expansion please refer to the Topic Guide, the Glossary, and the Index.

UNIT 3

Interpersonal Relationships

Six selections examine the dynamics of establishing sexual relationships and the need to make these relationships responsible and effective.

The concepts in bold italics are developed in the article. For further expansion please refer to the Topic Guide, the Glossary, and the Index.

vii

UNIT 4

Reproduction

Five articles discuss the roles
of both males and females in
pregnancy and childbirth and
consider the influences of the
latest birth control methods
and practices on individuals
and society as a whole.

The concepts in bold italics are developed in the article. For further expansion please refer to the Topic Guide, the Glossary, and the Index.

UNIT 5

Sexuality
through the
Life Cycle

Six articles consider human
sexuality as an important element
throughout the life cycle. Topics
include responsible adolescent
sexuality, sex in and out of
marriage, and sex in old age.

UNIT 6

Old/New
Sexual Concerns

Twelve selections discuss ongoing
concerns of sexual abuse, violence,
and harassment, gender roles and
issues, and sex in the media.

The concepts in bold italics are developed in the article. For further expansion please refer to the Topic Guide, the Glossary, and the Index.

The concepts in bold italics are developed in the article. For further expansion please refer to the Topic Guide, the Glossary, and the Index.

The following list of **Human Sexuality** article titles, article numbers (in parenthesis), and page numbers are listed alphabetically for convenience and easy reference:

The concepts in bold italics are developed in the article. For further expansion please refer to the Topic Guide, the Glossary, and the Index.

Topic Guide

This topic guide suggests how the selections and World Wide Web sites found in the next section of this book relate to topics of traditional concern to human sexuality students and professionals. It is useful for locating interrelated articles and Web sites for reading and research. The guide is arranged alphabetically according to topic.

The relevant Web sites, which are numbered and annotated on pages 6 and 7, are easily identified by the Web icon (◎) under the topic articles. By linking the articles and the Web sites by topic, this ANNUAL EDITIONS reader becomes a powerful learning and research tool.

TOPIC AREA	TREATED IN	TOPIC AREA	TREATED IN
Abortion	41. Blocking Women's Health Care 42. Last Abortion ◎ *1, 9, 16, 20, 21, 26*	Gender/Gender Roles (Continued)	31. Raising Sexually Healthy Kids 32. Breaking through the Wall of Silence 34. Joy of Midlife Sex 37. When Preachers Prey 38. Sex @ Work 45. Gender Blur ◎ *4, 5, 6, 9, 10, 14, 16, 17, 29, 32*
Abuse	2. Secrets and Lies 3. Another Planet 4. Where There Is No Village 35. Healing the Scars 36. These Women Uncovered Sexual Slavery in America 37. When Preachers Prey 38. Sex @ Work ◎ *30, 31*	Homosexuality/ Bisexuality	3. Another Planet 15. What Made Troy Gay? 16. Trans across America 17. Can Gays 'Convert'? 29. Where'd You Learn That? 32. Breaking through the Wall of Silence 40. Battling Backlash 45. Gender Blur 46. Sex in the Future ◎ *2, 7, 8, 9, 10, 16, 17, 24, 25, 29, 32*
Aging	5. World Made Flesh 10. Impotency 14. Not Tonight, Baby 22. 'It' Doesn't Just Happen 34. Joy of Midlife Sex ◎ *22, 23, 25*	Legal/Ethical Issues	2. Secrect and Lies 3. Another Planet 12. America: Awash in STDs 15. What Made Troy Gay? 16. Trans across America 17. Can Gays 'Convert'? 29. Where'd You Learn That? 32. Breaking through the Wall of Silence 35. Healing the Scars 36. These Women Uncovered Sexual Slavery in America 37. When Preachers Prey 38. Sex @ Work 39. New Fertility 40. Battling Backlash 41. Blocking Women's Health Care 42. Last Abortion 43. Is Sex a Necessity? 46. Sex in the Future ◎ *1, 2, 20, 26*
Birth Control/ Contraception	2. Secrets and Lies 3. Another Planet 4. Where There Is No Village 24. Protecting against Unintended Pregnancy 25. How Reliable Are Condoms? 29. Where'd You Learn That? 41. Blocking Women's Health Care 46. Sex in the Future ◎ *1, 9, 16, 18, 19, 20, 21, 28*		
Females/Female Sexuality	2. Secrets and Lies 3. Another Planet 4. Where There Is No Village 5. World Made Flesh 6. Feminism: It's All about Me! 9. Your Sexual Landscape 14. Not Tonight, Baby 18. 1997 Body Image Survey 19. Brain Sex 26. Pregnant Pleasures 31. Raising Sexually Healthy Kids 34. Joy of Midlife Sex 35. Healing the Scars 36. These Women Uncovered Sexual Slavery in America 37. When Preachers Prey 38. Sex @ Work 45. Gender Blur ◎ *3, 5, 6, 7, 8, 9, 10, 14, 16, 17, 32*	Males/Male Sexuality	1. In Search of Russia's "Strong Sex" 3. Another Planet 5. World Made Flesh 7. Men in Crisis 10. Impotency 11. Viagra Craze 15. What Made Troy Gay? 19. Brain Sex 20. Men for Sale 27. Six Dads Dish 29. Where'd You Learn That? 31. Raising Sexually Healthy Kids 37. When Preachers Prey 38. Sex @ Work 45. Gender Blur ◎ *7, 8, 9, 10, 13, 14, 15, 16, 17, 29*
Gender/Gender Roles	1. In Search of Russia's "Strong Sex" 5. World Made Flesh 6. Feminism: It's All about Me! 7. Men in Crisis 15. What Made Troy Gay? 16. Trans across America 18. 1997 Body Image Survey 19. Brain Sex 20. Men for Sale 22. 'It' Doesn't Just Happen		

2

● AE: Human Sexuality

The following World Wide Web sites have been carefully researched and selected to support the articles found in this reader. If you are interested in learning more about specific topics found in this book, these Web sites are a good place to start. The sites are cross-referenced by number and appear in the topic guide on the previous two pages. Also, you can link to these Web sites through our DUSHKIN ONLINE support site at *http://www.dushkin.com/online/*.

The following sites were available at the time of publication. Visit our Web site—we update DUSHKIN ONLINE regularly to reflect any changes.

General Sources

1. National Institutes of Health (NIH)
http://www.nih.gov
Consult this site for links to extensive health information and scientific resources. The NIH is one of eight health agencies of the Public Health Service, which, in turn, is part of the U.S. Department of Health and Human Services.

2. SIECUS
http://www.siecus.org
Visit the Sexuality Information and Education Council of the United States (SIECUS) home page to learn about the organization, to find news of its educational programs and activities, and to access links to resources in sexuality education.

Sexuality and Society

3. Human Rights Report: India
http://www.usis.usemb.se/human/india.html
Read this U.S. Department of State USIS (U.S. Information Service) report on India's human rights practices for an understanding of the issues that affect women's mental and physical health and well-being in different parts of the world.

4. National Organization of Circumcision Information Resource Centers (NOCIRC)
http://nocirc.org
This is the home page of the NOCIRC, which describes itself as "a nonprofit educational organization committed to securing the birthright of male and female children and babies to keep their sexual organs intact." It disseminates material about male and female circumcision.

5. Q Web Sweden: A Women's Empowerment Base
http://www.qweb.kvinnoforum.se/index.htm
This site will lead you to a number of pages addressing women's health issues and discussing societal issues related to sex. It provides interesting cross-cultural perspectives.

6. SocioSite: Feminism and Woman Issues
http://www.pscw.uva.nl/sociosite/TOPICS/Women.html
Open this University of Amsterdam Sociology Department's site to gain insights into a number of issues that affect both men and women. It provides biographies of women in history, an international network for women in the workplace, and links to family and children issues, and more.

Sexual Biology, Behavior, and Orientation

7. Bibliography: HIV/AIDS and College Students
http://www.sph.emory.edu/bshe/AIDS/college.html
This Emory University site contains an in-print bibliography of articles dealing with HIV/AIDS and college students. Some 75 articles addressing sexual behaviors and behaviors related to HIV/Aids, primarily from academic and professional journals, are listed.

8. The Body: A Multimedia AIDS and HIV Information Resource
http://www.thebody.com/cgi-bin/body.cgi
On this site you can find the basics about AIDS/HIV, learn about treatments, exchange information in forums, and gain insight from experts.

9. Healthy Way
http://www.ab.sympatico.ca/Contents/Health/GENERAL/sitemap.html
This Canadian site, which is directed toward consumers, will lead you to many links related to sexual orientation. It also addresses aspects of human sexuality over the life span, general health, and reproductive health.

10. Hispanic Sexual Behavior and Gender Roles
http://www.caps.ucsf.edu/hispnews.html
This research report from the University of California at San Francisco Center for AIDS Prevention Studies describes and analyzes Hispanic sexual behavior and gender roles, particularly as regards prevention of STDs and HIV/AIDS. It discusses gender and cultural differences in sexual behavior and expectations and other topics of interest.

11. James Kohl
http://www.pheromones.com
Keeping in mind that this is a commercial site with the goal of selling a book, look here to find topics of interest to nonscientists about pheromones. Links to related material of a more academic nature are included. Check out the diagram of "Mammalian Olfactory-Genetic-Neuronal-Hormonal-Behavioral Reciprocity and Human Sexuality" for a sense of the myriad biological influences that play a part in sexual behavior.

12. Johan's Guide to Aphrodisiacs
http://www.santesson.com/aphrodis/aphrhome.htm
"The Aphrodisiac Home Page" provides links to information about a multitude of substances that some believe arouse or increase sexual response or cause or increase sexual desire. Skepticism about aphrodisiacs is also discussed.

Interpersonal Relationships

13. American Psychological Association
http://www.apa.org/psychnet/
By exploring the APA's "PsychNET," you will be able to find links to an abundance of articles and other resources related to interpersonal relationships throughout the life span.

14. Bonobos Sex and Society
http://soong.club.cc.cmu.edu/~julie/bonobos.html
This site, accessed through Carnegie Mellon University, includes an article explaining how a primate's behavior challenges traditional assumptions about male supremacy in human evolution.

15. The Celibate FAQ
http://mail.bris.ac.uk/~plmlp/celibate.html
Martin Poulter's definitions, thoughts, and suggested resources on celibacy, created, he says, "in response to the lack of celibate stuff (outside religious contexts) on the Internet," and his perception of the Net's bias against celibacy can be found on this site.

16. Go Ask Alice
http://www.goaskalice.columbia.edu
This interactive site provided by Healthwise, a division of Columbia University Health Services, includes discussion and insight into a number of personal issues of interest to college-age people—and those younger and older. Many questions about physical and emotional health and well-being in the modern world are answered.

17. Sex and Gender
http://www.bioanth.cam.ac.uk/pip4amod3.html
Use the syllabus, lecture titles, and readings noted in this site to explore sexual differentiation in human cultures, the genetics of sexual differentiation, and the biology of sex roles in nonhumans.

Reproduction

18. Ask NOAH About Pregnancy: Fertility & Infertility
http://www.noah.cuny.edu/pregnancy/fertility.html
New York Online Access to Health (NOAH) seeks to provide relevant, timely, and unbiased health information for consumers. At this site, the organization presents extensive links to a variety of resources about infertility treatments and issues.

19. Childbirth.Org
http://www.childbirth.org
This interactive site about childbirth options is from an organization that aims to educate consumers to know their options and provide themselves with the best possible care to ensure healthy pregnancies and deliveries. The site and its links address a myriad of topics, from episiotomy to water birth.

20. Medically Induced Abortion
http://medicalabortion.com/index.htm
Access this home page of physician Richard Hausknecht to read his very detailed New England Journal of Medicine article about medical abortion using methotrexate and misoprostol. A bibliography is included.

21. Planned Parenthood
http://www.plannedparenthood.org
Visit this well-known organization's home page for links to information on the various kinds of contraceptives (including outercourse and abstinence) and to discussions of other topics related to sexual and reproductive health.

Sexuality through the Life Cycle

22. American Association of Retired Persons (AARP)
http://www.aarp.org
The AARP, a major advocacy group for older people, includes among its many resources suggested readings and Internet links to organizations that deal with the health and social issues that may affect one's sexuality as one ages.

23. National Institute on Aging (NIA)
http://www.nih.gov/nia/
The NIA, one of the institutes of the National Institutes of Health, presents this home page to lead you to a variety of resources on health and lifestyle issues that are of interest to people as they grow older.

24. Teacher Talk
http://education.indiana.edu/cas/tt/tthmpg.html
This home page of the publication Teacher Talk from the Indiana University School of Education Center for Adolescent Studies will lead you to many interesting teacher comments, suggestions, and ideas regarding sexuality education and how to deal with sex issues in the classroom.

25. World Association for Sexology
http://www.tc.umn.edu/nlhome/m201/colem001/was/wasindex.htm
The World Association for Sexology works to further the understanding and development of sexology throughout the world. Access this site to explore a number of issues and links related to sexuality throughout life.

Old/New Sexual Concerns

26. Abortion Law Homepage
http://members.aol.com/_ht_a/abtrbng/index.htm
This page explains the background and state of abortion law in the United States. Roe v. Wade, Planned Parenthood v. Casey, feticide cases, and statutes are among the important subects discussed.

27. Cyber Romance 101
http://web2.airmail.net/walraven/romance.htm
This interactive site explores a very '90s topic: relationships forged on the Internet. Browse here to hear various viewpoints on the issue. Advice columnists and psychologists add their perspectives.

28. Infertility Resources
http://www.ihr.com/infertility/index.html
This site includes links to the Oregon Health Sciences University Fertility Program and the Center for Reproductive Growth in Nashville, Tennessee. Ethical, legal, financial, psychological, and social issues are discussed.

29. Men's Health Resource Guide
http://www.menshealth.com/new/guide/index.html
This resource guide from Men's Health presents many links to topics in men's health, from AIDS/STDs, to back pain, to impotence and infertility, to vasectomy. It also includes discussions of relationship and family issues.

30. Other Sexual Violence Resources on the Web
http://www.witserv.com/org/ocrcc/resource/resource.htm
Open this useful site for links to other sexual violence pages. For example, it has a link to "Men against Rape," a site maintained by the D.C. Men against Rape organization, providing men's perspectives on sexual violence.

31. Sexual Assault Information Page
http://www.cs.utk.edu/~bartley/saInfoPage.html
This invaluable site provides dozens of links to information and resources on a variety of sexual assault–related topics: child sexual abuse, date rape, incest, secondary victims, and offenders.

32. Women's Studies Resources
http://www.inform.umd.edu/EdRes/Topic/WomensStudies/
This site from the University of Maryland provides a wealth of resources related to women's studies. You can find links to such topics as body image, comfort (or discomfort) with sexuality, personal relationships, pornography, and more.

We highly recommend that you review our Web site for expanded information and our other product lines. We are continually updating and adding links to our Web site in order to offer you the most usable and useful information that will support and expand the value of your Annual Editions. You can reach us at:
http://www.dushkin.com/annualeditions/.

www.dushkin.com/online/

Unit Selections

Key Points to Consider

❖ Is it harder or easier to be your gender today than it was for your parents' or grandparents' generations? Why? Do you think the changes in gender roles enhance or inhibit sexual relationships and intimacy? Why?

❖ What kind of sex education did you have in elementary school? In junior high? In high school? When do you think education about anatomy, physiology, and reproduction should start? Should the nature of the classes change as students get older? If so, how and why?

❖ Have you ever spoken to a young person from another culture/country about sexuality-related ideas, norms, education, or behavior? If so, what surprised you? What did you think about their perspective or ways?

❖ Will there always be "secrets" with respect to sex? Why or why not and is this desirable? What kinds of things have you kept or would you keep secret from peers, parents, employers, people in general, or partners?

❖ What do you make of the increased popularity of body-piercing, tattooing, and other body adornments for both genders and wider age groups?

 **Links**   **www.dushkin.com/online/**

These sites are annotated on pages 4 and 5.

People of different civilizations in different historical periods have engaged in a variety of modes of sexual expression and behavior. Despite this cultural and historical diversity, one important principle should be kept in mind: Sexual awareness, attitudes, and behaviors are learned within sociocultural contexts that define appropriate sexuality for society's members. Our sexual attitudes and behaviors are in large measure social and cultural phenomena. As articles were gathered for the last edition of the twentieth century, the veracity of the statements in the preceding paragraph was reinforced. More so than ever before the topics and issues discussed in the international media matched those found in the U.S. media. Although the cross-cultural perspective on sexuality is broader and more varied, it is becoming increasingly clear that, as the twenty-first century approaches, the gap between differences and similarities between people all over the world has indeed narrowed. As a result, an article found in an international magazine, *India Today International,* is not included in the first unit's cross-cultural section, but in the section devoted to its topic, impotency and sexual dysfunction.

For several centuries, Western civilization, especially Western European and, in turn, American cultures, have been characterized by an "antisex ethic." This belief system includes a variety of negative views and norms about sex and sexuality, including denial, fear, restriction, and the detachment of sexual feelings and behavior from the wholeness of personhood or humanity. Indeed, it has only been in the last 50 years that the antisex proscriptions against knowing or learning about sex have lost their stranglehold so that people can find accurate information about their sexual health, sexual functioning, and birth control without fear of stigma or even incarceration.

Sociologists and others who study human behavior agree that social change in beliefs, norms, or behavior is not easily accomplished. When it does occur it is linked to significant changes in the social environment and usually happens as a result of interest groups that move society to confront and question existing beliefs, norms, and behavior. Changes in the social environment that have been most often linked to changes in sexuality and its expression include the invention of the car, the liberation of women from the kitchen, changes in the legality and availability of birth control, the reconsideration of democratic values of individual freedom and the pursuit of happiness, the growth of mass media, and the coming of the computer age. The social groups that have been involved in the process of this sexual-social change have also been far-reaching. They include the earliest feminists, the suffragettes; Margaret Sanger, the mother of the birth control movement; mainstream religious groups that insist that "sexuality is a good gift from God"; publishers of sex education curricula for youth; pioneering researchers like Alfred Kinsey, Havelock Ellis, William Masters, Virginia Johnson and others; and a panorama of interest groups advocating changes, demanding rights, or both. Many events, people, and perspectives have played a role in sexuality beliefs and behaviors today.

Still it is clear that many things have changed with respect to sexuality and society. One of the most dramatic is from the 'don't-talk-about-it' to an 'everyone's-talking-about-it' communication norm. This year's examples range from baby-boomer women and menopause to President Clinton and oral sex. However, it is also clear that some things have not changed as much as we might expect, given the increased talk, information, and availability of birth control and other sex health products and services. It is not characteristic for the majority of people of any age to feel comfortable with and communicate about sexual feelings, fears, needs, and desires. Negotiating, even understanding, consent and responsibility seems even harder today than when we were not talking. The incidence of unplanned, unwed, and teenage pregnancies, sexually transmitted diseases (some life-threatening), molestation, incest, rape, and sexual harassment continue to be troubling. At the same time, despite more knowledge than ever before and the efforts of many in the educational, medical, and political spheres, the dream of healthy, positive, fulfilling sexuality still eludes individuals and society as a whole.

This unit overviews historical, cross-cultural, and current issues and trends in order to illustrate the connectedness of our values, practices, and experiences of sexuality. In so doing it is meant to challenge readers to adopt a very broad perspective through which their examination of today's sexuality, and their experience of it, can be more meaningful. Only in so doing can we hope to avoid a fear-based return to the "antisex ethic" of the past while striving to evaluate the impact and value of the social changes that have so profoundly affected sexuality at the dawn of the twenty-first century.

The articles in the first subsection, *Historical and Cross-Cultural Perspectives*, reveal some surprising contradictions and paradoxes in sexuality and society. The first two articles focus on gender roles, but they deal with modern-day male images and roles in Russia and Great Britain. The next two articles expose the often significant disparities between public and private realities regarding sexual dimensions of life. In "Secrets and Lies" the apparent success of Peru's governmental family planning programming is shown to have a darker side. The final article in this subsection, "Where There Is No Village: Teaching about Sexuality in Crisis Situations," addresses sex education needs of African refugee youth. Each article invites readers to question why cultures dictate and/or proscribe certain beliefs, values, and practices and how these belief systems can help or harm the individuals, the society involved, and/or humanity as a whole.

The four articles that make up the second subsection, *Changing Society/Changing Sexuality,* address pivotal issues of sexuality today. Each attempts to place these changes within a historic perspective while discussing the conflicting assessments and uncertain future of these changes. Bodies and what they mean and represent are (un)covered in "The World Made Flesh." The next two articles ring some warning bells about the current and future direction that gender roles, identities, and relationships seem to be taking.

Sexuality and Society

In Search of Russia's "Strong Sex"

By Anna Hoare

In an interview with *Novye Izvestiya,* Russian actress Alla Demidova recalled visiting the home of Vladimir ["Volodya"] Vysotsky, with whom she had acted in *The Cherry Orchard* and *Hamlet* {see **RL**, February 1998}. Demidova was met at the door by Vysotsky's wife, Marina Vladi, who was holding a drill. Marina, Demidova asked, slightly confused, what are you doing?

"I'm putting in nails in the bathroom," Vladi replied.

"But what about Volodya?"

"Oh, Volodya, he's lying around on the couch like a Russian *muzhik.*"

Then there is this story, as told by writer Karem Rashem: "The greatest soldier in the history of Russia was General Gorbatov. In his youth, he swore that he would speak only the truth under any circumstances until his death. When he was told before the war: tomorrow you will go out and announce before the regiment that your division commander is an enemy of the people, he went out and said: my division commander is *not* an enemy of the people. And he was sent to the *gulag.*"

These two sketches illustrate the conflicting images of Russian men in today's society. Tough, high-minded *muzhiks* or weak brats, spoiled by their women? In films and in fiction, you will find both pictures. And perhaps both are accurate. Certainly, the image of Russian men has changed since the Second World War, along with women's expectations. So what does this image look like today?

From Hero to Anti-Hero

Time was, there was a simple answer to the question "What do you want to be when you grow up?" Many Russian boys would have said "a soldier." Their role models—Vasily Gubanov, Alexei Batalov, Vyacheslav Tikhonov—were actors in World War II movies playing soldiers or spies. They were tough and stoic, their principles were uncompromising and

they were willing to lay down their lives for the motherland without question.

Karem Rashem, a proponent of traditional military values, said he still believes in this image of the soldier. "Why is the army maintained?" he asked rhetorically. "To strengthen the state, of course. An officer is its main support, its example of honor and dignity. Therefore, metaphorically speaking, his readiness to fight must be displayed everywhere and serve as an example for the entire male population of our country." In Rashem's opinion, a soldier is equated with a real man: " . . . the greatness of a soldier, of a real man, cannot exist without bondage, without sacred duties to his family, business and country."

Not surprisingly, young Russian men these days balk at such enormous responsibilities. To be expected to be a pillar of support to country and family, to carry the world on your shoulders—all of this is a bit too much to stomach. The army has been thoroughly discredited by the fiascoes in Afghanistan and Chechnya, and today's "heroes" of popular culture are much more likely to be successful young mobsters. According to the Editor-in-Chief of the Russian Edition of *Men's Health,* Ilya Bezouglyi, "the macho image has become stronger since *perestroika,* when this new class of mobsters appeared. It's a new, very visible slice of society—these bad guys who don't try to hide that they are bad guys. . . . A lot of Russian men from the middle class, lower middle class, they just look at these guys and they find that they are very attractive."

Of course, to young men who are struggling to get by, the lives of New Russian gangsters look like pure glamour. These "heroes" are in their 20s or, at most, 30s, they sport maroon jackets, drive Mercedes or BMWs and fling their money around in flashy nightclubs and on fancy girls. Who cares how they came by it! Several years ago, Bezouglyi said, it was all the rage for ordinary guys to dress up like mobsters and even adopt their mannerisms. And to some extent, this holds true

From *Russian Life* magazine, May 1998, pp. 8-16. © 1998 by *Russian Life.* (ph.800-639-4301) Reprinted by permission.

to this day. No wonder traditionalists like Rashem are bemoaning the state of contemporary Russian Morals.

New Style

But, thankfully, gangsters are not the only ideal Russian guys are striving for. For one thing, according to Yuliya Menshova, host of the popular TV talk show *Ya Sama* (On My Own), the image of a "real man" in Russia is no longer as categorical as it used to be. A middle class is springing up {see **RL**, November 1997}, she said, made up largely of young, urban males with a Western outlook and money to spend. As Bezouglyi noted: "a new population of Russian males has appeared during the last ten years ... there are enough young, ambitious, relatively successful career-oriented Russian males—professionals and young businessmen who care about their health, don't want to be like their parents. They want to live longer, they want to look better, and they care about things like grooming, health, sex, career, success . . . they're kind of tired of experimenting with their health and they're tired of all these extremes they've had to face. They're striving for a normal, stable, quiet life."

With such men, as with their gangster brothers, image is key. They buy up grooming products—cologne, aftershave, deodorant—like there's no tomorrow and spend a large proportion of their income on clothing (according to Bezouglyi, proportionally much more than Americans). "Russia is still a semi-Asian country," he said, "and image still means a lot here. They still try to show off, they still try to look better than they are, they're a bit more expansive . . ."

Presidential Press Secretary Sergei Yastrzhembsky is an example of one who has perfected his image. Known as a snappy dresser, his suits are impeccable, his tie collection impressive (it is said that his ties do not repeat themselves more often than once every three months). Looking at him, the words "refined" and "sophisticated" leap to mind. Yastrzhembsky is a connoisseur of wine and French cooking, as well as a long-time tennis player. He is also quick on his toes in the political arena and has been credited with smoothing over Yeltsin's gaffes and repairing the presidential image on many an occasion. In a poll taken last December, Yastrzhembsky's personal image-making showed its results: he was voted 19th among Russia's most influential political players—two notches above the Defense Minister.

Still, image is often reserved to clothes and grooming. Working out has yet to catch on in a big way, even though gym chains like Gold's and World Class are becoming increasingly popular among New Russians. Your average Ivan, on the other hand, is more likely to kick a soccer ball around with his friends on a Saturday, if he engages in any kind of exercise at all.

What Women Want

When it comes to women's expectations, Menshova feels that there is a world of difference between the image and the

> **"Over here, a man is still a man, and it's much easier to be a man here. You can be a total male chauvinist pig here and feel perfectly fine. It's very accepted—by women too."**
> —*Ilya Bezough*

truth: "It's no longer the case," she said, "that the man must earn money in order to be called a real man, it is no longer necessary to be the best, strong, to cope with all difficulties—things that women used to lay on men's shoulders." Now, she said, if a woman earns money, then inwardly, that woman is not terribly worried if her man is not the "locomotive of the family."

Outwardly, though, it's a different story. For, Menshova argued, women are not yet risking to express these thoughts out loud: "Nominally, the image remains the same, women still support the outward feeling that such a man is important to them, while inside, in essence, they have long been at peace with an equal situation—I earn money, my husband earns money, maybe I earn more than he does."

Menshova herself thinks of her father, Vladimir Menshov—director of the 1981 Oscar winner *Moscow Does Not Believe in Tears*, as embodying many of the traits of a "real Russian man." "He is very active, inventive, he takes the initiative, makes decisions. . . . With him, it is fun and interesting. . . . In this, his character coincides with the ideal of a man. The dream of Russian women, then and now, is Gosha in *Moscow Does Not Believe in Tears*. Papa shares many of Gosha's characteristics." In the film, Gosha is a jack-of-all-trades, by turns a gallant cavalier, an accomplished cook and the right guy to have around in a fight. In his own way, he is both macho and caring.

In the realm of romance, Moscow journalist Alla Pavlova listed spiritual conversations and walks under the moon as big turn-ons. She also had some rather sarcastic advice to give to potential suitors (evidently caused by bad date experiences in the past!): carry more money in your pocket than the cost of a metro token, don't expect to charm a woman while drunk, forget about your deep passion for computers or cars. And, oh yeah, don't forget to use deodorant.

In an interview with *Komsomolskaya Pravda*, feminist icon Maria Arbatova talked about the kind of man she finds sexually attractive: "Apart from his appearance, he must be a personality. I like realized men and not crybabies. As soon as a man begins to talk about how hard life is, all my erogenous zones atrophy."

But progressive women like Menshova and Arbatova hardly speak for all of Russia. For their social and economic positions give them the kind of freedom that most lack. As Bezouglyi put it, the majority of Russian women "are still very much dependent on their boyfriends or husbands. It's still like in the

States back in the '50s—they want to stay home, they're sick and tired of working in an aggressive environment full of sexual harassment, accidents, so they expect a lot of support from men. It's kind of hard to be a man in Russia these days because you not only have to be responsible for your family, financially and emotionally, you also very often find yourself being the only one who brings the money home, and women do expect that. . . . And, as anywhere else in the world, they expect men to be giving and sharing and emotional, but very tough at the same time."

"Of course," he added, "Russian females never pay on dates, never. Even women with high incomes . . . have told me that they sometimes offer to pay for themselves. But if a guy actually accepts this offer, forget it, they will never meet him again."

> **"I would not say that Russian men are particularly romantic because, in most cases, flowers, helping with a coat, etc., happen rather automatically, and they don't contain any especially romantic meaning . . . For me, it is even unpleasant because it is a stereotype . . ."**
>
> —*Yulia Menshova*

More Girls Than Boys

Russia has always suffered from a shortage of men (currently men make up only 47% of the total population). After the Second World War, in which 27 million Soviets were killed and the bulk of the casualties were male, this shortage was especially acute. There was even a popular song in the 1960s that went: *na desyat devchyonok po statistike devyat rebyat* ("according to statistics, there are only nine boys for ten girls"). In many ways, this "deficit" has placed Russian men in an enviable position. Not only are they sought after, they also have more choice. And yet, as Alexander Vorobyov, Editor-in-Chief of *Medved* (Bear) magazine, said: "when there are more women than men, a man has less stimulus to 'win his girl.' Although this is still a question of a man's ambition."

The deficit of men has other consequences as well. "We're kind of spoiled here," Bezouglyi admitted wryly. "People in the States, they watch their mouth much more, they behave themselves, political correctness, all that. Over here, a man is still a man, and it's much easier to be a man here. You can be a total male chauvinist pig here and feel perfectly fine. It's very accepted—by women too." Promiscuity among men is also quite accepted, if not outright admired. Many Russians, for instance, cannot understand what all the fuss is about when it comes to President Bill Clinton's ongoing sex scandals. Attitudes range from "Big deal!" to "Way to go, Bill!"

So, in many ways, Russia remains a traditional society. There is still the notion of men's work (outside the home) and women's work (taking care of the home, including everything from child care, to cooking, to—it appears—putting in nails in the bathroom), and a woman is expected to cope with these tasks whether or not she has a job outside the home.

One of the most visible of Russia's new generation of leaders—former Vice-premier Boris Nemtsov (38)—confessed in his book *Provincial* that he is lost in the kitchen and lives on omelets when his wife is away. And Vladimir Ardzhevanidze, Europe's Tae Kwan Do champion, who is half-Russian, half-Georgian, told *Ya Sama* magazine outright: "A woman should know her place. She should know her woman's business. . . . When I come home from work, everything should be tidied up and she should be waiting for me." A man, on the other hand, "is a hunter in life. He must achieve a woman . . ."

On the positive side, Russian men do believe in romantic gestures in their "pursuit" of women—from little things like extending a hand to help a woman off a bus, to gifts of flowers, chocolates or perfume. To many Western women, these gestures are a welcome surprise. But Menshova has her own view on the matter. "It is a question of upbringing. . . . I would not say that Russian men are particularly romantic because, in most cases, flowers, helping with a coat, etc., happen rather automatically, and they don't contain any especially romantic meaning. . . . For me, it is even unpleasant because it is a stereotype. We have this so-called candy period, when men without fail give champagne, a box of candy and flowers."

Another consequence of the shortage of males is intense competition among women for "the right guy." According to Bezouglyi, "there are many more so-called decent women—beautiful, good-looking, in good health and without bad habits—than men like this [in Russia]. . . . And the women have always been closer to Western standards." The obvious implication is that women spend more time on their looks because they have to, while men can get away with just being their "adorable selves."

More ominously, according to a Human Rights Watch report, 14,000 women die every year at the hands of their husbands or other family members in Russia. And the Interior Ministry reported that, in 1996, 80% of all violent acts were committed within the family. Most of these acts go unreported, as there is still a widespread belief that "if he beats you, he must love you." In another arena, ultranationalist Duma Deputy Vladimir Zhirinovsky obviously has no qualms about attacking female deputies during Duma sessions—and justifying his behavior by *their* lack of femininity (see Note Book).

Reverse Discrimination

But before labeling Russian men as macho monsters, the situation should also be looked at from another standpoint. As a matter of fact, there are quite a few public leaders who see Russian men as a victim of gender discrimination. There is the idea— propounded by the leader of the "Women of Russia" movement, Yekaterina Lakhova, among others—that the myth of the male as the head of the family, as an aggressive leader who has no right to show his softer side, is taking its toll on male health. In other words, men suffer from the stress of being placed first.

Take life expectancy. The Journal of the American Medical Association recently published a survey showing that, during the first half of the 1990s, the life expectancy of Russian men fell from 63.8 years to 57.7 (from 74.4 to 71.2 for women). This male-female differential—about 13 years—has no parallel in any developed country, and according to Lakhova, the mortality rate of working-aged men is currently almost the same as it was a century ago. Men in Russia are eight times more likely than women to have infectious diseases, and four times more likely to have tuberculosis. Their incidences of heart disease, alcoholism and suicide are the highest in the developed world. And drug abuse is on the rise among young men. In 1997, 20,000 young Muscovites were declared unfit to serve in the army for health reasons.

So what does all this have to do with discrimination? Well, for one thing, men are doing the majority of dangerous and harmful work in Russia (Lakhova stated that 79% of those injured in manufacturing are men). As comic Mikhail Zhvanetsky said, poking fun at today's business terminology: "If a man comes home from work beaten up, that's called small business. If he comes home killed, *that's* big business." Work-related stress can also lead to alcoholism and depression. "How many drinking bouts and divorces have been provoked by the principle that the man is the head of the family!" exclaimed Lakhova. And, partly because there is no place in Russian society for the nurturing male, men have almost no chance of being granted custody of children. A study conducted by the Russian State Statistics Committee in 1996 did not reveal a single case of a man taking a leave of absence to care for his children. The "Women of Russia" movement is currently working to get this practice changed and to lower the retirement age of Russian men to 55 (from 60 or 65). After all, you can't give a pension to someone who is already dead.

Adaptation and Desperation

A major factor contributing to the health problems of Russian men is the difficulty of adapting to a market economy. Men who formerly had no trouble supporting their families on a decent level are now struggling at or below the poverty line. Men in professions that used to be privileged and revered—

Some Thoughts on *Homo Muzhikus*

"Do you want me to tell you the truth about men? They have one brain convolution and you have two. You have to feel sorry for them. They're the weak sex."

Actress Nina Ruslanova (*Komsomolskaya Pravda*)

" ... I love men with stable habits. Not the best ones—maybe even extravagant ones—even better. But in the eyes of girlfriends, such a man can always be justified—he's an eccentric and with his peculiarities. But all the same a man, and in this lies his main strength ... So long as you are fighting his stupid habits, he's yours. As soon as you win, he leaves you. Why fight? It's better to forgive and prolong the pleasure."

Freelance journalist Yelena Levina (*Komsomolskaya Pravda*)

"Stanislav Yezhi Lets believed ... that out of the three things that bring a man pleasure (work, cars and women), the best is the dog. In my opinion, what brings men even more pleasure is money, or to be more exact, the process of obtaining it."

Yuri Katsman, Editor-in-Chief, *Dengi Magazine*

"I believe that we don't have any muzhiks among actors, that the strongest sex in Russia is women. All the same, the men contrive to play some sort of strong characters."

Stage actress Alla Demidova (*Novye Izvestiya*)

"My first husband—an opera singer—was well adapted to the socialist system and was absolutely helpless in the new one. Helplessness in the face of capitalism is a common trait of many ex-husbands."

Maria Arbatova, playwright and feminist icon (*Komsomolskaya Pravda*)

teachers, doctors, scientists—can barely make ends meet, and the shock is nasty. Those who are young, well-educated and enterprising enough may have an opportunity to turn to business. But for the others, there seems to be no place.

Many young people have trouble understanding the older generation's failure to adapt. "A real man," Menshova asserted, "is someone who has managed to get his bearings in this new life. To this day, they are still living in comparison with yesterday.... If you have already found your bearings, you want to snap your fingers in front of the guy's face and say: 'dear, we have lived for a very long time in another world, you've got to understand it, you have to adapt to it.' Moreover, it is terribly off-putting to hear... that the present day is something different. Let's go ahead and act in the present day."

Medved's Vorobyov formulated this idea slightly differently: "A real man," he said, "is someone who is capable of enduring any difficult situation. A transfer from one economic system to another is without a doubt an extremely complicated situation, and those who have accomplished this, they are truly well done, they are truly 'real men.' "

One excellent example of adaptation in today's Russia is opera singer turned entrepreneur Alexander Voroshilo. For many years, Voroshilo had a shining career on the stage of Moscow's Bolshoi theater. Then, in 1983, he caught pneumonia, which led to chronic bronchitis, and could hardly talk. Just like that, his career was over. Desperate for work, Voroshilo threw himself into the first opportunity—sausages—and today, he is the head of a sausage empire. In an interview with *Ogonyok* weekly, Voroshilo talked about how he embarked on his new life: "There was fear, but nothing else remained. Who besides me is to feed my family? If a person is talented... then he is most likely capable of mastering another business. The recipe for success is the same throughout the world. You place a goal in front of you and head toward it."

But Voroshilo's story is only one success out of many failures. According to Lakhova, only 10% of Russian males are currently capable of supporting their families. Many members of the *intelligentsia* are simply incapable of becoming taxi drivers. And understandably. As *Men's Health's* Bezouglyi recounted: "My father was an aerospace engineer all his life. He built up space technology in this country, worked for 30 years, and then when he was around 50, the whole program was just closed. That was a big tragedy for him... and he still cannot overcome it completely. I am afraid that for the next several years, life for him will not get easier, because now is not the time for this kind of people." Even Voroshilo himself confessed that he "suffered terribly" in making the switch to business: "Singing for me is the meaning of existence."

As a result of business dynamics in the new Russia, the younger generation often ends up supporting the older one. The drivers of BMWs are not doctors and lawyers in their 50s, as in the States, they are young guys in their 20s or 30s— mobsters or businessmen or both. "It's tough," Bezouglyi said, "it's a jungle situation, only the strongest survive."

"The strength of a man, of the army, of any stable society, is based on respect for yourself, for commanders and for the Fatherland."

—*Karem Rashem*

School of Life

Today, Russian men are required to complete two years of military service, although exemptions do occur for health reasons and for those who have completed higher education. Some say the army is a school of life, where men learn how to be men. Others call it a dangerous exercise in violence and emotional scarring. In Moscow alone, over 12,000 young men are reportedly hiding out from military service—about the same number the capital sent out to serve last year. Some are terrified by stories of hazing and accidents. Some see no point in serving for meager pay that comes months late. Others just don't see the point of serving at all when they can get away without it. Last year, according to Interfax, only five cases against draft dodgers made it to court in Moscow.

In many ways, these young men are lucky to have been born at a time when they have a choice. As Bezouglyi recounted: "When I was 18, there was no opportunity to escape this, simply because we had a war in Afghanistan, and everybody had to go (except for people in technical schools maybe)." He compared the experience to being sent to prison, yet said that the army taught him valuable and irreplaceable lessons about men's characters. "They call it a school of life," he said, "but it's a very ugly way to learn things about life."

Ugly, indeed. Even during peacetime, military life is full of dangers and hardships. Many young conscripts are undernourished, and in a recent study, over 70,000 were found to be mentally unstable. According to *The Moscow Tribune*, over 80% of potential conscripts plan to dodge the draft in 1998. Perhaps bowing to the inevitable, the Kremlin plans to reduce the army by 500,000 soldiers, to 1.2 million, by the end of 1998 and eventually abolish conscription in favor of a professional army.

The problems with today's army are very real. But, in the face of this, some young men continue to serve out of a sense of duty. And for those, young and old, who have fought for Russia, it must be tough to see the lack of respect for the army among today's youth. General-Major Viktor Nikulin, who is in charge of military recruitment in the Saratov region, maintained that, come what may, "military service remains the most important pursuit for men."

Duma deputy Stanislav Govorukhin also has a deep respect for the military. His documentary film entitled *The Russia We Lost* bemoans the loss of traditional religious and social ideals in Russia. Govorukhin's son volunteered for active duty in

Chechnya, where he lost a leg, and later made his own patriotic documentary about his experiences.

Meanwhile, the image of a military man continues to have some resonance with Russians even if much of the shine has rubbed off. General Alexander Lebed, who won himself a reputation as a no-nonsense commander in Moldova's Transdnestr region and came in a surprise third in the first round of the 1996 presidential elections, is widely respected. Fired as secretary of the Security Council (many feel as a scapegoat for Yeltsin's Chechnya policy), Lebed is now back in the spotlight as a candidate for governor of Siberia's Krasnoyarsk region (though he is trailing badly in the polls at press time). Russian women of a certain age consider Lebed's deep voice and uncompromising stance sexy. And even those who don't agree have to admit that he seems like a "real *muzhik*."

Lebed would almost certainly agree with Rashem's view that "it is important to understand that the strength of a man, of the army, of any stable society, is based on respect for your-self, for commanders and for the Fatherland. . . . A man who feels deep respect for the Defense Minister, the President is a true soldier in the highest sense of the word. . . . If an army wants to be victorious, it must honor its commander under any circumstances. This is also the deepest moral of a man not only in the army, but in society, in the church as well."

In Russia now, the men—and women—who would support such an extreme position are few and far between. Today, men are admired more for their language skills and business savvy than for their moral depth or unwavering loyalty. They are not expected to obey their leaders without question, or to sacrifice themselves like General Gorbatov. But one can hope (as does this female correspondent), when all this transitioning is through, that giving flowers will not be passe. And that getting up off the couch to help your wife pound in some nails will be the norm, rather than the exception.

—Vladimir Dernovoi also contributed to this article.

Peru has been heralded as a family-planning 'success story'. Since 1961 the country has reduced its fertility rate from six children per woman to three-and-a-half. But the line between planning families and controlling population is a fine one—as **Stephanie Boyd** found out when she met some of the 110,000 women who were sterilized last year.

Secrets and lies

LEOPOLDINA Vega hasn't felt well since her operation. Peeking out shyly from behind the door of her house, she is at first reluctant to talk about her experience. After some reassurance she finally consents to tell her story. The thirty-one-year-old mother of five complains of nausea, pain and fatigue. She speaks of health workers who bullied her into having her tubes tied. They said it would be so 'simple' her husband would not find out and she would be home working the same day. She describes the consent forms she signed but being illiterate did not understand. And she shudders when she tells how she and three other women were lined up on tables to be operated on the same day, one after another. Lastly she recalls the doctors who abandoned her after it was over, dropping her off at home and never returning.

... reproductive health was taken away from the women themselves once it was finally deemed 'important'

Reports she has seen recently on television of women who have died or suffered severe complications after being sterilized have made her anxious. 'My health isn't important,' says Leopoldina, her voice wavering. 'It's my children I worry about. Who will take care of them if I die?'

Residents say health workers tried to convince women with four or five children to consent to tubal ligations during a vaccination campaign last May.

Investigations by opposition politicians, local journalists and a US congressional subcommittee have uncovered numerous cases of coercion and abuse in poor communities across the country. Peru's Office of the Public Defender is investigating thirty-five cases of illegalities in tubal ligation operations, including nine deaths from alleged complications and unsanitary operating conditions. Doctors performed about 110,000 such sterilizations in Peru last year (more than three times the 1996 figure) and 10,000 vasectomies as part of a Government birth-control campaign.

Leopoldina's neighbour, Martha Mallón, has had problems urinating since she was sterilized. After her fifth child in June last year workers at the government clinic convinced her to have her tubes tied the following day. 'They said I would be able to care for my children better and that I would not have any more.' When she told her husband he was furious. After learning about the side-effects and consequences from the media she now regrets the whole thing.

The local press has labelled the campaign 'an attack on Peru's poor'. But the meaning didn't sink in until I went to visit the community where Leopoldina and Martha live. It's a small settlement tucked inside an up-market development called *La Molina*. This Western-style suburb is complete with paved roads, mowed lawns and convenience stores, while the two women live in rough shacks and collect water from a single tap at the bottom of the hill. The Government's logic was clear: their community was an eyesore and an unwelcome blight on its wealthy neighbours. Why should it be allowed to grow?

However, what struck me most about Leopoldina and Martha's community was not the poverty, but the possibilities. Its people are survivors, having left their homes in the Sierra during Sendero Luminoso's armed violence of the 1980s and built new lives in Lima. Although houses are without running water, the settlement is not a 'slum' and the people are not starving or malnourished. Their children play in streets which are free from garbage or sewage. Houses have electricity and many are equipped with televisions. Reforms like piped water, paved roads and a health clinic to provide real choices for family planning would not be difficult. But infrastructure would only encourage the inhabitants to stay. And the Government's response is clearly not about building futures, but about simple population control.

In February 1998 a delegation from Peru travelled to the US to testify before a Congressional Subcommittee on International and Human Rights Operations. Peruvian physician Héctor Chávez described the pressures on doctors to perform sterilization operations. Two women also testified—one claiming she was sterilized without her consent and the other that she was bribed with monthly food shipments.

Dr Chávez told the Subcommittee that women were not given adequate information about the irreversibility or the risks involved prior to their operations. He also said that many doctors disagreed with the sterilization campaign, suggesting they were pressured into performing the operations for fear of losing their jobs.

Chávez said his regional health department required full-time personnel to sterilize two patients a month and contract workers to sterilize three. Joseph Rees, chief council of the US Congressional hearing, concluded: 'I don't think there is any question that women in Peru, especially very poor *mestizo* [mixed race] women, have been misled into having sterilizations and that in some cases they were lied to, or offered food, in exchange . . .'

The Peruvian Government denies there are quotas and maintains that abuses are the fault of individuals and not the health system. A few weeks after Dr Chávez's delegation returned to Peru he was dismissed from his post for not 'fulfilling his duties'.

The media hype has brought forth opinions—and raised battle flags—from all sides of the reproductive health debate. Women's groups have long been at war with Peru's influential Catholic Church for its rigid stand against birth control and abortion rights. Church leaders are claiming their position protects women's health and rights, while the notion of 'family planning' is just another disguise to control women's bodies.

High-profile reports in the *New York Times, Miami Herald* and *Washington Post* have provoked international condemnation of the Government's campaign. And in the US there is also concern that American aid dollars may have been used to fund the sterilizations—though aid officials in Washington claim that this is not the case. Nonetheless, before the abuses were made public Peru's family planning program (one of the most ambitious in Latin America) received praise from both the UN Population Fund and the World Bank for reducing the country's population growth rate.

The Peruvian women's organization *Flora Tristan* is struggling to determine the number of women affected. Already hundreds have come forward claiming they were misinformed, tricked, pressured or offered gifts of money if they agreed to the operation. And it is not yet clear how much women's groups working in the field of reproductive health knew about the abuses—but kept silent—until the media safely broke the story. Although government agencies perform nearly 80 per cent of Peru's tubal ligations, non-governmental organizations (NGOs) often work loosely with government departments or are aware of what's happening in the communities where they work. Whether they receive direct government funding or not, NGOs in Peru can't function without Lima's consent. Treading too harshly on government toes is never wise.

But the dilemma for the women's groups goes beyond the compromising position of funding. Family-planning activists fear losing all they've worked for if donors become wary of funding programs or if a conservative backlash frightens women away from clinics and turns birth control back into a taboo subject.

The sterilization campaign was the first time the Government had run a women's health program without enlisting the help of NGOs or community groups. And this gets to the crux of the problem. After working for years to raise awareness about the importance of reproductive health, the issue was taken away from the women themselves once it was finally deemed 'important'. In President Fujimori's dictatorial style, the campaign was scripted to achieve maximum public-relations points: he announced it at the UN Women's Conference in Beijing in 1995.

Mary Vargas, a lawyer working with the Peruvian women's group *Demus,* says that women's health should be decentralized, taken from federal government and given to local groups who work closely with women and know their community's needs. Vargas cautions that fixating on numbers and population neglects the social aspect of women's reproductive health, which is heavily influenced by factors such as education, access to economic resources and legal protection.

It is these social and political factors that must be changed in order to create a fair and representative family planning program. Like other women's activists, Vargas argues that demographics and population control should not take precedence over women's right to control their own bodies. She insists that having access to reproductive health methods and proper information is 'a fundamental right for women everywhere'.

Stephanie Boyd *is the associate editor of Latin America Press, a weekly news publication based in Lima, Peru.*

For further information contact the Peru Support Group. e-mail: perusupport@gn.apc.org

Another **planet**

Anouk Ride reports on the mixed messages that teenagers are being given about sex and argues that young people have rights too.

YOU can't feel me up when I'm ten, then come back when I'm nineteen and tell me not to have sex with my boyfriend, Maria shouts loudly down the phone over the street noise of Baguio City, the Philippines.[1] She is not alone in decrying the contradictory and condescending views that adults hold about young people and sex.

According to global surveys young people everywhere feel they are ruled by adults who tell them how to behave—but then refuse to give them control over their own bodies and their own sexuality.[2] Nor do they protect them from exploitation. While the media, religious leaders and governments decry the fact that kids are having sex and 'family values' are breaking down, they have failed to protect young people from the dangers of unwanted and unsafe sexual relations.

This is universal. In the Majority World early and forced marriages, female genital mutilation and prostitution deny young men and women their own sexuality. In Africa, two million girls between seven and twelve are genitally mutilated and worldwide two million girls are introduced to the sex market each year.[3]

In Western countries kids are sent mixed messages by the media. They're told that early sexual initiation is bad, but are bombarded with images of teenagers as sexual toys. Who is cool in the fashion world? Models that are young and childlike. Fashion designer Calvin Klein recently popularized this image with ads depicting young women (such as British super-model Kate Moss) in provocative poses. Critics said this was an example of 1990s fashion excess—but Klein and most designers have used half-dressed, pouting teenagers to sell their clothes for years. Society sexualizes children—and then tells them sex is bad.

In many Western countries sexual abuse of children is rife. In the US victims below the age of ten account for 29 per cent of rape cases and 62 per cent of cases involve victims fifteen years old or less. And these

are reported cases only.[4] The overwhelming majority of abuse is by someone known to the victim. Often the very adults who are in positions of trust with young people—relatives, neighbours, parents—are those who destroy their self-esteem and disturb their sexual development.

Adults think young people need to be controlled. And society generally has the same view towards the poor, the uneducated and 'minorities' such as ethnic groups and

homosexuals. So young people from these backgrounds have even more societal pressures on their sexual behaviour. In the West the highest rates of teenage pregnancy are found among girls living in poverty with low education levels or job prospects. In Britain, in a poor district of East London, one in ten teenage girls gets pregnant while in the wealthier boroughs of Kingston and Richmond the rate is less than half that.[5] One in every ten births worldwide is to a teenage

---

Sex, drugs—and rights for all! A charter for young people's sexual rights.

Cheer up

Sexuality is part of normal teenage development, not a monster to be locked away and starved. Young people need a chance to grow into their bodies, understand their reproductive systems and be responsible in their sexual relations. Sex is about relationships, personal discovery—and fun.

Get real

Methods for contraception and prevention against STDs should be explained and discussed fully and in terms kids can understand by people they can relate to. Knowledge is not enough—they need support not judgement.

Boys *too*

Sex-education programs and services are not just for girls. Young men want to know sexual techniques, what to do to avoid pregnancy and information about STDs.

Right laws

Young people are entitled to contraception which is safe, legal, affordable and available. They have a right to be protected from disease.

Sex ed

Education of young people will only work if adults too learn about sex and young people's rights.

Parts Are Private

Parents should not overrule youth rights. Abuse of young people must be condemned. Privacy and confidentiality of services is essential.

7—letter word

Respect. If older people respect teenagers, the feeling will be mutual.

---

mother. Sometimes getting pregnant is the only way a teenager can boost her self-esteem and add a sense of purpose to her life.

Society perpetuates the powerlessness of girls through poverty, class or caste and lack of education. Hari from Nepal describes a girl from her village: 'Mona was pregnant with her seventh child, having married a 17-year-old boy at the age of 14. Being of a low caste, with no education, she didn't have any control over her own life. If she had been given the opportunity of education to make her own money and an awareness of her body, she would not have become the slave of tradition and society.'[2]

Many girls marry for money or protection: 'I got married because of a super-painful childhood, because my father was always hitting me,' said one Chilean girl.[5] Early marriage means that girls have little power within the relationship so cannot control if and when they have children.

And having babies before their bodies are fully formed puts them at risk of a range of life-threatening illnesses—the most common cause of death in teenage girls around the world.[3] Fistulae (a rupture between the bladder, rectum and vagina often caused by giving birth too young) is one horrific example. Girls are left infertile and incontinent and

become social outcasts. Inadequate access to safe contraceptives means that in places like São Paulo, Brazil, the number of young girls admitted to hospitals due to complications from unsafe abortions is greater than the number of births.

Even societies classified as democratic and liberal are far from accepting young people's sexuality, particularly when it is seen as not 'normal'. In Australia, where one of the best-selling, locally produced movies was *Priscilla, Queen of the Desert* and where Sydney's Gay and Lesbian Mardi Gras is the nation's biggest street party, research indicates that around a third of young

---

ACTION/READING

Women's Health Movement

The Asian-Pacific Resource and Research Centre for Women (ARROW), 2nd Floor, Block F, Anjung Felda, Jalan Maktab, 54000 Kuala Lumpur, Malaysia. Tel: +603 292 9913; e-mail: women@arrow.po.my An information and resource centre focusing on women and development. Reproductive rights is one of its main areas. **Committee on Women, Population and the Environment** (CWPE), c/o Population and Development Program, Hampshire College, Amherst, MA 01002, US. Tel: +1 413 582 5506; e-mail: cwpe@igc.apc.org Provides alternative analyses of the relationships between population poverty and environmental degradation and challenges both population control and anti-abortion forces. **International Reproductive Rights Research Action Group** (IRRRAG), c/o Women's Studies, Hunter College, CUNY, 695 Park Avenue, New York, NY 10021, US. Tel: +1 212 772 5682; e-mail: IRRRAG@igc.apc.org A grassroots research project on reproductive issues and women's rights, based in seven countries. The results are being published in *Negotiating Reproductive Rights: Women's Perspectives Across Countries and Cultures*, edited by Rosalind Petchesky and Karen Judd (Zed Books 1998). **International Women's Health Coalition** (IWHC), 24 East 21st St, New York, NY 10010, USA. Tel: +1 212 979 8500; e-mail: iwhc@igc.apc.org Supports projects and aid agencies aiming to promote high-quality women's reproductive health. **Women's Global Network for Reproductive Rights**, NZ Voorburgwal 32, 1012 RZ Amsterdam, The Netherlands,

Tel: +31 20 620 9672; e-mail: wgnrr@antenna.nl An autonomous international network campaigning for the right of women to decide whether, when and with whom to have children.

Family planning/United Nations

United Nations. Fund for Population Activities (UNFPA), 220 East 42nd St, New York, NY 10017, US. Fax: +1 212 557 6416. Website: http://www.unfpa.org The main UN organization dealing with fertility issues. Publishes The State of World Population report each year. **World Health Organization** (WHO), 1211 Geneva 27, Switzerland. Fax: +41 22 791 4870. Website: http://www.who.ch Produces the annual *World Health Report*. **International Planned Parent Federation** (IPPF), Regent's College, Inner Circle, Regent's Park, London NW1 4NS, England. Tel: +44 171 487 7900; e-mail: ippfinfo@ippf.attmail.com The largest non-governmental family-planning organization.

Worth reading . . .

Abortion: Between Freedom and Necessity, Janet Hadley (Virago 1996). A well-argued case for abortion which also acknowledges the difficulties and dilemmas. 'Population and reproductive rights'. Focus on Gender, Vol. 2, No. 2, June 1994 (Oxfam). A range of perspectives on reproduction in a Majority World context. *Our Bodies, Ourselves,* the Boston Women's Health Book Collective (Penguin 1996). A classic, recently updated. Pandora's Clock: *Understanding our Fertility,* Maureen

Freely and Celia Pyper (Heinemann 1993). A humorous look at the ambiguities and emotions surrounding pregnancy and birth. *Private Decisions, Public Debates: Women, Reproduction and Population* (Panos Institute 1994) has a range of articles by journalists from the Majority World. Panos (Tel: +44 171 278 1111; e-mail: panoslondon@gn.apc.org) also produces briefing papers on reproductive rights. *Population and Reproductive Rights: Feminist Perspectives from the South,* Sonia Corrêa and Rebecca Reichmann, (Zed Books/Kali for Women/DAWN 1994). A critical Southern view of the debates around population, reproduction and development. *Reproductive Health Matters* is a quarterly journal with in-depth analysis and up-to-date news on women's health and rights. (29-35 Farringdon Rd, London EC1M 3JB, England. Tel: +44 171 242 8686; e-mail: 100663.3504@compuserve.com) *Reproductive Rights and Wrongs: The Global Politics of Population Control,* Betsy Hartmann (South End Press 1995). A detailed and searing analysis of the politics and history of population control which argues for a more woman-based perspective. *Where Women have no Doctor: A health guide for women,* A. August Burns, Ronnie Lovich, Jane Maxwell, Katharine Shapiro (Hesperian Foundation 1997). A practical guide, useful for its down-to-earth explanations. *Women, Population and Global Crisis,* Asoka Bandarage (Zed Books, 1997). Places the population debate in a broad historical and social justice-oriented perspective. *The Legacy of Malthus* (forthcoming), Eric Ross (Zed Press 1998). A political economy critique of Malthusian theory and its applications in Europe and the South.

lesbians and gays have attempted suicide. The main cause of their depression was a common feeling that they lacked adult support.[6]

This is not surprising when some 'experts' are clearly living on another planet. One academic seriously proposed forced permanent contraception for ten- to seventeen-year-old girls worldwide. Meanwhile, Phyllis Schafly, an anti-feminist campaigner in the US, says: 'It's very healthy for a young girl to be deterred from promiscuity by fear of contracting a painful, incurable disease or cervical cancer or sterility or the likelihood of giving birth to a dead, blind or brain-damaged baby.'[7]

People often believe that if young people are taught about sex this will promote immorality and recklessness. But sexual-abstinence programs, popular in the US, have never been effective in delaying the onset of intercourse. Research indicates that increased information about sex encourages a later start to sexual relations, higher use of contraceptives and fewer sexual partners.[2]

Kids are having sex despite adult disapproval. 'Heavy-handedness, brainwashing and moralizing will not stop the young from engaging in sexual activity,' says Elmira from Kazakhstan.[2] In fact, improvements in nutrition have led to girls worldwide becoming fertile more than two years earlier than previous generations. So most young people have a longer period of sexual relations before marriage than their parents. In sub-Saharan Africa eight out of ten people below the age of twenty are sexually experienced as are seven out of ten teenagers in many developed countries and at least half of all teens in Latin America.

Although they are sexually active, young people are ill-equipped to deal with the consequences of sex. Without access to information, contraception and equal rights they have high rates of sexually transmitted diseases (STDs) and unwanted pregnancies. Half of all new HIV infections are among the 15 to 24 age group—predominantly in South-East Asia and sub-Saharan Africa. And one out of every twenty adolescents contracts an STD each year.

Almost all young people say that they need more information on all aspects of their sexual and reproductive health. More than three-quarters in a global youth survey were aware of the risks of STDs including HIV/AIDS. But a significant number of young people, particularly in Arab states and some parts of the Far East, believed STDs and AIDS were not a personal concern.

'STDs are only a problem for homosexuals, sex workers and drug addicts—it is scientifically proven,' said a young respondent reciting common knowledge in Yemen.[2] In India a study found most young people encountered sex earlier than in previous decades, but still thirty-six per cent of those interviewed had no idea what led to conception and only five per cent of them were using contraceptives.[8] Up to 60 per cent of adolescent births throughout the world are unplanned.

Many youth workers say that teenagers, due to the lack of sex education and an inability to talk with parents, rely on the media and friends for advice. Most young people feel awkward talking to their elders about sex. In a recent survey of youth in 54 countries more than half said they felt too embarrassed to discuss sex with adults.[2] 'Adults have got this ideology that young people are being rude if they express their thoughts, so sometimes I just feel like a stray, an alien' says Sarah from Botswana.[1]

But knowledge alone is not enough—young people, especially girls, need to feel empowered when it comes to sex.

One girl from Trinidad and Tobago says adamantly: 'If he does not have a condom, the woman should say: "If you don't have you can't get."'[1] But in practice it is difficult—in Canada one survey found although 85 per cent of youth claimed to be very knowledgeable about contraception, only 11 per cent of female university students and 19 per cent of male students always used condoms, which were seen as 'uncool'.[9] Girls and young women said they lacked the power to negotiate condom use and were subject to strongly held views about traditional male and female roles in sexual relationships.

Kids also need the law on their side. But often sex is illegal, with 15 or 16 being the average minimum age of consent. Shantal, a youth worker in Barbados, explains the dilemmas this can create: 'A mother wanted to have the partner of her 13-year-old daughter arrested for statutory rape. . . . The young girl said that she had not been raped and had willingly consented to sex. The young man, who was 21, was her boyfriend and she would never forgive her mother if she had him arrested. The case was eventually dropped because the girl refused to testify. Young people see themselves as sexual beings.'[1]

Young people are always going to have sex (or have it forced upon them). It is a denial of their rights to refuse them contraception and protection against STDs. What is needed when a 13-year-old goes to a clinic or to a doctor for contraception is clear information, support and counselling to ensure that the teenager is able to choose sexual relations and is confident of their control over the situation. It is a basic human right to have control over your own body. In fact, it may even be the one thing anyone can truly 'own'—so why deny this to people just because they are young?

Young people have identified their needs in order to ensure they are informed, safe and empowered in their sexual relations. Before heading off to meet her friends in Baguio City, Maria offers a final opinion. 'I am tired of being told what to do. I would like older people to listen to my experiences and my questions,' she says confidently. 'But change will be impossible if adults do not learn from us.'[1]

1. Interviews by Anouk Ride and International Planned Parenthood Foundation. Some of the names of people in this article have been changed.
2. *Generation 97* (International Planned Parenthood Federation 1997).
3. *Rights of women in relation to sexuality and reproductive health* (Swedish Association for Sex Education 1997).
4. *Reproductive Health Matters,* November 1996.
5. *Reproductive Health Matters,* May 1995.
6. *Sexuality and Youth Suicide,* (Sexuality and Youth Suicide Project, Australia, 1997).
7. Janet Hadley, *Abortion: Between Freedom and Necessity* (Virago 1996).
8. *The Sex Files* (Family Planning Association of India/Sex Education, Counselling and Training 1996).
9. *Sex and Reproductive Health Rights in Canada* (website by Katherine McDonald <http://www.hcsc.gc.ca/canusa/papers/canada/english/reprod.html>)

WHERE THERE IS NO VILLAGE: TEACHING ABOUT SEXUALITY IN CRISIS SITUATIONS

Nanette Ecker, M. A.
Director of Training and Education
The Global Institute for Training
Planned Parenthood of Nassau County
Hempstead, NY

We've all heard it. "It takes a village to raise a child." But what happens when there is no village?

As a sexuality education and reproductive health trainer working in Africa, I witnessed a country's destruction from tribal wars while I was managing projects in Liberia, a small, ruggedly beautiful nation formed by freed American slaves.

During a training I facilitated in the Liberian capital of Monrovia, we regularly monitored the radio for news of an impending invasion of young rebel soldiers. Whether discussing harmful effects of female genital mutilation (FGM) or ways to provide sexuality education, we hoped to make it without rebels invading the capital to riot the streets.

The United States Department of State urged all "non-essential personnel" to leave the country. I complied but soon planned to return to complete my work. I communicated with my Liberian colleagues in coded words about my plans. They told me that "the train was off the track." (In other words, "Don't come back.") This was only the beginning of the terror that would come to Liberia. I still don't know what became of many of my Liberian colleagues except for occasional letters I received from friends displaced in the nameless refugee camps which had sprung up in the border towns of Sierra Leone and Guinea.

Most humanitarian organizations have since withdrawn from the region. Of those people who stayed, some were slaughtered like lambs. The project coordinator with whom I worked had her arm broken by boy soldiers after they broke into her home in the middle of the night. Another colleague's farm was destroyed, commandeered, and turned into an army barracks for rebel troops. Even the compound of the United Nations Development Program—always gated, secured and considered untouchable—was

"An important first step is to create more awareness about adolescent refugee health."

stormed by rebels who murdered several of their staff in cold blood.

Part of my innocence about the inherent goodness of humankind died as a result of my experience in Liberia. My thoughts of the evil mankind is capable of in the name of tribal hatred haunted me in dreams and wakeful hours.

Seduced by ongoing work in the sub-Saharan region, I moved on to tackle other challenges. It wasn't until last June that fate again brought me face to face with the plight of adolescent refugees and their unheard cries of pain and suffering. I need to help tell their stories.

WHEN ELEPHANTS FIGHT, IT IS THE GRASS THAT SUFFERS

There is an old African proverb that says, "When elephants fight, it is the grass that suffers." The adage rang true as I returned home last June from Kenya.

The International Red Cross and the Red Crescent Societies (IRC) had asked me to conduct a training program on adolescent sexuality education and reproductive health for the staff of the humanitarian and relief agencies serving the refugee camps in the Great Lakes region—particularly those in Uganda and Tanzania, where refugee camps have sprung up in border towns that swell to hundreds of thousands of persons displaced from Rwanda, Burundi, and the Democratic Republic of Congo (formerly Zaire), as well as people fleeing from Sudan and Somalia because of genocidal war based on tribal and ethnic hatred.

The adolescent reproductive health and sexuality education training focused on those health workers engaged in work with young people enduring deprivations and daily terrors commonplace in the refugee camps. Many of the stories, told to me by these relief workers echoed the Liberian horror stories and once again told me agonizing tales of lost families, lost hope, and lost lives.

The district and regional medical officers, doctors, nurses, and family planning workers spoke of how displaced youth are sexually victimized in exchange for food, shelter, and protection. Many of these youths grow up in an artificial culture created by the tribal war forces that have torn apart the social fabric of the countries they have fled. They live in a nether world where "survival sex" ensures another day. Exploitative sex is inextricably linked to survival. Rape and sexual abuse sadly become the badges of courage worn as a rite of passage to adulthood.

Many of the relief workers shared with me their experiences with refugee youth. Story after story unfolded to reveal an almost universal, collective pattern of experiences. They told of girls who were sent by their guardians or families to collect food and provisions at distribution sites. These girls could accept a man's offer for sexual intercourse if he promised to buy her oranges. He would often pay her for all the oranges and "then some" if she allowed him to perform sexual acts with her. When she returned to her family with food and money in hand, they rarely questioned her. Rather, they praised her for being so "industrious." A recent issue of *Population Reports* entitled "People Who Move: New Reproductive Health Focus" (November 1997) states that "violence against women is widespread during refugee and internal displacement movements. When women and children move, they are often alone and powerless and thus at risk of becoming sexual prey."[1]

KEY ISSUES AFFECTING YOUTH IN REFUGEE CAMPS

The key reproductive and sexual health problems affecting refugee youth are compounded by the severe lack of resources and the basic need for survival within the refugee setting. Families live on top of each other in tents constructed from plastic sheathing.

In talking with the training participants about the plight and subsequent needs of these adolescents, they discussed cultural, gender-related, psychosexual, and economic factors that contribute to negative sexual attitudes and risky sexual practices that impact on the young people's reproductive and health status. Some of these factors are:

- *A virtual blackout of sexuality education and sexual health information and resources.* Discussion about sexuality is taboo. In years past, traditional cultural scripts encouraged extended family members to provide sexuality education for their youth. Rural-to-urban migration and the breakdown in traditional ways have stopped the transfer of sexuality-related knowledge.

- *A cultural limbo.* Many youth have left the familiar environment of their country of origin and its cultural and sexual scripts, but have not fully integrated into the host country. They have abandoned or forgotten their own country of origin's scripts, and they are left without the structure, both familial and cultural, to help them navigate through a value system upon which to base their sexual decisions and behaviors. As a result, they are growing up in a confused, muddled world during an already challenging developmental phase.

- *Exploitation of youth on a variety of levels.* For some families, unaccompanied minors are seen as a cheap form of labor. They become indentured servants used and exploited for work they can do to help the family unit survive. This can happen with nonrelatives who assume the role of foster parents, as well as by distant family members, who may be the only relatives left in the extended family. The unaccompanied minor taken into the family unit may provide a new source of sexual attention for the male head of the family. Since polygamy is practiced by many of the ethnic groups, a young female coming into a family circle often creates imbalance in a formally stable family unit. The result is jealousy and fear, which may lead to a bias in how commodities are distributed within the family. The best and biggest portions may go to those who are in good favor with the male head of household. And this may be based on sexual favoritism.

- *An abundance of dangerous myths and misinformation regarding AIDS, sexually transmitted infections (STIs), and pregnancy prevention.* Myths include the following: An individual can become infected with worms by having sexual intercourse with an elderly person; a man can cure an STI by having sexual intercourse with a virgin or a young girl; a person can improve his or her complexion just by having sexual intercourse. The Great Lakes region that borders Lake Victoria is known for having extremely high rates of HIV/AIDS and STIs. Many men are looking for a miracle cure. Traditional healers encourage men to cure themselves by having sexual intercourse with a young woman, who is unaware of how she is being used. This creates a great risk for many females in the camps who are victimized by men in their search for a cure.

- *Teenage, premature, and unintended pregnancies are common, and abortion is illegal.* Desperate adolescents often seek herbalists and other traditional healers for a clandestine abortion. These herbalists may use methods that are dangerous and that may result in sickness, infertility, and death. Serious infections from incomplete abortions are common and are frequently seen by relief workers.

- *Sexual behavior and actions are connected to power and control in the refugee camp situation.* A relief worker or other trusted adult often controls the flow and distribution of commodities within a camp. This person, with a leash on the lives of those whose existence depends on him, may be in a position to take emotional, physical, and sexual advantage of dependent youth. This unequal power dynamic often results in young people providing sexual favors in trade for the necessities for survival.

- *Unequal and stereotypical gender roles often result in dangerous sexual behavior and sexual violence.* These roles, like those in many countries, define females as inferior and submissive, and males as assertive and domineering. They perpetuate sexual abuse, molestation, sexual and domestic violence, and rape that is rampant in the camps.

- *Experimental sexual relationships have become a rite of passage for many youth who are left unsupervised, or who are now the head of household.* With few recreational programs and lack of educational opportunities, young people may engage in sexual relationships for recreational purposes and as a panacea against boredom, to fill the void left by a lack of parental affection, to establish their adult status, for popularity, and for curiosity.

- **Maternal child health and population/family planning services in the camps are minimal and are targeted toward adults.** There are several hundred thousand displaced people living in various degrees of squalor who are not receiving reproductive and sexual health intervention. Although many adolescents are in the camps, their exact numbers are unknown. *A Reproductive Health and Training Needs Assessment in Refugee Camps In Kigoma Region—Tanzania,* conducted by the International Federation of Red Cross in March 1997, states that "adolescent sexuality programs had not been established in any of the camps in spite of the many problems facing the youth such as STD/HIV infection and teen pregnancy." It also says that "youth were reluctant to visit Maternal Child Health/Family Planning (MCH/FP) clinics where adults, including their parents, go for services."[2] Most of the health needs of youth go unmet. There are no targeted programs for them within the camp that would help curtail the soaring pregnancy, HIV/AIDS, and STI rates through promotion of comprehensive sexuality education and the distribution of condoms and contraceptives.

- *A general tacit attitude of acceptance of child marriage exists within the camps.* The needs assessment report talks of many teen mothers in the camps who are unskilled in properly caring for their children. It says that there are many young women who marry immediately after their first menstrual cycles. The resulting premature childbirth often leads to complications such as the formation of Vesico-vaginal fistulae (VVF), which are small tears between the walls of the vagina and the bladder caused by childbirth before a young woman reaches full maturity.

- *Young people receive education through United Nations High Commission on Refugee (UNHCR)-sup-* *ported schools only through elementary levels.* The lack of education and literacy has profound effects on a young person's ability to attain a viable economic means of support and to achieve life planning and career goals. It has been well documented that individuals who obtain higher degrees of literacy and education have smaller families. They will have children that they are able to feed, to support, and to educate. There are many children and adolescents in the camps who are older than elementary school level age. They are left idle and their educational needs are left unmet. They often pass time by using bang (marijuana), sniffing glue, or using alcohol or other drugs. Some resort to trading sex for drugs, much like adolescents who trade sex for drugs in the urban crack houses in the United States. They are well aware that their future is bleak. They often suffer depression. The relief workers lack the counseling skills to address many of their problems.

The training that I provide through the Global Institute for Training (GIFT) helps doctors, clinicians, and relief workers focus on identifying adolescent social, emotional, reproductive, and sexual health problems that can be addressed through improved health service delivery and comprehensive sexuality education programs.

The bulk of the participants are painfully shy, embarrassed, and improperly trained in concepts surrounding such initiatives. In particular, they lack training related to human sexuality and sexual health needs specific to adolescents. They have not been exposed to information about sexuality; they have not addressed their lack of attitudinal comfort and confidence in discussing sexuality issues with youth; and they lack skills related to the counseling or health service needs of at-risk youth. The cultural constraints surrounding the discussion of sexuality issues are very powerful and point to the need for continued training and attitude clarification opportunities.

During GIFT training, I witnessed the fascinating transformation of participants into advocates of adolescent sexual health programs. Every day, we discussed and buried myths, identified key agents of change within the community, suggested strategies, and strengthened skills and comforts.

Yet, I know I cannot expect change overnight. It takes time to change negative attitudes toward sexuality that are strongly embedded in their culture. Change will only come through adequate resources and the subsequent transfer of the knowledge and skills necessary to implement programs.

We need advocates for change and a belief in the mission of helping youth to help themselves. There are no easy answers, no *ju-ju,* or as we say in the West, *no magic bullets.*

RECOMMENDATIONS FOR PROGRAM DEVELOPMENT

GIFT has developed a variety of steps to help those who work with youth, particularly displaced or refugee youth, to meet their emotional, academic, reproductive, sexual health, and sexuality education needs.

An important first step is to create more awareness about adolescent refugee health and their social, emotional, and health needs. This means working to initiate change at camp, local, and regional levels; within international donor, humanitarian, and relief organizational levels; and within the global community, including the international media.

An important second step is to gain support and understanding of the needs of adolescent refugees by working with individuals who are the key agents of change such as governmental and ministry officials; religious and spiritual leaders; village elders; school officials; youth leaders; traditional healers; doctors, traditional birth attendants, family planning and allied health professionals; and youth.

Action must be swift and widespread and should promote the agents of change in the refugee community to mobilize in support for adolescent sexuality education initiatives. Workers must integrate adolescent sexuality education initiatives within their ongoing job responsibilities.

Since opposition exists to providing youth with access to contraceptives and sexual health services, individual members of the community must publicly support such initiatives. Other recommendations include:

- *Organizational collaboration for the common good* that includes pooling staff, resources, talent, and time to ensure that programming is well integrated.
- *Training of grassroots educators* to work with parents or guardians in the camps to enhance sexuality education within families.
- *Training of peer educators* to provide youth with positive role models and important information.
- *Training of agencies and ministries* on adolescent reproductive and sexual health, human sexuality, gender role development, and violence prevention.
- *Standardizing resource materials around adolescent reproductive health programs and services* to help establish guidelines to keep workers on track through the process of needs assessment, strategic planning, program development, implementation, and evaluation.
- *Building an advocacy group to address opposition to sexuality education for youth.* The individuals who are key agents of change within the refugee, local, and international community have the ability to advocate for the creation of new policies, resources, programs, and services that focus on adolescent reproductive, sexuality, gender equity, sexual health, social and educational needs.

- *Involve youth.* Provide them with focus group opportunities so they can tell you what methods and interventions they think will prove most effective in dealing with their problems. Involve them in the design as well as in the delivery of such programs. They will prove powerful advocates and will exert a strong influence on the social norms adopted by their peers.
- *Create recreational and social programs to generate self-esteem and personal development among the youth.* Integrate sexuality education into these social and recreational programs. Provide youth-oriented health clinics where they can access contraception and condoms without fear of judgment or embarrassment. Try to enhance their future by providing more comprehensive educational opportunities and vocational training. In the process, keep the donor community informed and involved.

Yet the cries of the young still go unheard. Many refuse to pay adequate attention to the adolescent refugee crisis. This is not surprising in a world where the majority of cultures are uncomfortable dealing with sexuality, in general, and adolescent sexuality, in particular.

The first need is to recognize the problem. Yes, the relief workers are now more aware of the need for adolescent services. But these agencies have limited time, money, and resources. They are also overwhelmed trying to provide basic necessities. They lack the expertise to deal with the problems experienced by refugee youth in regard to sexuality and sexual health. But awareness is not enough. They also need adequate support for international family planning and education programs. Both established agencies and developed countries must answer the call.

We as sexuality educators cannot continue to overlook the needs of adolescents in refugee camps, when, in fact, they are in the most precarious situations—with no adults to protect them, no access to contraceptives or condoms, no feelings of control, no set cultural scripts, no knowledge of the dangers of unprotected sexual intercourse, and no way to refuse acts that may lead to their death from the very real threats of AIDS and complications from adolescent pregnancy and childbirth.

Whether or not there is a village need not matter. There still can be love. There still can be hope. People who care can make all the difference in the world. We must raise children to be happy, healthy, and informed. We are, after all, a global village, and the future must be made bright for all our children.

REFERENCES

"People Who Move: New Reproductive Health Focus," *Population Reports,* volume 24, 3, Nov. 1997.

M. Obaso and W. Musuya, *Reproductive Health, Training and MISP Kits Needs Assessment Report (Nairobi),* International Federation of Red Cross and Red Crescent Societies, March, 1997.

The **world** made
flesh

Bodies. Human bodies. We love them. We need them. But examine the body, and you will see a lot more besides, argues **Vanessa Baird.**

Along the white corridors are garish, coloured illustrations showing parts of the body I hardly knew existed, let alone cared about.

They take on particular significance now, some organs and their functions especially so.

We make our way, down one floor, to the operating theatre. Above its twin doors are strict instructions not to enter. A few yards away, opposite the doors, are a couple of tables with blue covered chairs. Here we sit and wait.

Not for the first time am I aware of a horrible congruence. I was in the early stages of putting together this issue of the **NI** on the theme of 'the body' and had just finished commissioning the main articles, when there was a phone-call saying that a close relative has been taken quite unexpectedly, seriously, ill.

He is now behind those swing doors, fighting for his life.

Strangely, during these hours, while his actual body is undergoing a massive medical assault, it's not his body that fills my con-sciousness. Maybe because it doesn't bear thinking about. But I don't think this is the only reason.

As I gaze out of the window, up to the dark, ragged fringes of fir trees on the snow-clad mountains, I think not of his body but of his love for snow. And as I watch the birds darting and weaving between the eves, their lives and gestures so vital yet vulnerable, it's his vitality, his spirit that fills my mind.

After ten hours in the operating theatre the surgeon comes out. The operation was very tricky, but it's worked. The patient has age and strength on his side.

The next day we visit him. The first thing he does, in between all the tubes, and without a moment's hesitation, is to beckon and kiss us each in turn.

And it's perfect. The simplest, most direct way of expressing all the love, fear, relief, hope, gratitude. Bodily communicating what desperately needs to be said, but would take volumes to say in words.

Body politics

Returning to Oxford I find, on my desk, the piles of books I'd started reading on 'the body'. It's a trendy, 'hip' area of study these days. Much of the work is being done not by biologists but by philosophers, psycho-analysts and feminist theorists, drawing inspiration from French thinkers such as Hélène Cixous, Jacques Lacan, Michel Foucault, Jacques Derrida or Luce Irigaray. Debates on the 'materiality' versus the 'discursivity' of the body abound. And a lot of it is frankly impenetrable to the general reader.

I flick open one of the less jargon-bound collections and read: 'The body of woman is the site where culture manufactures the blockade of woman.' My mind quietly boggles at the prospect. Another text offers: 'Poststructuralist discourse analysis engages with the extra discursive of social reality (social practices, institutions etc) and of *corporeal* bodies (their physical beings) . . .' Well, there you are.

I find it hard to relate these writings either to the feelings aroused by the personal experience of the body of a loved one at risk or to the subjects that lie at the heart of the *New Internationalist's* concerns. Issues like the right to the basic, vital things your body needs to survive: food, water, shelter, access to healthcare. The right not to have your body violated by others, be they oppressive regimes, employers or those with most clout within your family or community.

But there is a connection. These texts may not dwell on what bodies need, but they do examine what bodies 'mean'. And what bodies 'mean' in a particular culture or society actually plays a crucial role in determining who can have what they need in their lives and who can't.

More explicitly, inequalities in the world are established and maintained by the 'meaning' that we give different bodies.

It's often extremely crude. For example, in many parts of the world, if you are born with a female body you are automatically denied control over your own life. You are the possession of your father or your brothers or your uncles until you become that of your husband and later your sons. Inferiority is 'read' into your body at birth. Your very chances of survival may be affected. In Bangladesh girls have a 70-percent higher mortality rate than boys for the simple reasons that they are fed less and are less likely than their brothers to be taken to a health clinic if ill.[1]

Gender is not the only issue. Not so long ago—before 1994 to be precise—if you were one of the 30 million South Africans with a black-skinned body you had to live in designated areas and were not even allowed to vote in elections in your own country.

The stamping of inequality on our bodies occurs in an infinite variety of ways. If you are disabled you generally do not have the same rights to a job or to mainstream education as an able-bodied person. In many countries—Romania springs to mind—you are likely to be incarcerated in an institution at birth.

Body prejudice also comes in more subtle guises. It may be focused on what you actually do with your body. If you come from a class background in which it is usual to sell your bodily or manual skills rather than your cerebral abilities then the chances are you will receive lower wages and be less valued for the work you do. Unless, that is, you happen to enjoy the elevated status of a sports celebrity or supermodel.

Finally, your chances in life can be determined by whether your body conforms to your society's ideals of beauty. This has been particularly true for women. Without political or economic power, a woman is entirely dependent on male patronage and thus male ideas of how she should behave and appear. Typically, this is internalized by women and becomes an obsessive concern with physical appearance. It's not just a case of 'you are your body', but 'you are what your body looks like'. If you have any doubts about the continued power and prevalence of this, consult any magazine rack.

If we look at the body, we can see the world. If we look at how different bodies—black, white, male, female, rich, poor—are viewed, and what kind of privileges or privations that accrue to them, then we see a picture of the world of human, social and economic relationships. In this sense the body is 'the world made flesh'.

Skinny things and nipple rings

And look at bodies we do. For we are fascinated by them. Although most major religions in the world maintain that our temporal bodies are not the most important thing in life and it's our eternal souls that really count, body-consciousness rules supreme.

It makes sense in a way. Our bodies are our prime source of pleasure and pain, our first point of contact with the world. What would our lives in the world be without our bodies? They are a source of delight. Cultures and religions that have tried to deny the flesh have almost always lapsed into hypocrisy. Such regimes—be they Catholic or Puritan—become obsessed with the flesh, especially female flesh. The women in Tehran or Kabul trying to navigate kerbs and potholes via the tiny permissible slits in their veils, are at the sharp end of such denials.

The joys of physicality may be simple, like feeling the air on your face as you step out on a Spring morning. The cold smoothness of a stone. The rugged bark of a tree. The exhilaration of water. The comfort of the bodies of loved ones. The intimacy of loving eroticism. The magic of sex.

The body is also an amazingly powerful medium for transmitting information and emotions between living creatures. Even when people are speaking to each other face-to-face, two-thirds of their communication is non-verbal body-language.[2]

But our fascination with the body far exceeds these simple functions and pleasures. It can also be a very potent zone of self expression, giving scope to tremendous creativity on the one hand, dreary uniformity on the other. It has lead to extraordinary feats of dance and athletics, and dazzling displays of imagination when it comes to adornment.

International and popular culture bombards us non-stop with body consciousness. Beautiful bodies are used to sell almost anything. And there's a lot of money to be made in the products and services of the body business, be they the provision of fashionable 'energy' drinks or cosmetic surgery. As Jeremy Seabrook says in his article *Of human bondage* (see "New Internationalist," April 1998) human bodies are the world's biggest cash crop. The body is both the means of industrial production and the market for its products.

What the body business most profitably taps into is our use of our bodies to identify ourselves. This need is fundamental and universal. Tribal markings are everywhere to be seen: in the etched cheeks of a Yoruba villager in Southern Nigeria and the pierced nipple of a gay teenager in a Liverpool night-club; in the pure-silk sari of the Bombay socialite and the designer tie of the Wall Street financier.

With the globalization of the world economy, and the aggressive marketing of 'cool' body images, the definitions of desirability and available identities seem to become increasingly narrow. The young and trendy wear Billabong cult clothing, be they in Brisbane or Bogotá. And traditional aesthetics are rapidly being replaced by a Westernized, globalized image.

Nowhere is this more painfully expressed than in the hyper-slender model for women, the 'Barbie-doll' look that has swept the world. Recently there have been reports of anorexia—previously thought to affect only white middle-class teenagers—among young black women in Southern Africa. 'In African culture beauty is traditionally associated with round bodies but as Western culture creeps into this society, so anorexia is affecting more and more Africans,' quotes Tsitso Rampuku, reporting from Lesotho, where there has been a spate of recent cases.

The young and trendy wear Billabong, be they in Brisbane or Bogotá

Across the border, in South Africa, it's a similar story. Malinda Motaung, a nurse working in Bloemfontein, says she has noticed a big increase in an illness that was unknown in her clinic five years ago. Mampho Mokhethe, mother of a 17-year-old

anorectic, blames this on the way young urban women are bombarded with images of beautiful and successful women. 'And almost without fail, they are thin,' she says. 'The subtle message is: if you want to get ahead, you had better look like supermodel Naomi Campbell.'[3]

Anorexia has to do with more than fashion. It has to do with power. Although a few males are affected, it's mainly a female problem. For many young women, eating is the area in which they feel they can have real control. US academic Susan Bordo quotes Aimee Liu, an ex-anorectic recreating her mindset at the time of her illness: 'Energy, discipline, my own power will keep me going. I need nothing and no-one else . . . I will be master of my own body, if nothing else, I vow.'

Like the flesh-denying ascetic, the anorectic's ability to live with minimal food makes her feel powerful and worthy of admiration in a world from which, at the most profound level, she feels excluded and unvalued.[4]

The terrible irony is that it is so self-defeating. As Bordo points out, the symptoms of anorexia isolate, weaken and undermine its sufferer, as she turns the life of the body into an all-absorbing fetish. In effect she capitulates to patriarchy's traditional demand that women limit themselves and live in a shrunken world.

Ultimately others—principally medical professionals—intervene, and take control.

The body in parts

Few encounters require that we willingly submit our bodies to a group of strangers, to examine, prod, poke, inject and even cut open. But that, in theory, is what we do when we cross the threshold into a doctor's surgery or a hospital. If you are in pain or in danger it's only natural to want someone to make you better, to magic the trouble away. You may feel so grateful to that person that you don't question too closely the magic they are using, or its premise. The power we hand over to our chosen healers is really quite astounding when you stop to think about it.

Until the 1970s the authority of orthodox Western medicine went virtually unchallenged. Although it borrows much of its terminology from the Classical Greeks, it does not use the same premise that mind, spirit and body are interconnected. Rather it uses the Cartesian notion that mind and body are quite separate entities and the body is but a kind of biological machine.

This mechanistic view has given birth to the stereotype of the consultant zooming in on an organ or a condition, ignoring the person it belongs to and then talking to colleagues about it in technical language the patient doesn't understand. This is not just the hackneyed stuff of comic movies. Although slowly changing, it's still the experience of many people around the world when they come into contact with the medical profession.

Medical anthropologist Nancy Scheper-Hughes reports that poor people in Brazil fear that health professionals will 'steal their organs' for transplant. This fear is in a sense realistic, but it can also be seen as a symbolic response to a medical approach that has scant regard for the integrity of the human being.

In the rich world, too, there is growing disenchantment with Western medical system that treats people as though their bodies were machines, with parts that may go wrong and need discrete and specific treatment.

This has fed the growth of 'holistic' approaches and alternative therapies. Most popular are acupuncture, homeopathy and osteopathy. More than one in three people in Britain has consulted an alternative health practitioner, and similar figures apply in Australia, Canada and the US. Even the World Health Organization has criticized doctors for failing to accept acupuncture as a useful complementary medical technique.

Many argue that the boom in alternative medicine is giving patients choice and more power over their own bodies. This is debatable, as some alternative practitioners can be even more interventionist and paternalistic than orthodox doctors.[5]

But the idea that mind, body and spirit are interconnected, and that they have their own self-healing mechanisms, is gaining currency even in the most unexpected quarters.

I recall the surgeon who operated on my relative. He had said prior to the operation that during it he would be doing half the work, the patient would be doing the other half. And as I watched the birds and thought of the flow of his mind, body and spirit, this felt absolutely right.

One body, one world

We tend to think of the body as an entity with firm contours. In fact it is mainly fluid: two-thirds of it is water. If we thought of our bodies more in this way, I wonder what difference it would make. Would our thinking about our bodies be less hard and possessive? Would we think in terms of sharing an economy of vitality? Would we think differently about inner and outer, about self and other, about the boundary between your body and my body?

The word 'body' is not always personal and individualistic. It can also be used to describe a collection of people. It's long been recognized by ethicists that belonging to a 'social body' makes it possible to equate one's own good with that of another and thus to refrain from mutual injury, violence and exploitation. Why shouldn't the terms of reference be expanded to include the universal body, the international body of humanity?

Let's conclude with a little holistic exercise. The world is a body, your body. The top half of your body, the Northern part, say, gets all the goodness it needs to survive and more. In some parts it's actually quite bloated.

The bottom half, the Southern part, say, is in a state of perpetual struggle to get what it needs to survive. It has plenty of vitality, is capable of joy, but somehow it never gets quite enough goodness or nourishment in relation to the energy it expends just to stay alive.

In between the two, somewhere below your belly, is a belt. A very tight belt. It has to be that way, you are told, because your Northern body and your Southern body are different.

Not a very healthy state of affairs. Might it not be a good idea to loosen the belt a bit, let some of the goodness and nourishment flow around the whole body? Wouldn't Northern and Southern body benefit from this?

Your toes would probably agree.

1 United Nations, *Women: Challenges to the Year 2000,* New York, 1991. 2 Alan Pease, *Body Language,* Sheldon Press, 1997. 3 Tsitso Rampuku, 'Health fears as slimming mania hits Africans', Gemini News Service, London, 1997. 4 Susan Bordo, *Unbearable Weight: Feminism, Western Culture and the Body,* University of California Press, 1993. 5 Dr Vernon Coleman, *Spiritpower,* European Medical Journal, Barnstaple, 1997.

FEMINISM
IT'S ALL ABOUT ME!

Want to know what today's chic young feminist thinkers care about? Their bodies! Themselves!

By GINIA BELLAFANTE

GROWING UP IN WASHINGTON STATE DURING THE '70S, Courtney Love didn't care much for the women's-movement rallies her mother attended. "I'd wonder why nobody on these marches was wearing heels," she has said. But with its days of flat shoes and fiery protest behind it, feminism is clearly more attractive to Love now. Earlier this year, the angry rocker turned Versace model and movie star showed up at the Ms. Foundation's 25th-anniversary bash at Caroline's Comedy Club in New York City. A busy celebrity, she couldn't stay long. Springing up to leave midway through the event, she announced, "Can you believe it? Here I am with Gloria Steinem, and now I'm off to dinner with Milos Forman!"

The Ms. party was one of many in a hectic season of feminist nightlife in Manhattan. In April came *Show,* a living work of art by Vanessa Beecroft designed to humanize media images of female beauty and thus somehow invest women with power. The invitees gathered in the rotunda of the Guggehheim Museum in Manhattan to view 15 bikini-clad models staring into space atop their high heels. But the glitziest affair in recent

months was a reading of *The Vagina Monologues,* a performance piece about female private parts by Eve Ensler that attracted Uma Thurman, Winona Ryder and Calista Flockhart, among others. The actresses had come to raise money to fight domestic violence, but the cause seemed lost amid the event's giddy theatrics. Featured were Marisa Tomei on the subject of pubic hair (sample line; "You cannot love a vagina unless you love hair"); Glenn Close offering an homage to an obscene word for female genitalia; and, finally, the playwright delivering three solid minutes of orgasmic moaning. The *Village Voice* called it "the most important and outrageous feminist event" of the past 30 years.

Fashion spectacle, paparazzi-jammed galas, mindless sex talk—is this what the road map to greater female empowerment has become? If feminism is, as Gloria Steinem has said for decades, "a revolution and not a public relations movement," why has it come to feel so much like spin?

Steinem isn't the person to answer that question. The doyen of second-wave feminism startled many in March when she penned an op-ed piece for the New York *Times* arguing that

 From *Time,* June 29, 1998, pp. 54-60. © 1998 by Time Inc. Magazine Company. Reprinted by permission.

THEN AND NOW

In the '70s, feminism produced a pop culture that was intellectually provocative (O.K., maybe not Helen Reddy). Today it's a whole lot of stylish fluff

MAGAZINES

THEN The voice of the movement, Ms. magazine dissected women's roles, status and pay **NOW** The voice of the "new girl order," Bust sarcastically dissects often wacky sexual exploits

MOVIES

THEN When her husband leaves her, Jill Clayburgh gets a life in an *An Unmarried Woman* **NOW** In *My Best Friend's Wedding,* neurotic Julia Roberts badly wants the altared state

TELEVISION

THEN The essence of level-headedness, Mary Richards was a shoulder to lean on **NOW** The essence of flightiness, Ally McBeal can't even manage to lean on her sandaled self

ACTIVISM

THEN Gloria Steinem and pals took to the streets to protest male violence and Vietnam **NOW** Glen Close and Whoopi Goldberg perform *The Vagina Monologues*

MUSIC

THEN Brassy-voiced Helen Reddy earnestly declared, "I am woman, hear me roar!" and while you're at it, "Watch me grow. See me standing toe to toe" **NOW** The Spice Girls peddle girl power—short skirts and sass. "Yo, I'll tell you what I want, what I really, really want," as their famous lyric puts it

ART

THEN Judy Chicago's vagina motifs honored famous women **NOW** Vanessa Beecroft's *Show* makes bored models a display

BOOKS

THEN French's yearning women shed husbands and old roles and ventured on to find their independent selves **NOW** Fielding's party-loving Bridget tries shedding weight and bad habits, all in the hope of finding Mr. Someone

THEN A literary scholar and "saucy feminist," Greer railed against a culture that made women objects **NOW** A wannabe saucy feminist, Wurtzel pleads for "difficult" women and fusses over who's pretty

---

the allegations of a sexual dalliance between the President and a 21-year-old intern were nothing to get worked up about. If the stories were true (and she believed they were), then Clinton was guilty of nothing more than frat boyishness, Steinem wrote. *Backlash* author Susan Faludi also made excuses for the President, writing in the *Nation* that along with other powers, women have gained "the power to forgive men." And in the places where you would expect feminist indignation to be thriving—the élite liberal colleges of the Northeast—TIME found in numerous interviews that it isn't. On the Clinton sex scandal, Barnard College senior Rebecca Spence says, "As a self-defined feminist, I should be outraged, but I'm not."

Conservatives have an easy explanation for these forgiving attitudes toward the President's private treatment of women. They say Clinton-loving feminists, as if following the how-to-catch-a-man *Rules* manual, have chosen to overlook the faults of a man who has been their best provider. Ideals be damned for the President who vetoed the ban on partial-birth abortions.

But political allegiance is only part of the story. If women's leaders seemed to ignore some of the murkier questions raised by the Clinton scandal—for example, what does consensual sex mean between two people so unequal in power?—it is in part because feminism at the very end of the century seems to be an intellectual undertaking in which the complicated, often mundane issues of modern life get little attention and the narcissistic ramblings of a few new media-anointed spokeswomen get far too much. You'll have better luck becoming a darling of feminist circles if

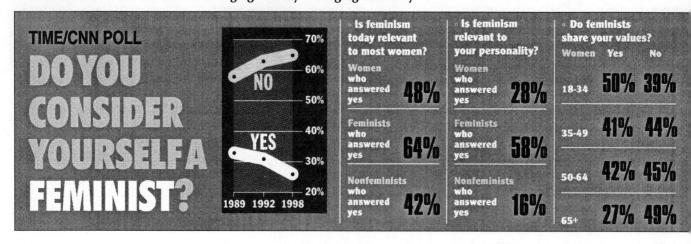

you chronicle your adventures in cybersex than if you churn out a tome on the glass ceiling.

W HAT A COMEDOWN FOR THE MOVEMENT. IF women were able to make their case in the '60s and '70s, it was largely because, as the slogan went, they turned the personal into the political. They used their daily experience as the basis for a critique, often a scholarly one, of larger institutions and social arrangements. From Simone de Beauvoir's *Second Sex* to Betty Friedan's *Feminine Mystique* to Kate Millett's *Sexual Politics*—a doctoral dissertation that became a national best seller—feminists made big, unambiguous demands of the world. They sought absolute equal rights and opportunities for women, a constitutional amendment to make it so, a chance to be compensated equally and to share the task of raising a family. But if feminism of the '60s and '70s was steeped in research and obsessed with social change, feminism today is wed to the culture of celebrity and self-obsession.

It is fair to ask why anyone should be worried about this outcome. Who cares about the trivial literary and artistic pursuits of a largely Manhattan-based group of self-appointed feminists? They're talking only to one another, after all. But the women's movement, like many upheavals before it, from the French Revolution in 1789 to the civil rights movement in the U.S. and even the uprising in Tiananmen Square, would be nowhere without the upper-middle-class intellectual élite. Feminism didn't start in the factory. It started in wood-paneled salons, spread to suburban living rooms, with their consciousness-raising sessions, and eventually ended up with Norma Rae. In fact, that trajectory is its biggest problem today—it remains suspect to those who have never ventured onto a college campus. A TIME/CNN poll shows what most people already suspect—that education more than anything else determines whether a woman defines herself as a feminist. Fifty-three percent of white, college-educated women living in cities embrace the label. Fifty percent of white women with postgraduate training and no children do the same. But feminism shouldn't

be punished for its pedigree. We would never have had Ginger Spice if we hadn't had Germaine Greer.

And that brings up another reason why the flightiness of contemporary feminism is a problem. Some would argue that if the women's movement were still useful, it would have something to say; it's dead because it has won. Some wags have coined a phrase for this: Duh Feminism. But there's nothing obvious about the movement's achievements. It's true that we now have a woman crafting America's foreign policy (Madeleine Albright), that a woman is deciding which Barbie dolls to produce (Jill Barad, CEO of Mattel) and a woman (Catharine MacKinnon) pioneered the field of sexual-harassment law (which is turning into real dollars for real women, as Mitsubishi Motors evidenced two weeks ago with its record $34 million payment to women on the assembly line). It's also true that women are joining together for their own, big-draw rock tours and that we now have "girl power," that sassy, don't-mess-with-me adolescent spirit that Madison Avenue carefully caters to. So yes, the women's movement changed our individual lives and expectations, and young women today acknowledge this. A hefty 50% of those from ages 18 to 34 told the pollsters in the TIME/CNN Survey that they share "feminist" values, by which they generally mean they want a world in which they can choose to be anything—the President or a mother, or both.

But that doesn't mean that American society is supporting them much in their choices, and this is where the pseudo-feminists of today could be of help. The average female worker in America still earns just 76¢ for every dollar a man earns, up 17¢ from the '70s but still no cause for rejoicing. And for most women, the glass ceiling is as impenetrable as ever. There are only two female CEOs at FORTUNE 500 companies, and just 10% of corporate officers are women. Day care, a top priority for both middle-class women and less fortunate mothers maneuvering through welfare reform, still seems a marginal issue to feminist leaders. Under the heading Key Issues on the website of the National Organization for Women, day care isn't even mentioned.

Instead, much of feminism has devolved into the silly. And it has powerful support for this: a popular culture insistent on offering images of grown single women as frazzled, self-ab-

What is your impression of feminists?		What is the main problem today facing women that men don't face?	Do the following describe feminists?						
			Work for equal rights	Work for equal pay	Work against sexual harassment	Support abortion rights	Work for affordable day care	Don't respect married stay-at-home moms	Don't like most men
1989 / **1998** **Favorable** 44% / 32%		Inequality in the workplace **34%**	**Women who answered yes** 85%	85%	81%	72%	65%	44%	37%
Unfavorable 29% / 43%		Difficulties balancing work/family **12%**	**Feminists who answered yes** 93%	93%	92%	71%	83%	28%	23%
From a telephone poll of 721 adult American women taken for TIME/CNN on May 16-19 by Yankelovich Partners Inc. Sampling error is ±6.8% and for Nonfeminists is ±4.6%.		Lack of quality child care **7%**	**Nonfeminists who answered yes** 83%	84%	78%	75%	60%	50%	44%

sorbed girls. Ally McBeal is the most popular female character on television. The show, for the few who may have missed it, focuses on a ditsy 28-year-old Ivy League Boston litigator who never seems in need of the body-concealing clothing that Northeastern weather often requires. Ally spends much of her time fantasizing about her ex-boyfriend, who is married and in the next office, and manages to work references to her mangled love life into nearly every summation she delivers. She has fits in supermarkets because there are too few cans of Pringles. She answers the question "Why are your problems so much bigger than everyone else's?" with the earnest response "Because they're mine." When Ally gets any work done, how she keeps her job, why she thinks it's O.K. to ask her secretary why she didn't give her a birthday present—these are all mysteries. Ally probably wouldn't seem so offensive as an addition to the cast of *Seinfeld,* but because this is a one-hour drama filled with pseudo-Melissa Etheridge music and emotional pretense, we are meant to take her problems more seriously than George Costanza's. "Ally McBeal is a mess. She's like a little animal," notes Nancy Friday, a sex-positive feminist if ever there was one. "You want to put her on a leash." And what does Ally's creator David Kelley have to say about Ally as a feminist? "She's not a hard, strident feminist out of the '60s and '70s. She's all for women's rights, but she does not want to lead the charge at her own emotional expense." Ally, though, is in charge of nothing, least of all her emotional life.

As if one Ally McBeal character was not enough, America is discovering another, the heroine of an enormously hyped novel called *Bridget Jones's Diary,* by British author Helen Fielding. The book, a best seller in England for months, is a sometimes funny but ultimately monotonous chronicle of a year in the life of an unmarried thirtysomething London editor whose thoughts never veer far from dating, the cocktail hour and her invariably failed attempts at calorie cutting. A typical Bridget reflection: "Cannot face thought of going to work. Only thing that makes it tolerable is thought of seeing Daniel again, but even this is inadvisable since am fat, have spot on chin, and desire only to sit on cushion eating chocolate and watching Xmas specials." Few women alive haven't dwelled on relationships or their appearance, but most manage to concern themselves with other things too. The problem with Bridget and Ally is that they are presented as archetypes of single womanhood even though they are little more than composites of frivolous neuroses.

ALLY MCBEAL AND BRIDGET JONES ARE THE PRODUCT of what could be called the Camille Paglia syndrome. In her landmark 1990 book, *Sexual Personae,* author Paglia used intellect to analyze art, history and literature from classical times to the 19th century and argue that it is men who are the weaker sex because they have remained eternally powerless over their desire for the female body. It is female sexuality, she said, that is humanity's greatest force. Her tome helped catapult feminism beyond an ideology of victimhood.

In the heated atmosphere of early-'90s gender politics, in which Anita Hill accused Clarence Thomas of sexual harassment before an audience of millions, Paglia quickly began turning up all over the media voicing her controversial opinions on the sex wars. Feminism wasted time trying to persuade us that men are tameable, she proclaimed. Relish sexual power, she told women, but don't go to frat parties expecting men to be saints. The argument was powerful and full of merit, but deployed by lesser minds it quickly devolved into an excuse for media-hungry would-be feminists to share their adventures in the mall or in bed. So let us survey the full post-Paglia landscape.

Out this spring is Lisa Palac's *The Edge of the Bed,* in which the author suggests that pornography can be liberating because X-rated movies were sexually freeing for her. "Once I figured out how to look at an erotic image and use my sexual imagination to turn desire into a self-generated orgasm, my life was irrevocably and positively changed," writes Palac. The subtext of her book is that sexual self-revelation is groundbreaking in itself. But of course it isn't. It's at least as old as the '70s. That decade gave us, among other things, the erotic art of feminist group-sex advocate Betty Dodson and a Now-sponsored sexuality conference that covered the subject of sadomasochism. And it gave us Erica Jong's titillating *Fear of Flying,* as well as Nancy Friday's 1973 best seller, *My Secret Garden,* which celebrated female sexual fantasies.

Beyond Palac, there are other young postfeminists who have launched careers by merely plucking from and personalizing Paglia's headline-making ideas. The latest addition to the women's-studies sections of bookstores, *Bitch: In Praise of Difficult Women,* features on its cover a topless picture of author Elizabeth Wurtzel. Beyond it lies a seemingly unedited rant in which Wurtzel, billed on her book jacket as a Pagliaite, demands for herself and womankind the right to be rapacious, have fits and own more than one Gucci bag. "I intend to scream, shout, throw tantrums in Bloomingdale's if I feel like it and confess intimate details of my life to complete strangers," she writes. "I intend to answer only to myself."

Then there is 29-year-old Katie Roiphe, who appeared on the scene with her 1993 book, *The Morning After,* arguing that heightened date-rape awareness on college campuses was creating a culture of sexual fear and hysteria. She has gone on to write articles that excuse bad male behavior and tout her own desirability. In a piece that appeared in the January issue of *Vogue,* she told the story of an affair she had had with a teacher when she was 16. "In that first moment of thinking, maybe he likes me, there is a blossoming of feminine power," she wrote. "I remember first learning from my 36-year-old that I had the ability to attract a man." The implication is that such relationships empower young girls because this one, she feels, was good for her. (Roiphe is currently expressing her feminine power as a model for Coach leather goods.)

The most fussed-about young poet of the moment is Deborah Garrison, whose new collection, *A Working Girl Can't Win,* revolves around a quintessentially self-absorbed postfeminist. Again we get a picture of a career woman in her 20s who doesn't feel pretty enough and who fantasizes about life as a sexpot. "I'm never going to sleep/ with Martin Amis/ or anyone famous./At twenty-one I scotched/ my chance to be/ one of the seductresses/ of the century,/ a vamp on the rise through the ranks/ of literary Gods and military men,/ who wouldn't stop at the President:/ she'd take the Pentagon by storm/ in halter dress and rhinestone extras," Garrison writes in "An Idle Thought." (It could be retitled "Oh, How I Would Have Put You to Shame, Monica Lewinsky.") Garrison's efforts won her a book blurb from feminist columnist Katha Pollitt, who described the poems as "brave, elegant, edgy."

EVEN THOSE FEMINISTS WHO DON'T NECESSARILY embrace Paglia's world view seem to have inherited the postfeminist tic of offering up autobiography as theory. A 1995 anthology of young feminist thought, *To Be Real,* compiled by Rebecca Walker, is a collection of airy—sometimes even ludicrous—mini-memoirs meant to expand our understanding of female experience. She introduces the material by explaining that she first felt guilty about putting together such an introspective, apolitical book. But, Walker says, she resisted the pressure

"to make a book I really wasn't all that desperate to read." An essay by Veena Cabreros-Sud tells us how empowering it can be to have random fistfights with strangers. And there's the interview with model Veronica Webb titled "How Does a Supermodel Do Feminism?," in which she explains that while the fashion industry may make women feel inadequate, there is a physically deformed little girl she knows "who actually has more self-confidence than I do."

Feminist author Naomi Wolf's most recent book, 1997's *Promiscuities,* draws on what she and her friends experienced growing up to make the point that female longing is dangerously suppressed in our culture. She argues that the world would be a better place if we celebrated women's sexuality the way so many ancient peoples did. "Confucius, in his Book of Rites," she writes, "held that it was a husband's duty to take care of his wife or concubine sexually as well as financially and emotionally." It seems to have eluded Wolf that ancient Chinese women might have aspired to something better than life as a concubine.

Then there is the matter of *Bust,* the hip magazine of the moment. Created by Debbie Stoller, a 35-year-old who holds a doctorate in women's studies from Yale, and Marcelle Karp, a 34-year-old TV producer, *Bust* is a magazine intentionally written in teenspeak but meant for female readers in their late 20s and early 30s. It was developed as an antidote to magazines like *Cosmopolitan,* which present female sexuality so cartoonishly. However noble the intent, the message is often lost in the magazine's adolescent tone: read about an adult woman's first-time vibrator discoveries or a scintillating account of lust for delivery men in an article titled "Sex with the UPS Guy." Of the magazine's purposely immature tone, Stoller says, "Women have been forced into roles as women and now they're rebelling." But in the end, *Bust* offers a peek-aboo view of the world of sex that leaves one feeling not like an empowered adult but more like a 12-year-old sneaking in some sexy reading behind her parents' back.

Bust, which began as a photocopied 'zine, is essentially a product of alternative culture's Riot Grrrl movement, an effort by new female bands in the early '90s to reclaim the brash, bratty sense of self-control that psychologists claim girls lose just before puberty. And in many ways, the movement succeeded, as any fan of Sleater-Kinney and even the Spice Girls will tell you. But even in the world of pop music, with the spirit of girl power behind it, the concept of feminism is often misapplied. Look how the label is tossed about: female singers like Meredith Brooks and Alanis Morissette are installed as icons of woman power (alongside real artist-activists like Tori Amos) simply because they sing about bad moods or boyfriends who have dumped them. In the late '60s, when the label was applied more sparingly, no one thought to call Nancy Sinatra a feminist, and yet if she recorded *These Boots Are Made for Walkin'* in 1998, she'd probably find herself headlining the Lilith Fair.

Part of the reason for Riot Grrrl's impact is that it often focused on the issue of childhood sexual abuse. Not only did the songs relate harrowing personal experiences but the band members started 'zines and websites through which teenagers who had been molested could communicate with one another. Riot Grrrl's concerns paralleled those of feminists in the grownup world who, around the same time, also became preoccupied with sexual abuse and self-help (even Steinem got in on the act with her 1992 book, *Revolution from Within).* But many of those grownups, who called themselves feminist therapists, ended up attaching themselves to the bizarre fringes of the sexual-recovery movement. "Women weren't looking at their lives and saying, 'I'm stressed because I'm getting no help at home,' they were saying, 'I'm stressed out because my family molested me in the crib,'" explains social psychologist Carol Tavris. "The feelings of powerlessness many women continued to have in the early '90s got attached to sex-abuse-survivor syndrome." When Tavris debunked self-help books on incest-survivor syndrome in the New York *Times* Book Review in 1993, she received a flood of letters from feminist therapists calling her a betrayer.

If feminism has come to seem divorced from matters of public purpose, it is thanks in part to shifts in the academy. "Women's studies, a big chunk of it at least, has focused increasingly on the symbols of the body and less on social action and social change," explains Leslie Calman, a political-science professor and director of the Center for Research on Women at Barnard College. Moreover, gender studies, the theoretical analysis of how gender identities are constructed, have become increasingly incorporated into women's studies or turned into rival departments of their own. In April, Yale University renamed its Women's Studies Department the Women and Gender Studies Department.

It's not surprising that Old Guard feminists, surveying their legacy, are dismayed by what they see. "All the sex stuff is stupid," said Betty Friedan. "The real problems have to do with women's lives and how you put together work and family." Says Susan Brownmiller, author of *Against Our Will,* which pioneered the idea that rape is a crime of power: "These are not movement people. I don't know whom they're speaking for. They seem to be making individual bids for stardom." It's easy to dismiss the voices of Old Guard feminists as the typical complaints of leaders nostalgic for their days at center stage. But is Ally McBeal really progress? Maybe if she lost her job and wound up a single mom, we could begin a movement again.

Men In CRISIS

Throughout our history, *Ladies' Home Journal* has written about the sometimes maddening but always fascinating relationship between men and women. Now, for our **115th Anniversary,** we bring you this excerpt from best-selling author Gail Sheehy's new book, *Understanding Men's Passages.* From her blockbuster *Passages,* which provided a map to adulthood, to what has become a bible on menopause, *The Silent Passage,* Sheehy has helped us navigate the transitions of life. Here, she sorts out the challenges besetting men today.

By Gail Sheehy

Headlines and books trumpet the notion that manhood is on trial—or that it is dead altogether. The forties, which ought to be the peak decade in the lives of most men, are often filled with anxiety, dread and isolation. No less an icon than Clint Eastwood calls himself the "last cowboy." Robert Kincaid, the protagonist of *The Bridges of Madison County*—whom Eastwood played in the film of the same name—describes himself as obsolete: Computers and robots, he says, have replaced men of courage. Meanwhile, women's magazines instruct their readers in how to satisfy their own rising expectations: "Seize the Night!" they urge. "Your Sexual Peak Is Now!"

"Men in their forties feel quite threatened and attacked," says John Munder Ross, Ph.D., a pioneer in men's studies who teaches psychoanalysis and human development at the New York medical schools of Columbia, Cornell and New York University, and the author of *The Male*

Paradox (Simon & Schuster, 1992). "On the work front and at home, they feel expendable. Women begin to look for positive changes in their forties, when their years of total parenthood are winding down. They become more invested in their careers, and often initiate separation from their mates. Men are much more dependent, and they have greater separation anxiety than they like to acknowledge."

Changes in the landscape

It is commonly believed that men are hardwired to act aggressively and suppress emotion, and in fact it is true that

in studies of temperament, one of the most striking gender differences is a man's ability to remain cool under physical attack. Yet there is also a basic need for intimacy that becomes more persistent as a man grows older.

What confuses this natural process for men today is the erosion of traditional male roles and privileges. For tens of thousands of years, men were warriors and hunters, dominant over women and indispensable as breadwinners. Their brawn was admired and feared. But in the past few decades—an evolutionary eye-blink—men have been asked to cool their aggressiveness, share their

In recent decades, Sheehy says, men have been asked to cool their aggressiveness and share their emotional secrets

emotional secrets and be more polite about their sexual predation.

To make matters worse, millions of men at all social levels who expected to be secure by midlife are

ing as a way for men to reassert a male preserve and adopt a status symbol that is considerably cheaper than a luxury car. During the next four years, the sales of premium ci-

what constitutes the code of manliness today. As one beefy blond Gen-Xer of twenty-eight raised in the American West says, with noticeable envy, "With my parents, there was a relationship of clear dominance and submission. My dad acted with godlike certainty. I mean, he assumed prerogative. My mother assumed it was her role to show deference." He summed up the dilemma: "There are no rules for how to be a man today."

When men today struggle to live up to the traditional mold of masculinity, they are trying to accomplish the big impossible. For some time now, women have been defying all the stereotypes with which they grew up, and they are measurably happier in midlife than any previous generation has been. It is time that men recognize that their old roles and rules are virtually impossible to live up to in the contemporary world. Trying to do so only limits their otherwise exhilarating possibilities for custom-designing a happier middle life.

"There are no rules for how to be a man today," says one twenty-eight-year-old

seeing their jobs disappear or their marriages disintegrate. The participation of adult males in the workforce is down from 87 percent in 1948 to just over 75 percent now.

Furthermore, American men in every age group under sixty-five have watched their income (in constant dollars) remain flat, decline or show only modest gains over the past two decades, while women's has steadily climbed. And the more economically independent women become, the less likely they are to remain in a miserable marriage.

Given these role-shattering changes, the historical model of masculinity is blurred at best. As in any era of profound change, there is a predictable backlash.

Sometimes a cigar is more than a cigar

The scene is The Big Smoke, in San Francisco, at the Embarcadero Center. A thousand men are here to smoke big cigars, sip booze, get a little buzz and show off. Big steak-and-potatoes men with slaphappy smiles strut around the display booths. At the center of the swirl is the short, thick figure of Marvin Shanken, the prescient editor of *Cigar Aficionado*. When he launched his magazine in 1992, the antismoking wave was at its peak and the cigar market had dropped like a stone. But Shanken understood that men were famished for ways to express their maleness. He saw cigar smok-

gars more than doubled, and circulation and ad sales for Shanken's magazine followed suit.

Of course, the cigar-smoking trend does not seriously address the confusion over a code of manliness appropriate to today. It is an elite version of a larger movement among men who feel displaced, disappointed and "dissed." Men need action-oriented ways and places they can get together with other men; many of those opportunities have been lost as a result of laws—justified and long overdue—against sexual discrimination.

"The Big Impossible"

Men's problem with defining their masculinity is an eternal one. In aboriginal North America, for example, among the nonviolent Fox tribe of the Iowa area, real manhood was described as "the Big Impossible." It was an elevated status that only an extraordinary few could achieve.

A man is *made* a man. Manhood is not something he's born with but something he earns. Anthropologist David D. Gilmore, in a cross-cultural study, finds that on every continent, among everyone from simple hunters to sophisticated urbanites, boys must pass a critical threshold, through harsh testing, before they can gain the right to be called men. There is no single line that, once passed, confers manhood, as menstruation marks womanhood for girls.

Even young men in their late twenties admit they are confused about

Honor among men

"What men need is men's approval," notes playwright David Mamet. Traditionally, men have demonstrated their masculinity through displays of honor in the fields of sports, politics, business and war—all fields that until very recently excluded women. No matter how the roles of men have changed, one cultural truth remains: Men care most about what other men think of them. Their greatest fear is of being dominated or humiliated by a stronger man, particularly in front of other men. How then do they continue to demonstrate their manliness in middle life, even as their physical strength wanes and as the need arises to listen to and accommodate others in order to fulfill leadership roles?

Through sports, for one thing. The average American man watches twenty-eight hours of TV a week, much of it sports. Basketball, baseball, football and soccer are more than games. They constitute a culture—arguably, the dominant male culture today.

In a fascinating book called *The Stronger Women Get, the More Men Love Football* (Harcourt Brace & Co., 1994), Mariah Burton Nelson, a former professional female basketball player, points out that "manly sports comprise a world where men are in charge and women are irrelevant at best. . . . Sports offer a . . . world where men, as owners, coaches and umpires, still rule."

Sports also permit shared passion between men. It is most often the over-forty guys in the stands at games who shriek and groan and weep, uncovering raw emotions they would contain in front of other men in almost any other setting.

More important, true athletic heroes are champions at emotional control. If they weren't able to psych themselves up, control their anxieties, channel their anger and blot out the jeers of the crowd, they would never have the concentration necessary to kick that crucial field goal or come back from losing the first set. As Nelson writes, "When they fight, the fighting is deliberate masculine theater, not a momentary loss of control. The decision to [lose one's temper] involves rational considerations: not losing face, trying to win games, fulfilling expectations of fans and teammates and appearing on the evening news."

Current models of manhood

Men are finding ways to bolster themselves in this time of confusion, sometimes shifting back and forth among the following expressions of manliness, depending on mood or circumstances.

One of the strongest trends of the nineties is the reversion to the pre-feminist, pre-Alan Alda form, **Resurgent Angry Macho Man (RAMM)**. The RAMM movement encourages a man to return to his primitive nature as the wild man with fire in his belly and a strong arm to put women back in their place. The prototype is the American cowboy. The tough loner who shoots from the hip, doesn't need love, doesn't stick around with women and doesn't react to loss was a cultural ideal through the 1950s. John Wayne, who has held up as a symbol of manhood for several generations, remains an inspiration to men of the RAMM type. As described by Garry Wills in his book *John Wayne's America* (Simon & Schuster, 1997), Wayne is the very embodiment of the country's receded frontier, "untrammeled, unspoiled, free to roam."

The opposite philosophy is represented by the **Sensitive New Age Guy (SNAG)**, initially a man who discovered his nurturing side unexpectedly (or by default, as in the film *Kramer vs. Kramer*). In the extreme version, he switched roles and assumed the prerogatives of Mr. Mom. He expected his kids and wife to idealize his contribution, his hours would remain discretionary, and he wouldn't be responsible for mortgage payments. Or, having fought for custody after divorce, he was determined to prove he could outdo Mom. The results among men who actually try to perform this role without work outside the home are mixed. They can usually develop the necessary empathy and patience to care for the kids, but forgoing career ambitions and male posturing may eventually make them feel emasculated. And they often find themselves left behind by women, who desert them to seek wider horizons themselves.

However, many successful men in midlife have disclosed to me that they yearn to enjoy a period as Mr. Mom. This is an important cultural change, still small, but growing. It could be a very healthy way for a man in transition to exercise his nurturing side and feel useful while he is figuring out a new direction.

The currently popular Hollywood model of the SNAG is a successful but egocentric Yuppie who almost loses what is most important but is saved in the end by growing out of his macho posturing. The zany putty-face Jim Carrey scored a big hit with *Liar Liar*, which features a driven lawyer whose five-year-old son magically transforms a narcissis- tic no-show into a sensitive hands-on father.

Another expression of manliness is the **Dominant Male Model (DOM)**. These men are the world-beaters, the wunderkinder, the high achievers who have to be on top to be happy. In contemporary terms, they were the hotshot bond traders of the greedy eighties so memorably labeled by Tom Wolfe as Masters of the Universe. In the nineties they are personified by the rogue elephants of the information and entertainment worlds: Bill Gates, Rupert Murdoch, Donald Trump.

Yet a fourth philosophy is the **Messenger of God** model (MOG), propounded by a new wave of evangelism, which calls upon men to band together in spiritually inspired mass movements that bear a great resemblance to twelve-step programs. Men are recruited to these movements by powerful autocratic figures: Louis Farrakhan, for example, the militantly anti-Semitic Muslim who presided over the Million Man March, or Bill McCartney, the messianic former football coach who created the Promise Keepers. Both of these movements tap into a longing for ideals, discipline, spiritual guidance and a resurgence of male authority. They appeal particularly to boomers and Gen-Xers, with their use of rock music, an athletic "uniform," martial speeches, the pointed exclusion of women and permission for heterosexual men to show love for one another. Adherents recite vows to become better fathers, husbands and community leaders and dedicate themselves to restoring Scriptural values.

A true grassroots movement is the **Partner and Leader** model **(PAL)**. Men are finding ways to bond in small groups that form spontaneously—through a school or church connection, among men cruelly downsized at a workplace or shut out of their children's lives as noncustodial fathers. In these smaller groups, men are encouraged to act as partners as well as leaders, rather than being led by any higher authority. They are not bonding for the historical purpose of attacking or defending turf, but as chosen brothers who can offer each other support and solace or aid in unlearning the socialization that keeps them locked up with inscrutable feelings and secret failings.

These groups are not usually religious, but there are reverberations among men in the Christian communities, who are being called by their churches to find new meaning in service and community leadership. Wives are welcomed as full partners. The new manhood ideal here is servant-leader. Christian counseling is blended with psychotherapy. The call is to spiritual transformation, stressing the movement from success to significance.

Reinventing manhood

In truth, no man is just one of these types. Men's lives today call upon a full range of capacities—from brute force to gentle empathy—and it is no longer necessary or useful to lock oneself into the old stereotypes. With military confrontations increasingly being replaced by trade wars, men have a greater chance to develop new "manly arts."

To speak of the end of manhood is both absurd and destructive. What is needed is a new definition of manliness, one that celebrates the strengths of the post-patriarchal male in midlife and uses his individual gifts. Such ideals are indispensable to the healthy functioning of any culture, to give men a purpose in life regardless of their age, and urgently necessary to bind men psychologically into the family and the community.

Gail Sheehy
For over two decades, this noted journalist and author has helped us to understand the adult life cycle. "Men in Crisis" excerpted from her new book, *Understanding Men's Passages* (Random House, 1998)— is her take on the state of modern manhood.

Unit Selections

Key Points to Consider

❖ How do you rate yourself with respect to knowing how your body works sexually on a scale from one (very uninformed, not even sure of correct names for my parts and processes) to six (well-informed and can troubleshoot sexual health conditions and figure out how to improve sexual response)? What has held your score down or increased it?

❖ If you or your sexual partner were experiencing a sexual problem, would you prefer it to have a physical, an emotional, or an interactional cause? Why?

❖ How have (or would) you react if a friend confided in you that he or she was having sexual functioning problems, for example, erections or painful intercourse problems? What if the person confiding in you was a coworker? A stranger? Your mother or your grandfather? Who would you talk to if it were you with the problem and what response would you want from the other person?

❖ It is rare for people to wonder why someone is heterosexual in the same ways as we wonder why someone is homosexual or bisexual. What do you think contributes to a person's sexual orientation? Do you think it is possible for people not to feel threatened by sexual orientations different from their own? Why or why not?

 **Links**   **www.dushkin.com/online/**

7. **Bibliography: HIV/AIDS and College Students**
   http://www.sph.emory.edu/bshe/AIDS/college.html

8. **The Body: A Multimedia AIDS and HIV Information Resource**
   http://www.thebody.com/cgi-bin/body.cgi

9. **Healthy Way**
   http://www.ab.sympatico.ca/Contents/Health/GENERAL/sitemap.html

10. **Hispanic Sexual Behavior and Gender Roles**
   http://www.caps.ucsf.edu/hispnews.html

11. **James Kohl**
   http://www.pheromones.com

12. **Johan's Guide to Aphrodisiacs**
   http://www.santesson.com/aphrodis/aphrhome.htm

These sites are annotated on pages 4 and 5.

Human bodies are miraculous things. Most of us, however, have less than a complete understanding of how they work. This is especially true of our bodily responses and functioning during sexual activity. Efforts to develop a healthy sexual awareness are severely hindered by misconceptions and lack of quality information about physiology. The first portion of this unit directs attention to the development of a clearer understanding and appreciation of the workings of the human body.

Over the past decade and a half, the general public's awareness of, and interest and involvement in, their own health care has dramatically increased. We want to stay healthy and live longer and know that to do so, we must know more about our bodies, including how to prevent problems, recognize danger signs, and find the most effective treatments. By the same token, if we want to be sexually fit and to continue being sexually functional as we age, we must be knowledgeable about sexual health care. *Annual Editions: Human Sexuality 99/00* has an expanded section that can help readers do what they need to do today to be healthy, happy, sexy older men and women in the twenty-first century.

As you read through the articles in this section, you will be able to see more clearly that matters of sexual biology and behavior are not merely physiological in origin. The articles included clearly demonstrate the psychological, social, and cultural origins of sexual behavior as well.

Why we humans feel, react, respond, and behave sexually can be quite complex. This is especially true regarding the issue of sexual orientation. Perhaps no other area of sexual behavior is as misunderstood as this one. Although experts do not agree about what causes our sexual orientation—homosexual, hetero-sexual, or bisexual—growing evidence suggests a complex interaction of biological or genetic determination, environmental or sociocultural influence, and free choice. In the early years of this century, sexologist Alfred Kinsey's seven-point continuum of sexual orientation was introduced. It placed exclusive heterosexual orientation at one end, exclusive homosexual orientation at the other, and identified the middle range as where most people would fall if society and culture were unprejudiced. Since Kinsey, many others have added their research findings and theories to what is known about sexual orientation. John Money, a Johns Hopkins University researcher, who for the last 30 years has done research and writing on what he calls the sexology of erotic orientation, asserts that we should consider orientation as even more multidimensional than Kinsey's continuum. He stands with others who suggest that we pluralize our terms in this area: human sexualities.

That the previous paragraph may have been upsetting, even distasteful, to some readers emphasizes the connectedness of psychological, social, and cultural issues with those of sexuality. Human sexuality is biology, behavior, and much, much more. Our sexual beliefs, behaviors, choices, even feelings and comfort levels, are profoundly affected by what our culture prescribes and proscribes, which has been transmitted to us by the full range of social institutions and processes. This section begins our attempt to address these interrelationships and their impact on human sexuality.

The subsection *The Body and Its Responses* contains four informative and thought-provoking articles that illuminate the interplay of biological, psychological, cultural, and interpersonal factors that affect sexual functioning. Opening with intriguing current findings on chemical and sensual aphrodisiacs or lust-enhancers, it continues with a trio of articles that could serve as owners' manuals for female and male bodies. "Your Sexual Landscape" provides straightforward information on external female genitalia, points out signs of health and concern, and explains self-examination and medical exams. The last two articles "Impotency: Growing Malaise," from *India Today International,* and "The Viagra Craze," from *Time,* educate readers about male functioning, dysfunctioning, and the range of causes and treatments.

The subsection *Hygiene and Sexual Health Care* contains three articles that address a variety of sexual health concerns and factors that often hinder sexual desire and/or functioning. The first two articles focus on sexually transmitted diseases with "America: Awash in STDs" and "Hepatitis C: A Silent Killer" providing a combination of up-to-date factual information and examinations of social and political issues involved in, and perhaps hindering, efforts at containing these health crises. The last article addresses ongoing sexual functioning or "horizontal fitness" in positive, practical ways. The "Getting Your Groove Back" table in the last article covers the range of libido killers and what to do about them in a very usable, down-to-earth way.

The *Human Sexualities and Orientation* subsection contains three articles that dramatically demonstrate the changes that have occurred during the last decade with respect to sexual orientation. In the past few years, growing numbers of scientific findings have identified biological, genetic, and hormonal differences between heterosexual and homosexual people. However, these findings have not significantly weakened an American culture often called fundamentally homophobic (or homosexual-fearing). At the same time, more gay, lesbian, bisexual, and transgendered people have publicly acknowledged their orientation and have become more visible in the public eye via popular magazine stories, television, and movies. They are asserting their desires to be understood and accepted. In this subsection readers will meet some of these people, as well as some of their families, supporters, and critics. At the end, readers can make their own predictions about whether the first decade of the new century will bring a greater understanding and acceptance of the wide range of human sexualities, further entrenchment of homophobia, or an increased polarization of both.

Sexual Biology, Behavior, and Orientation

Recipes for Lust

Scientists had long dismissed aphrodisiacs as worthless.

Then studies revealed that some actually do what folklore and

herbalists claimed. Here's a guide to what works—and what doesn't.

BY MICHAEL CASTLEMAN

Old beliefs die hard—especially when they promise to add zing to our sex lives. The rhinoceros has been hunted to near-extinction partly because its powdered horn is believed to boost virility. (It doesn't.) And the legendary "Spanish fly"—actually made by pulverizing a Mediterranean beetle—is merely a urinary tract irritant that can be poisonous in large doses.

So until recently, scientists insisted that nothing ingested, inhaled, or injected could possibly have the amatory effect promised in that old rock song, "Love Potion #9," whose narrator "started kissing everything in sight" after downing an herbal brew. The sad fact is that there are many more ways to kill sexual interest than enhance it. But while science has still not identified anything that charms reluctant objects of desire into ripping off their clothes, a surprising number of herbs, drugs, and foods have physiological effects that just might make reluctant paramours more receptive to erotic invitations.

The reputations of most alleged aphrodisiacs can be traced to one of three sources: ancient myths, medieval medical theory, and traditional herbal medicine. The term "aphrodisiac" itself comes from Aphrodite, Greek goddess of beauty and love. In mythology, when Uranus, ruler of the heavens, was killed in a battle among the gods, his flesh fell into the sea and Aphrodite was created from it. Ever since the tale arose, products of the sea have been considered sex stimulants—especially oysters, whose fleshy moistness bears some fanciful resemblance to the female genitalia.

Such resemblances lie at the heart of the Doctrine of Signatures, a dubious medical philosophy that reigned in the Middle Ages. The idea was that God had blessed his children with natural remedies that announced their utility by their appearance, or "signature." Plants with heart-shaped leaves were prescribed for heart disease, yellow flowers were used to treat jaundice, and so on. Using the same "logic," plants with phallic parts—carrots, for example—were considered virility boosters, according to George Armelagos, Ph.D., a professor of anthropology at Emory University and author of *Consuming Passions: The Anthropology of Eating*. Similarly, anything soft and moist—peaches, oysters, ripe tomatoes—were linked to the vagina and considered aphrodisiacs for women. The theory held sway from China to Africa, where rhino horns looked phallic enough to spur the belief that they were sex stimulants. The head ornaments of other animals also gained reputations as aphrodisiacs—and gave us a term for feeling sex-starved, "horny."

Meanwhile, in herbal medicine any plant containing a stimulant gained a reputation as a sex enchancer. Before Arab caliphs visited their harems they sipped coffee, which of course contains caffeine. Montezuma and Casanova fortified themselves for sex by drinking another caffeinated beverage, hot chocolate. In addition, many herbs with action on the urinary tract gained reputations as aphrodisiacs, particularly irritants like Spanish fly and diuretics like saw palmetto.

BEYOND FOLKLORE

Until the early 1980s, most scientists had dismissed all traditional aphrodisiacs as quaint frauds whose powers had less to do with sex than suggestion. In some cases, they're right: Nothing even remotely libidinous has ever been discovered about the herb damiana, despite its scientific name, Turnera aphrodisiaca. "It's very difficult to separate aphrodisiacs' effects on the mind from their effects on the body," notes Varro Tyler, Ph.D., a recently retired professor of pharmacognosy (natural medicine) at Purdue University. "Sexual enjoyment involves the mind as much as the body, so anything people consider arousing becomes arousing."

But with all due respect to the power of suggestion, researchers are now finding that several traditional aphrodisiacs do stimulate more than just the imagination:

• **YOHIMBE.** For centuries the bark of the West African yohimbe tree was reputed to restore erections to impotent men. And studies during the 1980s showed that a chemical in the tree's bark, yohimbine, indeed raises erections in some men by increasing blood flow to the penis. About 10 years ago the Food and Drug Administration (FDA) approved yohimbine as a treatment for impotence. The herbal extract is now available in five prescription drugs: Yocon, Ahprodyne, Erex, Yohimex, and Yovital. The herb quebracho also contains yohimbine.

However, some medical naysayers have continued to assail yohimbine as worthless. While a recent review of 16 studies shows that yohimbine is effective, the skeptics may be right about the yohimbine sold in health food stores. In 1995 the FDA sponsored a study of 26 over-the-counter yohimbine products, including Super Man and Hot Stuff. The yohimbine content of yohimbe bark is 7,089 parts per million (ppm), but the concentrations found in the tested products ranged from less than 0.1 ppm to 489 ppm, probably not enough to have much effect. If you want yohimbine's benefits, go with a prescription drug.

• **OYSTERS.** These shellfish are exceptionally rich in zinc, a mineral intimately related to male sexual health. Men with zinc-deficient diets are at high risk for infertility, prostate problems, and loss of libido. University of Rochester researchers have successfully restored sperm counts in infertile men using zinc supplements. Besides oysters, whole grains and fresh fruits and vegetables also contain this mineral.

• **WILD YAM.** This tuber's age-old reputation as a treatment for gynecological ailments was partially validated by the finding that it is a potent source of diosgenin, a chemical resembling female sex hormones. Though there's still little evidence that it boosts sexual desire, many herbalists tout wild yam salves for vaginal dryness, which makes intercourse uncomfortable for many women.

• **GINSENG.** The Chinese and Koreans insist that ginseng boosts sexual desire. Several Asian animal studies suggest that ginseng stimulates sexual function, and a Russian study shows it to be effective in treating impotence. But American scientists remain skeptical, including noted herbal medicine expert James Duke, Ph.D., author of *Ginseng: A Concise Handbook.*

• **CAFFEINE.** If your honey's thoughts turn to dreamland just as yours turn to dallying, a cup of coffee just might keep him or her awake long enough to make the most of the evening. University of Michigan urologist Ananias Diokno, M.D., found that compared to those who did not drink coffee, regular java drinkers were considerably more sexually active. But the finding may simply reflect caffeine's ability to keep the Sandman at bay until the end of the 10 o'clock news, rather than any boost in sexual desire per se.

• **CHOCOLATE.** Chocolate contains not only caffeine but also phenylethylamine (PEA), dubbed "the molecule of love" by sexual medicine specialist Theresa Crenshaw, M.D., author of *The Alchemy of Love and Lust.* A natural form of the stimulant amphetamine, PEA is actually a neurotransmitter. Both love and lust increase blood levels of PEA, but after a heartbreak the levels plummet. Although chocolate contains high levels of PEA, critics contend that it gets metabolized so quickly that it couldn't have much libidinous effect. Perhaps, but giving chocolates has become a worldwide courtship ritual. P.S.: The artificial sweetener, NutraSweet, also contains PEA. Maybe lovers should forget the champagne and toast one another with goblets of Diet Coke.

• **GINKGO.** Ginkgo is the latest arrival among sex-promoting herbs. It has no traditional reputation as an aphrodisiac, but research shows that it improves blood flow through the brain. Widely used in Europe to treat stroke and poor circulation in the brain, ginkgo also boosts blood flow into the penis. In one study, 50 men with erection impairment caused by poor penile blood flow were given 240 milligrams of a standardized ginkgo extract daily for nine months. Thirty-nine (78 percent) regained their erections, including all those who had previously been helped by impotence drugs.

HORMONAL HELP

Every knows testosterone is the primary male sex hormone. It's only a short leap to the notion that extra testosterone might give men a sexual boost. It does—but *only if you're deficient.* Few men are. "Testosterone has been one of the most abused and over-prescribed medications for male sexual dysfunction in medical history," insists Crenshaw. She compares the hormone to oil in a car: If you have enough, adding more doesn't make your car run better. In fact, extra testosterone may throw the body's hormonal circuitry out of whack, increasing irritability, aggression, blood pressure, and hair loss. But like a car low on oil, supplemental testosterone can restore sexual functioning in men who are truly deficient (See

"Patching Up Testosterone," PSYCHOLOGY TODAY, February 1997).

Testosterone is not just for men, however. The ovaries produce it in small quantities, and the hormone is responsible for female libido. But at menopause women's testosterone production declines. Studies have shown that women who supplement replacement female sex hormones with a little testosterone feel more energetic and libidinous. Unfortunately, the hormone may also cause acne, aggressiveness, oily skin, and possibly liver damage. In other words, it should not be taken impulsively. But Crenshaw considers testosterone "promising" for carefully screened women who suffer unusual libido loss of menopause.

Another possible hormonal contributor to sex drive is dehydroepiandrosterone (DHEA), a precursor of both estrogen and testosterone. Recently DHEA has become the biggest supplement fad since melatonin, fueled by media hype that it improves mood, increases energy, prevents cancer and heart disease—and boosts libido.

Crenshaw calls DHEA a "natural aphrodisiac." Her studies show that in young women DHEA levels are "significant predictors" of sexual thoughts, desire, and masturbation. But she believes that the hormone may be less important for men, suggesting that guys "are so overwhelmed by testosterone that the DHEA effect is insignificant by comparison." However, another researcher says that DHEA doesn't do much sexually for either men or women. Samuel Yen, M.D., a professor of reproductive medicine at the University of California at San Diego, gave people 50 milligrams of DHEA a day for three months. They reported a greater sense of well-being, but no extra sex drive.

DHEA's safety is equally controversial. Some studies show that DHEA prevents liver tumors in animals, while other studies show that it causes them. If you opt for DHEA, it's available over the counter at many health food stores.

IN THE REALM OF THE SENSES

Mention "aphrodisiacs" and most people think only of herbs or drugs. But that view is as limited as the missionary position. "The most neglected ingredient of great sex is the backdrop," Crenshaw says. "Instead of making love on a deep-pile carpet by a roaring fire in a ski chalet with a magnificent view, people are in a dark bedroom on musty sheets when they're exhausted. For ordinary sex to become great, the setting is crucial. Arouse your senses—all five of them."

Take smell. What's the aroma of lust? Cinnamon, reports Alan Hirsch, M.D., neurologic director of the Smell and Taste Research Foundation in Chicago. Hirsch fitted male medical students' penises with gauges that detected erection and then exposed them to dozens of fragrances.

The only one that got a rise was the smell of hot cinnamon buns. But other aromas can also add sensuality to sex. Try scented candles on your night table, flowers, or a new perfume.

Lovers should also remember to think visual. Many sex therapists recommend X-rated videos as aphrodisiacs. Most men need little convincing, but many women consider traditional male-oriented pornography demeaning. Some years ago, former porn starlet Candida Royalle launched Femme Productions to produce X-rated videos aimed specifically at women. Femme videos feature plenty of "action," but the characters also have loving relationships and some emotional complexity.

According to two recent studies, Royalle's female sensibility is a major turn-on for women. University of Connecticut psychologist Donald Mosher, Ph.D., showed 395 college students one of six X-rated videos—three traditional male-oriented tapes, and three Femme programs. Most men found both types equally arousing. Women, however, clearly preferred the Femme programs, reporting considerably more intercourse afterward than those who watched the traditional pornography.

A similar study at the University of Amsterdam delved deeper, as it were, into the participants' sexuality. In addition to filling out a survey, female undergraduates were fitted with tampon-like devices that measured vaginal engorgement, an indication of sexual arousal. In the survey arm of the study, the women greatly preferred the Femme programs. But both types of videos elicited similar vaginal reactions, suggesting that feelings of sexual arousal are often more subjective than objective.

For a free catalog of Femme videos, call 1-800-456-LOVE. Another source of woman-oriented erotic videos is The Sexuality Library; call (415) 974-8985.

Finally, lovers shouldn't forget their sense of touch. "Every square inch of the body is a sensual playground," sex therapist Louanne Cole says. "It's sad that so many lovers explore only a few corners." To discover the sensuality of the whole body, try a hot bath or shower together using a fragrant herbal soap. Bathing is a wonderfully arousing prelude to lovemaking. The warmth relaxes muscles made tense by the daily grind. And soaping and drying each other can be a marvelous whole-body turn-on. For extra enjoyment, drape your towels over a radiator or pop them into the dryer so they'll be warm when you use them.

Aroused By Intimacy

Okay, so you've got a roaring fire in the hearth, cinnamon-scented candles, a pot of ginseng tea, and a plate of oysters on the coffee table. Now what? Next try the board game, "An Enchanted Evening." It's a delightfully sensual aphrodisiac-in-a-box.

"An Enchanted Evening" began in 1979 as a kiss-and-make-up offering from then-37-year-old Barbara Jonas of

BEWARE THE **SEX** KILLERS

If you want to rev up your sex life, first make sure you don't shut it down. Many everyday items can interfere with pleasure in the sack:

- **ALCOHOL.** In *Macbeth*, Shakespeare wrote that this substance "provokes the desire, but takes away the performance." Truer words were never penned. When people of average weight drink more than two beers, cocktails, or glasses of wine in an hour, alcohol interferes with erection in men and impairs sexual responsiveness in women. Drink too much, and all you'll do in the prone position is pass out.

- **TOBACCO.** Smoking narrows the blood vessels, impairing blood flow into the penis in men and increasing their risk of erection impairment. In women, the same mechanism limits blood flow into the vaginal wall, decreasing lubrication.

- **ANTIDEPRESSANTS.** Antidepressants work—but at a price. All except one (see below) carry a considerable risk of sexual side effects: loss of desire and difficulty reaching orgasm in both sexes, impaired erections in men, and lubrication problems in women. Currently the most popular antidepressants are the selective serotonin reuptake inhibitors (SSRIs): Prozac, Zoloft, and Paxil. According to Jamie Grimes, M.D., chief of outpatient psychiatry at the Walter Reed Army Medical Center in Washington, D.C., SSRIs cause sex problems in more than half of those who use them. Sex-impairing side effects also occur among older antidepressants like Elavil, Tofranil, and Nardil.

  If you take an antidepressant what can you do to preserve sexual function? Jacob Katzow, M.D., a Washington, D.C., psychiatrist, says a lower dose might reduce sexual side effects while preserving antidepressant benefits. Or try a "drug holiday." Anthony Rothschild, M.D., a psychiatrist at MacLean Hospital in Belmont, Massachusetts, had 30 couples—each with one member taking an SSRI and reporting loss of sexual function or desire—go drug-free on weekends, from Thursday morning to Sunday at noon. Among the 20 taking Paxil or Zoloft, half reported better sexual

functioning and more desire over the weekend, and only two said they felt more depressed. But of the 10 taking Prozac, only one reported sexual improvement, probably because Prozac takes longer than other SSRIs to clear from the blood.

Another option is to ask your physician about switching to Wellbutrin (bupropion). For reasons that remain biochemically unclear, it has no sex-impairing side effects.

- **OTHER LEGAL DRUGS.** An enormous number of prescription and over-the-counter medications—even the antihistimines people take for allergies—can cause sexual impairment. "If a drug label says, 'May cause drowsiness,'" says sexual medicine specialist Theresa Crenshaw, M.D., "it can impair sexual desire or performance." John Morganthaler, director of the Sex/Drug Interaction Foundation in Petaluma, California, estimates that up to 20 percent of all sex problems are caused by drug side effects or interactions. He recommends asking your doctor and pharmacist about this possibility every time you get a prescription.

- **ILLICIT DRUGS.** There's a good reason why narcotics and tranquilizers are called "downers." That's what happens to the sexual interest of people who use them. But "uppers" are no better. Amphetamines and cocaine stimulate sexual desire, but impair orgasm, making sex decidedly frustrating. With regular use, desire fades as well.

The most sexually unpredictable illicit drug is marijuana. Some say it enhances lovemaking. Chemically, it just might. Pot increases blood levels of phenylethylamine, a neurotransmitter associated with love and lust. But marijuana makes other people withdraw or become anxious or irritable, which can ruin sex.

Finally, all illicit drugs involve risk of involuntary intimacy with the legal system. Fear of possible arrest causes anxiety, and anxiety takes the joy out of sex.—*M.C.*

Scottsdale, Arizona, to her husband, Michael. Today, it's one of the nation's best-selling adult board games. (It's available at game stores and lingerie shops nationwide, or call 1-800-776-7662.) "An Enchanted Evening" begins with each player writing a secret wish for later than evening. Then you roll dice and draw game cards. Some are "talk" cards that ask open-ended questions designed to celebrate your relationship: "You have lunch with a long-lost friend who asks, 'What attracted you to your spouse?' What did?" Others are "touch" cards with deliciously ambiguous directions: "Kiss your spouse in a place that's soft and warm." The first one around the board—if the players get that far—wins his or her wish.

"An Enchanted Evening" made a believer out of Marty Klein, Ph.D., a Palo Alto, California, marriage counselor. "When I first heard about it, I felt totally cyni-

cal. But I thoroughly enjoyed it. It encourages the kind of playful touch and supportive communication most couples stop sharing after a while. And it shows a profound understanding of how intimacy and sexual desire go hand in hand."

They do, indeed. Which just goes to show that the world's greatest sex-stimulant is that crazy, wonderful emotion called love. Without love's special magic, sexual enhancements can fall flat. But for couples who share that intimate, chemical bond, aphrodisiacs, defined broadly, can transform lovemaking from "eh" to ecstatic.

Michael Castleman is a San Francisco–based health writer. His latest book is Nature's Cures *(Bantam).*

Your Sexual Landscape

For too long, women and doctors have maintained an uneasy silence about what goes on below the beltline. It's time we got comfortable with our own anatomy—

our health depends on it

By Beth Howard

Vagina. There, I've said it. This simple three-syllable word is no tongue twister—but it leaves even the boldest of us sputtering.

And it's not just talking about vaginas that makes women nervous. Many of us can't bear to *look* at our anatomy. The vagina is the locus of our most profound feelings about intimacy. No wonder it's shrouded in mystery and shame, or that the men in our lives often know their way around our bodies better than we do.

Until recently even medicine was guilty of keeping the vagina under wraps. Research on vulvar-vaginal disorders (the vulva is the external genitalia) is nearly nonexistent, says Libby Edwards, M.D., a vulvar-disease specialist at the Carolinas Medical Center in Charlotte, NC. And medical training on the subject is notoriously scanty. Even the obvious specialties limit their scope. Gynecologists tend to focus on the internal reproductive organs; urologists on urinary tract problems. Most dermatologists stop short of the vulva. "Thanks to sexual taboos, this area has been virtually ignored," says Peter Lynch, M.D., chairman of dermatology at the University of California

at Davis and one of the field's few specialists in vulvar dermatology.

Medicine may be neglecting women, but we are often our own worst enemies when it comes to vaginal health. "*Vagina* is a dirty word. Women don't think about taking care of their vaginas," says Sharon Hillier, Ph.D., director of reproductive infectious disease research at Magee-Women's Hospital at the University of Pittsburgh. Add the shame factor, and you've got the setup for a stalemate: Doctors don't ask about vaginal problems, and women don't tell.

But times are changing. Spurred by new data about vaginal health, gynecological researchers have begun to advocate a newer, friendlier way of thinking about the vagina. Not simply a place for penises, babies and tampons, this four-inch-deep tunnel is also home to a variety of microscopic organisms that conspire to make it as delicately balanced an ecosystem as a tropical rain forest. When the system is running properly, friendly bacteria called lactobacilli constantly manufacture hydrogen peroxide, in effect churning out tiny bits of bleach to keep not-so-friendly organisms in check. Left to itself, the vagina is one of the cleanest surfaces on the body.

The idea of a naturally clean vagina is so at odds with women's beliefs and society's stereotypes that Dr. Hillier has embarked on a virtual vagina campaign. "The healthy vaginal ecosystem," she declares, "is an endangered habitat."

IRRITANTS AND INFECTION:
Preserving a Pristine Environment

As with other ecological disasters, we can blame ourselves when the vagina's natural balance is upset. We have unsafe sex, take antibiotics (which kill off healthy bacteria) or mistakenly use nonprescription yeast cures when we don't really have yeast infections.

Ironically the primary culprits are often products aimed at helping women feel "fresh." Douches, vaginal deodorants and scented panty liners contain chemicals that can irritate the searchers reported in the *Journal of Infectious Diseases* last November that tampons did not adversely affect the vaginal ecosystem.

Not only can some vaginal products cause internal trouble, but they also can result in external redness or itching and derail sex. What to do: Stop using the product and let the ecosystem's natural cleanup squad restore things to normal. Vulvar irritation often comes in the form of dermatitis: dry, itchy skin that may be due to tight or chafing clothes combined with the moisture of normal vaginal secretions. The solution: loose-fitting clothes. Your doctor may prescribe a steroid ointment if the problem persists.

BACTERIA, VIRUSES AND YEAST:
Stopping an Ecological Disaster

The good news for women of all ages is that the vagina has a natural tendency to restore itself—to a point: Dis-

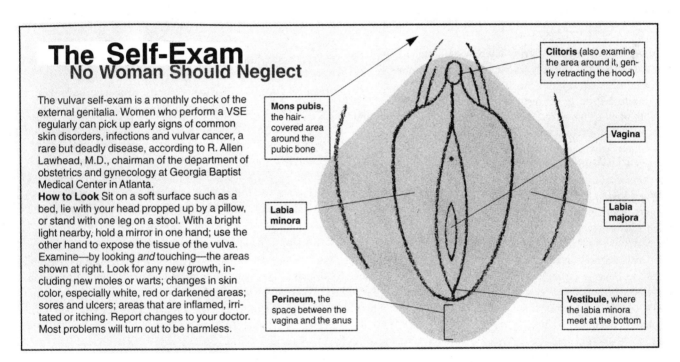

The Self-Exam
No Woman Should Neglect

The vulvar self-exam is a monthly check of the external genitalia. Women who perform a VSE regularly can pick up early signs of common skin disorders, infections and vulvar cancer, a rare but deadly disease, according to R. Allen Lawhead, M.D., chairman of the department of obstetrics and gynecology at Georgia Baptist Medical Center in Atlanta.

How to Look Sit on a soft surface such as a bed, lie with your head propped up by a pillow, or stand with one leg on a stool. With a bright light nearby, hold a mirror in one hand; use the other hand to expose the tissue of the vulva. Examine—by looking *and* touching—the areas shown at right. Look for any new growth, including new moles or warts; changes in skin color, especially white, red or darkened areas; sores and ulcers; areas that are inflamed, irritated or itching. Report changes to your doctor. Most problems will turn out to be harmless.

Mons pubis, the hair-covered area around the pubic bone

Labia minora

Perineum, the space between the vagina and the anus

Clitoris (also examine the area around it, gently retracting the hood)

Vagina

Labia majora

Vestibule, where the labia minora meet at the bottom

vaginal walls and disrupt the normal flora. A study of 182 women done at the University of Washington in Seattle found that women who routinely douched for hygiene were four times as likely as those who didn't to lose their healthful lactobacilli. "Douching can upset the ecosystem in much the same way as putting weed killer on the lawn can kill the underlying lawn," Dr. Hillier says. "It has no medical benefits," and it's actually associated with an *increased* risk for pelvic inflammatory disease.

Fortunately tampons seem to have little effect on the vagina. Today's less absorbent, natural-fiber tampons are far safer than the super-absorbent synthetic ones that spurred cases of toxic-shock syndrome in the early 1980s. Re-

charge combined with odor, particularly a fishy odor, is almost always a tip-off to the presence of an infection that can make intercourse painful and require medical attention. "Normal secretions are not foul or fishy," says David E. Soper, M.D., director of the division of benign gynecology at the Medical University of South Carolina in Charleston. The wise course of action is to become familiar with these sex stoppers before they strike. (For a list of common complaints, see "The Infection Connection."

The problem is, some women blame bad hygiene for their symptoms. Doctors are often party to the cover-up: In a recent survey by the National Vaginitis Association, nearly 50% of gynecologists said that even when they found evidence of the most common infection, bacterial vaginosis, they treated it only if patients complained of symptoms.

A vaginal infection won't always be diagnosed during a routine gynecological visit, notes Jill Maura Rabin, M.D., head of urogynecology at Long Island Jewish Medical Center in New Hyde Park, NY. The Pap smear is not designed to detect vaginal infections. That's why it's important to speak up about symptoms such as odor and discharge, especially because unchecked infections now appear to be more dangerous than previously believed. Bacterial vaginosis, for example, has recently been linked to a higher rate of pelvic inflammatory disease, pregnancy complications and postoperative infections.

Viruses present an altogether different threat to vaginal health and sexual pleasure, so it's also crucial to bring any herpes blisters or genital warts to a doctor's attention. (For information about how to examine yourself, see box on previous page.

AGE-RELATED DRYNESS:
Changes in the Terrain

Sometimes discomfort during intercourse is not a symptom of infection but the primary problem. Its most common cause is vaginal dryness. Some women develop premenopausal dryness due to a drop in estrogen or as a result of hysterectomy, chemotherapy or the use of antidepressants, antihistamines and some hormonal contraceptives. "And after menopause, nearly all women experience dryness," says Geoffrey Redmond, M.D., a Cleveland endocrinologist and author of *The Good New About Women's Hormones.*

When the ovaries stop producing estrogen, the vaginal lining gets drier and thinner, making it vulnerable to irritation, which can result in pain during sex. The vulva and the vagina also become less elastic, although regular stimulation—through either masturbation or intercourse—may reduce this change, according to Beverly Whipple, Ph.D., an associate professor in the department of nursing at Rutgers University in Newark, NJ.

For a quick fix, drugstores display a variety of slippery substances designed to keep your love life gliding happily along. Gels are used just before sex, while liquid moisturizers can be applied as often as needed. Choose a water-soluble product; oil-based ones can upset the vaginal ecology and erode latex used in diaphragms and condoms.

Lack of moisture puts a damper on intimacy. But the right lubricant can keep things gliding along.

The best solution for postmenopausal women, though, is estrogen replacement. "The minimal dose that protects women against heart disease and osteoporosis may not be enough to adequately relieve thin, dry tissue," says Dr. Redmond. You'll have to speak up if you want your doctor to fine-tune treatment. One offbeat solution is the Reality female condom. Anecdotal reports suggest some women are using it to protect thinning tissues during intercourse.

Menopause produces other vaginal changes. The vagina begins to narrow and shorten, and the rugae—tiny ridges that help the vagina expand at childbirth and enhance its gripping effect during sex—gradually disappear. For many women, pelvic muscle strength decreases with age. This may reduce the sensation of friction during intercourse. Some women turn to cosmetic surgery to tighten the vaginal opening, but "this should be a last resort," says Linda Brubaker, M.D., director of urogynecology and reconstructive pelvic surgery at Rush-Presbyterian-St. Luke's Medical Center in Chicago. For most women, exercises or physical therapy can strengthen the pelvic muscle.

Women who undergo a hysterectomy may notice that the vagina feels different during intercourse, because the cervix is routinely removed during the surgery, according to Dr. Whipple. Many doctors don't tell patients to expect this, and women may not realize that they can ask for cervix-sparing surgery. "Studies support the fact that if the cervix is left, women don't report a change in sexual response," she says.

If menopausal changes aren't to blame for sexual discomfort, the source may be vulvodynia or vaginismus, two painful problems that can affect women of any age. Vulvodynia is a set of chronic symptoms—burning, rawness, stinging or irritation of the vulva and the vaginal opening—with an unknown cause. (For more information, contact the National Vulvodynia Association in Silver Spring, MD, at 301–299–0775.) Vaginismus, an involuntary spasm of the vaginal muscles that occurs before or during penetration, also causes extreme pain. It's often related to fear or anxiety about sex.

Finding the Elusive G Spot

The G spot usurped the clitoris as the focus of sensual pleasure in the 1980s, when researchers reported that orgasm often results when a small area beneath the front of the vaginal wall is stimulated. It's easiest to find your G spot when you're kneeling. You or your partner can insert two fingers about halfway into the vagina and explore the front wall until you find a patch of tissue that begins to swell. (Use your other hand to press on the lower abdomen just above the pubic hair.) Stimulation produces a pleasant sensation for most women and often leads to orgasm, reports Beverly Whipple, Ph.D., an associate professor in the department of nursing at Rutgers University in Newark, N.J. Once you've located the G spot, you and your partner can try different positions to improve his contact with the area during lovemaking.

The Infection Connection

Here's how to cope with the most common vaginal infections that strike women in midlife:

The culprit	The symptoms	The cure
Bacterial vaginosis, an overgrowth of normal vaginal bacteria.	Thin grayish or white discharge that has a foul, fishy odor. Possible itching and irritation.	The prescription drugs metronidazole or clindamycin. Avoid nonprescription yeast drugs—they could make matters worse.
Yeast infection, an overgrowth of the *Candida* fungus.	Odorless white, cottage cheese—like discharge and itching.	If you're sure it's yeast, try an over-the-counter yeast fighter; otherwise, see your doctor. Eating yogurt that contains live *Lactobacillus acidophilus* cultures may reduce the risk of future infections.
Trichomonas, a parasite usually transmitted during sex.	Frothy, yellow-green fishy-smelling discharge; itching, painful urination or intercourse.	Prompt treatment with the prescription drug metronidazole for both you and your partner.
Herpes simplex virus, which can be transmitted sexually even in the absence of blisters.	Itching, stinging sores on the vulva or in the vagina.	There is no cure, but prescription antiviral drugs can reduce outbreaks and to some extent protect a partner from infection.
Human papillomavirus, which can be sexually transmitted.	Vaginal warts which may itch or burn after sex.	Certain types of HPV place women at above-average risk of cervical cancer, so most growths are surgically removed.

Whether it's the pain of vaginismus or the annoyance of a yeast infection, doctors are taking vaginal symptoms more seriously. "There is a transition from seeing them as a nuisance to seeing them as a threat to women's health and psychological well-being," says Dr. Hillier. As more physicians fight to clean up the vagina's public image, this under-appreciated part of our anatomy will no doubt be seen as less mysterious—and more marvelous.

Your next step? See the box for advice on how to use vulvar self-exams to get acquainted with your body. Debra Gussman, M.D., a Denver gynecologist, puts it this way: "If you don't know what you look like, how are you going to know everything's okay?"

Beth Howard lives in New York City and is writing a book about sexual wellness for women.

IMPOTENCY
GROWING MALAISE

A silent, embarrassing affliction sweeps Indian bedrooms, with men from all age groups and social classes desperately turning to doctors for cures

By MADHU JAIN, SUBHADRA MENON
and RAMESH VINAYAK

Lalit Bhasin is the kind of man most men envy. Just a year ago he would have thought so too. At 39, the suave, successful banker had a well-turned out wife and two precocious children, swung a mean club on the golf course. But a few months ago, things began to go wrong in the bedroom. The worst thing that could happen to a man happened to him: he became impotent. "It drove me nuts," confesses Bhasin. "I had money, but without my virility I was only half a man."

He didn't see a connection but whistle-stop work schedules and jetting round the globe chasing deals and dreams had sapped his sexual vitality. And so began a nightmarish odyssey: rounds of quacks and charlatans. It took Rs 25,000 and a great desperation before Bhasin finally summoned courage to seek medical help. Bhasin's ordeal is not unique. In fact, it has become particularly common. The proverbial headache is getting to be the male preserve. One out of every 10 Indian males could be impotent, according to a survey of 1,500 men done in Delhi by the Alpha One Andrology Centre at Aashlok Hospital. "Impotence is a silent epidemic that is sweeping across the nation, the average victim being a middle-aged male otherwise healthy and successful," says the centre's director, urologist Vikram Sharma. Big city hospitals estimate that one out of every five to eight patients is impotent—or, as the politically-correct term goes, suffers from erectile dysfunction (ED). A recent seven-year study by the Marital and Psychosexual Clinic at the Post-Graduate Institute of Medical Education and Research (PGIMER), Chandigarh, concluded that 77 per cent of its 464 new patients suffered from ED or premature ejaculation—or both. And so, in clinics across the nation, amazed doctors watch as determined wives, mothers, even mothers-in-law, drag in their men. Women no longer content with lying back and being mere baby machines want satisfaction. Borne on the beams of unseen satellites, images of a loud, new female sexuality are displacing traditional roles of silent fertility. They see hard bodies and seemingly endless energy.

"The meta message coming from the media is that you have to have a huge erection and keep it for a long time," says Radhika Chandiramani, clinical psychologist. "The young man often fantasises about what an erection should be like, compares it with the real situation, after which anxiety sets in and that is the most deflationary thing that can happen."

As the traditionally boorish, sexually self-centred Indian male is called upon to prove his mettle, he's getting a bad case of performance anxiety. Like Sanjay Lal, a small-time Delhi doctor in his early 30s. His problem is a transformed wife who demands more creativity in the bedroom. When they married six years ago, Ranjana was a small-town girl barely able to string together two sentences in English. But she soon found a Professor Higgins in her female boss (an IIM graduate) in the multinational company where she works as a secretary. The two women discussed their sexual lives, and their conversations began to resound in the Lal bedroom. The fights began: she resented the fact that he never asked her where she wanted to be touched and her language took on the intonations of her other role model: the revenge-seeking heroine in the popular afternoon soap Shanti. For someone brought up in the-man-knows-best environment, this was crippling for Lal. He stopped making love.

This new female demand is particularly—and poignantly—difficult to meet, given the hectic pace of the daily treadmill of life. The pressures of competition, the race to earn more money and consumerism are all drives that relegate sex to the back-burner. The winds of liberalisation, in a sense, are chilling Indian bedrooms. Nitin Bose, a 42-year-old executive, narrates with frustration how unceasing ambition and a pursuit of the good life put him out to pasture—sexually. His love life was reduced to an infrequent tension-filled 10-minute tryst after an exhausting 16-hour day. Two children and six years into his marriage, Bose's mind and body finally gave up. He just couldn't do it any more.

Anecdotal evidence confirms that the affliction plagues urban and rural India, the rich and the poor, the young—and yes, even older men in search of sexual reawakening. D. Narayana Reddy, a consultant on sexual medicine at the Dega Institute in Chennai, says that he

STUDIES SHOW THAT ONE OUT OF EVERY 10 MEN IN INDIA IS IMPOTENT.

now sees at least 15 patients a day; back in 1982, he had just 37 patients for the whole year. Rajiv Gupta, a consultant psychiatrist in Ludhiana, says that the number of patients reporting impotency has increased three to four times in the past decade. Dr Prakash Kothari, head of the sexual medicine department at Mumbai's KEM Hospital, says that impotence has increased by 15 per cent a year in the past two to three years. In Lucknow, A. K. Agrawal, head of the department of psychiatry at the King George Medical College, says: "There is a growing fear of impotence among rural and urban people here." It's a trend in line with what happens to men in the developed world. In the US, the National Institute of Health estimates that as many as 30 million men suffer from ED. That staggering figure has given rise to a market for impotence cures that runs into billions of dollars.

In India, the cures mushroom on the pavements, restricted only by the imaginations of those who create the formulations. Street-corner quacks have always plied Indian males with elixirs. But driven by the exploding demand for magic potions, street medicine has gone mainstream: packaged and over-the-counter in chemist shops in their new quasi-pharmacological avatars. The remedies are wild and varied. From "rooster's flesh fried in crocodile semen" (a recipe from the classic ayurveda text Charaka Samhita) to more prosaic repackaged roots like 303.

The street experts and "sexologists" with gloriously luxuriant moustaches have clinicians and doctors worried. Harjeet Singh, a leading Lucknow psychiatrist, is convinced that the "so-called sexologists" are a major factor in the increasing fear about impotency. "An average patient ends up paying Rs 25,000 to Rs 40,000 without having an erection," says Singh. "Since they spend huge sums of money on advertisements, pamphlets and hoardings to lure customers, they must be recovering it from the hapless patients."

Are more and more men getting impotent? Or, are they just more open about it and seeking help? Doctors and psychiatrists are divided on this. Reddy believes that a larger number of men are seeking help because we now live in more liberated times: "Social taboos are disappearing and there's a greater awareness in the younger generation." On the other hand, Ajit Avasthi of PGIMER says quite unequivocally: "What we are diagnosing is not even the tip of the iceberg."

Impotency cuts across age groups and classes. At the Alpha One Centre, the youngest patient is 18 years old, the oldest 72. Last week, a 75-year-old businessman walked into the Out-Patient Department of PGIMER and,

TREATMENT OPTIONS

INJECTIONS: Direct injections of drugs like postaglandin stimulate blood flow into the penis.
Cost: Less than a rupee for a shot.
Flip side: Drug has to be injected just before sex.

VACUUM DEVICES: Vacuum created by plastic cylinder, which is held in place by a plastic ring, allows erection.
Cost: Rs 30 to Rs 50.
Flip side: Harmful to keep ring in place for long.

SURGICAL PENILE IMPLANTS: A penile prosthesis is inserted into the penis. This is a permanent cure.
Cost: Rs 1.3 lakh (implant); Rs 10,000 (surgery).
Flip side: Prolonged erection in some cases.

ORAL DRUGS: Viagra is an approved drug which increases blood flow and sustains erection.
Cost: Rs 500 a tablet.
Flip side: Unavailable here; few side-effects.

EXPLODING MYTHS

MISCONCEPTION	FACT
■ There are not many Indians who suffer from impotence.	One out of every 10 Indian men is impotent, the incidence could be higher in metros.
■ Once you discover you are impotent, there is nothing you can do about it.	There are treatments for all kinds of impotence. Success rate: 80%–100%.
■ It's all in your head. Psychological factors contribute to impotence.	No. Almost two-thirds of cases have physiological causes like diabetes and high BP.
■ One must accept impotence as a natural step in the ageing process.	For most older men, impotence is a result of some physical disorder that can be treated.
■ You should not talk about it.	You must—with your partner and doctor.
■ Impotence means that you cannot have children.	Impotence is not being able to have an erection and has little to do with fertility.
■ Masturbation in younger years can cause impotence later in life.	Masturbation does not cause impotence. It only creates a false sense of guilt.
■ Sexual intercourse saps one's vitality.	In most cases it is the other way round.
■ Marriage can help overcome the problem.	It doesn't. In most cases, it makes the situation worse due to performance anxiety.
■ If one kind of treatment fails, then there is no way out.	There are various methods of treatment. One of them is bound to work.

without batting an eyelid, narrated his problem to Dr S. K. Sharma, who heads the urology department. "I want sex," he told Sharma, "but my organ has lost its erection." He had already done the rounds of quacks and spent a minor fortune in search of the elixir of love. Finally, he went away happy, after the installation of the Vacuum Erection Device. Another Rs 15,000—but all for love.

The changing age profile surprises doctors. Dr Achal Bhagat, psychotherapist at Delhi's Indraprastha Apollo Hospital, observes a gradual shift from the younger men coming in for premature ejaculation and ED to men in their 30s and even older. "There has been a marked increase in the age group of 45–69," he says.

So what is this typical patient like? He's likely to be around 40–45 years old and in a second relationship—the first not having worked out. He is also likely to be fairly successful, smokes, drinks a bit, may chew paan masala and is a little tubby. He's had a good sex life, but lately he isn't so sure. "While in the 30-year-old and the 45-year-old there may be some loss of libido,

this 60-year-old has no loss of libido, only a loss of erection," says Bhagat.

There are two kinds of impotency: primary and secondary. Primary impotence occurs early in sexual life, whereas men who cannot achieve erection after a certain age suffer from what is called secondary impotence. Whether primary or secondary, ED falls into two categories—physical and psychological. Physical impotence is when the patient has some defect or is suffering from a disease. It could be damaged blood vessels leading to insufficient blood supply to the penis. It could be a nerve damage because of a spinal injury or diabetes. It could be due to drugs taken for depression, hypertension, an allergy or a cardiac condition.

Drug-induced impotence could account for as much as 25 per cent of the total cases of ED, says Dr Mandeep Bajaj, endocrinologist at the Apollo Hospital. Hormonal imbalances—like the creeping presence of Prolactin, a hormone for lactation in women sometimes found in men—could also lead to the inability to have an erection. So could excessive alcohol consumption or smoking. According to international health protocols, smoking just two cigarettes can lead to a decreased ability to have an erection. Such physical causes of impotence, however, are completely curable (see box on treatment options).

A major emerging worry is diabetes. Studies by Dr S. M. Sadikot, a consulting endocrinologist and andrologist at the Jaslok Hospital and Research Centre in Mumbai, have shown that at least 28 per cent of male diabetics complain of total ED, while more than 45 per cent suffered from a significant degree of the problem. According to Bajaj, there is a 30 per cent to 75 per cent higher prevalence of impotence amongst diabetic men compared with the general population. The diabetic suffers from a combination of damage to the blood vessels and nerves because of high blood sugar. Impotence may often be the first symptom of diabetes and requires preventive management. Bajaj sees an earlier onset of diabetes in India because of altered lifestyles which are increasingly sedentary, encourage high-fat diets and fast foods.

Sometimes, it's all in the mind. While Dr Rupin Shah, director of the Centre for Male Reproductive and Sexual Medicine at Mumbai's Bhatia General Hospital, maintains that "almost two-thirds of all cases of impotence in India stem from psychological causes", Sadikot insists that the reverse is true. "A precise understanding of the physiology of erections and their nervous, vascular and hormonal control makes us realise that in the vast majority of cases (70 percent–75 per cent), the cause is organic (physiological)," says Sadikot. Doctors are putting their minds together to resolve the mind-or-matter debate. The new speciality of andrology uses a battery of specialists: psychiatrists, urologists, endocrinologists, surgeons, neurologists and gynaecologists.

The most damaging aspect of impotence is that it creates a vicious cycle of anxiety and depression, which in turn aggravates the problem. Newly weds especially are susceptible to what is called "honeymoon impotence". India, according to Shah, is "the country of unconsummated marriages". Every week, he counsels at least five new couples who haven't ever had sexual intercourse. He estimates that 45 per cent of all men who have a sexual problem are impotent.

Stress and depression are also major psychological triggers. The stereotype of the business executive who comes home mentally and physically exhausted. Love in the time of the stopwatch can kill desire. Indeed, as Dr Jitender Nagpal, consultant psychiatrist at Delhi's Vidyasagar Institute of Mental Health, observes, if the romantic aspect of sex goes missing in these hurried times, the quality of the

ANDROLOGY WHICH COMBINES PHYSICAL AND PSYCHOLOGICAL CURES IS THE BEST BET.

sexual lives of couples will suffer. "They end up being spectators to each others' anguish rather than performers," says Nagpal. There's also an impotence of convenience. Loss of erection in the late 20s and 30s, say psychiatrists, can become a vehicle to express anger and difficulties in a marriage. It could be "situational impotence". "Impotence is definitely a problem where marital conflicts remain unresolved," says Reeni Singh, a family and marital therapist with the Sampark Counselling Centre at Delhi's Modi Hospital. "For instance, if there is tension between the mother-in-law and the daughter-in-law, some husbands tend to become impotent." Add to this the fear of having contracted AIDS. Typically, after an indiscreet sexual encounter a man may worry so much about picking up the disease that often he is unable to perform later.

What surprises doctors the most is not just the openness about a subject that was once considered taboo, but also who's bringing in the men. Wives often bring their husbands, but now an increasing number of mothers and mothers-in-law are taking their sons and sons-in-law for treatment. "Earlier, barely 5 per cent of women would reluctantly accompany their husbands to a sexologist," says Dr Raj Brahmbhatt, consultant with the Family Planning Association of India, "but today, one in every five ED cases is actually brought in by the wives." Previously, after two children, people were content to kiss their sex lives goodbye. Now, thanks to the media, they're still interested at 60.

So the mamas have also become players. An old woman from rural Punjab actually took her son-in-law to Ludhiana's M.D. Memorial Hospital and did most of the talking to Dr P. P. S. Gill, about how the newly married man was unable to have an erection. In another instance, a mother dragged her 20-year-old son, who had been married just the day before and could not "perform", to urologist Dr Rohit Bhargava. "Mothers even ring up and ask about how the therapy is going," says Bhagat.

What compounds the problem are the various myths surrounding impotency—most of them deep-rooted and ingrained in society (see box on Exploding Myths). Much of this arises from a simple fact. "For a man," says Brahmbhatt, "his ego lies in his penis." For most men, the guilt of masturbation during adolescence could become a trigger for impotence. It stems from a general ignorance about the subject, lack of proper sex education and a generally conservative society.

As a result, the myths persist. For instance, a lot of people believe that impotence is something one has to accept as part of ageing. Erection, say doctors, has nothing to do with age, at least in the physiological sense. If you retain normal testosterone levels and adequate blood supply, there is no reason why you can't have one even at 60 or 70. "What does change is the attitude to sex and sharing, which often reduces the frequency of erection," says Sharma. In some older men, a lowering of testosterone levels can also create impotence. "You need all the right hormones in the right amounts for sexual desire and erection," says Dr R. Ahlawat, urologist at Apollo Hospital. After 40, most males show hormonal decline, although the rate can vary from person to person. Hormone replacement therapy can work for such people, but doctors warn that in some cases it can lead to prostrate cancer.

For Vivek Nair it wasn't as simple as hormones. Defective vessels restricting blood flow to his penis had made the 27-year-old teacher impotent. Nair despaired over the fact that he could never have a normal sex life until he reached the right doctor. A surgical implant solved his problem. Today, diagnosis is fast, decisions for the kind of treatment regime are taken quickly, and within days the patient is normal. Such implants are just one of the many options available for treating physical impotence. And each one has its merits and demerits. Sharma of Alpha One explains, "The most sophisticated implant enables a patient to manipulate the timing and duration of the erection by just pressing a synthetic sac placed in his scrotum." This regulates the flow of a saline solution into the two cylinders of the prostheses and erection takes place. Of course, this treatment is not always affordable as it can cost anywhere between Rs 1.75 lakh and Rs 2 lakh.

Which is why doctors have long been hoping for an oral drug that can cure impotence. "Can't I just pop a pill and be fine, doctor?" is a question Indian physicians have to answer very often. Recently, the US Food and Drug Administration cleared a drug called sildenafil, trade name Viagra, developed by the pharmaceutical giant Pfizer, to cure impotence. But it may be months before it is available here, subject to approval by the Drugs Controller of India. More importantly, a dose for a single erection will cost about Rs 500. "We are cautiously optimistic about the drug and its side-effects and potential for misuse would have to be kept in mind," says Sharma. Popping a pill to become potent would be wishful thinking for most Indians, at least for now. Meanwhile, the only way out might be a combination of physiological and psychological therapy. The shrinking world may have some bearing on impotency but it is also part of the cure: already, enterprising men in Mumbai are getting their relatives in the US to send them Viagra, while others are seeking the wonder drug through the Internet. But the ultimate aphrodisiac still remains elusive. Superman will have to wait.

—with FARAH BARIA, FARZAND AHMED and
S. SENTHILNATHAN

Names of patients have been changed to protect their identities.

THE VIAGRA CRAZE

A pill to cure impotence? Afflicted men are saying Yesss! But is this the end of sex as we know it?

By BRUCE HANDY

Besides its phony name, funny shape and unappetizing color, what's not to like about Viagra, the new pill that conquers impotence? Could there be a product more tailored to the easy-solution-loving, sexually insecure American psyche than this one? The drug, manufactured by Pfizer, went on sale three weeks ago, finally giving talk-show hosts something other than Bill Clinton and Pamela Lee to crack smarmy jokes about.

Spurred, perhaps, by just that sort of publicity, would-be patients have been besieging urologists' offices and sex clinics—men both genuinely dysfunctional and merely dissatisfied, skulking around in hopes of achieving "better" erections through chemistry. Already, a kind of Viagra connoisseurship is beginning to take hold. "The hundreds are absolutely incredible," says a very satisfied user, referring to the drug's 100-mg maximum-strength dosage, "and the effect lasts through the following morning." What else can one say but *Vrooom!* Cheap gas, strong economy, erection pills—what a country! What a time to be alive!

"We've always been waiting for the magic bullet," says Dr. Fernando Borges of the Florida Impotency Center in St. Petersburg, where he has been working with sexually dysfunctional patients for 21 years. "This," he says, "is pretty close to the magic bullet." The very day Viagra became available, Dr. John Stripling, an Atlanta urologist, churned out 300 prescriptions with the help of a rubber stamp he had had the foresight to purchase. At the Urology Health Center in New Port Richey, Fla., which participated in the drug's clinical trials, the waiting time to see a doctor for a Viagra consultation is a month. Not that this has stopped motivated patients. "We've been inundated with emergencies," says Dr. Ramon Perez. "Pain in the kidney. Blood in the urine. But when they get in here, they just want to ask us about Viagra. It's amazing. These people have been impotent for three years, and they cannot wait another few days."

"It's the fastest takeoff of a new drug that I've ever seen, and I've been in this business for 27 years," says Michael Podgurski, director of pharmacy at the 4,000-outlet Rite Aid drugstore chain. After a brief lag, the drug is now being prescribed at the rate of at least 10,000 scripts a day, outpacing such famous quick starters as the antidepressant Prozac (which went on to become one of the biggest-selling drugs in America) and the baldness remedy Rogaine (which has been something of a disappointment after its initial blaze of popularity).

The run on Viagra has been abetted by the likes of David Michael Thomas, a Mil-

HOT NEW DRUGS
Prescriptions dispensed during first two weeks on the market

Viagra	(impotence)	36,809
Propecia	(baldness)	5,500
Lipitor	(cholesterol reducer)	2,203
Evista	(bone-density regulator)	1,624

Source: IMS Health

waukee, Wis., osteopath who advertises his services on the Web at *www.penispill.com* and who allegedly prescribed Viagra to some 700 patients after cursory $50 telephone examinations. At a license-suspension hearing in front of Wisconsin regulatory officials last week, Thomas agreed to stop the practice. (Normally a diagnosis of impotence involves a rigorous physical exam, blood tests and an extensive sexual history.) Other entrepreneurs have been offering prescriptions directly over the Internet.

Even supporters of the pill worry about hyped expectations. "People always want a quick fix," complains Dr. Domeena Renshaw, a psychiatrist who directs the Loyola Sex Therapy Clinic outside Chicago. "They think Viagra is magic, just like they thought the G spot worked like a garage-door opener." In the wake of fen/phen and Redux, the diet-drug

treatments that were pulled from the market last year after it was learned that they could damage heart valves, caution would be advisable with Viagra. But so far the side effects seem comparatively slight and manageable: chiefly headache, flushed skin, upset stomach and curious vision distortions involving the color blue. Pfizer, leaving nothing to chance, has even requested and received the Vatican's unofficial blessing for Viagra. All in all, a happy ending for American men, their partners and especially Pfizer stockholders, who have seen the value of their shares jump nearly 60% this year alone.

Yet there's something unnerving about Viagra too, not so much on the face of it (the drug's merits appear to be manifold; doctors think it might even improve the sexual response of postmenopausal women) but in the broader philosophical implications. Is sexuality, like the state of happiness or male-pattern baldness, just one more hitherto mysterious and profound area of human-beingness that can be pharmaceutically manipulated, like any other fathomable construct of enzymes and receptors? Another looming question: Since Viagra is taken—at prices ranging from $8 to $12 a pop—not on a day-in, day-out basis but only when one actually wants to have sex, will HMOs and other insurers soon be telling us how much sex is reimbursable? Sufficient? Normal? Necessary?

And what about the impact on the freighted social interactions we euphemistically refer to as dating? "I bet that within a year, you'll see women's magazine articles saying, 'How to Tell If It's You or Viagra,'" says James R. Petersen, who has written the *Playboy* Advisor column for the past 22 years. He adds, "I think Viagra is going to be as monumental as the birth-control pill." No less an authority than Bob Guccione, publisher of *Penthouse* magazine, believes the drug will "free the American male libido" from the emasculating doings of feminists. And not only that. According to Guccione, "the ability to have sex by older men will make them healthier and live longer. It will fool the biological clock when men are still active in the later years. It is a very signifi-

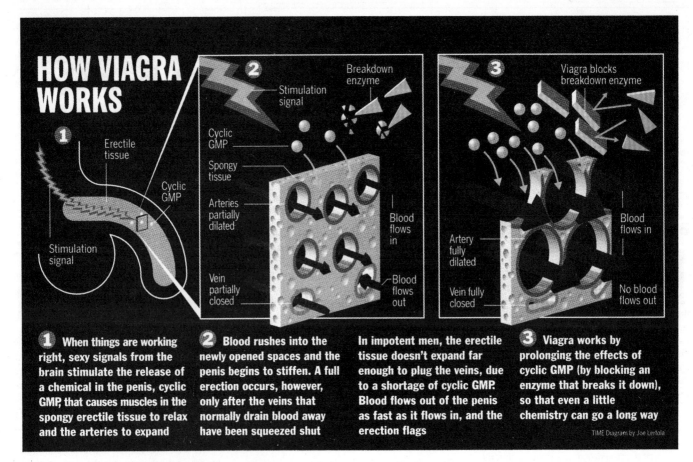

HOW VIAGRA WORKS

1 When things are working right, sexy signals from the brain stimulate the release of a chemical in the penis, cyclic GMP, that causes muscles in the spongy erectile tissue to relax and the arteries to expand

2 Blood rushes into the newly opened spaces and the penis begins to stiffen. A full erection occurs, however, only after the veins that normally drain blood away have been squeezed shut

In impotent men, the erectile tissue doesn't expand far enough to plug the veins, due to a shortage of cyclic GMP. Blood flows out of the penis as fast as it flows in, and the erection flags

3 Viagra works by prolonging the effects of cyclic GMP (by blocking an enzyme that breaks it down), so that even a little chemistry can go a long way

TIME Diagram by Joe Lertola

cant effect of the drug that many haven't contemplated." There isn't any actual scientific evidence to back up Guccione's claims, but he does do a nice job of illuminating two important subtexts of Viagra's appeal: the chimeras of undiminishable power and perpetual youth.

Of course, the overt appeal is pretty compelling too.

In the past decade there have been great advances in the treatment of impotence, which is now seen by most therapists, in most cases, as a physiological rather than a psychological problem, rejecting the medical establishment's long-held view. The word impotence itself, like "frigidity" for women, is considered suspect in many circles; the more politically correct—or at least clinical—term is erectile dysfunction, or ED, as it is commonly abbreviated. Inspired by a 1992 National Institutes of Health Conference and landmark 1994 study on the problem, the diagnosis has been defined more broadly, from the rather strict criterion of inability to get an erection, period, to the somewhat more elastic and subjective criterion of inability to get an erection adequate for "satisfactory sexual performance." This has led to a tripling of the number of men estimated to be impotent in this country—some 30 million according to the NIH, half of whom are thought to be under the age of 65. ED is associated with age; it affects about 1 in 20 men ages 40 and up, 1 in 4 over 65.

From a drug manufacturer's point of view, this burgeoning of the potential market has coincided quite nicely with the development of pharmaceutical treatments. (At least two more impotence pills are in the pipeline from different companies.) Before Viagra, the most promising therapies involved putting gel suppositories in the urethra and injecting drugs directly in the base of the penis. The downside is not hard to grasp. "You can imagine the look most patients gave when I told them they would have to stick a small needle into the most sensitive portion of their body," says University of Chicago urologist Dr. Gregory Bales. The good news is that the erections resulting from such injections can last an hour or more, even after orgasm, though depending on one's taste and circumstances, this too could be a downside. Other treatments, which involve vacuum pumps, penile implants and penis rings, are no less awkward or, to get to the heart of the matter, no more conducive to the spontaneous, unselfconscious, beautiful sex that Calvin Klein ads imply is our daily right.

The promise of Viagra is its discretion and ease of use. Doctors recommend taking the pill an hour before sex, which might lead to some wastage among overly optimistic users but shouldn't otherwise interfere too greatly with the normal course of coital events. An even greater advantage, or at least a more naturalistic one: unlike the injectable

drugs, which when efficacious produce an erection regardless of context (famously proved by Dr. Giles Brindley, a leading British impotence researcher, who once demonstrated a successful experiment treatment by dropping his trousers in front of hundreds of astonished colleagues at a conference), Viagra merely paves the way for the *possibility* of arousal. Erections must still be achieved the old-fashioned way, whether through desire, attraction, physical stimulation, the guilty thrill of an illicit affair, page 27 of *The Godfather* or what have you.

Loyola psychiatrist Renshaw offers the instructive example of a couple who came to see her the day after the man had taken Viagra for the first time: "They went to bed to wait for something to happen and fell asleep while they were waiting. They forgot to have foreplay. They expected an instant erection." The next night, after Renshaw gently reminded them about the importance of stimulation, they had intercourse for the first time in three years.

During the drug's clinical trials, which as a rule tend to have rosier outcomes than real life, Pfizer reported a 60%-to-80% success rate, depending on the dosage (compared with a 24% success rate for placebos). The anecdotal evidence is even more compelling, if one can put up with a certain amount of crowing. Earl Macklin, a 59-year-old security guard in Chicago, has suffered from impotence on and off for 10 years as a result of diabetes. The first two times he tried Via-

THE DOWNSIDE OF VIAGRA

Viagra may help millions of men—and even some women—but it is not a sexual cure-all. It is not an aphrodisiac; it will not work in the absence of desire. Nor will it make a normal erection harder or make one last longer. It will not, in and of itself, save a marriage. In fact, there are some risks to taking Viagra that everyone, whether sexually dysfunctional or merely dissatisfied, should consider before rushing to the pharmacy:

■ **HEADACHES** One out of 10 men in the clinical trials developed blinding headaches that grew more severe at higher doses.

■ **SEEING BLUE** Because the eyes contain an enzyme similar to the one on which Viagra works in the penis, about 3% of users develop temporary vision problems, ranging from blurred vision to a blue or green halo effect.

■ **BLACKOUTS** Viagra can trigger sudden drops in blood pressure, and there is a risk that men who take it in combination with nitroglycerin or other antihypertensive drugs could faint or go into shock.

■ **PRIAPISM** Although it never happened in the trials, there is a theoretical risk that men with sickle-cell anemia, leukemia or urethral inflammation could, when taking Viagra, develop priapism (defined as an erection that lasts four hours or more). Untreated, priapism can lead to tissue damage and even impotence.

■ **COITAL CORONARIES** Sometimes impotence is an early indicator of heart disease, diabetes and some types of cancer. Taking Viagra could mask these life-threatening conditions. Men with coronary problems who have not had sex for many years should consult their doctors before putting too much strain on a weakened heart.

■ **ABUSE** Nobody knows the long-term effects of large doses of Viagra, especially on men who take it for the wrong reason. Although it is a relatively safe drug, there is a possibility that users will become psychologically dependent on it, unable to achieve an erection without Viagra.—**By Christine Gorman**

gra, it produced minimal results; the third time he was able to have intercourse with his girlfriend for the first time in their four-month relationship. "I've been using it every day since then," he says (four days later) with a conspiratorial chuckle. "It makes me feel like I'm in my 30s again." Macklin's insurance company has notified him that it won't be reimbursing him, so, he says, "I'll limit myself to 20 pills a month."

Tom Cannata, a 43-year-old accountant from Springfield, Mass., has been taking Viagra for the past three years as a trial subject. He was suffering from partial impotence brought on, he believes, by years of bicycle riding (an activity, it should be noted, that is not universally held to be a cause of impotence). Cannata was able to achieve erections but felt that they "should have been stronger and much longer-lasting." Viagra worked for him the first time and has worked ever since. "Not only is the frequency of our sex greater," he says, "but for me it is much more intense than it was without the medication. The quality is so much better. Much firmer, stronger erections. And the orgasm is much more explosive." So pleased has Cannata been with the results that he was inspired, he says, to go out and buy a sports car not long after beginning the drug—indicating, perhaps, a soon-to-boom, Viagra-inspired market for souped-up cars, Aramis, oversize stereo equipment and other accoutrements of the virile life-style.

Some patients TIME queried had no reaction to Viagra whatsoever. Others have had more ambiguous experiences. Consider Irving Mesher, a 73-year-old retired New York City firefighter, who currently lives at a family-owned nudist resort in Pennsylvania's Pocono mountains. He describes himself as "sexually motivated" and "very active." Thanks to injection therapies (prostate-cancer treatments six years ago left him "semihard"), he has been having sex—by his account—as often as three or four times a week with several girlfriends in their 20s. Still, he was eager to try Viagra. Taking a 50-mg dose the first time, he was pleased with the results: "About as hard as it can get." However, a subsequent experiment with a 100-mg pill backfired, having no beneficial effect, as did a return to 50 mg. Mesher nevertheless plans to continue with Viagra, inspired, perhaps, by the example of his 70-year-old best friend Frank, who took the drug last week and "turned into a monster." The two are planning to invite several friends to a Viagra party.

As Mesher's story suggests, and many doctors insist, more isn't necessarily more with Viagra. Known to chemists by the less evocative name of sildenafil (the word Viagra, redolent of both "vigor" and "Niagara," had been kicking around Pfizer for years, a brand name in search of a product), the drug began life as a heart medication designed to treat angina by increasing blood flow to the heart. Sildenafil, it turned out, wasn't so

good at opening coronary arteries, but happy test subjects did notice increased blood flow to their penises, a side effect brought to Pfizer's attention when the test subjects were reluctant to return their leftover pills. The medication works by suppressing the effect of the naturally occurring enzyme phosphodiesterase type 5 (PDE5), which causes an erection to subside after orgasm by breaking down the body chemical known as cyclic GMP. It is cyclic GMP that initiates the muscular and vascular changes that lead to an erection in the first place. While PDE5 is always present in the penis, cyclic GMP is produced only during arousal. The catch in impotent men is that they may not produce enough cyclic GMP to temporarily "win out" over the PDE5. Thus the efficacy of Viagra: by strong-arming PDE5, it allows a little bit of one's cyclic GMP to go a long way.

One more nugget of possibly boring but crucial biochemistry: the erectile tissue in the penis has a finite number of receptors for cyclic GMP. This means that a normally functioning man with adequate levels of the chemical shouldn't get any more bang for his buck by gobbling Viagra; the variations anyone feels in his or her sexual response are due to factors outside the drug's purview. At the same time, Pfizer hasn't done any testing of the drug on nonimpotent men to prove the point, but it's hard to imagine that biochemical nitpicking is going to stop people from experimenting. Certainly it will be hard for wet blankets and smarty-pants to compete with the siren calls coming out of sex clinics around the country from men "feeling 18 again."

"If you can have an erection naturally, you probably won't need Viagra," says Thomas Burnakis, pharmacy clinical coordinator at Baptist Medical Center in Jacksonville, Fla. "It's not going to make your erection harder or last longer. But I can guarantee you that if you walk in and say, 'Doc, I'm having trouble keeping my flag up,' most physicians are not going to insist on testing. What's to keep you from using it? Absolutely nothing. And just as with fen/phen, while a lot of doctors said they would not give that drug, a lot of clinics were prescribing it. It's going to be a moneymaking procedure. They'll give you a cursory exam, charge you for that and write the prescription"—a prediction that has already been borne out on the Internet. According to Pfizer, there's no evidence that overeager users could develop a physical addiction to Viagra. But as for a psychological addiction, that is uncharted territory.

It is because of the potential for abuse and, more to the point, the traditionally seedy associations that cling to impotence remedies (witness the ads in the back of low-rent men's magazines for spurious Spanish fly, hard-on creams and the like) that drug companies have only recently turned their attention to sexual dysfunction. This would account for the tone

WHAT'S BEING SAID ABOUT VIAGRA BY THE FAMOUS ... AND THE NOT SO FAMOUS

■ "Even if a man has an erection from floor to ceiling and can keep it that way for an hour, it will not be pleasurable for a woman if he is not sexually literate. There has to be an education process to go with this drug. On the positive side, by the year 2004 there will be 90 million grandparents in the U.S., and for them, this will be a boon."
—**DR. RUTH WESTHEIMER,** *sex adviser*

■ "It is frightening to be a male these days. We are a performance-oriented society, and sex has always been to the woman's advantage. For sex to occur, all she really has to do is lie there."
—**NANCY FRIDAY,** *author of* The Power of Beauty *and* Men in Love

■ "Feminism has emasculated the American male, and that emasculation has led to physical problems. This pill will take the pressure off

men. It will lead to new relationships between men and women and undercut the feminist agenda. It will free the American male libido much the same way the Pill did."
—**BOB GUCCIONE,** Penthouse *publisher*

■ "The astounding success of Viagra testifies, I think, to how integral the erection is to men's self-worth. The penis is a weapon, and much of society has been aimed at controlling it. But it is also a lewdly lyrical thing. It is man's most honest organ. It is either up or down, and you can't lie about it."
—**GAY TALESE,** *author of* Thy Neighbor's Wife, *is writing a book about the penis*

■ "The erection is the last gasp of modern manhood. If men can't continue to produce erections, they're going to evolve themselves right out of the human species. I want men to re-examine, really re-

examine why they need this pill. Because they do need it, they need it right now. They need it to bolster themselves. They need it to stiffen their erections. It's like the steel that they would get if they were at war."
—**CAMILLE PAGLIA,** *postfeminist social critic*

■ "I've waited seven years for a real erection. This little pill is like a package of dynamite; you don't know if you're going to diffuse the little sucker or if it's going to explode in your face."
—**RONALD MARROCCO,** *a 55-year-old diabetic from St. Petersburg, Fla.*

■ "There was significantly more lubrication. I did get a slight headache last night and in the morning, and I had major facial flushing during sex and afterward."
—*a Seattle nurse who experimented with Viagra without telling her husband*

■ "Not only is the frequency of our sex greater, but for me it is much more intense than it was without the medication. The quality is so much better. Much firmer, stronger erections, and the orgasm is much more explosive, much more satisfying."
—**TOM CANNATA,** *a 43-year-old accountant from Springfield, Mass.*

■ "I've been using it every day. It makes me feel like I'm in my 30s. I don't worry about the risks."
—**EARL MACKLIN,** *a 59-year-old security guard in Chicago*

■ "I hear that it works for 2 out of 3 men. Maybe I'm the one."
—**TYRONE,** *a 48-year-old city employee in Chicago with diabetes who has tried Viagra twice, so far with no real improvement*

adopted by Pfizer chairman and CEO William Steere even as he figuratively licks his chops over the potential market in "aging baby boomers." He is careful to point out that "quality-of-life drugs are gene-based just like those for serious medical conditions. In areas like impotence, aging skin, baldness and obesity, the science is just as profound as if you were working in cancer, asthma or anti-infectives." In other words, Viagra is sober stuff and not at all akin to Sy Sperling's Hair Club for Men.

Along related lines, a brochure for Pfizer employees points out that while "jokes and puns are often used in conversation about sexual health topics . . . you can redirect humorous remarks to more appropriate discussion by not joining in the humor and pointing out the seriousness of the subject matter, reminding the people with whom you speak that ED is a significant medical con-

dition that affects the lives of millions of men and their partners." This is true, of course. It also speaks to the tricky questions of taste and exploitation that Pfizer will have to navigate in marketing the drug. So far, without an official launch or virtually any promotion, Viagra is doing fine. But why hold back? Advertisements will begin appearing in medical journals in about six weeks, followed by consumer ads this summer. A company spokesman says they will be "tasteful and emotional, emphasizing [impotence] as a couple's condition." One can imagine.

At any rate, it's an emphasis that should remind us that human sexuality is far too rich and complex for the entire subject to be balanced on the delicate fulcrum of an erection. As with the debate in psychiatry between traditional talk therapists and their more pharmacologically minded colleagues,

controversy over Viagra and its cousins may well provoke a rift among sex researchers. Raymond Rosen, a professor of psychiatry at the Robert Wood Johnson Medical School in Piscataway, N.J., makes the obvious but necessary point that Viagra will not be the final word on sexual dysfunction or dissatisfaction: "There's a danger that we could lose sight of the fact that a lot of sexual problems relate to poor relationships or poor self-esteem or anxiety, depression or other factors." Or as Petersen, the *Playboy* adviser, puts it, "You can take an angry couple and give them Viagra, and then you have an angry couple with an erection." Oddly, that's reassuring.

—*Reported by Edward Barnes and Lawrence Mondi/New York, Wendy Cole/Chicago, Greg Fulton/Atlanta and Arnold Mann/Washington*

America: Awash in STDs

by Gracie S. Hsu

A "hidden epidemic" is stalking America, according to the Institute of Medicine, a branch of the National Academy of Sciences.

More than 25 infectious diseases transmitted by unprecedented rates of promiscuous extramarital sexual activity are infecting at least 12 million Americans annually.

At current rates of infection, at least one in four Americans will contract a sexually transmitted disease (STD) at some point in life.

The United States bears the dubious distinction of leading the industrialized world in overall rates of STDs.

Two-thirds of the 12 million new cases a year are among men and women under age 25. Indeed, about 3 million teenagers—one in four sexually experienced adolescents—acquire an STD each year.

STDs should concern Americans because they can cause such serious consequences as cervical cancer, infertility, infection of offspring, and death. Most people are unaware that

• an estimated 100,000 to 150,000 women become infertile each year as a result of an STD;

• half of the 88,000 ectopic pregnancies that occur each year are due to a preexisting STD infection;

• 4,500 American women die each year from cervical cancer, which is almost always caused by an

STD called the human papilloma virus (HPV).

'STEALTH' DISEASE

"I don't think people understand how common some of these serious consequences are, particularly infertility," says Patricia Donovan, senior associate at the Alan Guttmacher Institute (AGI), a nonprofit research corporation specializing in reproductive health.

"Seventy-five percent of women with chlamydia don't have any symptoms. They don't know until 5 years later, when they have serious pelvic pain, or 10 years later, when they can't get pregnant, that they had this STD that would have been easily curable."

STDs such as chlamydia, gonorrhea, syphilis, and trichomoniasis are nonviral and therefore curable if detected early enough. Other STDs, however, are viral and have no cure. These include HPV, genital herpes, sexually transmitted hepatitis B, and the human immunodeficiency virus, or HIV, which is responsible for 90,000 cases of AIDS annually, a figure that was dramatically expanded in 1993 over previous years due to an official redefinition of AIDS.

As many as 56 million individuals—more than one in five Ameri-

cans—may be infected with an incurable viral STD other than AIDS.

STDs are "a tremendous problem," says W. David Hager, president of the Infectious Diseases Society for Obstetrics and Gynecology.

"Last fall, a *New England Journal of Medicine* article found that slightly over 21 percent of Americans over age 12 are herpes simplex virus positive," Hager says. "That equals 45 million people.

"Furthermore, huge numbers of coeds on college campuses have HPV. Ninety-five percent of all cervical cancer and dysplasia [abnormal growth of organs or cells] are caused by HPV. And this may only be the tip of the iceberg."

The Institute of Medicine (IOM) estimates that the annual direct and indirect costs of selected major STDs, in addition to the human suffering associated with them, are approximately $10 billion. If sexually transmitted HIV infections are included, the total rises to $17 billion.

Medically, experts agree that the main risk factor for contracting an STD is promiscuity.

PROMISCUITY'S PERIL

"Having more than one lifetime sexual partner connotes risk," says Shepherd Smith, president of the Institute for Youth Development

This article originally appeared in *The World & I*, June 1998, pp. 56-61. Reprinted by permission of *The World & I*, a publication of The Washington Times Corporation. © 1998.

The Hidden Epidemic

→ The United States leads the industralized world in overall rates of STDs.

→ STDs can cause cervical cancer, infertility, infection of offspring, and death.

→ As many as 56 million Americans (more than one in five citizens) may be infected with an incurable viral STD other than AIDS, such as genital herpes or hepatitis B.

→ Annual costs of selected major STDs are about $10 billion. Including sexually transmitted HIV, the total rises to $17 billion.

COURTESY OF THE INSTITUTE FOR YOUTH DEVELOPMENT

■ *Promiscuity skeptic:* Shepherd Smith, president of the Institute for Youth Development, says, "The more [sexual] partners, the more risk [for contracting STDs]. It's that simple."

(IYD). "The more partners, the more risk. It's that simple."

Compared with men and women who have had only 1 partner, those who report 2–3 partners are 5 times as likely to have had an STD; those with 4–6 lifetime partners are 10 times as likely; and the odds are 31 times greater for those who report 16 or more partners.

But Americans today are far more promiscuous than in the past. One big reason is that people are initiating sexual intercourse at younger ages, which usually leads to a higher number of partners during their lifetime.

According to a national poll of more than 11,000 high-school-aged youths, 54 percent said they were sexually active, compared with 29 percent in 1970. The proportion of 15-year-olds who have had sex has risen from 4.6 percent in 1970 to 26 percent. And almost one-fifth of the sexually active teens say they have had four or more partners.

In urban areas, the percentage of sexually experienced women aged 15–19 who reported four or more sex partners increased from 14 percent in 1971 to 31 percent in 1988.

"Sexual behavior is putting a sizable portion of high school students at risk," says Richard Lowry, an adolescent-health expert at the federal Centers for Disease Control and Prevention (CDC).

Having several partners is especially dangerous for teenage girls, he says, because studies show that they often have an immature cervix, which may be more easily infected.

While experts agree that promiscuity is a major risk factor, liberals and conservatives generally hold very different values regarding promiscuity. Conservatives usually believe that promiscuity in and of itself is unhealthy and should be prevented by advocating abstinence until marriage and faithfulness within marriage.

Liberals usually argue that promiscuity already exists, that it results from legitimate personal choices, and that it is not necessarily something that can or should be prevented. Rather, people should be educated about their risks so that they can protect themselves with condoms if they choose to have more than one sexual partner.

CONSERVATIVES: PREVENT PROMISCUITY

To conservatives, America's STD epidemic is really a problem of promiscuity, a symptom of society's moral decline, which began with the 1960s sexual revolution.

Joe McIlhaney, president of the Medical Institute for Sexual Health in Austin, Texas, says that "the reason there are more [sexually transmitted] diseases now than 30 years ago is because the ethics and values of society have changed."

There has been, he says, "a weakening of values, not just those having to do with sex, but also of other values like respect, responsibility, integrity." He says parents are not teaching their children these values strongly anymore.

Hager concurs. "Family breakdown and the loss of a great deal of family identity," he says, have contributed to a problem he's seeing become more common among young women: "A majority of young women that we see with STDs come from a situation where they are seeking the love and intimacy that they have missed in their homes."

To reverse the moral decline, conservatives advocate reinstating the traditional values of abstinence until marriage and faithfulness within marriage.

First, "parents should give unambiguous messages regarding appropriate sexual conduct," says the IYD's Smith.

Research shows that parents have the biggest impact of anyone on kids' behavior. And, according to the National Longitudinal Study on

The STD Tidal Wave

STD	Consequences of Infection	Estimated New Cases Annually	Estimated Costs (1990)
Pelvic Inflammatory Disease (PID)	Infertility, ectopic pregnancy	1 million	$4.2 billion
Chlamydia	PID, infertility, ectopic pregnancy; neonatal eye infections; infant pneumonia and chronic respiratory problems	4 million	$781 million
Gonorrhea	PID, infertility, ectopic pregnancy; in newborns causes blindness, septic arthritis, meningitis	1.1 million	$288 million
Genetal Herpes*	Babies exposed at birth may die or suffer neurologic damage	200,000–500,000 (31 million currently infected)	$145 million
Trichomoniasis	Vaginal discharge	3 million	Unknown
Urethritis		1.2 million	Unknown
Human Papilloma Virus (HPV)*	Cervical cancer	500,000–1 million (24–40 million currently infected)	Unknown
Epididymitis	Fever, chills, groin pain	500,000	Unknown
Hepatitis B*	Liver cancer	100,000–200,000 (1.5 million currently infected)	Unknown
Syphilis	Stillborn children; in infants, congenital syphilis	120,000	Unknown
HIV*	Death, greater susceptibility to other diseases	40,000 (1 million currently infected)	Unknown

*NONCURABLE STDs

SOURCE: ALAN GUTTMACHER INSTITUTE

Adolescent Health, the largest-ever survey of American adolescents, kids were more likely to abstain from sex if their parents encouraged them to wait until marriage and discouraged birth control.

Kids also need to know that "sex within marriage is truly worth waiting for," Smith continues. "The NORC [National Opinion Research Center] study in Chicago found that the most sexually satisfied Americans are those who are in monogamous married relationships."

Second, "educators and medical professionals need to come around and help the parents to avoid disease and have a consistent message," says McIlhaney. He suggests that schools teach a character-based sex education program, because "values are the foundation on which good character is built."

"Young people will behave at the level of greatest expectation," says Hager. "If your expectation of young people is that they will engage in sexual activity, you aren't teaching them appropriate restraints.

"If your expectation of young people is that they can abstain, your educational program and expectations will give them enough hope that they will be able to abstain."

LIBERALS: PREVENT UNPROTECTED SEX

Unlike conservatives, liberals think that preventing promiscuity is unrealistic and not even necessarily desirable.

Instead, they envision a culture where people are open and comfortable with their sexuality so each person would be able to negotiate with his sexual partner about what he wants or doesn't want from sex. Preventing promiscuity, therefore, is not the goal; preventing unprotected intercourse is.

COURTESY OF CAMPAIGN FOR OUR CHILDREN

■ *Advertising abstinence:* **Various groups and localities have begun to run billboard ads, such as this one in Maryland, promoting abstinence as a way of stemming the STD epidemic.**

To liberals, the problem of high STD rates stems from Americans' inability to talk about sexuality and provide factual sex education in the home, school, and health care setting.

Peggy Clarke, president of the American Social Health Association, the only nongovernmental organization devoted to fighting STDs, says that the reason STDs are flourishing is that "we, as a culture, have not been good at dealing with sexuality."

"We need to raise people's skills in talking about sexuality and becoming more comfortable with it," says Kent Klindera, director of the HIV/STD education department at Advocates for Youth. The message that humans are "sexual beings" has to come from all sectors of society, he says, including "schools, churches, the mass media."

For example, Klindera conducts a peer education program through the Episcopal Church. His workshops help young people build better communication skills around their sexuality, whether it be through condom negotiation or abstinence role playing. He says if young people can communicate better about their

sexuality, they'll be able to prevent the spread of STDs.

Liberals say that the best way to prevent STDs among the sexually active is to use condoms. They claim that condoms are "very effective" in preventing disease if used correctly every time. Thus, they want condoms to be distributed in schools, and they advocate increased funding for clinics that distribute condoms.

The AGI's Donovan says television networks should air condom ads to educate people about the risks of unprotected sex.

Planned Parenthood sums up the communication and condoms message this way: "Talk with your partners before the heat of passion, and use a condom every time!"

THE VALUES BATTLEFIELD

Conservatives say that the liberal approach is ultimately self-defeating, primarily because the underlying problem of promiscuity is not addressed. They also believe condoms are a poor substitute for true prevention, citing the following reasons:

1. Sending the implicit message that sex outside marriage is permis-

sible will increase the number of people choosing to have sex with multiple partners.

2. Talking explicitly about sexuality piques curiosity and increases the likelihood of sexual experimentation.

3. Condoms provide only partial protection at best. Studies show that condoms have a 12–16 percent failure rate at preventing pregnancy after one year of using the devices. And while pregnancy can only occur a few days during the month, an STD can be transmitted any time a person has sex. Studies also indicate that condoms provide no detectable protection against HPV, genital herpes, or chlamydia.

4. It is unrealistic to expect people to use condoms consistently and correctly with every act of intercourse for a long period of time. McIlhaney says that the highest rate of condom use is a little more than 50 percent, and this was among adults who knew their partners were HIV-positive and whose participation in a research study exposed them to constant encouragement to use condoms. He also cites a 1997 *CDC Update* that said that if people do not use condoms

effectively 100 percent of the time, the outcome would be the same as if they were not using condoms at all.

Liberals say that their approach is superior to the conservatives' for the following reasons:

1. Promiscuity exists, and a "just say no" message is an inadequate and unrealistic response. Conservatives have no response, liberals say, for those who choose to be sexually active outside marriage.

2. Condoms provide very effective protection against STDs. When asked about the 12–16 percent pregnancy failure rate of condoms, liberals respond that such a rate reflects "typical use." Perfect use of condoms, they say, results in an annual pregnancy rate of only 2 percent. They are also adamant about the effectiveness of condoms in preventing STDs. Planned Parenthood says that latex condoms offer "good protection" against many STDs, including gonorrhea, HIV, syphilis, and

> "Seventy-five percent of women with chlamydia don't have any symptoms. They don't know until . . . 10 years later, when they can't get pregnant," says an Alan Guttmacher Institute official.

chancroid, and "some protection" against HPV and genital herpes.

3. Their approach does not impose moral absolutes on people's sexual behavior. Choosing abstinence is just as fine an option as choosing to be sexually active using condoms. It is more important that people be open and comfortable with their own sexuality.

In the final analysis, liberals are right in saying that not everyone is going to practice abstinence until marriage and faithfulness within marriage.

Conservatives are also accurate in saying that far from everyone who engages in sex with multiple partners is going to use condoms consistently and correctly 100 percent of the time.

But ultimately, the debate is more about values than science. It's about whose ideas about human sexuality, family, and lifestyle will prevail.

And that is a question only the American public can answer.

Gracie S. Hsu is a policy analyst specializing in adolescent sexuality and life issues at the Family Research Council, a Washington, D.C.-based research and educational organization.

HEPATITIS C:
A silent killer

There is no vaccine. No truly effective treatment. And the death toll is rising

BY NANCY SHUTE

Janet Gobeille Crenshaw didn't suspect a thing when, eight years ago, she got a letter from the Red Cross after donating blood. "Please don't come back," she recalls the letter saying. "See your doctor. You've tested positive for hepatitis C" "I thought, 'Well, what's that?'"

Her doctor told her not to worry about it, and she didn't. It wasn't until last summer that Crenshaw, a computer systems analyst for IBM in Dallas, decided she'd better find out something about the disease that had led to the rejection of her blood. She didn't like what she found.

Hepatitis C is a killer. About 10,000 people die of the disease each year, and the death toll is rising. It has infected four times as many people as has HIV, the virus that causes AIDS. At least 4 million Americans have it—2 percent of the population. "Hepatitis C is a grave threat to our society," Surgeon General David Satcher warned a congressional subcommittee this spring. "Many Americans infected with hepatitis C are unaware they have the disease."

What makes hepatitis C even more frightening is that while the public and the medical community have focused on AIDS, hepatitis C, a virus transmitted by exposure to contaminated blood, has lurked largely unknown. People seldom get sick when first infected with the virus, unlike what happens with its cousins hepatitis A and B. Instead, the microbe quietly damages the liver, an organ with many vital functions, for 20 years before symptoms emerge. People like Crenshaw, 49, who contracted the disease in 1981 through a blood transfusion, are only now becoming sick.

> # Hepatitis C infects 4 million people in the United States—four times as many as does HIV

"Hepatitis C is an insidious disease," says Willis C. Maddrey, a hepatitis specialist at the University of Texas Southwest Medical Center. "It creeps up on you."

Though the number of new hepatitis C infections is dropping, thanks to efforts that began in 1990 to screen the virus from the blood supply, the number of people falling ill is rising. Officials with the federal Centers for Disease Control and Prevention predict that in the next 10 years the hepatitis C death toll will triple, eclipsing that of AIDS. The costs—financial, social, and emotional—will be huge. Health care already costs more than $600 million a year, according to Satcher. And no one can calculate the value of someone like Janet Crenshaw to her family.

Her experience isn't unusual. She never would have known she was infected if she hadn't been a blood donor. Last year, when she finally connected with a doctor who knew something about the disease (many family doctors aren't up to speed on hep C), a liver biopsy revealed fibrosis, scarring caused by the virus. (like Crenshaw, 60 percent of those now infected are in their 30s and 40s; many of them will become chronically ill in the prime of their lives.)

Crenshaw, married just two years with two teenage stepdaughters, read enough to know that the odds are 8 in 10 that she will develop chronic hepatitis with some inflammation of the liver, and 1 in 5 that she will develop cirrhosis, which kills liver cells and impairs the organ's ability to perform vital tasks such as filtering toxic substances from the blood. Liver cancer is a 1 to 5 percent risk; that risk increases by as much as 4 percent a year with cirrhosis. The treatment for cancer and cirrhosis is a liver transplant. But last year 10,000 names were on the list for transplants, and only 4,000 organs were available. "I married a widower," Crenshaw says. "The last thing I want is for him to go through that again.'

Last fall, Crenshaw started on alpha interferon, a naturally occurring protein that is the primary treatment for hepatitis C. For four months she injected herself three nights a week after dinner. Her hair fell out; she felt achy and tired, as with an endless bout of the flu. Interferon is notorious for inducing flu-like symptoms and depression; 5 percent to 10 percent of patients are so miserable they quit the treatment. Crenshaw kept working, but she tucked a pillow and blanket in the car so that she could slip out of the office and nap.

And after all that, the interferon didn't work. Unfortunately, that's not unusual; interferon clears the virus from the bloodstream for only about 20 percent of patients. Two months ago, Crenshaw started treatment with Infergen, a bio-engineered version of interferon that was approved by the FDA last October. Last week, she found out that she had no response to the Infergen, either. She's continuing treatment in the hope it will work over time. "The last thing I want to do is accidentally spread it to someone. I worry about passing it to my husband. In the back of my mind, it's always there."

The virus's origins remain mysterious, but it probably first spread widely during World War II. Blood transfusion, then a new technology, was common on the battlefield, and sterile equipment was rare. In the 1960s, researchers began noticing liver problems among people who had had transfusions. But it wasn't until the 1970s that scientists were able to differentiate a new strain. "We found there was a third kind of hepatitis, which we called non-A, non-B hepatitis," says Robert Purcell, an NIH researcher who led the effort to study the new virus. "We thought [its identity] would be resolved very quickly." That was in 1975. It wasn't until 1989 that a biotechnology firm replicated part of the virus and created the first blood test for it. Hepatitis C remains largely a mystery; it is one of the RNA viruses, which are less well understood than are DNA viruses, and it has defied efforts to grow it in a test tube. Like HIV, it mutates its protein coating to disguise itself from the body's immune defenses; there are at least six different genotypes of hepatitis C, and more than 30 subtypes. Unlike HIV, it doesn't attack the immune system, making victims less prone to secondary infections that plague AIDS patients. The HIV virus also progresses more quickly, and is more lethal.

AIDS preoccupation. But AIDS has played a role in the hepatitis C story. Critics of the government's response to hep C, including former Surgeon General C. Everett Koop and members of Congress, say public-health authorities let themselves get preoccupied with AIDS and failed to alert the public to this other threat. Others say it would have been irresponsible to inform people if there was no way to help them. "There isn't a lot we've been able to do," says Miriam Alter, chief of epidemiology for hepatitis at the CDC. Reliable tests weren't available until 1990; and, Alter adds, "therapy has been very disappointing for most people."

Now the federal government is making its first public moves against the disease. The Department of Health and Human Services is finalizing a rule requiring blood banks and hospitals to notify people who likely contracted hepatitis C through transfusions between January 1988 and June 1992. This is cumbersome; the institutions must first search their databases for blood donors who later tested positive for hepatitis C, then search again for patients who got blood from those donors, an estimated 300,000 people. Notices won't go out for at least six months.

But many more people got transfusions before 1992, and those people will not be individually notified. In any event, transfusions account for only 7 percent of hepatitis C infections. The government hopes to alert the millions of other probable hepatitis C carriers with a $4 million public-education campaign.

Junkies. Most Americans remain in the dark about hepatitis C and how it spreads. And the authorities don't know all risk factors, which adds to the confusion. The medical community has traditionally considered hepatitis C a "junkie's disease," because it's easily spread by sharing intravenous needles. Blood transfusions before 1990, kidney dialysis, clotting factors for hemophilia, and organ transplants also are known risk factors. People who received blood before 1970, when hospitals quit using commercially provided blood, face a greater risk of infection than do those transfused later. Paid blood donors were often Skid Row denizens with high rates of hepatitis and other infectious diseases.

The CDC says 10 percent of transmissions are unexplained, and more than 50 percent of cases are linked to intravenous drugs. David Crosby, 1960s rocker and heavy drug user, had a liver transplant in 1994 as a result of hep C. But many people who merely experimented with IV drugs may have become infected, too. "These are [now] solid citizens who just played around in the late '60s or early '70s," says Emmet Keeffe, a professor of medicine at Stanford Uni-

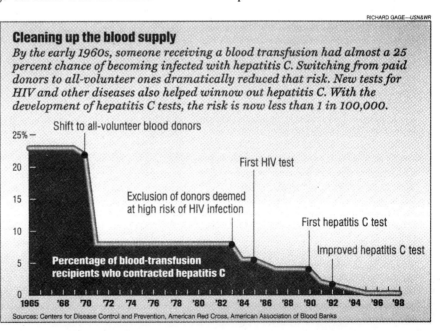

RICHARD GAGE—USN&WR

Cleaning up the blood supply

By the early 1960s, someone receiving a blood transfusion had almost a 25 percent chance of becoming infected with hepatitis C. Switching from paid donors to all-volunteer ones dramatically reduced that risk. New tests for HIV and other diseases also helped winnow out hepatitis C. With the development of hepatitis C tests, the risk is now less than 1 in 100,000.

Shift to all-volunteer blood donors

First HIV test

Exclusion of donors deemed at high risk of HIV infection

First hepatitis C test

Improved hepatitis C test

Percentage of blood-transfusion recipients who contracted hepatitis C

25% — 20 — 15 — 10 — 5 — 0

1965 '68 '70 72 '74 '76 '78 '80 '82 '84 '86 '88 '90 '92 '94 '96 '98

Sources: Centers for Disease Control and Prevention, American Red Cross, American Association of Blood Banks

The ABCs of hepatitis

Hepatitis A and B, both viruses that affect the liver, were identified following World War II. Since the 1970s, doctors had been aware of a virus that was neither A nor B, but it was not until 1989 that hepatitis C was identified. Other viruses have been identified more recently.

FORM	TRANSMISSION	SYMPTOMS	TREATMENT	NEW INFECTIONS PER YEAR
Hepatitis A	Contact with something, usually food or water, contaminated by the feces of an infected person.	Flu-like symptoms such as fatigue, abdominal pain, loss of appetite, nausea, diarrhea, dark urine, and jaundice (yellowing of the skin and eyes). But some infected people have no symptoms.	Bed rest and increased intake of fluids. Infections can be prevented if immune globulin, which is a preparation of antibodies, is given within two weeks of exposure to the virus. Vaccines are available.	Up to 200,000
Hepatitis B	Direct contact with infected blood or bodily fluids, such as from sharing drug needles or having sex with an infected person. Babies can be infected by their mothers during birth.	Jaundice, fatigue, abdominal and joint pain, loss of appetite, nausea, and vomiting. Can lead to cirrhosis of the liver and liver cancer, however most people infected with the virus do not develop chronic infection. Some people never develop symptoms.	The drug interferon reduces the chance of a return of the disease and can be effective in about 30 percent to 40 percent of patients. A vaccine has been available since the early 1980s.	Between 150,000 and 300,000
Hepatitis C	Shared drug needles, sexual contact and blood transfusions prior to 1992. Babies can get the disease from their mothers during birth.	Most people never experience acute symptoms such as fatigue, abdominal pain, loss of appetite, jaundice, nausea, and vomiting. Can cause chronic liver damage, cirrhosis of the liver, and liver cancer.	Interferon. When that is not effective, doctors try Rebetron, a combination of drugs made up of interferon and ribavirin. There is no vaccine.	Between 28,000 and 180,000
Hepatitis D	Intravenous drug use, sex with an infected partner, and from mother to baby. But it can only be contracted by people who also are infected with hepatitis B.	Jaundice, fatigue, abdominal and joint pain, loss of appetite, nausea, and vomiting. Produces chronic liver-damage symptoms that are similar to hepatitis B only more severe.	Interferon is used for some people. The vaccine for hepatitis B is effective in stopping the transmission of hepatitis D, too, but only in people who are not already infected with hepatitis B.	About 5,000
Hepatitis E	Contaminated water from the feces of infected humans. It is not commonly contracted in the U.S.	Inflammation of the liver leading to loss of appetite, nausea and vomiting, fever, fatigue, and abdominal pain. Many people who contract it have no symptoms.	No vaccine. Doctors encourage bed rest and drinking extra fluids.	Few U.S. cases

Sources: The Centers for Disease Control and Prevention, the American Liver Foundation, and the Food and Drug Administration. Compiled by Stacey Schultz

versity. Snorting cocaine, which many people thought safe, is also risky, it turns out. Microdroplets of blood dislodged when a coke straw bumps the delicate capillaries inside the nose can be passed on the end of the straw.

Richard Wallace wonders whether he's among those paying the price for the sins of youth. A 43-year-old St. Petersburg, Fla., businessman, he found out he has hep C after a blood test in 1991 for more life insurance following

the birth of his second child. Wallace figures he got the disease from a surgical procedure he had as a child, or perhaps from trying cocaine as a young man. Since then he has married, had two children, built a successful bakery-supply business, even joined the Rotary Club. The business is gone now; he sold it when he realized the hepatitis was progressing quickly. He also sold his house, buying a smaller one that took less maintenance. He hasn't been able to work since October, and a new regime licensed this month, combining interferon with ribavirin, an antiviral, failed to lower his high viral load. He's now trying high daily doses of Infergen and plans to try whatever new treatments come along. "I've got to protect myself," Wallace says. "If I slip into cirrhosis, it's the no-return point."

The CDC recently attributed 20 percent of hepatitis C cases to sexual transmission. Having multiple partners appears to be a risk, but the virus is not easily sexually transmitted, unlike HIV. And the transmission rate among monogamous partners is quite low, around 3 percent. Another 10 percent of cases are from blood transfusions or exposure at work or home; surgeons, nurses and emergency workers are at risk from blood splashes and needle sticks. Country singer Naomi Judd says she got hepatitis C while working as a nurse before she became famous. Hepatitis C carriers are cautioned not to share razors or toothbrushes. "Everybody is at some risk for hepatitis C," says Andi Thomas, founder of Hep-C Alert, an activist group in Florida. "You're not safe just because you've lived a safe and sane life."

U.S. veterans appear to have higher rates of hepatitis C than the civilian population. In a recent six-week survey, 20 percent of patients at the Washington, D.C., VA Medical Center tested positive for hepatitis C; 10 percent tested positive at the San Francisco VA hospital, and half of the VA's liver-transplant patients have the disease. Dr. Thomas Holohan, chief of patient-care services, says that "veterans have a higher incidence of drug use than the civilian population," and that Vietnam veterans were more likely to have been exposed to blood during transfusions and evacuations. Last week, the Department of Veterans Affairs sent its doctors a directive to screen all their patients for any of 10 factors, including tattoos and "intemperate alcohol use," then test those with risk factors for virus antibodies. Within the next month, the VA also will issue formal treatment guidelines.

Testing, testing. Federal health officials say anyone with a major risk factor should get tested for hepatitis C. So should people who show elevated liver enzymes on a standard blood test (but those can also rise from having a glass of wine the night before). Because it can take from two to six months after infection for a hepatitis C blood test to register positive, and because no blood test is 100 percent effective, there is still a slight risk of transmitting hepatitis C through the blood supply. Someone who suspects they might have hepatitis C

should not donate blood. (For free information, contact the American Liver Foundation at 888-443-7872 or www. liverfoundation.org.)

People who find out they have hepatitis C face the question of whether or not to get treatment. It's not an easy decision. A 1997 report from the National Institutes of Health recommends that patients with elevated liver enzymes and fibrosis be treated with interferon but said it's unclear whether people with mild cases, or those with advanced disease, will benefit. Drinking alcohol can exacerbate the disease, and doctors recommend quitting, or cutting back to one drink a day.

Many drug companies, enticed by a global market of 170 million potential customers, are working on new hep C treatments. A vaccine is nowhere on the horizon because it's very hard to come up with enough variations to attack the virus's many forms. But some potential treatments look promising, particularly protease inhibitors similar to those that have proved so successful with AIDS. The drugs could disrupt the virus's enzymatic processes and block its replication. But clinical trials are at least several years off. Until we have better weapons to use against hepatitis C, we have to learn to live with it.

With E. F Licking and Stacey Schultz

not tonight, baby

AFTER 13 YEARS OF PASSIONATE SEX WITH HER HUSBAND,
ONE SISTER STRUGGLES WITH A SUDDEN LOSS OF DESIRE
AND ITS EFFECT ON HER ONCE-VIBRANT MARRIAGE

BY D.Y. PHILLIPS

RAYMOND FORGOT TO KISS ME BEFORE HE LEFT FOR work this morning. Again. Another little thing he thinks I don't notice. But I do. It's always the little things. For instance, the way he looks at me now when he comes home at night, the warm and familiar glow in his eyes gone. The easy sharing of our day has been replaced by distance, like a sulking stranger who lurks between us. Sometimes I glance up and my eyes catch his, and for a fleeting moment I see something else, something I don't want to see. I see his hurt.

I am a 44-year-old woman who has been happily married for 13 years—and I have lost my libido. It all started with my decision to undergo a hysterectomy. Just the mention of the word can conjure up visions of once sensual and vibrant women slowly being robbed of their femininity because they've been stripped of a uterus. Breasts, courageously struggling along, finally give in and hang their heads in despair. Vaginas evict all moisture and refuse to cooperate. Mood swings as unpredictable as hurricanes sweep down from some mysterious place, wreaking havoc on husbands, lovers, family and friends.

With such a bleak prognosis, a hysterectomy was definitely something I feared. Raymond and I have always enjoyed an active sex life, and I wanted it to stay that way. Still, after months of indecision, I chose the operation to remove fibroids—benign tumors of the uterus—so inflamed they bled for weeks on end. That operation changed my life.

Looking back, I can see how easy it is to become a victim of circumstances. I was living in my own dream world, aspiring to become a writer. I was so wrapped up in my stories that I didn't pay much attention to the fact that I was literally bleeding to death each month. Not until I began to have embarrassing accidents at work—accidents so severe they often forced me to go back home to change my clothes—did I start to worry. Visits to gynecologists revealed that the excessive bleeding was caused by several small fibroid tumors in my womb. "It's nothing to be too concerned about," I was told by each of the four gynecologists I consulted. "Fibroid tumors are very common, especially among Black women."

Common or not, the idea of a tumor, big or small, growing somewhere inside me was unnerving, not to mention inconvenient and occasionally painful. My regular gynecologist suggested that I consider having my uterus removed. After all, she reasoned, I was already the mother of two daughters, and at 42 didn't plan on having more children. I wasn't convinced. I found the idea of having such a vital organ removed disconcerting. And I had another concern: My husband, Raymond, and I weren't quite teenagers with racing hormones, but we were pretty darn close—lovemaking was often the highlight of our weekend. I feared a hysterectomy would change all that.

Friends were no help. They'd say: "Girl, don't let those people take your uterus out. You

From *Essence*, July 1998, pp. 73-73, 136-138. © 1998 by Essence Communications, Inc. Reprinted by permission.

HOW TO GET YOUR GROOVE BACK

Whether you've gone a few weeks, months or even years without any sign of your libido—relax. You're not alone. Experts say a lack of sexual desire is a common complaint among women and men. But if you're not interested in faking it and you're tired of being celibate, you *can* rekindle your internal fire. Here's how.—SHEREE CRUTE

PROBLEM	SYMPTOMS	POSSIBLE SOLUTIONS
RELATIONSHIP TROUBLES	You're bored, harboring resentments and anger or holding a grudge against your partner.	Remember that sex will never be delicious if you and your partner are emotionally estranged. To heal the relationship, try talking things out or consider couples therapy. And do make time for romance. If boredom is the problem, don't be afraid to spice things up by exploring sexual fantasies with your partner, making love in unusual places, trying sex toys or renting a sexually stimulating video.
STRESS OR EXHAUSTION	You're tired and irritable, and sex is the last thing on your mind.	Take care of yourself. Ask your lover to help out with an aromatherapy massage. Sip a little kava-kava herb tea to ease the tension. Daiana tea may also help you feel sexy, but stick to 1 to 2 teaspoons per cup and no more than 3 cups per day. (Too much can raise blood pressure.)
DEPRESSION	Listlessness and a total lack of interest in sex and other activities you normally enjoy.	Professional support and counseling can help you reclaim your emotional and sexual health.
PERIMENOPAUSE AND MENOPAUSE (These naturally occur between ages 35 and 50 but may also result from removal of the ovaries or from other health problems.)	Waning levels of the hormones estrogen, progesterone and even testosterone (dubbed "the hormone of desire") can make it difficult to become aroused, or make intercourse painful due to vaginal thinning and dryness.	To ease menopausal symptoms, ask your doctor about the pros and cons of hormone-replacement therapy, including estrogen-testosterone combinations. Or try the natural approach: Vitamin E oil, teas or herbal formulas with dong quai, black cohosh, vitex or fenugreek seed may help (be sure to clear these with your doctor). To combat vaginal dryness and thinning, try borage oil (taken orally), creams with estrogen and lubricants like Astroglide or Replens.
MEDICATIONS	Many drugs, including Prozac and treatments for hypertension, can cause a lack of libido.	Ask your doctor if it is possible to change your medication, or at least reduce doses.
HEALTH ISSUES	Diabetes, sickle cell and other illnesses that affect circulation or hormones can cause vaginal dryness and a lack of arousal.	Exercise, eat lots of fruits and vegetables, and be sure to stick to your treatment regimen. If you can manage your health challenge effectively, chances are good that your sex life will get back on course.

better get a fourth or fifth opinion." And then there was: "Girl, you know how a man feels when his woman ain't all woman no more. Especially a Black man. Things change." This remark, an innocent observation from a longtime friend, irritated me the most. I knew she meant well, but I was furious with her and had to bite my tongue to keep from telling her off. How dare she assume that my marriage to Raymond was based on just sex! How dare she imply that my husband wouldn't continue to be loving and understanding if I needed to have my uterus removed!

In the weeks that followed, I investigated various nonsurgical options, including herbal remedies and holistic treatments, but nothing seemed to promise the relief that a hysterectomy did. As I weighed whether or not to have the surgery, my symptoms worsened. I began to have frequent intense headaches, I lacked energy and I never knew when the bleeding would start—at work, at the market, while visiting a friend. I was terrified of sitting on anyone's furniture, thinking I might arise and find beneath me a pool of crimson.

It remains a mystery to me how a woman can lose so much blood each month and still be walking around. Finally Raymond said, "Baby, just do what you have to do. As long as you're well—that's the important thing." With his blessing, I decided to go ahead with the operation.

But before I could have the surgery, doctors discovered through preoperative blood work that I was dangerously low in hemoglobin (the iron-rich pigment in red blood cells that transports oxygen all over the body). My blood was thin and watery, and I was anemic to boot. Immediate surgery was out of the question. Instead, I was placed on iron supplements three times a day and given a series of shots to prevent me from having a menstrual cycle for three months.

"I want you to understand," my doctor told me as I sat on the examination table, "there will be side effects from the shots. They will shut down your hormone production and stop you from bleeding, and you will go into premature menopause. I thought, *No periods for three whole months! How bad can it be?* After bleeding so much for so long, I was in seventh heaven. But after heaven came hell.

Hell showed up in the form of strange mood swings that made friends and family look at me with a cautious eye. Was I glad, mad or sad this time? And my poor husband: I still loved him with all my heart, but the sight of him coming through the door in the evening sometimes made me want to pull my hair out by the roots and run screaming from the room. Though I had once welcomed his gentle caress on my leg or my bottom, now I sought ways to move away from his touch. The kisses-for-no-reason that we used to enjoy didn't seem a big deal now. If we did, fine;

if we didn't, fine. My nights were no better. On a cool night when I was just about to slip into a peaceful sleep, it would seem as if somebody deliberately set the bed on fire. I would break out in a sweat, burning up from the hell I couldn't escape. I'd endure one, two, maybe three minutes of heat. Hot. So, so hot. And then it was gone.

Three months later, my blood thickened and enriched by the regimen of iron supplements and the cessation of bleeding, my doctor performed the hysterectomy. I healed quickly: In five weeks I was my old self—almost. It's been more than a year now, and I'm back to my regular nine-to-five routine. I am much calmer knowing that I will no longer bleed through my clothes or leave stains on chairs. But something isn't right between Raymond and me. I know it has to do with my lack of sexual desire, but I don't know exactly how to correct it. Raymond's hands moving along my body used to start the fire. But not anymore. Now I find ways to avoid sexual intimacy. I don't miss sex. In fact, I rarely think about it these days. If the place between a woman's thighs could be likened to a fireplace, my embers have all died out. No ashes are left smoldering. Sexually, I am cold and dead.

I visit my gynecologist, seeking a solution to my problem. "Did they take out my libido along with my uterus?" I want to ask her. "Did it just slip out, unnoticed, in the operating room?" What I say is "I don't have any desire now, no lust, no libido." I want the doctor to see my desperation, yet I can't help but wonder if she truly understands. My gynecologist, a wonderful and efficient woman, must be in her sixties. Can she still remember what it was like to be touched and loved with a runaway passion? For that matter, can I?

"You just need to give yourself more time," she tells me. Her eyes

have a little twinkle to them. "Remember, we didn't remove your ovaries, so you should still have your supply of hormones. Give yourself some time."

So I am giving myself time, waiting for a semblance of the old libido to return. I'm saddened to think that I may never be the same ooh-baby-let's-get-it-on-now freak mama that Raymond so loved. I wish I could call the hot and steamy feelings back to the place where my libido once lived, but I can't. I ask myself: *How can I expect Raymond to desire me when I can't return the feeling?* And then come the more difficult questions: Are love and sex really one and the same? Have we as active sexual females been misled all these years into believing that lust and love are two different things? If I don't desire my husband sexually, does it mean that I no longer love him? Even worse, will he cease to love me?

As I contemplate all this, I listen to the emptiness of the house without Raymond in it, and I realize that I am looking forward to his return. Outside my window, the morning clouds, gray and cryptic, still hold the sky hostage. Yet birds chirp merrily in the humid air. They remind me that I have to be strong in the face of this difficulty, that I have to think positively.

I decide that when Raymond comes home this evening, I'll put my cards on the table. We'll talk to each other about what our marriage means to us and how we can find enough spiritual love to continue. In the meantime, I feel like picking up the phone and calling my doctor. We have a running joke these days; as soon as she hears my voice, she knows the question I will ask her: "So tell me, Ms. Doctor, have you seen my libido?"

D.Y. Phillips is a writer who lives in Los Angeles.

What Made Troy Gay?

By Deborah Blum

When Troy DeVore told his mother he was gay, his wife was with him.

The couple had driven eight hot sweaty hours in their little unair-conditioned car—470 near-silent miles—from the central California coast north to the dusty valley town of Redding. They reached Troy's mother's home near midnight, damp, exhausted, and anxious to get the words out and over with. They hadn't called to say they were coming.

As soon as Sandi DeVore opened the door, her son hauled her off to the back bedroom. For some time Sandi had felt that Troy was withdrawing into some unreachable distance. He wouldn't talk to her. She couldn't figure out why. All she knew was that she was worried to death about him. Now, without preliminaries, he blurted it out. "Mom, I'm gay." He had no idea what she would do or say. And then, he recalls, "My mother went and hugged my wife; well, she's my ex-wife now. And I thought, What? Shouldn't she be hugging me? But my mother said she thought my wife needed comforting more. Because she thought my wife was going to blame herself."

Mother and son both remember it that way: the first hug going to his wife, like a charm to be used against grief and guilt. Next Sandi DeVore turned to her son and took him in her arms and said, "Are you sure?" as if those words were another charm, against reality.

Today that question—"Are you sure?"—makes them both laugh. Since that breakaway moment in the summer of 1987, Troy has embraced homosexuality with exuber-

> **Scientists once would have pointed to his mother's personality. Now they think her DNA holds the strongest clue.**

ance. At age 32, he runs the public health program at Sacramento's Lambda AIDS Response, a gay nonprofit agency where he teaches safe sex to teenagers. He's cheerfully comfortable with himself, a big man (standing 6 foot 6 and weighing "too much and I'm not saying anything more") with a reddish beard, clear blue eyes, a quick laugh, and a style of dress that emphasizes jeans, T-shirts, and body piercing. He's filled his office with a furry mix of stuffed teddy bears. He wakes up every morning to a bear-shaped alarm clock playing Walt Disney's Winnie-the-Pooh theme song. Knowing what she now knows about Troy, Sandi wonders, How could I not have seen?

But she hadn't seen, and neither had Troy's wife or his father. And like any unwelcome secret unveiled within a family, this one rippled outward into a flood of blame. His father, long divorced from his mom and already on poor terms with Troy, was so furious when he heard about Troy's coming out that the two haven't spoken since. Meanwhile Troy's wife, Kathy, reacted just as Sandi had sensed she would, insisting that she'd somehow turned Troy toward men. As their marriage foundered, Sandi recalls, "Kathy was just so upset."

And Sandi? Sandi, as any mother might, blamed herself.

Sandi, now 50, shares much with her son. She's also tall, also red haired and blue eyed, and her enthusiasm for Troy's life now matches his. But in the months after he came out, what she mainly felt was a profound sense of personal failure. Like most parents of her generation, she'd received the message that homosexuality was a mother's legacy. "I'm a real strong person. I have a strong personality. Was I so dominant that I pushed him into this?" she recalls wondering late at night, turning the circumstances over and over in her mind.

In hindsight, such worry looks painfully unnecessary. Over the past decade a new generation of researchers has uncovered evidence about what drives and shapes sexual orientation, particularly for men. And though there are still unanswered questions, this much seems certain: Sexual orientation is largely innate, dominated by genetics perhaps less powerful than the chromosomal information that dictates physical attributes, such as height, but strong compared with heredity's influence on other behaviors. Scientists estimate that a solid sense of self-worth is perhaps 30 to 40 percent inherited, which allows for powerful environment influence; shyness, perhaps 50 percent; height, perhaps 90 percent. Male sexual orientation, according to the new estimates, may be as much as 70 percent determined at birth.

There's a measure of comfort in this research. It has helped explain the uncomfortable feeling of difference experienced by many gays from an early age. It has raised hope that antigay sentiment can be relegated to the dustheap of prejudices. It has consoled mothers like Sandi DeVore. But it has not come without an irony attached. For if this research is correct, the genes that drive homosexuality are inherited from mothers.

NO ONE IS SURE, but the most reliable estimate—based on surveys of sexual behavior, which probably underestimate—is that 2 to 3 percent of men and not quite 2 percent of women have a same-sex orientation. That's 5 million Americans. Some hide it, desperately, from their parents. Some parents, with equal desperation, refuse to listen. Most gay children and their parents, though, do face the facts together. And from all accounts, one of the first questions parents ask themselves concerns blame: Was it something I did?

For decades scientists answered this question with a highly judgmental yes. Freud had posited that the cause was a domineering mother, an assertion that prompted millions of women over the years to wonder, as Sandi did, whether being a meeker person would have made the child grow up straight. Psychologists also theorized that gays were the product of weak or emotionally distant fathers, or of neurotic family life. Little tested, these explanations became popular wisdom; moreover, the American Psychiatric Association kept homosexuality in its diagnostic manual of mental disorders until 1973.

Such theories—no more than speculation, really—fell away when actually tested. In a study of 1,500 homosexuals and heterosexuals done by the Kinsey Institute in the 1970s, researchers found no evidence that a mother's personality or the quality of family life influenced sexual preference. Children of strong-willed mothers and timid mothers, from happy families and unhappy ones, were equally likely to turn out straight or gay. And while gay men tended to have more distant relationships with their fathers, the researchers theorized that fathers were more apt to turn away from gay sons.

The Kinsey study did more than discredit the myth of the "guilty" parent, however. It provided a compelling portrait of a group of people who were distinctive from an early age. The gays in the study reported playing differently from other children of their gender. Asked, "Did you specifically enjoy girls' activities, such as hopscotch, playing house, or jacks?" half of the gay men responded yes, compared to 12 percent of the straight men. Most gay men but few straight men reported disliking team sports, while 67 percent of the lesbians but only 18 percent of the straight women said they'd cringed at dolls and dress-up. Later studies involving interviews with the parents of gay subjects, conducted without telling them what their children had said, affirmed these childhood differences.

By chronicling such visible early behaviors, the Kinsey study suggested genetics was involved. But it took the pioneering work of psychologist Michael Bailey of Northwestern University and psychiatrist Richard Pillard of Boston University to put that notion on solid ground.

Working together in the early 1990s, they did a series of studies on families of gay men and women. Among identical twins, if one brother was gay, the other brother was gay 52 percent of the time. Among fraternal twins, the rate was 22 percent. The numbers were essentially the same for women. Homosexuality, Bailey and Pillard had found, fit the classic profile of inheritance: The more genetically alike someone was to a gay sibling, the more likely that person also was gay.

Inspired by these findings, Dean Hamer, a geneticist at the National Cancer Institute, wanted to tease out how the transfer might work. He knew that the men Bailey and Pillard studied had an unusually high number of gay male relatives on the mother's side. So he examined the genealogy of 40 families with at least two gay brothers to see if the same pattern emerged. It did: While the father's side showed no pattern, male cousins and uncles on the mother's side were two to three times more likely to be gay.

Whatever genes might be involved, Hamer figured, would be on the X chromosome—the one men get from their mothers. And when he scanned the X of the gay brothers, in 82 percent of his samples he found distinctive genetic markings in one region. He repeated the study, this time looking at the DNA of gay brothers, straight brothers, and lesbian women, and again got significant results: Sixty-seven percent of the gay brothers had the same markings on the X. But the surprise was that the straight men also shared telltale markings at that spot, only these imprints differed from those found in the DNA of gay men. On the lesbians' X chromosomes, however, the region showed no consistent marks.

Hamer couldn't say exactly what he'd found. It wasn't a "gay gene," and it didn't apply to women. Still, it was a genetic region clearly involved in setting male sexual preference. Put together with the work from Bailey, Pillard, and others, Hamer's study signaled a new era in the science of sexual orientation. BORN GAY, trumpeted the cover of *Time*.

TROY DEVORE'S CHILDhood is the textbook case outlined by these researchers. He was a boy who—against everything in his environment—preferred dolls to trucks, girl playmates to boys, domestic games to sports. He was five, Troy recalls, when he developed a crush on television actor Chad Everett. "The signs were there," he says, "if anyone had known to look."

His first-grade teacher wrote on his report card that Troy was the type of boy who stopped to smell the flowers. "I ran into her years later, and she said she'd always suspected I was gay," he says. His female cousins remember that he would borrow their Barbies and other dolls, and wouldn't join backyard ball games. Says Sandi, "His friends were girls rather than boys. And the boys he did like were ones that needed some help. He had a blind friend. He had a friend in a wheelchair."

When he was a freshman in high school, he developed his first major crush. Feeling attracted to a boy terrified him. Beating up "faggots and queers" was a hot topic of discussion in the locker room after gym class. "In the showers it was always, you know, you show me yours, I'll show you mine, and then the topic of faggots would come up." He dated girls. He tried to be one of the guys. But he was different. And, in his mind, he couldn't do anything about it.

After Troy graduated from high school, he drifted, taking aimless and easy work until he fell into a friendship with a waitress at a fast-food restaurant. Kathy was pregnant and wasn't going to marry the father of her child. She seemed to be the answer to Troy's problems. "I asked her to marry me. I wanted kids. I really like kids. She wanted to be married. We both had ulterior motives, I guess." His stepdaughter was born in 1984, and he and his wife had a daughter together in 1986. The family moved to the central coast, where Troy and Kathy managed a small oceanfront motel.

By this time his mother was deeply concerned about him. "I couldn't put a finger on what was different about Troy," says Sandi. "But I was afraid he was going to die, to kill himself. He kept having these accidents, you

know? He hit a tree when he was driving. I kept thinking he wasn't going to make it."

Then a gay couple staying at the motel became estranged, and Troy found himself consoling the partners. Before long he was spending so much time with the men that his wife, in a fury, accused him of sleeping with male guests and, further, of being gay himself. "Yes, I guess I am," he said, shocked into telling the truth. Kathy insisted he tell his mother.

In the months and years after Troy came out to her, Sandi experienced the harrowing series of emotions familiar to many parents of gays. "The first six months were the hard ones," she says. "I even asked him if he thought he was going through a phase. I hear that lots of parents ask that question."

She found herself grieving the loss of the life she had hoped for him, terrified that he would contract AIDS, and ashamed that for all those years she'd failed to see her own son as he was. "I was going back through old photos, and I found a picture of him as a toddler, sitting on the floor playing with three Barbie dolls," she says. "But I just didn't look. Your mind just won't go there." On top of all that, the idea that her pushiness had driven her son from mainstream life wouldn't leave her alone.

"Then one day we were having an altercation, and he wasn't taking anything off me," she says. "And I realized that there was no way I was so overbearing that I could take away from him just being Troy." Finally she agreed with Troy. He was born different. She'd had nothing to do with it.

When Hamer's studies splashed across the newspapers, however, Sandi found she couldn't escape responsibility after all. "Troy called me right away," she remembers. "He said, 'I knew they'd find a way to blame you.'"

"It's funny," she says. "I had always just thought, Is he gay because of me? I never thought about it being my family."

HOW MANY members of Sandi's family are gay can't be established; Troy is the only one who is out of the closet. Still, Troy and Sandi see a clear pattern. Across three generations of her large and far-flung family, they say, they've noted relatives who are both secretive about their sexual preferences and uneasy with them. The one relative who has come out to Sandi and Troy agrees with them. "There are many in our family that I believe to be gay that have never acknowledged it to anyone, not even themselves," says the relative, who has lived with a same-sex companion for years and who spoke on the condition of anonymity.

> When the "gay gene" made headlines, Troy called his mom. "I knew they'd find a way to blame you."

Despite the progress made by researchers, no one knows how the genes that help determine homosexuality work. One notion is that they are but slightly altered versions of the genes that propel most of us toward the opposite sex. Some scientists theorize that in males a testosterone release that starts around age four somehow organizes brain cells toward opposite-sex orientation. Perhaps, they say, the genes in homosexual boys prompt the same urge only in a different direction. Or the so-called gay genes could code for behaviors that in turn have an impact on sexual preference. Seen from that angle, the genes could be ones that encourage nonconformist behavior, say, or promote the flouting of authority. Or they could influence all of the above.

What's more, environmental or cultural triggers can't be ruled out. Scientists now know that nature and nurture push and tug at each other throughout our lives. Even something as genetically driven as height can be nudged by real-world factors—stunted by malnutrition or stress hormones. What in a child's life may sway his sexual preference? What he eats? His first playmate? No one has the foggiest idea. Even without answers to such questions, says Daryl Bem, a psychologist at Cornell University who studies the causes of homosexuality, all of us should accept that both environment and genes are at work—and that, when it comes to orientation, a parent's actions aren't the key.

"I don't think parents have very much to do with it," Bem says. "It may be that you have a boy with strongly feminine traits and that may mean he's likely to grow up gay. Really your only choice is whether you want him to grow up happy and well adjusted or miserable and neurotic."

THAT TROY grew up miserable is a truth neither Troy nor Sandi avoids. It is the motive, as if they need one, behind their respective struggles: in Troy's case to advocate for gay rights and in his mother's case to support Troy. "Troy was raised with three very macho stepbrothers," says Sandi, her voice flat with the sound of unwelcome memories. "There were rumors. That was really hard for him. He would never, never have wanted his brothers to think he was gay."

Hiding from his brothers wasn't even the most painful part of the past. Troy recalls a high school field trip to an amusement park during which his one good friend at the time declared that he'd heard the gossip that Troy was gay. "He said he wasn't going to mess around with any faggots and to leave him alone."

Troy sits in the courtyard of a Sacramento coffeehouse as he calls up this memory. A mimosa tree arches above

him. The bright morning filtered through the leaves makes a pattern on his face, a design of shadow and light. It doesn't disguise hurt. Troy likes to laugh, but he looks back now without even smiling. "It took years to get over that one," he says. "There isn't a choice in this. If I could have chosen, I would have chosen to be straight. Life is so much easier when you're straight."

"God," Sandi says, "Can you imagine how hard it was for Troy?"

Mother and son have become close in the years since Troy announced that he was gay. Sandi marches in gay pride parades and hosts parties for Troy's friends. Troy is engaged to a man he's been seeing for more than a year; Sandi is planning the wedding. She also helps out with his daughter and step-daughter, both of whom he is helping to raise. Sandi and Troy talk now about everything, including the family history and how his father blames them both for the shame, as he sees it, of having a gay son. Sandi and Troy have a tacit agreement: no more secrets, no more panicky confessions. It all comes out between them.

For his part, Troy hopes that the new scientific understanding of homosexuality will alter attitudes, allow for tolerance. In this he joins those who note how left-handedness, once considered a perversion to be weeded out, became quickly disconnected from a moral position once it was understood as a biological trait.

> Sandi, who's seen Troy hurt, challenges anyone who would change him. "God doesn't make junk," she says.

Sandi, like any mother who's seen a child hurt, is less trusting. She worries that people who hate the very idea of homosexuality will call for ways to "cure" the problem with some futuristic gene therapy or by injecting kids with hormones. The idea infuriates her. "God doesn't make junk," she says. "My son is not defective."

All around her she comes across minds in need of widening. In the small conservative California town where she lives, she challenges people who begin grumbling about gays. "I jump in right away, before they say something they're going to feel bad about. I tell them that my son is gay. And they, well, they usually say that it's okay, as long as he doesn't touch them." She begins to laugh, but it fades into a sigh.

"You know, it doesn't make any difference where the homosexuality came from," she says. "There is no sense looking for someone to blame. Troy is what he is. I just feel proud that he is a good parent, a good teacher, and not a judgmental person."

She smiles. "He learned that from me."

Deborah Blum is a professor of journalism at the University of Wisconsin at Madison and the author of Sex on the Brain.

TRANS ACROSS AMERICA

Watch out, Pat Buchanan. Ridiculed for years, "transgenders" are emerging as the newest group to demand equality

By JOHN CLOUD ST. LOUIS

WHEN JAMES MADISON WAS URGing his young nation to refrain "from oppressing the minority," he was talking about "other sects," not other sexes. Shannon Ware, an engineer from St. Louis, Mo., who began life as Craig Ware but now lives as a woman, would grant that much. But since a high school civics teacher inspired her, she has clung to the belief that social change is possible, that America is elastic enough to accommodate all minority groups—even when the minority is as caricatured and misunderstood as hers.

Ware is "transgendered," which means her mental gender—her deepest awareness of her identity—doesn't correspond to the parts she was born with. Though she has become an activist in the past year or so, Ware struggled with these feelings for years. Now, at 45, she is happy with her inner and outward selves, the latter feminized with hormones and women's clothes. Ware isn't yet "transsexual," but she does plan to undergo what doctors call "sex-reassignment surgery" when she and her beau David can afford it; it will cost about as much as their new Nissan.

Since transsexuals burst on the scene in the 1950s, when a G.I. went from George to Christine Jorgensen, journalists have periodically revisited the subject in tones varying from the dryly medical to the hotly sensational. But today many forms of gender nonconformity have actually become mainstream. In the past five years, several movies, plays, tabloid shows and famous cross-dressers like RuPaul have moved drag from the fringes of gay culture to prime time. Even *Teletubbies*, a show for toddlers, features Tinky Winky, a boy who carries a red patent-leather purse.

Less noticed, however, is that gender nonconformists have been working together, with some remarkable successes, to build a political movement. Their first step was to reclaim the power to name themselves: transgender is now the term most widely used, and it encompasses everyone from cross-dressers (those who dress in clothes of the opposite sex) to transsexuals (those who surgically "correct" their genitals to match their "real" gender).

No one knows how many transgendered people exist, but at least 25,000 Americans have undergone sex-reassignment surgery, and the dozen or so North American doctors who perform it have long waiting lists. Psychologists say "gender-identity disorder" occurs in at least 2% of children; they experience discomfort with their assigned gender and may experiment with gender roles. Some of these people turn out to be gay; most don't. The overlapping permutations of gender and sexuality can get baffling, which is why transgender activist Riki Anne Wilchins simply declared "the end of gender" in her recent book, *Read My Lips*. Wilchins believes that male-female divisions force constructed social roles on all of us and create a class of the "gender oppressed"— not only transgenders but also feminine men, butch women, lesbians and gays, "intersexed" people (hermaphrodites) and even people with "alternative sexual practices." (Marv Albert, meet your leader.)

In the early '90s, transgenders started forming political groups, mostly street-level organizations, which picketed the American Psychiatric Association, for instance, for using the gender-identity-disorder diagnosis. Previously, transgenders appeared as figures in the early gay-liberation movement: it was cross-dressing men—their "hair in curls," as they chanted—who threw the first rocks in the 1969 Stonewall riots in New York City's Greenwich Village. But as the gay movement went mainstream, it jettisoned transgenders as too off-putting.

Transgenders faced practical obstacles to organizing themselves separately. Most couldn't simply dress as a member of the opposite sex without getting beaten or fired. Many felt pressured to undergo expensive genital and cosmetic operations, which doctors wouldn't perform unless the patients also underwent years of psychiatric treatment. After the surgery, some had to move to find a new job and start a new life. Political organizing was a luxury.

Today medical rules are getting more relaxed. Some transgenders still elect to have full operations, but others (especially the young) express gender their own way, perhaps just with clothing or hormone treatments or with partial surgery. Increasingly, they simply refuse to discuss their private parts. "What's important is hate crimes and job discrimination," says Shannon Minter, a female-to-male transgender and civil rights lawyer. "Why does everyone want to talk about my genitals?"

Governments and employers are starting to listen. Although just one state, Minnesota, has a law protecting transgenders from job and housing discrimination, cities all over the country (including San Francisco, of course, but also Seattle and, as of last year, Evanston, Ill.) have passed similar legislation. Recently the California assembly approved a bill to increase penalties for those who commit crimes against transgenders; the bill awaits senate approval.

Lawyers with the Transgender Law Conference have helped pass statutes in at least 17 states allowing transsexuals to change the sex designation on their birth certificate, which means their driver's license and passport can reflect reality. (One unintended consequence: legal marriages between people who have become the same sex.) In Missouri, the house judiciary committee met in March to discuss the state's first civil rights bill to include "sexual orientation"—defined to include gender "self-image or identity." Illinois and Pennsylvania considered similar

SHANNON WARE

AGE 45

PROFESSION
Engineer

BIO
After years of silence, Ware came out as transgendered to family and friends—and became an activist

SHANNON MINTER

AGE 37

PROFESSION
Lawyer, National Center for Lesbian Rights

BIO
After an internal debate, the center supported Minter's decision to live as a man

bills. None passed, but "we were happy to get the issue out there," says activist Ware.

Many transgenders are furious that the biggest gay lobbying group in the U.S., the Human Rights Campaign, opposes adding transgenders to the Employment Nondiscrimination Act, a gay job-protection bill that has been pending in Congress since 1994. But the Campaign is coming around. Last year it helped arrange a meeting between transgender activists and Justice Department officials to discuss anti-trans violence (a 1997 survey of transgenders found that 60% had been assaulted). The Campaign is also lobbying for a bill that would give U.S. district attorneys the authority to handle state crimes involving bias against "real or *perceived* . . . gender." Transgenders have their own D.C. presence, Gender PAC. It sponsored its third Lobby Day on Capitol Hill in April, when more than 100 transgenders met members of Congress. A state-focused group called It's Time America! has chapters in half the states. And of course, transgenders are talking about staging a march on Washington—de rigueur for any minority going mainstream.

Businesses are paying attention. Computer firm Lucent Technologies has added "gender-identity characteristics or expression" to its equal-opportunity policy. The University of Iowa has similar language, and in February, Rutgers adopted more limited

protections for "people who have changed or are in the process of changing" their sex. Last year Harvard allowed an incoming female-to-male freshman to live on a male dorm floor. Campus groups have asked the college to formally protect transgenders, but Harvard being Harvard, the university is studying the issue. Transgenders are pushing ahead in the courts as well. In a little-noticed but groundbreaking case last year, a Minnesota male-to-female transsexual won Social Security "widow's benefits" following her husband's death in 1995. The Social Security Administration declined to grant them at first but reversed itself after the woman appealed, with the A.C.L.U.'s help.

The most important victories are often won outside the public arena. A little over a year ago, Shannon Ware was the host of a constituent meet-and-greet for her state representative. Over coffee and snacks, Ware introduced Representative Patrick Dougherty, a moderate Democrat and devout Roman Catholic, to several transgenders. He was set to consider legislation that would make it difficult for transsexuals to gain even partial custody of their children after a divorce. For Ware, it wasn't an academic issue. She was once married and has a daughter, Elizabeth. Though the 13-year-old and her mom have been "totally cool" about her transition from Craig to Shannon, Ware knew others weren't as lucky as she was. Another Missourian, Sharon (né Daniel), has fought her ex-wife for six years for the right simply to visit her two boys.

The low-key meeting at Ware's house worked. Dougherty listened as she and several others told their stories. Some had lost jobs, some had been rejected by family, all felt battered by a society that insists that biology is destiny. Dougherty left seeing no reason to attack these folks with a new law. A few days later, he quietly let the legislation die in his committee.

Can Gays *'Convert'*?

A controversial series of ads claims that homosexuals aren't born that way, and can change. A look inside the 'ex-gay' movement, and the elusive science of sexual orientation.

BY JOHN LELAND AND MARK MILLER

In a town house in northwest Washington, D.C., Anthony Falzarano calls for a show of hands. "How many of you," he asks, "were raped, molested or sexualized as children?" More than half of the 20 men and three women raise their hands. Falzarano, 42, is neatly dressed, a former architectural restorer who talks with the reassuring cadences of a motivational speaker. For the last hour or so, he has recited Scriptures and talked about his own life—about his rather glamorous turns in the New York gay scene of the 1970s, about his Christian reawakening, about his wife and two children. Now he urges the others to talk.

"My name is Dave," begins one. "It's been a good week. I haven't had any lapses into masturbation for more than a month." Shannon, 27, has not had a good week. He started a new job, and already, he says, "people are buzzing. 'Is the new guy gay?'" Falzarano admonishes, "You're still sending out mixed signals." The secret sharers are mostly in their 20s and 30s, racially mixed, united in purpose: they want desperately, some painfully, not to be gay.

They have come to the Transformation Ministries branch of Exodus International, a nondenominational Christian fellowship dedicated to helping homosexuals change their orientation. Touting strict Scriptural reading and a discredited theory of childhood development, Exodus was until recently one of the better-kept secrets in the American church. Then on July 13, in conjunction with conservative groups like the Christian Coalition, it started taking out full-page ads in major newspapers (including The Washington Post, NEWSWEEK's sister publication). In gentle, loving language, smiling "ex-gays" offered the bold promise: we changed, so can you. Gay advocates fumed. "This is a deliberate campaign ... to make homophobia acceptable," argues Anne Fausto-Sterling, a professor of biology and women's studies at Brown University. The mainstream psych community bridled: therapy to change sexual orientation, says Gregory Herek, a research psychologist at the University of California, Davis, "doesn't have any scientific basis." For the ad's sponsors, the uproar was golden. "We've done 37 interviews in the last 10 days," exults Falzarano, who describes himself as "one of the top five 'ex-gays'." After years of daytime-TV indignities, ex-gays like John and Anne Paulk of Colorado Springs—a former drag queen and a former lesbian, now married with a son—were working prime time.

The ads come just as factions within the Republican Party are battling over gay rights. Senate leader Trent Lott recently likened homosexuality to alcoholism and kleptomania, and blocked a vote to allow James Hormel, who is gay, to become ambassador to Luxembourg. The Republican-controlled House voted to deny certain federal funds to any city that required contractors to provide health benefits to gay partners. But just last week, defectors within the party helped defeat a GOP bill to rescind President Bill Clinton's anti-discrimination order for gays in the federal government.

At Falzarano's ministry, such political machinations are lost on people like Shannon. He has led a complicated life. At his first meeting, he wore mascara and outrageous dress. "I was *flaming*," he says, conspiratorially. Raised in a strict Pentecostal home, with a violent, drug-addicted father, he "got into the lifestyle"—Exodus-speak for homosexuality—at the age of 14. By 20, he says, "I wanted a change. I [believed] I was an awful, damaged product in God's eyes." He returned to the church, quickly married and fathered a child, but eventually started seeing men again. Earlier this year, with a second child on the way, he brought himself to an Exodus meeting. He was dubious—"I thought they were all fakers"—but desperate. "At first, I came because I didn't want to waste more of my wife's life. I really, really enjoyed the gay lifestyle. But now I want to come out of this for myself. I'm tired of homosexuality being my identity."

For more than a century, therapists, churches and groups like the Aesthetic Realists have tried to change gays by means including drugs, electroshock and even testicular transplant. One Masters and Johnson treatment taught gay men how to make con-

Straight Views, Gay Views: By the Numbers

In two national polls, NEWSWEEK compared the general public's opinions on gay issues with those of the gay community. Though there's more common ground than in recent years, the two groups still disagree strongly about some hotly debated issues.

Overall population:
33% say that homosexuality is something people are born with, not the result of upbringing or environmental influences

Gay respondents:
75% say they believe homosexuality is something people are born with, not due to upbringing or environmental influences

Overall:
56% say that gay men and lesbians can change their sexual orientation through therapy, will power or religious conviction

Gays:
Only 11% say that gay men and lesbians can change their sexual orientation through therapy, will power or religious conviction

FOR THIS SPECIAL NEWSWEEK POLL, PRINCETON SURVEY RESEARCH ASSOCIATES CONDUCTED TELEPHONE INTERVIEWS WITH 602 ADULTS JULY 30–31, 1998. THE MARGIN OF ERROR IS +/-4 PERCENTAGE POINTS. FOR THE OPINIONS OF HOMOSEXUALS, PRINCETON SURVEY RESEARCH ASSOCIATES CONDUCTED TELEPHONE INTERVIEWS WITH 502 GAY MEN AND LESBIANS JULY 28–30, 1998. RESPONDENTS WERE RANDOMLY DRAWN FROM LISTS COMPILED BY STRUBCO INC. OF 750,000 WHO ASSOCIATED THEMSELVES WITH GAY OR LESBIAN INTERESTS AND ACTIVITIES. THOSE WHO IDENTIFIED THEMSELVES AS HETEROSEXUAL WERE EXCLUDED FROM THE SURVEY. THE MARGIN OF ERROR IS +/-5 PERCENTAGE POINTS. SOME RESPONSES NOT SHOWN. THE NEWSWEEK POLL © 1998 BY NEWSWEEK, INC.

versation and eye contact with women. But after the American Psychiatric and Psychological associations voted in the 1970s that homosexuality was not a disorder, most therapists got out of the sexual-conversion business. Last year the American Psychological Association officially declared "reparative therapy" scientifically ineffective and possibly harmful. Its guidelines strongly discourage such therapy as unnecessary. The public is less convinced. In a new NEWSWEEK Poll, 56 percent said gays could become straight; 11 percent of gays agreed.

Exodus, founded in 1976, has taken up the call. With 83 chapters in 35 states, the group claims to have "touched" 200,000 lives, though it keeps no figures on how many people have gone through treatment. "I don't know of anybody who can do it on their own," says John Paulk, the national board chairman. Exodus rejects what members call the "homophobia" of censorious conservative churches; rather, the idea is to help gays become healing members of the congregation. The "homosexual lifestyle," the group contends, is a sin, though not of the sinner's choosing—a neat distinction in a culture loath to accept blame for anything.

The group offers a tidy explanation for homosexuality. Boys with absent fathers, girls with absent mothers, get stuck in developmental limbo and seek masculine or feminine fulfillment through sex with members of their own gender. By recognizing this deficiency, and through prayer, individuals can replace some gay desires with same-sex friendships. Or so the theory goes. Heterosexual desire may or may not follow. Along the way, Exodus workshops encourage gay men to "butch up" through sports, and lesbians to unleash their inner heterosexual through dress and makeup.

"Recovery" might mean anything from a heterosexual marriage to abstinence. Temptation alone, the group counsels, is not a sin. As one ex-gay man puts it, "I still struggle with attraction [to men]. But I don't see attraction as a problem, because people are attractive." Ministries claim success rates of about 30 percent, but have allowed no long-term studies. The failures on the other hand, have been most importune. Two of Exodus International's founders, Michael Bussee and Gary Cooper, fell in love and left the organization in 1979. In all, 13 Exodus ministries have had to close because the director returned to homosexuality.

Exodus's claims take up an unresolved scientific debate. In the early '90s, three highly publicized studies seemed to suggest that homosexuality's roots were genetic, traceable to nature rather than nurture. Though the studies were small and the conclusions cautious, many gay groups embraced the news. We're born this way, they announced, don't judge us. More than five years later the data have never been replicated. Moreover, researchers say, the public has misunderstood "behavioral genetics." Unlike eye color, behavior is not strictly inherited; it needs to be brought into play by a daunting complexity of environmental factors. "People very much want to find simple answers," says Neil Risch, a professor of genetics at Stanford. "A gene for this, a gene for that. . . . Human behavior is much more complicated than that." The existence of a genetic pattern among homosexuals doesn't mean people are born gay, any more than the genes for height, presumably common in NBA players, indicate an inborn ability to play basketball. Isolating environmental factors of homosexuality has proved equally elusive: in blind psychological evaluations, gays are indistinguishable from straight peo-

ple. Most scientists postulate that homosexuality results from some combination of genes and environmental factors, possibly different in each individual. But, admits biologist Evan Balaban, "I think we're as much in the dark as we ever were."

Matt, 20, thinks he knows the answer. A junior at a Los Angeles university, Matt is articulate, casually chic in a retro surfer shirt. Since 1997, he has been a patient of psychologist Joseph Nicolosi, the leading exponent of the secular approach called reparative therapy. Matt had his first homosexual experience in college—unsatisfying, but not traumatic. His parents urged him to see Nicolosi. "I basically hated Joe at first. I thought he was full of s—." He agreed to continue treatment, he says, "just to talk through the issue. I didn't expect to change."

Nicolosi considers himself a maverick in a profession held captive by the gay political lobby. He is the executive director of NARTH, the National Association for Research and Therapy of Homosexuality, a small band that steadfastly maintains that homosexuality is a disorder that can and should be treated. NARTH represents "the fringe of the mental-health establishment," says psychologist Herek. Nicolosi's patients, most controversially, can be as young as 3 years old. Like Exodus, he trumpets his success rates, but has done no long-term follow-up study. "I don't have time," he says.

Still skeptical, Matt read Nicolosi's book "Reparative Therapy of Male Homosexuality." "It could have been written about my family," he says—distant father, very attentive mother, no interest in sports. Matt started to come round. He looked into mainstream "gay affirmative" therapies, which hold that gay tensions derive from "internalized homophobia." Nicolosi had an answer to each. "It was a battle of theories, and Joe's really convinced me more." Matt says his attractions to men have diminished. He still hasn't dated a woman, but feels confident that the move is "imminent. I want to make sure I'm ready."

Despite Matt's experience, both Nicolosi and Exodus stress that the process isn't for everybody. People who are gay and happy won't find it useful. "We have to work with people who are broke and ready," says Anita Worthen, a counselor at New Hope Ministries in San Rafael, Calif. "We can't drag them off the streets." Worthen's own son is gay and not in therapy. At her ministry, she and her husband, Frank, try to warn off the less stalwart. "You don't want to come in and fail at one more thing."

Critics accuse NARTH of preying on the vulnerable. "It intensifies conflict," says psychiatrist Susan Vaughan, the American Psychoanalytical Association's spokesperson on gay issues. "Being celibate, or trying to have sex with the opposite sex, can lead to anxiety and depression." James Campbell, 37, now an ordained Methodist minister, said his therapist tried to exploit his fear of AIDS, and goaded him to "remember" an incident of molestation he now isn't sure happened. Since leaving therapy, he says, "my acceptance of myself as a gay man saved my life and any relationship I had with God."

There is a middle ground between the camps—between the ex-gay claim that anyone can change and the opposing contention that no one can. The psychologist Patricia Hannigan has argued that individuals can, in the face of strong religious conflict, lay down their own laws. "If the foremost priority in one's life is religious faith, then personal happiness might come from conforming to faith rather than from pursuing sexual orientation." She likens gay Christians in reparative therapy to priests who have taken a vow of celibacy.

At Transformation Ministries, Falzarano asks the men to describe their distant fa- thers, an assortment that runs from abusive drug addict to benign workaholic. "So you see," he says, nodding, "we didn't all show up in this room by accident." He is building up to something, and raises his voice a notch. "Homosexuality is not a lifestyle we chose. It was inflicted on us as children. Most churches don't realize we were molested. Most churches don't realize we didn't bond with our fathers."

This is the payoff. There is strength in unity, strength in grievance and in rejection. Few identities in America are more marginal than ex-gay. In here there is community. After a pop hymn, the group members hug or shake hands. Then they head off into the night, perhaps less lonely than when they came in.

With CLAUDIA KALB, PATRICIA KING, THOMAS HAYDEN *and* MATTHEW COOPER

Unit Selections

Key Points to Consider

❖ What do you feel about your body? How often do you check your appearance in the mirror? How often do you wonder what you look like when you are engaging in intimate or sexual behavior? What impact do you feel these behaviors have on you and your relationships?

❖ What do you see as the greatest barriers to attaining satisfying intimate relationships? Are some people destined to fail at establishing and/or maintaining them? Explain who and why.

❖ What makes male-female intimacy difficult to achieve? Have you learned any lessons about yourself and the opposite sex "the hard way"?

❖ Do we as a society focus too little or too much on sexual mechanics—sexual parts and acts? List at least six adjectives you find synonymous with *great* sex.

❖ If you had to lose one of your senses *for sex only*, which would it be and why? Is this the same sense you would choose to do without if it were all-encompassing? Why or why not?

❖ What are the circumstances within a relationship that would most likely contribute to your decision to leave? Has your pattern been to decide too fast or too slowly, that is, have you after-the-fact regretted a decision to leave a relationship that may have been salvageable? Or have you stayed too long in a relationship that is/was unhealthy? Explain your answers to the best of your ability.

❖ Why does intimacy seem more difficult to achieve in the 1990s than in previous generations? If you had a time machine, would you prefer to go back in time, forward in time, or stay where you are as you search for intimacy? Explain your reasons.

 **Links** | **www.dushkin.com/online/**

13. **American Psychological Association**
    http://www.apa.org/psychnet/
14. **Bonobos Sex and Society**
    http://soong.club.cc.cmu.edu/~julie/bonobos.html
15. **The Celibate FAQ** *http://mail.bris.ac.uk/~plmlp/celibate.html*
16. **Go Ask Alice**
    http://www.goaskalice.columbia.edu
17. **Sex and Gender**
    http://www.bioanth.cam.ac.uk/pip4amod3.html

These sites are annotated on pages 4 and 5.

Most people are familiar with the term "sexual relationship." It denotes an important dimension of sexuality—interpersonal sexuality, or sexual interactions occurring between two (and sometimes more) individuals. This unit focuses attention on these types of relationships.

No woman is an island. No man is an island. Interpersonal contact forms the basis for self-esteem and meaningful living. Conversely, isolation results in loneliness and depression for most human beings. People seek and cultivate friendships for the warmth, affection, supportiveness, and sense of trust and loyalty that such relationships can provide.

Long-term friendships may develop into intimate relationships. The qualifying word in the previous sentence is "may." Today many people, single as well as married, yearn for close or intimate interpersonal relationships but fail to find them. Despite developments in communication and technology that past generations could never fathom, discovering how and where to find potential friends, partners, lovers, and soul mates is reported to be more difficult today than in times past. Fear of rejection causes some to avoid interpersonal relationships, others to present a false front or illusory self that they think is more acceptable or socially desirable. This sets the stage for a game of intimacy that is counterproductive to genuine intimacy. For others a major dilemma may exist—the problem of balancing closeness with the preservation of individual identity in a manner that satisfies the need for both personal and interpersonal growth and integrity. In either case, partners in a relationship should be advised that the development of interpersonal awareness (the mutual recognition and knowledge of others as they really are) rests upon trust and self-disclosure—letting the other person know who you really are and how you truly feel. In American society this has never been easy, and today some fear it may be more difficult than ever.

These considerations in regard to interpersonal relationships apply equally well to achieving meaningful and satisfying sexual relationships. Three basic ingredients lay the foundation for quality sexual interaction: self-awareness, understanding and acceptance of the partner's needs and desires, and mutual efforts to accommodate both partners' needs and desires. Without these, misunderstandings may arise, bringing anxiety, frustration, dissatisfaction, and/or resentment into the relationship. There may also be a heightened risk of contracting AIDS or another STD (sexually transmitted disease), experiencing an unplanned pregnancy, or experiencing sexual dysfunction by one or both partners. On the other hand, experience and research show that ongoing attention to these three ingredients by intimate partners contributes not only to sexual responsibility, but also to true emotional and sexual intimacy and a longer and happier life.

As might already be apparent, there is much more to quality sexual relationships than our popular culture recognizes. Such relationships are not established by means of sexual techniques or beautiful/handsome features. Rather, it is the quality of the interaction that makes sex a celebration of our sexuality. A person-oriented (as opposed to genitally oriented) sexual awareness, coupled with a whole-body/mind sexuality and an open, relaxed, even playful, attitude toward exploration make for equality in sexuality.

The subsection *Establishing Sexual Relationships* opens with an article that addresses the real starting point of intimate relationship potential: how people feel about themselves and their bodies. This follow-up to an earlier body image survey contains some troubling findings. The next two articles, "Brain Sex and the Language of Love" and "Men for Sale," use different styles and approaches, but both tackle the gender issues and behaviors that have the potential to increase attraction, kindle romance, lead to exciting relationships, or undermine all of these.

Although the subsection *Responsible Quality Sexual Relationships* opens with an article whose title asks a question "Should You Leave?" that seems the antithesis of long-term relationships, this article and the next one in the subsection include compelling wisdom about how to maintain true intimacy. Both combine research, the advice of experts, and the experiences of real people to address a range of issues and events that have the potential to nurture or derail relationships. The final unit article, "Celibate Passion: The Hidden Rewards of Quitting Sex," provides a thought-provoking challenge to our often complex and contradicting cultural beliefs about sex and intimacy. Readers are encouraged to use the articles in this unit as a backdrop of perspectives and experiences that can assist all of us in considering, comparing, and improving our interpersonal and/or sexual relationships.

The 1997 Body Image Survey Results

BY DAVID M. GARNER, PH.D.

For the past three decades, women and, increasingly men have been preoccupied with how they look. But the intense scrutiny hasn't necessarily helped us see ourselves any more clearly. While as individuals we are growing heavier, our body preferences are growing thinner. And thinness is depicted everywhere as crucial to personal happiness. Despite the concerns of feminists and other observers, body image issues seem to be only growing in importance.

When most people think of body image, they think about aspects of physical appearance, attractiveness, and beauty. But body image is so much more. It's our mental representation of ourselves; it's what allows us to contemplate ourselves. Body image isn't simply influenced by feelings, and it actively influences much of our behavior, self-esteem, and psychopathology. Our body perceptions, feelings, and beliefs govern our life plan—who we meet, who we marry, the nature of our interactions, our day-to-day comfort level. Indeed, our body is our personal billboard, providing others with first—and sometimes only—impressions.

With that in mind, Psychology Today decided it was time for another detailed reading of the state of body image. The landmark PT national surveys of 1972 and 1985 are among the most widely cited on the subject. We wanted to try and understand the growing gulf between actual and preferred shapes—and to develop the very revealing picture that can be seen only by tracking changes over time. We asked David Garner, Ph.D., to bring his vast expertise to our project. Garner, the director of the Toledo Center for Eating Disorders, is also an adjunct professor of psychology at Bowling Green State University and of women's studies at the University of Toledo. He has been researching and treating eating disorders for 20 years, heading one of the earliest studies linking them to changes in cultural expectations for thinness. From measurements of *Playboy* centerfold models and Miss America contestants, he documented that these

Who Responded to the Survey		
Some of your vital statistics:		
	WOMEN	**MEN**
Total number	3,452	548
Average age	32	35
Actual weight	140	180
Desired weight	125	175
Height	5'5"	5'11"
Caucasian	87%	82%
College grad +	62%	54%
Income: $50,000 +	39%	38%
Heterosexual	93%	79%
Bisexual	4%	8%
Health problems	36%	30%

How You Describe Yourselves		
What you have to say about yourselves		
	%WOMEN	**%MEN**
Relationship-oriented	75	63
Career-oriented	62	56
Happy person	69	66
Spiritually-oriented	66	53
Feminist	55	20
Traditional values	44	43
Athletic	33	45
Pro-choice	73	64
Politically conservative	21	28
Strong belief in astrology	16	14

A Very Revealing Picture: Psychology Today's 1997 Body Image Survey Findings

Many of our survey results astounded even us veteran observers of the body wars. Among the most important findings:

• Body image is more complex than previous research suggests. It's influenced by many factors, including interpersonal factors, individual factors such as mood, and physical factors like body weight. Cultural pressures also play their part. Which factors are most important vary from person to person.

• Body dissatisfaction is soaring among both women and men—increasing at a faster rate than ever before. This is the great paradox of body preoccupation—instead of insight, it seems to breed only discontent. But a revolution in the way women see themselves—or, more accurately, *want* to see themselves—may be brewing.

• How important is it for people to be the weight they want? Fifteen percent of women and 11 percent of men say they would sacrifice more than five years of their lives to be the weight they want. Twenty-four percent of women and 17 percent of men say they would give up more than three years.

• Among young women ages 13 to 19, a whopping 62 percent say they are dissatisfied with their weight. And it gets a bit worse with age: Sixty-seven percent of women over age 30 also say they are unhappy with how much they weigh.

• While body hatred tends to stay at about the same level as women age, today's young women may be more vulnerable to self-disparagement as they get older. They are being initiated into feelings of body dissatisfaction at a tender age, and this early programming may be difficult to undo.

• Body dissatisfaction afflicts those women who describe themselves as feminists (32 percent) as well as those who say they are more traditional (49 percent). Nevertheless, feminist beliefs seem to confer some behavioral protection: Feminists say they are less willing to use drastic measures like vomiting to control their weight.

• Physical factors, such as gaining weight, are the most common cause of negative feelings about the body. Nevertheless, relationships also have an impact. If your mate doesn't think you look great, you're likely to feel devastated.

• Pregnancy is increasingly being seen not as a normal body function but as an encumbrance to body image. And some women say they are choosing not to have children for this reason.

• More than 75 percent of women surveyed say that menstruation, another normal body function, causes them to have negative feelings about their bodies.

• Bad moods wreak havoc on women's feelings about their bodies. Women get caught in a vicious spiral: emotional distress causes body loathing; disgust with their body causes emotional distress.

• Teasing during childhood or adolescence has an indelible effect on women's feelings about their bodies. Women say that the negative fallout can last for decades—no matter what shape they're currently in.

• What's a quick way to feel good about your body? Good sex. The survey found that in general, good sexual experiences breed high levels of body satisfaction.

• Sexual abuse is an important contributor to body dissatisfaction—but only women who have been sexually abused think so. Other women don't grasp the damage abuse can do to feelings about the body. The experience of sexual abuse seems to create a divide that mirrors the general cultural debate over the validity of allegations of sexual abuse.

• What's the most reliable way to develop positive feelings about your body—to say nothing of boosting your health? Respondents say it's exercising—just for the pleasure of it.

• Curiously, most people say that when it comes to weight control, exercising does not boost body satisfaction. Only women who are very heavy disagree.

• It's no longer possible to deny the fact that images of models in the media have a terrible effect on the way women see themselves. Women who have eating disorders are most influenced by fashion models.

• A model backlash has already begun. Although images of fashion models are intended to inspire identification and emulation, more than three out of ten women say they make them feel angry and resentful. They make more than four out of ten women feel insecure. Women say they are dying to see models that are more representative of the natural range of body types.

"model women" had become significantly thinner from 1959 to 1979 and that advertising for weight-loss diets had grown correspondingly. A follow-up study showed the trend continuing through the late 1980s.

Garner, along with Cincinnati psychotherapist Ann Kearney Cooke, Ph.D., and editor at large Hara Estroff Marano, crafted five pages worth of questions and in our March/April 1996 issue we asked you how you see, feel, and are influenced by your bodies. The response was phenomenal: about 4,500 people returned questionnaires from every state, not to mention Europe, Israel, Puerto Rico, Pakistan, Saudi Arabia, South Africa, New Zealand, Peru, Australia, Japan, and China. Ten months after the questionnaire hit the newsstands, responses are still com-

Extreme Weight Control

To control my weight during the past year, once a week or more:

	%WOMEN	%MEN	EATING DISORDER*	NO EATING DISORDER
Induced vomiting	6	1	23	1.5
Abused laxatives	6	3	17	3
Took diuretics	5	4	10	4
Used diet pills	12	6	20	9

*Women identifying themselves as having a diagnosed or undiagnosed eating disorder.

ing in. Many of you supplemented your surveys with pages pouring out heart and soul. And though you could reply with complete anonymity a whopping two-thirds chose to include names, addresses, and phone numbers. Some of you even included pictures!

Our statistical analyses were conducted on the first 4,000 responses—3,452 women and 548 men (86 percent women, 14 percent men)—a much wider gender split than in our readership as a whole, which is 70 percent women and 30 percent men. (See "Who Responded to the Survey" below.) The predominantly female response clearly says something about the stake women have in this topic. Participants were primarily Caucasian, college-educated, in their early to mid thirties, middle-income, and heterosexual. Women who responded range in age from 13 to 90 and weigh between 77 and 365 pounds (89 women weigh 100 pounds or less; 82 women weigh more than 250 pounds). Men range in age from 14 to 82 and weigh between 115 and 350 pounds. You describe yourselves as relationship-oriented, pro-choice, intellectual, politically liberal, and spiritual. At the top of your worry list are financial matters and romantic relationships. A significant segment described health problems that vary from relatively minor ailments to cancer and AIDS.

Appearing to Be Dissatisfied

The 1997 Psychology Today Body Image Survey shows there's more discontent with the shape of our bodies than ever before. Okay, there are some things we like about our appearance: height, hair, face, feet, and the size of our sex organs generate the most approval. In the span between face and feet, our primary sex organs are a small oasis of favor amidst a wasteland of waist land. Apparently there's little pressure to change the things that we can't see or change. Of course, these areas tend not to be repositories for the accumulation of fat, that object of abhorrence. In contrast, the negative focus remains on our visible attributes, the ones that display fat—the ones that can presumably be controlled or corrected with enough self-discipline.

Fifty-six percent of women say they are dissatisfied with their overall appearance. Their self-disparagement is specifically directed toward their abdomens (71 percent), body weight (66 percent), hips (60 percent), and muscle tone (58 percent). Men show escalating dissatisfaction with their abdomens (63 percent), weight (52 percent), muscle tone (45 percent), overall appearance (43 percent), and chest (38 percent).

Weight dissatisfaction means one thing to men and something entirely different to women. The overwhelming majority of women—89 percent—want to lose weight. How much? The average woman's weight is 140 pounds; the preferred weight is 125 pounds. Only 3 percent of the women who say they are dissatisfied with their bodies want to gain weight; 8 percent want to stay the same. By contrast, 22 percent of the men who say they are dissatisfied with their bodies want to *gain* weight. (See "Men and Body Image.")

The survey also shows a correlation between body dissatisfaction and body weight—those who are more dissatisfied tend to be heavier. In fact, the average weight of the most dissatisfied women is about 180 pounds; the least dissatisfied weigh in at 128 pounds. Both groups have an average ideal weight that's lower than their actual weight; however, in the former group it's fifty pounds away from reality compared with three pounds for the least dissatisfied.

What Shaped Your Body Image When You Were Young?

Some of the facts that figure into body image:

	%WOMEN	%MEN
PHYSICAL		
My personal feelings about weight	58	35
INTERPERSONAL		
Being teased by others	44	35
My mother's attitude about my body	31	13
My father's attitude about my body	23	11
Positive sexual experiences	26	28
Sexual abuse	18	7
CULTURAL		
Movie or TV celebrities	23	13
Fashion magazine models	22	6
Sports figures	7	16

The Weight of Influence:
Factors Fostering Positive Body Image

What's instrumental in making you feel good about your body?

	%WOMEN	%MEN
PHYSICAL		
Exercising regularly	64	62
Losing weight	62	39
Feeling thin	53	24
Accepting my body the way it is	50	36
Wearing flattering clothes	46	21
INTERPERSONAL		
Compliments on my appearance	48	44
Love from another person	43	44
Positive sexual experiences	40	41
Good relationships	33	34
EMOTIONAL		
Confidence in my abilities	39	38
Feeling effective as a person	39	36
Meditating	11	9

How important is it for people to be the weight they want? We put the question in stark terms and asked, "How many years of your life would you trade to achieve your weight goals?" The findings are astounding: Fifteen percent of women and 11 percent of men say they'd sacrifice more than five years of their lives; 24 percent of women and 17 percent of men say they would give up more than three years. These answers make us regret not testing the extremes and offering 10- and 20-year options. Still, we can confidently conclude that a significant minority of you believe life is worth living only if you are thin.

A rather drastic measure of weight control is cigarette smoking. Statistics reveal that smoking is on the rise among young women. Robert Klesges, Ph.D., and colleagues at the University of Memphis have repeatedly shown that smoking is used by many women for weight control. While we didn't specifically ask whether you smoke, we did ask whether you smoke to control your weight. About 50 percent of women and 30 percent of men say they puff away to control the pounds.

Body dissatisfaction has very different implications for people depending upon how heavy they are. Among those well above normal weight, body dissatisfaction is a painful expression of despair, but understandable given the cultural stigma of being fat. However, an equivalent amount of self-loathing on the part of thin people suggests a different type of problem—distortion on top of dissatisfaction. Thin women distort reality by seeing themselves as fat. Today this type of distortion is rampant and has become the norm. It explains why so many women are susceptible to eating disorders, where the pursuit of thinness is driven by faulty perceptions rather than reality. One hundred and fifty-nine women in our sample are extremely underweight—and 40 percent of them still want to lose weight. Many have eating disorders, to be described later.

Age and Body Image

A number of national studies have shown that body weight is increasing among American adults. Moreover, epidemiologic studies find that body weight increases with age. For both men and women it tends to increase during the first five decades of life, then decline on the way to our inevitable destiny. Although the pattern of gradual weight gain during adulthood recently sparked a public health frenzy leading to such programs as C. Everett Koop's Shape Up America, an analysis of 13 major studies of weight change by Reuben Andres, M.D., of the Gerontology Research Center in Baltimore, Maryland, found that people who put on some pounds during adulthood survive longer than those who maintain or even lose weight.

The Weight of Influence:
Factors Fostering Negative Body Image

What's instrumental in making you feel bad about your body?

	%WOMEN	%MEN
PHYSICAL		
Gaining weight	66	37
Not exercising regularly	44	36
Looking at my stomach in the mirror	44	33
Looking at my face in the mirror	16	15
A certain time in my menstrual cycle	29	–
INTERPERSONAL		
My partner's opinion of my appearance	40	29
Being around someone critical	32	19
Someone rejecting me	26	24
Relationships not going well	24	21
Negative sexual experiences	20	16
EMOTIONAL		
Not feeling confident	22	18
Being in a bad mood	15	9

Our findings confirm that body weight usually increases with age. On average, both men and women tend to put on five to ten pounds per decade, a trend that stops between the ages of 50 and 59. Weight declines slightly after age 60.

Since satisfaction with our appearance is so closely tied to how much we weigh, particularly for women, it's logical to assume that our self-disparagement would gradually increase over a lifetime. But that's not what we found. The youngest women, ages 13 to 19, are both the thinnest and the most satisfied with their appearance, however 54 percent of them are still dissatisfied. The number barely increases to 57 percent among women ages 20 to 29. And it remains at around this level, even though women gained five to ten pounds each succeeding decade.

We can't say for sure how these young women will feel as they get older; a survey, of course, taps different women at each age, not the same women over time. Nevertheless, the magnitude of self-hatred among young women is astonishing. Despite being at a weight that most women envy they are still plagued by feelings of inadequacy. The good news is that even though women gain weight with age, they don't become more dissatisfied as they get older. In fact, there's some evidence that as they age they gain insight and appreciation of their bodies' abilities.

Induction into our culture's weight concerns is happening for women at younger ages. Girls today not only have more weight concerns when they're young, they also lack buffers to protect their psyches. Kids don't know themselves well and have not yet developed many competencies to draw on. It's easier for them to look outside themselves to discover who they are—and find themselves lacking. While we may not be able to draw conclusions about them based on the experiences of older women, we can only hope that over time they develop the insight of this 55-year-old woman from Pennsylvania: "From age 15 to 25, I was very concerned about my body image and went on many diets. As I matured, I realized that personality and morals are more important than how you look and stopped beating myself up and accepted my body. Now I don't worry about my weight but I do eat healthfully and exercise moderately."

In contrast to women, only 41 percent of young men ages 13 to 19 say they are dissatisfied with their appearance. The figures stay about the same for men ages 20 to 29 (38 percent), then spike to 48 percent among 30- to 39-year-olds. They decline again for the 40 to 49 age group (43 percent) and increase for men ages 50 to 59 (48 percent). Again, in contrast to women, a significant proportion of dissatisfied men want to *add* body mass, not lose it. But the critical point is that men as a group are more satisfied with their appearance, although the number who are tormented about their weight and shape appears to be growing.

The Locus of Focus

Because we were interested in discovering what was most instrumental in creating positive and negative feelings about your bodies, we asked how your body image is influenced by certain aspects of physical appearance: gaining weight, feeling thin, looking at your face in the mirror, looking at your stomach in the mirror. Exercise was also included, because we use it to change our body weight and shape.

Do Fashion Models Influence
How You Feel About Your Appearance?

What's the media's impact on how we see ourselves?

	%WOMEN	Extremely Satisfied Women	Extremely Dissatisfied Women	%MEN
I ALWAYS OR VERY OFTEN:				
Compare myself to models in magazines	27	17	43	12
Carefully study the shapes of models	28	18	47	19
VERY THIN OR MUSCULAR MODELS MAKE ME:				
Feel insecure about my weight	29	12	67	15
Want to lose weight	30	13	67	18
Feel angry or resentful	22	9	45	8

We assumed focusing on features like the face and the stomach—the latter the bearer of fat and of children—would produce highly-charged feelings, both good and bad. However, we were specifically interested in trying to understand the relative impact of different physical features on body feeling—the locus of focus. We also wanted to measure how physical aspects of appearance stack up against interpersonal factors, such as being rejected, receiving compliments, being teased, and sexual experiences, as well as emotional components, like feeling effective as a person and over-all happiness.

When it comes to what causes negative feelings, gaining weight is at the top of the list for everyone: two-thirds of women and about a third of men say it's a very important cause of their disapproval of their bodies. And the stomach, not the face, is the prevailing locus of disapproval for both men and women. Looking at your stomach in the mirror is an extreme downer for 44 percent of women and 33 percent of men—compared to the face, which was a downer for 16 percent of women and 15 percent of men.

Women are hit with a very specific source of body antipathy: more than 75 percent say that "a certain time in the menstrual cycle" is an important cause of negative feelings about their bodies. And a fear of fatness may be perverting women's attitudes toward pregnancy and childbearing. About a third of women say that, for them, pregnancy itself is an important source of negative body feelings.

If these feelings are strong enough, it's only reasonable to assume that they may affect some women's decisions to have kids. As one 25-year-old Maryland woman offers: "I love children and would love to have one more—but only if I didn't have to gain the weight." A 43-year-old woman from Georgia proselytizes against pregnancy: "I tell every young girl that if they like the way their body looks, don't get pregnant. It messes up a woman's body."

While interpersonal factors are the cause of negative feelings about the body for fewer people, they are highly influential for a significant minority. Forty percent of women and 29 percent of men say their partner's opinion about their appearance is very important to their body image. About a quarter of all respondents say the same goes for someone rejecting them. Thus there's a major connection between the way we feel about our body and the way we perceive others feel about it. One 54-year-old New York woman says: "Since my partner sees me as beautiful, I feel beautiful." This interpersonal connection seems to take root early, as a 17-year-old woman from New York explains: "My partner's feelings about me and my looks mean everything to me. If my mate had an unfavorable opinion, that would be devastating."

What impact does our mood have on our feelings about our body? The survey, as well as other research, suggests a potentially deadly two-way self-perpetuating process. When we feel bad about anything, our body satisfaction plummets, and when we hate our body, our mood takes a dive. A 39-year-old Connecticut woman captures the vicious cycle: When I'm in a bad mood about anything, I get more critical of my body. When I am more critical of my body, I lose confidence in my abilities." A 35-year-old woman from Pennsylvania illustrates the process: "When I am in a bad mood about something else, my focus often goes right to my body weight and I either feel fat or I obsess about food."

The connection between mood and body is critical; it suggests that body dissatisfaction is not a static entity but rather is governed, at least in part, by our general emotional state. When we feel bad about something else, our bodies get dragged down in the negative tide.

Among the many aspects of body image we looked at was the role of certain life orientations. For example, we compared women who call themselves feminists with those who view themselves more traditionally. There are no differences between the groups in average body weight. But 32 percent of feminists, compared with 49 percent of traditional women, are strongly dissatisfied with their overall appearance. When asked more specifically about their weight, 24 percent of feminists and 40 percent of traditional women are extremely dissatisfied. The differences translate directly into behavior—twice as many traditionally oriented women vomit to control their weight as women claiming to be feminists. It appears that feminist beliefs confer some behavioral protection.

When we asked what leads to positive feelings about your bodies, the results generally mirrored the findings about negative feelings, but there are some interesting differences. Weight-related factors tended to top the list of sources of positive feelings, paralleling the results for negative feelings. Exercise generated the greatest source

The Big Bad Body

The dissatisfaction we feel toward our bodies has not only risen since 1972, the rate at which it's rising is accelerating:

| | 1972 Survey% | | 1985 Survey% | | 1997 Survey% | |
	WOMEN	MEN	WOMEN	MEN	WOMEN	MEN
Overall appearance	25	15	38	34	56	43
Weight	48	35	55	41	66	52
Height	13	13	17	20	16	16
Muscle tone	30	25	45	32	57	45
Breasts/chest	26	18	32	28	34	38
Abdomen	50	36	57	50	71	63
Hips or upper thighs	49	12	50	21	61	29

of positive feelings. But moderate exercise, we found, goes a long way. People who exercise a lot do not seem to feel any better than those who exercise moderately.

And while both men and women identify a few circumstances that could crash their feelings about their bodies, you point out more factors that bolster it. About twice as many people judge sexual experiences as a source of good feelings rather than bad. For both sexes, interpersonal and emotional factors more often serve to reinforce, not punish. This is encouraging news; it implies that there are many avenues for us to improve our feelings about our bodies.

When we asked what shaped your body image during childhood and adolescence, most women and a significant minority of men reiterate the cultural theme that thinness is the key to happiness. But interpersonal factors also weigh heavily on most of us during development, and women rank them more important than men.

For many, teasing during childhood or adolescence had a crushing effect on body image. So much so that the extent of the damage can't be captured by a questionnaire. The narratives paint a graphic picture of the pain. As one 59-year-old Illinois man recounts: "Being teased when I was a child made me feel bad about my body for years and years." A 37-year-old woman from

Ohio admits: "No matter how thin I become, I always feel like the fat kid everyone made fun of." An 18-year-old Iowa woman says: "The memories absolutely haunt me and make me feel like something is wrong with me."

By far, however, the dominant factor that regulates our feelings about our appearance is our body weight—actual body weight as well as attitudes about it. The weight of this influence is staggering compared to other factors. Body weight alone accounts for 60 percent of our overall satisfaction with our appearance; all other physical features combined add only 10 percent more to our level of satisfaction. This suggests a simple solution—just change your weight and happy times will follow. Unfortunately, it's not that simple.

Exercise: The New Holy Grail?

Virtually everyone surveyed says they exercised during the past year—97 percent of both sexes. And exercise gets high marks when it comes to breeding positive body feelings (by a narrow margin for women, a substantial majority for men). Seventy-six percent of women and 86 percent of men report exercising at least two hours a week; 20 percent of women and 27 percent of men exercise five or more times a week for at least 30 minutes. There's a modest relationship between the amount of time spent exercising and satisfaction with appearance, and this is stronger for men than women.

On the surface, it appears that exercise is an uncomplicated remedy for achieving harmony with our bodies. But a closer look at our findings tempers this conclusion. More than 60 percent of women and 40 percent of men indicate that at least half of their workout time is spent exercising to control their weight. And for a significant proportion of both sexes—18 percent of women, 12 percent of men—all exercise is aimed at weight control.

But all that exercise is not leading to body satisfaction, since 88 percent of these women and 79 percent of these men say they are dissatisfied with their appearance. By contrast, among those who exercise for weight control less than 25 percent of the time, only a third are dissatisfied with their appearance. For many women, exercise is simply one more weapon in the weight-control war, a practice that mutes its ability to boost body satisfaction.

However, heavier women say the more they exercise, the bigger the boost to body satisfaction. Among women who weigh more than average, 30 percent of those who exercise more than five times a week are satisfied, compared to 20 percent who exercise less than once a week.

Whether or not exercise is effective as a method of weight control, it does tend to make us feel better about our appearance. It also improves both health and mood.

Men and Body Image

In general, men say they are more satisfied with their bodies than women. And weight plays a less important role in shaping their feelings about their bodies. A little over 12 percent of the men who responded to our survey say they're gay. In general, gay men are more concerned about their weight and have more eating concerns.

	%ALL MEN	%GAY MEN	%WOMEN
I am extremely or somewhat satisfied with my body	57	44	44
Gaining weight is very important in making me feel bad about my body	37	46	66
Feeling thin goes a long way toward making me feel good about my body	24	34	53
Do you ever diet?	58	70	84
Have you ever been diagnosed with an eating disorder?	3	9	14
Do you think you have an eating disorder but haven't been treated?	5	17	14
DO YOU USE:			
Diet pills	5	12	10
Laxatives	2	6	4
Diuretics	3	8	4
Vomiting	1	3	4

Sex and Body Image

Sexual experiences affect our body image, and our body image affects our sexual liaisons. You describe this reciprocal relationship poignantly. Body image affects sexual experiences: "The less attractive I feel, the less I desire sex," says a 31-year-old woman from Louisiana. "If at all possible I avoid sex; however, if it should happen, I am unwilling to let go. I have the feeling I may be vulgar to my partner."

Sexual experiences affect body image: "A bad sexual experience makes me feel embarrassed about my body," admits a 19-year-old Texas woman. Sexual abuse amplifies this self-abasement: "Having been sexually assaulted brought a lot of body hatred, and a desire to not have a body," a 24-year-old woman from Illinois says.

As has been the case for so many other variables in the 1997 Survey, weight gets in the middle of the picture. One 20-year-old Missouri woman states: "I try to lose weight for boyfriends. When I am fat, I know that no one wants to be with me. I feel like unless I have a good body, no decent guy wants me!"

The connection between sexual experiences and body image is affirmed in our overall findings. More than a third of all men (40 percent) and women (36 percent) say that unpleasant sexual experiences are moderately to very important in causing negative feelings of their body. But an even greater percentage—70 percent of men and 67 percent of women—feel that good sexual experiences contribute to satisfactory feelings about their bodies. Few believe they are irrelevant (6 percent of men and 7 percent of women).

Twenty-three percent of women consider sexual abuse moderately to very important in having shaped their body image in childhood or adolescence. That's twice the number of men—10 percent—who think so, perhaps reflecting the difference in rates of abuse between men and women. But the vast majority of men (85 percent) and women (74 percent) declare that it's almost or completely irrelevant, no doubt indicating their lack of personal experience.

The personal accounts of some respondents leave no doubt as to the devastating effects of sexual abuse. An 18-year-old woman says: "As a young child, I was sexually abused by my father. I grew up feeling as though there was something inherently dirty and evil about my body." Abuse is clearly a dominant factor in body image for members of both sexes, but it's not ubiquitous, unlike such factors as teasing by others (73 percent of women and 57 of percent men) and personal feelings about weight (79 percent of women and 56 percent of men).

Intriguingly, those who are dissatisfied with their bodies are much more inclined to view negative sexual experiences as important than those who are body-satisfied. Only 15 percent of women who are extremely satisfied with their bodies say that negative sexual experiences are very important in determining their body image (42 percent say that negative sexual experiences are completely irrelevant). In contrast, 41 percent of body-dissatisfied women regard negative sexual experiences as very important (only 16 percent say they are completely irrelevant). The same is true for men.

Sexual and physical abuse are important contributors to body dissatisfaction—but again primarily it's women who have been sexually abused who think so. Sexual abuse is judged very important by 30 percent of women who are extremely body-dissatisfied, versus 13 percent of the extremely body-satisfied group. Women who feel good about their bodies and have not been victims of abuse just don't grasp the damage abuse can do to feelings about the body.

EXTREME WEIGHT CONTROL

Eating disorders occur when a person's intense preoccupation with their "fatness leads them to extreme measures to control their weight. Considerable research indicates that anorexia and bulimia are outgrowths of a negative body image and, further, that today's epidemic increase in eating disorders is related to the intense pressure put on women to conform to ultraslender role models of feminine beauty.

A remarkable 84 percent of women and 58 percent of men report having dieted to lose weight. A sizable proportion of respondents say they have resorted to extreme and dangerous weight-control methods in the last year: 445 women (13 percent) and 22 men (4 percent) say they induce vomiting; more than a third of each of these groups vomit once a week or more. Fourteen percent of women (480) and 3 percent of men (16) say they have actually been diagnosed with eating disorders. Among the very underweight women in our survey, 31 percent (49) indicate they have been diagnosed with an eating disorder. And 11.5 percent of women and 2 percent of men say they have an eating disorder but have never received treatment, although the type of eating disorder was not specified.

Vomiting was more common among those who say they have been diagnosed (23 percent), less common among those who identify themselves as having untreated eating disorders (11 percent). Perhaps most surprising is that 1.5 percent of women (38) vomit for weight control and don't feel they have an eating disorder!

Laxative abuse for weight control is common among those diagnosed with eating disorders (17 percent) and those self-identified (9 percent). It is also reported by 3 percent of women (72) who don't feel they have eating disorders.

Vomiting and laxative abuse seem to be increasingly accepted as "normal" methods of weight control. And eating disorders themselves have become the object of envy gaining celebrity status with each new high-profile victim. There's even evidence that eating disorders acquire a positive patina with media exposure—even it it's

Altering Your Image: Strategies from the Trenches

One of the major goals of the 1997 Body Image Survey was to learn more about how people have remade their image. Though we anticipated receiving a few brief suggestions, we were inundated with your personal accounts of change. We have summarized your suggestions but kept your words. Try and discover what factors play a role in your struggle with your body. And be deliberate about creating a lifestyle that increases your chances for ending the war with your body.

1. Develop criteria for self-esteem that go beyond appearance. One way to make appearance less important is to develop other benchmarks for self-evaluation. A 51-year-old woman from California summarizes the approach: "By achieving in other areas, balancing successes and failures, searching where positives are possible." A 53-year-old Washington man says, "focusing on succeeding at work, participating in sports, and friendships have helped me overcome my negative body feelings."

2. Cultivate the ability to appreciate your body, especially how it functions. One middle-aged woman writes: "I have often wanted to write an article called 'I Have a Beautiful Body.' No, I don't look like Jane Fonda. I look like a normal 46-year-old woman who has had three children. But my body is beautiful because of all it does for me. I have two eyes that can see, a large nose for smelling, a large mouth for eating and smiling, two hands that can hold and hug, two breasts that have nursed three sons, an abdomen that was home to three babies, two legs that can walk everywhere I want to go, and two feet to take me there."

"I have extremely red hair and as a child I hated it because it was so different," says a 20-year-old woman from California. "I have come to realize that my hair is a beautiful and exotic part of me. Now I cherish it."

3. Engage in behavior that makes you feel good about yourself. "When I have negative thoughts and feelings about my physical appearance, I try to behave in ways that will turn them around, like exercise and buying a piece of clothing that enhances my appearance," says a 30-year-old Missouri woman.

"Although Rubenesque at age 54, I currently model nude for a local university art school, meditate daily to focus inward, and enjoy dancing, swimming, archery, art, and my writing projects," says a Georgia woman.

4. Reduce your exposure to noxious images. "I stopped buying fashion magazines completely when I was about 24," says a 30-year-old woman from Michigan. "Comparing myself to the models had a very strong and negative impact."

"One of the things that helped me become more accepting of my body was the realization that it was okay to be female," says a 67-year-old woman from Ohio. "It sounds hokey, but watching old movies starring Sophia Loren and Ava Gardner helped. These women had shoulders, and breasts, and hips, and are some of the sexiest women I have ever seen."

5. Exercise for strength, fitness, and health, not just weight control. "When I was able to stop focusing on how my body looked and began experiencing what it could help me accomplish—climbing, swimming, cycling, surviving in the wilderness—it made me feel extremely satisfied," says a 28-year-old woman from Louisiana.

"About a year ago I started walking every day for about an hour," says a 22-year-old woman from New York. "Because I was walking I felt so good. I also lost 10 pounds, but that didn't matter. My attitude changed because I cared about my health."

6. Seek out others who respect and care about your body; teach them how to talk about and touch your body. "The most recent experience that has helped has been a lover," says a 67-year-old Ohio woman. "He makes me glad to be in this body with this shape and these dimensions."

7. Get out of abusive relationships. "If my partner didn't like my appearance, he would no longer be my partner," says a 31-year-old woman from Alabama. "I eliminate the negative."

8. Identify and change habitual negative thoughts about your body. "I constructed a tape of positive self-talk with personal goals and feelings I want to achieve," says a 25-year-old Washington woman. "When I have a bad attitude about my body, I pop in my tape. It really helps improve my self-image."

"When I look in the mirror at my body I always try to say nice things rather than cringe," continues the wise-beyond-her-years 25-year-old.

9. Decode more complicated thoughts about the body. Are negative thoughts and feelings about your body distracting you from other issues that are really bothering you? A 60-year-old woman writes: "A factor that has helped me come to terms with my body was recognizing that much of my relationship problems had more to do with shyness and lack of social skills than physical appearance. Once I worked on my people skills, I found that I worried less about my appearance."

10. If you can't get over your bad body image, consider seeking professional help. "I was bulimic for 12 years," says a 36-year-old woman from Oregon. "My recovery was based on individual counseling, support from friends, and a hell of a lot of hard work on my part."

11. Control what you can, forget about what you can't. "As far as negativity about my physical appearance," says a 33-year-old woman from Michigan, "I've had one simple rule: work on improving what you can realistically change, and don't spend time worrying about the rest."

negative—and that actually helps spread them by social contagion. This was driven home by a patient I recently saw. When told she really didn't meet the diagnostic criteria for an eating disorder, she burst into tears. "I tried so hard to get an eating disorder, to be like [a high profile gymnast]," she lamented, "but I guess I can't even get this right."

Not surprisingly, one of the keys to helping people overcome eating disorders is fostering the development of a positive body image. Unfortunately, this means swimming against the cultural stream, as it's extremely hard to avoid ubiquitous thin-is-beautiful messages. Studies of prime-time television indicate that programs are dominated by people with thin body types and thinness is consistently associated with favorable personality traits. But one of the most interesting aspects of the psychology of appearance is that not everyone succumbs to the same pressures.

MEDIATING SELF-PERCEPTION

The media play an important role as a cultural gatekeeper, framing standards of beauty for all of us by the models they choose. Many observers, including eating-disorder specialists, have encouraged producers and editors to widen the range of beauty standards by including models more representative of real women. But often they respond by saying that more diversity will weaken sales; recently Vogue magazine acknowledged the outrage toward gaunt fashion models—but denied there's any evidence linking images of models to eating disorders.

The 1997 Body Image Survey gathered direct information on this issue and more generally on the media's impact on self-perception. The results are nothing short of fascinating. Forty-three percent of women report that "very thin or muscular models" make them feel insecure about their weight. This is true for only 28 percent of men. Just under half of women (48 percent) indicate very thin models make them want to lose weight to look like them; 34 percent of men agree. Though drawn to and driven by the image of fashion models, 34 percent of women declare they are angry and resentful at these presumed paragons of beauty, as are 15 percent of men.

The impact of the media, however, is somewhat selective, affecting most strongly those who are dissatisfied with their shape, and who are generally heavier and farther away from the cultural ideal. Women who are extremely satisfied with their weight compare themselves to and study the shapes of models less than half as often as women who are body-dissatisfied.

Even more striking, 76 percent of the women who are dissatisfied with their bodies say that very thin or muscular models make them feel insecure about their weight very often or always (versus 12 percent of body-satisfied women). Sixty-seven percent also say models make them want to lose weight (versus 13 percent of body-satisfied

women), and 45 percent say models make them angry or resentful (versus 9 percent of body-satisfied women).

Similarly, those who say they've been diagnosed with an eating disorder report being highly influenced by fashion models. Forty-three percent compare themselves to models in magazines; 45 percent scrutinize the shapes of models. Forty-nine percent say very thin models make them feel insecure about themselves, and 48 percent say they "make me want to lose weight to be like them."

Clearly, body satisfaction, a rather rare commodity, confers relative immunity to media influence. But the existence of a large number of women who are drawn to media imagery but resent the unreality of those images is cause for concern. It suggests they are experiencing an uncomfortable level of entrapment. We wonder how long it will take for their resentment to be unleashed full force on the fashion industry and/or the media—and in what form.

Women and, to a lesser degree, men are not only affected by images in the media, they also want to see themselves represented differently. They're clamoring for change and willing to put their money on their predilections. The overwhelming majority of all respondents—93 percent of women, 89 percent of men—want models in magazines to represent the natural range of body shapes; 82 percent of women assert they are willing to buy magazines containing heavier models, as do 53 percent of men, even though most still believe that clothes look better on thin models.

One 30-year-old woman captures the feeling: "The media portray an image of the perfect woman that is unattainable for somewhere between 98 to 99 percent of the female population. How are we supposed to live up to that standard that is shoved in our faces constantly—I hate it."

THE SHAPE OF THINGS TO COME

More than ever before, women are dissatisfied with their weight and are fighting it with relentless dieting and exercise. Thinness has become the preeminent yardstick for success or failure, a constant against which every woman can be measured, a gauge that has slowly permeated the male mentality. Yet the actual body weight of women in the U.S. has increased over the last 30 years, and consumer pressure for weight-loss products is surging.

Research shows that dieting to lose weight and fear of fatness are now common in girls as young as nine years old—and escalate dramatically during adolescence, particularly among those at the heavier end of the spectrum. The risk of developing an eating disorder is eight times higher in dieting 15-year-old girls than in nondieting 15-year-old girls.

The 1997 Body Image Survey results and cumulative clinical experience suggest there is merit to becoming comfortable with yourself even if you don't conform to current cultural body-size ideals. Some people are naturally fatter, just as others are naturally thinner. Despite a $50 billion-a-year diet industry; conventional treatments for obesity are an abysmal failure. Traditional dietary and behavioral treatments may have an effect in the short term, but they do not produce lasting and clinically significant amounts of weight loss. They are no match for the genetic and biological factors that regulate body weight. They certainly reinforce the myth that weight loss is the preferred route to improve self-esteem. Perhaps the wisest course is to get plenty of exercise—and accept yourself the way you are rather than try to mold yourself into a narrowly defined and arbitrary ideal, no matter how widely pictured it is.

Preoccupation with body image is undoubtedly not good for our mental health, but it also seems to be a metaphor for something larger in the culture—if we could only figure out what. Over a decade ago, the late social critic Christopher Lasch argued that our culture of mass consumption encourages narcissism, a new kind of self-consciousness or vanity through which people have learned to judge themselves not merely *against* others but *through* others' eyes. The "image" projected by possessions, physical attractiveness, clothes, and "personality" replace experience, skills, and character as gauges of personal identity, health, and happiness. We are thrown into a chronic state of unease, perfect prey for an array of commercial "solutions."

Psychiatrists and psychologists have also weighed in on the meaning of body image issues. At the 1996 meeting of the American Psychological Association, Yale psychiatrist Alan Feingold, M.D., received an award for detailing differences in body-image pressures on men and women. Dr. Feingold contends that pressure on women to look good is not only growing but reflects intensified competition for dwindling resources; after all, looks confer a kind of status to women. Others point to role conflicts for women; power issues; a mother-daughter generational rift; and the possibility that in a world of rapidly shifting realities, we seize on the body as an island of certainty—numbers on a scale represent quantifiable accomplishment. Perhaps it's all of these; the body is a big screen on which we now project all of our anxieties.

BRAIN SEX AND THE LANGUAGE OF LOVE

Robert L. Nadeau

If we can believe the experts, the standard for healthy intimacy in love relationships between men and women is female, and maleness is a disease in desperate need of a cure. Men, say social scientists, have a "trained incapacity to share" and have learned to overvalue independence and to fear emotional involvement. Female friendships, claim the intimacy experts, are based on emotional bonding and mutual support, and male friendships on competition, emotional inhibition, and aggression.[1] Social scientists have also pathologized maleness because men typically view love as action, or doing things for another, while women view love as talking and acknowledging feelings.

In fairness to the intimacy experts, what they say about differences in the behavior of men and women has been well documented. Numerous studies have shown that men feel close to other men when working or playing side by side, while women feel close to other women when talking face to face.[2] Male group behavior is characterized by an emphasis on space, privacy, and autonomy, and female group behavior by a need to feel included, connected, and attached.[3] Male conversation tends to center around activities (sports, politics, work), and personal matters are discussed in terms of strengths and achievements. Female conversation, in contrast, is more likely to center around feelings and relationships, and there is considerably less reluctance to reveal fears and weaknesses.

Men and women also appear to experience intimacy in disparate ways. In men's relationships with other men, the index of intimacy is the degree of comfort and relaxation felt when engaged in activities, such as helping a friend move furniture or repair cars. Even when men comfort one another in crisis situations, like the loss of a family member or a spouse, it is physical presence, rather than intimate talk, that tends to be most valued.[4]

The index for intimacy among women is the extent to which personal feelings can be shared in a climate of mutual support and trust. What tends to be most valued in these interactions is confirmation of feelings as opposed to constructive criticism and advice. When women are asked to describe the benefits of such conversations with other women, they typically mention relief from anxiety and stress, feeling better, and a more enhanced sense of self-worth. Although women also express intimacy by doing things for other women, the doing is typically viewed as an occasion for verbal intimacy.[5]

The response of males to depression also favors action, or a tendency to "run" when overcome with sadness, anxiety, or dread. And when men talk about their depression in therapy, they typically "rush through" an account of their emotions and describe depression with action metaphors, such as "running in place," "running wide open," and "pushing the edge."[6] When women are clinically depressed, they are more willing to talk about their feelings, to find opportunities to do so with other women, and to seek help in talk ther-

1. Mirra Komarovsky, *Blue-collar Marriage* (New York: Vintage, 1964).

2. D. Goleman, "Two Views of Marriage Explored: His and Hers," *New York Times*, 1 Apr. 1989.

3. C. Gilligan, *In a Different Voice* (Cambridge, Mass.: Harvard University Press, 1982).

4. Scott Swain, "Covert Intimacy: Closeness in Men's Friendship," in B. J. Reisman and P. Schwartz, eds., *Gender in Intimate Relations* (Belmont, Calif.: Wadsworth, 1989).

5. Robin Lakoff, *Talking Power: The Politics of Language* (New York: Basic Books, 1990).

6. Catherine Riessman, *Divorce Talk: Women and Men Make Sense of Personal Relationships* (New Brunswick, N.J.: Rutgers University Press, 1990).

This article originally appeared in *The World & I*, November 1997, pp. 330-339. Reprinted by permission of *The World & I*, a publication of the Washington Times Corporation. © 1997.

The human brain, like the human body, is sexed, and differences in the sex-specific human brain condition a wide range of behaviors that we typically associate with maleness or femaleness.

apy. Women also typically disclose the sources of depression in detailed narratives that represent and analyze experience. And while men tend to respond to clinical depression by running or moving, women tend to respond with sedentary activities like uncontrollable crying, staying in bed, and compulsive eating.

The sex-specific patterns that lie beneath the diversity of these behaviors reduce to a male orientation toward action and a female orientation toward talking. Why is this the case? According to the intimacy experts, it is entirely a product of learning and one of the primary sources of male pathology. As psychologist Carol Tavris puts it, "The doing-versus-talking distinction in the emotional styles of males and females begins in childhood, when boys begin to develop what psychologists call 'side by side' relationships, in which intimacy means sharing the same activity—sports, games, watching a movie or a sports event together." Girls, in contrast, "tend to prefer 'face to face' relationships, in which intimacy means revealing ideas and emotions in a heart-to-heart exchange."[7]

The problem is not, as a best-selling book would have us believe, that women are from Venus and men from Mars. It is that we have only recently come to realize something about the legacy of the evolution of our species on planet Earth. Throughout virtually all of our evolutionary history, men and women

lived in small tribes of hunter-gatherers where the terms for survival were not the same. We have long recognized that the different terms for survival, along with mate selection, account for sexual differences in the human body. But only in the last few decades have we discovered that the legacy of our evolutionary past is also apparent in the human brain. The human brain, like the human body, is sexed, and differences in the sex-specific human brain condition a wide range of behaviors that we typically associate with maleness or femaleness.

THE LEGACY OF THE HUNTER-GATHERERS

The family album containing the record of our hunter-gatherer evolutionary past is DNA, and the legacy of that past begins to unfold following the union of sperm and ovum. Normal females have two long X chromosomes, contributed by each biological parent, that closely resemble one another. Normal males have a long X chromosome, contributed by the mother, and a short Y chromosome, contributed by the father. Although each sperm and ovum contributes half of the full complement of forty-six chromosomes, the ovum provides all of the cytoplasmic DNA.

A fetus will develop with a female brain unless a gene on the Y chromosome, known as SRY, is expressed about the sixth week of pregnancy and triggers the release of testosterone in the gonads. The testosterone transforms the developing

fetus into a male by interacting with genes that regulate or are regulated by the expression of SRY. The result is a kind of chain reaction in which genes involved in the determination of maleness are activated in a large number of cells. But since the levels of hormones vary across individual brains, the response of brain regions to the presence of hormones is highly variable.

Many of the sex-specific differences in the human brain are located in more primitive brain regions, and they condition male and female copulatory behavior, sexual orientation, and cyclic biological processes like menstruation. Sex-specific differences also exist, however, in the more recently evolved neocortex or in the higher brain regions. The neocortex looks like a redundantly folded sheet and contains 70 percent of the neurons in the central nervous system. It is divided into two hemispheres that process different kinds of information fairly independently, and each communicates with the other via a 200-million-fiber network called the corpus callosum. While the symmetry is not exact, structures in one hemisphere are mirrored in the other. Thus we have two parietal lobes, two occipital lobes, and so on.

In people with normal hemispheric dominance, the left hemisphere has executive control. This hemisphere manages linguistic analysis and expression, as well as sequential motor responses or body movements. The right hemisphere is responsible for perception of spatial relationships, faces, emotional stimuli, and prosody (vocal intonations

7. Carol Tavris, *The Mismeasure of Women* (New York: Simon & Schuster, 1992), 251–52.

While males talk about their status in terms of simple descriptions of individual skills and achievements, Tannen says, females do so with complicated descriptions of overall character.

that modify the literal meaning of a word).[8] The two frontal lobes of each hemisphere, located behind the forehead, integrate inputs from other brain regions and are closely associated with conscious decision making. This portion of our brain, which occupies 29 percent of the cortex, has undergone the most recent evolutionary expansion.

8. S. F. Wietelson, "Neural Sexual Mosaicism: Sexual Differentiation of the Human Temporo-Parietal Region for Functional Asymmetry," *Psychoneuroendochrinology* 16:1–3 (1991): 131–55.

9. Wietelson, "Neural Sexual Mosaicism," 137–38.

10. I. Jibiki, H. Matsuda, et al., "Quantitative Assessment of Regional Blood Flow with 1231–IMP in Normal Adult Subjects," *Acta-Neurol-Napoli* 15:1 (1993): 7–15, and F. Okada, Y. Tokumitsu, et al., "Gender and Handedness-Related Differences in Forebrain Oxygenation and Hemodynamics," *Brain Research* 601:1–2 (1993): 337–47.

11. S. P. Springer and G. Deutsch, *Left Brain, Right Brain* (San Francisco: W. H. Friedman Co., 1985).

12. Ruben Gur, quoted in Gina Kolata, "Men's World, Women's World? Brain Studies Point to Differences," *New York Times*, 28 Feb. 1995, C1.

13. Melissa Hines, "Gonadal Hormones and Human Cognitive Development," in Jacques Balthazart, ed., *Hormones, Brain and Behavior in Vertebrates* (Basel, Switz.: Karger, 1990), 51–63.

14. Susan Phillips, Susan Steele, and Christine Tanz, eds., *Language, Gender and Sex in Comparative Perspective* (Cambridge, Eng.: Cambridge University Press, 1987); and David Martin and H. D. Hoover, "Sex Differences in Educational Achievement: A Longitudinal Study," *Journal of Early Adolescence* 7 (1987): 65–83.

15. Deborah Tannen, *You Just Don't Understand: Women and Men in Conversation* (New York: Ballantine Books, 1990), 77.

One piece of evidence that suggests why the brains of women and men tend to process information differently involves the corpus callosum, or the network of fibers connecting the two hemispheres. A subregion of this network, the splenium, is significantly larger in women than in men and more bulbous in shape.[9] More connections between the hemispheres in female brains could be a partial explanation for another significant discovery—both hemispheres are normally more active in the brains of females.

Computer-based imaging systems, such as positron emission tomography (PET) and magnetic resonance imaging (MRI), allow scientists to assess which areas of the brains of conscious subjects are active. All of these systems use advanced computers to construct three-dimensional images of brains as they process various kinds of information. Studies based on advanced imaging systems have revealed that cognitive tasks in the female brain tend to be localized in both hemispheres,[10] and that the same tasks in the male brain tend to be localized in one hemisphere.[11] Other recent studies using this technology have revealed sex-specific differences in the brain regions used to process language and sex-specific differences in feedback from more-primitive brain regions.[12] What this research suggests is that differences in the communication styles of men and women are not simply the product of learning.[13] They are also conditioned by differences in the sex-specific human brain.[14]

YOU JUST DON'T UNDERSTAND ME

While none of the intimacy experts, to my knowledge, attribute differences in the conversation styles of men and women to the sex-specific human brain, there is a growing consensus that it is extremely difficult to eliminate these differences. In the bestseller *You Just Don't Understand: Women and Men in Conversation*, Deborah Tannen claims that while men use conversation "to preserve their independence and negotiate and maintain status in a hierarchical social order," women use conversation as "a way of establishing connections and negotiating relationships."[15] Based on this assumption, Tannen makes the case that there are some large differences in the languages of men and women.

Men, she says, are more comfortable with public speaking, or "report talk," and women are more comfortable with private or "rapport talk." Men use language that is abstract and categorical, or communicate in "messages," and women use language that conveys subtle nuances and hidden meanings, or communicate in "metamessages." Similarly, men respond to problems with concrete solutions and suggestions, and women respond with empathy and an emphasis on community.

Competitive males, claims Tannen, favor "commands," or statements that indicate what should be done without qualification, while consensus-building females favor "conditional propositions," or statements prefaced with words like "let's," "we could," and "maybe." And while males talk about their status in terms of simple descriptions of individual skills and achievements, Tannen says, females do so with complicated descriptions of overall character.

This sparse theoretical framework, however, does not account for the enormous popularity of Tannen's book. What most impresses readers are the conversations that Tannen uses to illustrate the distinctive character of the languages used by men and women. The following exchange occurs when a husband indicates that he did not get enough sleep:

> **He:** I'm really tired. I didn't sleep well last night.
> **She:** I didn't sleep well either. I never do.
> **He:** Why are you trying to belittle me?
> **She:** I'm not! I'm just trying to show you I understand!

"This woman," says Tannen, "was not only hurt by her husband's reaction; she was mystified by it. How could he think she was belittling him? By 'belittle me,' he meant 'belittle my experience.' He was filtering her attempts to establish connection through his concern with preserving independence and avoiding being put down."[16]

In a discussion of the differences between messages and metamessages, Tannen quotes from Anne Tyler's novel *The Accidental Tourist*. At this point in the narrative the character Macon has left his wife and moved in with a woman named Muriel. The conversation begins when Macon makes an observation about Muriel's son:

> "I don't think Alexander's getting a proper education," he said to her one evening.
> "Oh, he's okay."
> "I asked him to figure what change they'd give back when we bought the milk today, and he

didn't have the faintest idea. He didn't even know he'd have to subtract."
> "Well, he's only in second grade," Muriel said.
> "I think he ought to go to private school."
> "Private schools cost money."
> "So? I'll pay."
> She stopped flipping the bacon and looked over at him. "What are you saying?" she said.
> "Pardon?"
> "What are you saying, Macon? Are you saying you're committed?"

Muriel then tells Macon that he must decide whether he wants to divorce his wife and marry her, and that she will not put her son in a new school when he could be forced to leave if Macon returns to his wife. Confused and frustrated by Muriel's attack, Macon responds, "But I just want him to learn to subtract." The problem, writes Tannen, is that "Macon is concerned with the message, the simple matter of Alexander's learning math. But Muriel is concerned with the metamessage. What would it say about the relationship if he began paying for her son's education?"[17]

Some reviewers of Tannen's book have rightly complained that these differences are made to appear too categorical. But they also concede, along with the majority of other reviewers, that Tannen has disclosed some actual disparities in the languages used by men and women. How, then, does Tannen account for these remarkable differences in the manner in which men and women linguistically construct reality? She claims that younger children "learn" these languages from older children in single-sex groups on the playground.

WHY MEN CAN'T ALWAYS TALK LIKE WOMEN

When we examine what Tannen says about differences in the languages used by men and women in the light of what

we know about the sex-specific human brain, it seems clear the differences are not simply learned. Report talk and messages may reflect the orientation toward action associated with higher reliance on the primitive region of the limbic system in the male brain and with an orientation toward linear movement in abstract map space in the neocortex.

Although the usual biological explanation for the male tendency to give commands is higher levels of aggression, this linguistic habit also seems consistent with the manner in which reality tends to be constructed in the male brain. Commands may reflect the bias toward action and the organization of particulars in terms of movement between points in map space. All of which suggests that men may perceive commands, as opposed to requests, as more consistent with their sense of the real and as a more expedient way to solve problems.

The relationship between the two hemispheres in the female brain tends to be more symmetric, and there is a greater degree of interaction between these hemispheres. Since linguistic reality in the brains of women seems to invoke a wider range of right-brain cognitive functions, this may enhance awareness of emotionally relevant details, visual clues, verbal nuances, and hidden meanings. This suggests that the female brain tends to construct linguistic reality in terms of more extensive and interrelated cognitive and emotional contexts. If this is the case, all aspects of experience may appear more interdependent and interconnected, and this could contribute to the tendency to perceive people and events in a complex web of relation. Perhaps this is why the language of women tends to feature a more profound sense of identification with others, or why this language seems more "consensual."

Rapport talk may reflect this sense of identification and satisfy the need to feel interconnected. And metamessages, which allow analysis of single

---

16. Tannen, *You Just Don't Understand*, 51.

17. Quoted in Tannen, *You Just Don't Understand*, 175.

events to be extended through a complex web of relation, also seem consistent with the manner in which the female brain tends to construct reality. Since this reality seems more consensual, women may be more inclined to regard decision making as consensual and to prefer "us" instead of "I." Higher reliance in the female brain on the portion of the limbic system associated with symbolic action could also contribute to these tendencies.

Since the male brain tends to construct reality in terms of abstract solutions and sequential movements in map space, men probably perceive action as more commensurate with their sense of the real. If action in the reality of males seems more "actual" than talking, this could explain, in part at least, why men are more inclined to associate intimacy with shared activities, to respond to depression with action, and to describe feelings with action metaphors.

Neuroscience also suggests why women seem to believe that emotions are conveyed more through talking than action. If reality as it is constructed in the female brain features a more extended network of perceptions, memories, associations, and feelings, then the real could be more closely associated with language. This could also explain why women favor "rapport talk," or conversations about the personal and the private. If this talk is more commensurate with the actual character of reality in the female brain, women more than men might de-pend on conversation to reinforce their reality.

More emotional content in female constructions of reality could also explain why women are more inclined to equate talking with feeling, and to view caring actions that are not accompanied by verbal expressions of feeling as less than authentic. And if linguistic constructions of reality in the female brain feature a broader range of emotional experience, women may have less difficulty, on average, disclosing, describing, and contextualizing feelings.

A NEW VIEW OF THE LANGUAGE OF LOVE

The use of qualifiers like "on average," "tends," "may," "probably," and "might" in the description of behavior associated with the sex-specific human brain is not a concession to political correctness. It is the only way to fairly characterize the differences. There is nothing in this research that argues for a direct causal connection between sex-specific brains and the behavior of men and women. Every human brain is unique and becomes more so as a result of learning, and there is more variation between same-sex brains than opposite-sex brains. What is most striking in virtually all of the research on the sex-specific human brain is not differences between the emotional and cognitive processes of men and women but the amazing degree of overlap, or sameness. And while nature may play a larger role in conditioning same-sex behavior than we previously realized, nurture, or learning, remains the most vital part of the equation.

Although many of the behaviors in the litany of male pathology are obviously learned and subject to change, the tendencies associated with the sex-specific male brain cannot be erased in the learning process.

This means that the assumption that love is not love unless men must think, feel, and behave like women in love relationships is not, in the vast majority of instances, realistic. Consider, for example, the primary reason why women seek a divorce. When divorced women are asked to explain the failure of a marriage, the common refrain is "lack of communication," or the unwillingness of the ex-husband to talk about or share feelings.[18] In one recent study, over two-thirds of the women surveyed felt that men would never understand them, or that the men in their lives would remain forever clueless about the lives of women.[19] And yet numerous studies have also shown that women view men who deviate from the masculine norm by displaying or talking openly about emotions as "too feminine" and "poorly adjusted."[20]

Recognizing discrepancies in reality as it "tends" to be constructed in the brains of men and women does not frustrate the desire of men and women to communicate better with their partners. In fact, the opposite is true. Awareness of the discrepancies makes it much easier to negotiate differences and to communicate to our partners how they might better satisfy our expectations and desires without recourse to blame and anger. And this could lead to a greater willingness to embrace two additional assumptions about human reality that have been grandly reinforced by brain science—the total reality is that of both men and women, and the overlap or sameness of the realities of men and women is far greater than the differences.

18. Thomas Wills, Robert Weiss, and Gerald Patterson, "A Behavioral Analysis of the Determinants of Marital Separation," *Journal of Consulting and Clinical Psychology* 42 (1974): 802–11.

19. Survey by Yankelovitch Partners, 1993.

20. See, for example, John Robertson and Louise Fitzgerald, "The (Mis)treatment of Men: Effects of Client Gender Role and Lifestyle on Diagnosis and Attribution of Pathology," *Journal of Counseling Psychology* 37 (1990): 3–9.

Robert L. Nadeau is a professor at George Mason University. This article is based on his most recent book, S/he Brain: Science, Sexual Politics and the Feminist Movement *(Praeger, 1996).*

exclusive men FOR SALE

We challenged 3 advertising agencies to create a campaign to make men more appealing

BY CARYS BOWEN-JONES

1 Selling their sex drive

SAATCHI & SAATCHI, NY: The Saatchi team—five women led by creative director Meg Rogers—agreed that they'd been saddled with a flawed product and considered ways to improve it. "We thought, well, we could attach a vacuum to his foot to make him more appealing, but that's not very realistic," Rogers recalls. So they decided to concentrate on the product's redeeming features.

The team brainstormed for men's possible selling points. "We came up with dozens: they're cute, they take the tops off pickle jars, they keep your feet warm at night, etc. But we kept coming back to the same thing—they will do anything for sex," says Rogers. Worried that her team had failed to come to grips with the true nature of the product, Rogers assembled a focus group made up of men in the agency. "We asked them what they thought women should like about them as a gender. Number Two on their list was, 'We'll kill bugs for you.' Number One? 'We'll do anything for sex.' "

"Suddenly the light switched on," says Rogers. " 'Yes!' We thought, 'men will do anything for sex.' How many times have we had our apartments moved or our cars fixed by men? It's because men love women, and because they love sexuality, that women have a certain power.' "

They'd cracked it. Suddenly this product, with its boundless sex drive, looked like something they could sell. They wrote a creative brief, just as they would for a bar of soap or a box of corn flakes. And the message was

the same as for cereal or soap: "When used correctly, men can improve the quality of your life."

The next step was to create a piece of advertising. "We'd been saying things like 'guys help you move' and 'guys carry your bags,' " says Rogers. "That pointed to an innate quality in men that says, 'If I lift heavy objects for you, I may get sex.' "

And so the image of a naked man hoisting a crimson sofa was born. "This approach is meant to be a bit flirtatious—teasing back, if you will," says Rogers. "Women have become so used to being portrayed as sex objects, and here the tables are turned. It's humorous because that's how you have to look at the relationship between men and women. You have to laugh at it. It's an age-old, very comedic dance between the sexes."

2 Imagine life without men

MAD DOGS & ENGLISHMEN, NY: Mad Dogs art director Carol Holsinger liked the idea of an ad that would buff up the image of the contemporary male. "I thought, 'Men get a bad rap. Maybe they're really not that awful' " she says. Copywriter Deacon Webster felt the same: "Men seem to be the battered item of the day. Everybody's taking potshots at them." But when they began casting around for men's marketable features, they were hard pressed to find any. It was difficult, Holsinger confesses.

They toyed with promoting the masculine talent for "fixing stuff." They noodled with his sex appeal. But most of the qualities they

 From *Marie Claire*, March 1997, pp. 64-67. © by Marie Claire. Reprinted by permission.

MEN®

Because you can't train your cat to do this.

Without men, there'd be no reason to stop eating. Ever.

MEN®

listed didn't seem likely to persuade consumers to try the product. "A lot of the things we were coming up with were negative—men eat up all the beef jerky, drink a lot of beer, and make more money than women," he explains.

Holsinger, who teaches an advertising course at the School of Visual Arts in New York, decided to throw open the brief to her students and see if they could think of something nice to say. They could. One student, David Polle, depicted a woman appraising her reflection in a mirror and asking her husband, "Do I look fat?" "No, darling," replies her husband, more loyal and obedient than any pet could ever be. "Men. Because you can't train your cat to do this," ran the tag line. Holsinger liked it. "It's a classic exchange between a man and a woman. I think women believe men like really skinny women. But women actually judge themselves a lot more harshly than men do. I think this ad makes men look good."

Webster, meanwhile, came up with what he calls the "oversized lady" ad. Like Holsinger, he believes that the pressure to be thin comes more from women themselves than from men. "The ad is obviously a joke," says Webster. "Women say, 'Oh, life without men would be a lot better because we could eat all we want.'" That, argues Webster, is patently not true: In a man-free world, a lot of women would continue to diet and exercise as furiously as ever. Webster hopes that women will laugh at the ad's sarcasm while reflecting on its message—that men aren't always guilty of bullying women into diet and exercise. And when they laugh, they will like men better and will say to themselves, "Oh, those guys aren't so bad after all."

3 A love letter to women

DEUTSCH, INC., NY "One of the first things we did was try to figure out what the hell was the matter with men," says art director Chris Van Oosterhout. With his creative partner, copywriter David Graham, he came up with a litany of masculine failings: Self-absorption. Childishness. Flirting. Fear of crying. The two produced some ads which promised guys could change—then dumped them. A New, Improved Man, they decided, was not what women really wanted. "We made up our minds that there isn't an awful lot wrong with men. Women are already pretty satisfied with

Woman,

I know you sometimes have doubts about me. About my feelings for you. I know you sometimes think the very qualities that make me a man, make me a pig. I'm not soft and sensitive like you. I'm self absorbed. I'm callous. I'm a slob. I'm afraid to cry. I forget what I promised. I act like a child. I flirt when I shouldn't. I take you for granted. So I thought I should tell you my feelings so you'd know why I love you and that might remind you why you love me. We are two halves of an amazing creature. I love how we fit together so perfectly despite our very different proportions and angles. I love the feeling of your small delicate hand in my big clumbsy paw. I love the way you know just when I need a hug. I love how you forgive me. I love how you can coax out the small boy hiding behind my macho exterior. I love how you make me feel strong and protective. I love being your best friend. I love being your opposite. I love how you make me a better human being. I love you woman. I love being your other half.

Love, Man

them—otherwise there wouldn't be relationships," says Graham.

"The vast majority of women love the vast majority of men. It would be artificial to try and reinvent Man and put bells and whistles on him and say, 'Now do you like him?'"

"Yeah, we've got some bad habits," agrees Van Oosterhout, "but there's nothing really wrong with us. After beating our heads against the wall trying to think of how we could improve men, we began to think that women love men for what they are, including some of the stupid, awkward things. We decided that you don't really have to sell a man to a woman. What you do is find the piece of Man that women really love, and reveal it."

So what is this "piece of Man" which makes him so appealing? Graham explains: "Our argument is that whatever physical characteristics a man has, whatever race he is, whatever background he comes from, at his core he has a love of women and a desire to express that love. We think that's what women find appealing in a man—his willingness to confess, to say, 'I love you.'"

This, the pair insist, is Man's true nature. "It shows the way men really think about

women, not the stereotypical 'big breasts and nice ass.' That might be said among men, but it's bull—," says Van Oosterhout.

So their ad became a love letter—an intimate piece of communication from Man to Woman in which Man unveils his feelings without his friends there to snigger at him. He not only owns up to his vices and declares his love for Woman, he also explains why he loves her. It is, he argues, because they are two complementary halves of a perfect whole. It's because of their differences that they get along so well. "In this letter you get the sensitivity of Man," says Van Oosterhout. "It's his true self, without the guy thing, without the social veneer," adds Graham.

"I think women make men much better, and I think men make women better. It's a symbiotic relationship," says Van Oosterhout. "A lot of what's in the ad comes from the way I feel about my girlfriend and the way David feels about his wife. It's personal and it's universal. We could have done a wacky, gimmicky ad, but it would have been hollow for your soul. We hope this one makes you feel you're genuinely being sold on Man, instead of him being sold to you with a coupon.

Should *You* Leave?

HERE THE AUTHOR OF **LISTENING** TO **PROZAC** TURNS HIS EAR TO **PEOPLE** ON THE THRESHOLD OF LEAVING A **ROMANTIC** RELATIONSHIP. BUT GIVING **ADVICE** TO SUCH FOLK, HE FINDS, ISN'T AS STRAIGHT-FORWARD AS YOU **MIGHT** THINK.

BY PETER D. KRAMER, M.D.

"How do you expect mankind to be happy in pairs when it is so miserable separately?"
—Peter De Vries

YOU ARE IN A DIFFICULT RELATIONSHIP, ONE THAT FEELS painful to stick with or to leave. You imagine there is something particular a psychiatrist can offer—perhaps the fresh perspective of a neutral observer. You want to know how your relationship looks from the outside. Is your partner impossible, or do you bring out the worst in others? Are you too tolerant, or too demanding? If you could decide which view to accept, you would know just how to behave. You have had it with the slow, self-directed process of psychotherapy; you want a frank and immediate response, an expert opinion.

I am sympathetic toward your wish for immediacy and plain talk. But often people who ask for advice in such matters are really looking for someone to blow up at when the rules indicate they should leave, but they dearly want to stay. Or perhaps you want permission. Sometimes a child can skate only when a parent is on the ice right beside; the parent becomes the child's nerve or guts, even the stiffness in the child's ankles. You may need what the child skater needs: additional self. If this is what you require of me, you will tell me what you already know you should do, and I will confirm your conclusions. But if you have a good supply of self, then the choice you are confronting must be a difficult one, or else you would have already made a decision.

I take it that you are in love, or have been, or think you might be in time. Love, not operatic passion: Those who are swept off their feet rarely ask questions. And since you go to the trouble to seek an expert opinion, you must value the investment of emotion and the crea-tive effort you have put into your relationship. Intimacy matters to you, shared experiences, time together. And you imagine that people should and can exercise control in affairs of the heart.

To this picture I might add that you already know the conventional wisdom. Television, romance novels, late-night radio call-in shows, and self-help books all provide exposure to the tenets of psychotherapy. Characters advise one another continually: Walk away from abuse. Don't bet on actively reforming an alcoholic. Communicate. Compromise on practical matters. Hold fast to your sense of self. Take emotional crises to be opportunities for growth. Expect and accept imperfection. No one is a stranger to these commonplaces.

But you hope to be an exception. You feel different enough to ask whether the conventional bromides illuminate your special predicament. Perhaps you fear that you are inept at judging partners, so that when it is time for others to leave, you should stay, because you will do no better next time. Or you are more vulnerable than others, less able to bear transitions. You have been telling yourself as much, and you hope that a neutral observer will agree.

IRIS'S STORY

HERE IS HOW I IMAGINE WE COME TO MEET. THE BELL RINGS, and you are at my office door. "Iris," I say, not concealing my surprise. My daughter used to play on the same soccer team as your nephew, and I remember admiring your spirit while your marriage and publishing career were unraveling. You assure me that you are not here for psychotherapy. You want help with a predicament.

You have not done well with men, you say. Your large-boned and angular stature, and what they call your fierceness, scares them off. Those few who are attracted to tough women don't give support when you need it,

HOW CAN YOU **STAY** *WITH A* **MAN** *WHO SEES* **YOU** *THIS* **WAY?** *AND YET YOU ARE* **TEMPTED** *TO.*

hate any sign of vulnerability—or are outright sadists. Randall seemed the sole exception. He is a man with enough confidence to enjoy forthright women and enough awareness of his own wounds to allow for frailty.

Randall courted you vigorously, tried to sweep you off your feet. He has given you the happiest two years of your life. He is sweetly handsome, separated, en route to divorce. Having grown up in a difficult family in a neighborhood that chews up its children, he now works with wayward youth. Best of all, unlike your ex-husband, who publicly humiliated you with a younger woman, Randall loves you alone.

At least that's what you thought until two weeks ago, when you went to download your e-mail. You received an extraordinary bundle of messages, all forwarded from bunny@univ.edu. You knew who this Bunny was: a touchy-feely social worker who runs a clinic Randall consults to. She had sent you the modern equivalent of the stack of letters, tied in a ribbon, deposited on the wife's dressing table. Although there was no evidence in the e-mail that Randall had slept with Bunny, he had revealed a few of your intimate secrets—enough to make you physically sick. And in his postings, Randall kept referring to you as Prickly Pear—barbed on the outside, tender within—the same term he had once used for an ex-girlfriend. You suddenly understood his m.o.: commit to one woman, then denigrate her to another.

When you felt able to stand, you left work, stopped for a moment at a florist, and drove to Randall's condo. Once there you shoved your purchase, a small cactus, into the open lips of the disk drive on his PC. For good measure, you erased his hard drive and threw his modem in the oven and set it to self-clean. You packed your clothes and bathroom

paraphernalia. Then you pulled a jar of gravy from the fridge. You spread the contents onto Randall's favorite rug and left his dog Shatzi to do her worst.

As you drove home, you were overcome with the awareness that you love Randall as you have never loved another person. And indeed, since then Randall has done all of the right things. He's broken off contact with Bunny, plied you with flowers, called the lawyer and directed that his divorce be set in motion, resumed treatment with his therapist and invited you in for joint sessions. But you realize that you are in one of the classic bad arrangements between lovers. Ran-

HEADS **I STAY,** *TAILS* **I LEAVE . . .**

For most of human history, the question of whether to leave a long-term relationship was almost irrelevant. Marriage was seen as an unbreakable contract, and the economic perils of a solo existence made abandoning one's partner difficult, particularly for women. Throw in legal and religious restrictions against divorce and leaving simply wasn't an option. As late as 1930 famed psychiatrist Karl Menninger refused to advise women to leave their husbands—even in cases of repeated philandering or abuse.

Today, most of the social and practical impediments to leaving have fallen, but the decision to do so remains psychologically daunting. "There's no litmus test you can give a partner that determines whether you should leave, or whether this person is good partner material," notes family therapist Diane Sollee, M.S.W. So figuring out whether to leave remains a complex and intensely personal calculation incorporating issues ranging from the philosophical—How happy am I?—to the profoundly practical: Can I find somebody better?

The upshot: Nobody can give you a definitive formula for when to try to salvage a relationship and when to move on. But here are some issues to keep in mind:

THAT'S MY STORY AND I'M STICKING TO IT

When pondering whether to leave, most people retrace the history of their relationship, taking a mental inventory of the good times and the bad. But there's a hidden pitfall in this technique, notes University of Minnesota psychologist William J. Doherty, Ph.D., author of *Soul Searching: Why Psychotherapy Must Promote Moral Responsibility.* The problem: Our memories tend to be biased by how we're feeling at the moment. So when people are feeling pessimistic about their relationship, says Doherty, they "unconsciously put a negative spin on everything—how they met, why they got married." And they're more likely to overlook happier times.

Let's say you and your spouse eloped right after high school. If you're feeling hopeless about the relationship at the moment, you're especially likely to describe the elopement as the act of two impulsive, foolish kids. "But two years earlier, when you were feeling better about the relationship, you would have told the story in a whole different way," says Doherty. Instead of viewing your teenage marriage as impulsive, you might have fondly remembered it as an exceedingly romantic act by two people passionately in love.

This memory bias colors the relationship history you present to friends, family, counselors, and other confidants. So these individuals may wind up advising you to pull the plug on a relationship that isn't as bad as you've portrayed. (The same bias, of course, gives you an unrealistically rosy view of your relationship during good times.) And even if you don't consult others, your own ruminations on whether to leave will be similarly slanted. None of this means that your relationship history is irrelevant to the decision to leave—only that the evidence may not be as clear-cut as you initially think.

dall is behaving like a naughty boy who buries himself in the skirts of the mother he has injured and sobs apologies. Looking back, you see that even your tornado-like attack on his apartment was only an enactment of his basic fantasy: woman as avenger. How can you stay with a man who sees you this way?

And yet you are tempted to. That there is something flawed about Randall makes him seem more accessible, less puzzling. Now that his flaws are laid out, you feel pecu-

liarly well-matched with him. After the fall, he seems more truly yours. You feel alive when you are with Randall. You still trust and admire him. Besides, you want to sustain this complex, intimate liaison you have done so much to nurture. Are you mad? Do these things ever work?

To say the obvious—that you must leave a man who has been dishonest, contemptuous, and incapable of commitment—doesn't seem to suffice. I know too little about you to answer the question you are asking, which is not whether most people should leave in these circumstances (they should) but whether you and Randall form an exception. I am taken with the odd detail that you feel more comfortable with Randall after the fall; to you, it is a relief to know that for all his kindness he is as crazy as you. I like your argument that even after the betrayal, there remains in your ledger a balance of trust in Randall's column. And since you are indicating that you have every intention of letting the relationship proceed, I feel unmotivated to throw myself in your path. You're making a bad bet, but I have seen worse bets succeed.

"To go ahead with the relationship will require all of your skills," I say. Business skills, people management skills, negotiation skills, every skill you possess. But you can risk continuing the relationship if you make that risk an occasion for your own maturation, for attaining something you can bring with you if the relationship fails, as it likely will. If you can be single-minded about what you need, and if you can let him be who he is—in that delicate combination of self-assertion and caring and disengagement, there will be hope that you will grow and that he will then grow to meet you.

HOW MOTIVATED IS YOUR PARTNER?

"Assessing whether you should leave may require assessing whether you have tried to stay," notes psychiatrist Peter Kramer, M.D., What he means is that relationships take work, and that couples often abandon relationships that would be successful with a little more effort. Indeed, adds Sollee, it's ironic that couples who are expecting a baby "will take months of classes to get ready for that one hour in which the mother pushes out the baby, but they don't take the time to [get counseling] on how to keep the marriage alive."

Given that every relationship requires effort, the fact that a relationship is somewhat rocky is not in itself a sign that a couple should split. What's more important, says Peter Frankl, M.D., a psychiatrist at New York University School of Medicine, is how motivated the partners are to give each other a chance to work out viable solutions to their particular problems. This motivation, says Frankl, is the best predictor of whether a troubled relationship will succeed. "I've turned around some marriages that were on the brink of divorce," he says. But if your partner isn't motivated to put some work into the relationship, the odds of success fall—and leaving may make more sense.

ADVICE DEPENDS ON THE ADVISOR

Visit three different doctors for your sore throat and you're likely to get similar diagnoses and treatments. Ask three different therapists whether you should leave your ailing relationship, however, and the advice you get may differ dramatically. The reason: a therapist's speciality—marriage counseling, individual therapy, groups—is linked to his or her feelings about commitment.

Marriage and family therapists are, by nature, inclined to keep people together. "I would never advise a couple to divorce," says Atlanta psychiatrist Frank Pittman, M.D., who feels that telling people to end a marriage is akin to advising a parent to put a child up for adoption. "You don't do it, especially when there are kids involved." (Pittman *did*, feel comfortable, however, advising a pair of newlyweds to break up when he learned that the wife had cheated on her husband during the honeymoon.)

On the other hand, individual therapists, whose training in treating troubled relationships may range from extensive experience to a single seminar in graduate school, are more likely to see a relationship as something that should be sacrificed if it interferes with a client's happiness. "I read a case study of a woman who stayed with the same analyst through five marriages," says Sollee. "And that analyst helped end all five marriages." Minnesota's Bill Doherty calls such cases "therapist-assisted marital suicide," noting that by repeatedly asking their clients whether they are happy, "the therapist is basically saying, 'Why do you stay?' "

Because therapists typically maintain a neutral stance with regard to what a client does—the better to appear objective—these philosophical differences on the importance of saving relationships may not be immediately apparent. But they're always present, warns Doherty. The lesson for those who seek counsel from therapists: Keep in mind that the advice you get may be more of a reflection of your therapist's personal values than a scientifically valid assessment of the "correct" thing to do.—P.D.

WHY STAY?

AS A THERAPIST, I LEAN IN THE DIRECTION of reconciliation. I lean that way in part because of my experience that simple interventions sometimes suffice to hold together couples who seem on the verge of separation, and that those repaired relationships proceed ordinarily well. Moreover, second marriages do not seem gloriously better than first marriages, or if they do, it is

I **LIKE** *YOUR* **ARGUMENT** *THAT*
EVEN **AFTER** *THE* **BETRAYAL**
THERE REMAINS A BALANCE OF **TRUST.**

often because the second marriage benefits from efforts or compromises that might as readily have been applied to the first.

People tend to choose partners who operate at an emotional level similar to their own. To stay with a flawed relationship thus may entail tacit acknowledgment of your own limitations. And coming to grips with your limitations, and those of your relationships, is an important form of personal development. If you are loyal and slow to say goodbye, I might say leave, because leaving would represent facing your fears. But if your tendency is to cut and run, I lean towards staying and altering perspective. If you leave, will you find greater satisfaction elsewhere? Most relationships, after all, are practice. That's why, in a culture that allows dating, people have more relationships than they have marriages. Not only because they're finding the right person, but because they're learning how to do it.

SANDY AND MARK

PERHAPS YOU HAVE LITTLE IN COMMON WITH IRIS. YOUR STORY is simpler, quieter. As you enter my office, I am aware of a critical sensibility. You approve, I think, of the framed photographs of the walls, though you squint at one and judge it prosaic.

In your soft voice, you say that you have known almost from the start that there were problems in your marriage. Now that you have the chance, you are determined to get a little help about whether to stay on.

You and Mark married just after high school and then moved from your hometown. It has always been Mark-and-Sandy: People run the words together, like warm and sunny or, lately, cool and cloudy. You shared fine taste, an appreciation of the arts and of the art in daily life. Having seen enough fighting and drinking in your own families as you grew up, you promised implicitly to protect each other from any more indignities.

Then you panicked when Mark leaned on you in his childish way. He resented the stress of competition on the job and the pressures associated with being a breadwinner, and would come home feeling unappreciated. In childhood, you had the responsibility for the care of your brothers, and you never felt you could do right by them. You lacked confidence that you could make another person feel better. So merely to think of Mark heading home worn out and hungry for affection made your day seem black. When he walked through the door and saw you

already drained, he would shrink away. You felt his withdrawal as another sign of your inability to give or elicit nurturance. You became hopeless and more needy than Mark could bear. I hope you will not feel diminished when I say yours has been a marriage between melancholics.

But you maintained the marriage in its early years by carrying on affairs with married men. To you, an adoring man is solace from the isolation Mark imposes. Although you felt dirty, in your bluest states you were buoyed by these dalliances. You felt that you had no choice, that life is too bleak without at least the pretense of admiration. As a result of these affairs, you were more emotionally available for Mark, and your support allowed Mark to do better at the office. And what surprised you through the course of these events is how much tenderness you continued to feel for Mark. He tries hard in a world he is not made for, and sometimes he succeeds.

Over the past couple of years, your odd jobs—making up gift packages in pharmacies and florist shops, designing window displays for boutiques—have turned into a career. Your work in a fabric shop led to requests that you consult on interior design. A former lover has begun small-scale commercial production of your decorated mirrors, boxes, and picture frames. This good luck has allowed you to feel secure month in, month out. There are no more lovers, though with your patron the door is open, especially now that his own marriage is headed for divorce.

For a while Mark seemed to disapprove of your commercial success, as if you had gone over to the enemy, the movers and shakers, in a way that were disloyal to your joint view of the world. Now Mark has told you he has a platonic girlfriend. He needed you to know of his near-peccadillo, because for him it throws the marriage into question. You know he does not really want a lover. He is asking for reassurance that you, despite your success, still want him. Lately, however, you have found yourself thinking that here is an opportune moment for you to leave.

I recognize this crisis—change in a member of a depressive couple. Marriages between emotionally sensitive people can be models of the best human beings are capable of. But the result can also be a stifling sort of peas-in-a-pod marriage such as yours, one made overtly stable by an implicit promise never to change, never to move toward the wider world. Although the stalemate

If YOU ARE **LOYAL,** *I MIGHT SAY*
LEAVE, *BECAUSE*
LEAVING **REPRESENTS**
FACING YOUR **FEARS.**

is often broken when a patient is "transformed" by medication, career success such as yours can have this function too. Now you are over your depression, and the question is whether you should stay.

This is a moment for remarriage or separation. Since you care so deeply for Mark and admire so many of his qualities, and since you have come so far with him, you may choose to let the marriage play itself out further. You could suggest to Mark that he seek treatment for depression, although what seems to be at issue is personality style rather than illness. If you stay put, you may next find Mark turning angry, which I would consider progress. Or you may find instead that he will move forward to join you, and you will be able to judge, after these many years together, whether a period of real marriage is possible.

Are you thinking of divorce and marriage to your patron entrepreneur? How could you not be? This is a frequent response to recovery from prolonged depression—entry into a highly "normal" marriage, one focused on pleasure rather than ideals, on the future rather than the past. This solution has its dangers. The patron may be someone who enjoys and demands dependency in a wife, while you take pride in your hard-earned autonomy, your quiet toughness and firm balance. And yet I have seen such relationships work. Perhaps your entrepreneur will treasure you and challenge you and rejoice with you in the bounty of life, and you will hold on to what is precious in your sadness without having sadness possess you.

The only apt advice is to say that you will need to fiddle with this problem as you have with others, quietly, from around the edges, at your own pace. You will need to be an artisan, here as elsewhere, and to rely on your unerring sense of the fitting. You seem someone who would prefer to find just the right time for leaving and to craft your exit in a way that pleases you—if you are to leave at all.

MATTER OF TRUST

How does a person whose faith in his or her partner has been breached decide whether to stay? Hungarian psychiatrist Ivan Boszormenyi-Nagy refers to what he calls "residual trust." Loss of trustworthiness, he observes, is rarely absolute. Each relationship contains an invisible slate or ledger of give and take, what I might call a "trust fund." Partners deposit trustworthy acts, earn merited entitlement, and owe due obligations. Strong balance sheets make stable marriages. But if one partner continually overdraws the account, the other will feel justified in retaliating or leaving—though other factors, such as good sex, excessive guilt, or power arrangements, might complicate the decision.

An additional complication is that people are poor bookkeepers. They attribute credits and debts to the wrong accounts. In Nagy's view, ethical relations are in-

tergenerational. A child is due reliable care by his parents and is owed restitution if he doesn't get it, but once he reaches adulthood there is no one appropriate from whom to seek it. So the deprived child will enter adulthood with a destructive sense of entitlement. In marriage, this creates further injustice, since it is not the spouse who created the imbalance in the books. Perhaps you demand excessive loyalty because you have been treated disloyally elsewhere, just as your wife demands support that she has been denied elsewhere. If you treat the other unjustly, however, the relationship will be further depleted of resources of trust.

NORA

What made you ask for a consultation is something that will sound trivial. Philip gave you a public tongue-lashing at a recent party, and the hostess took you aside. Nora, she said, if you will not stay here with me tonight and tell Philip goodbye, you must at least promise that you will see someone else.

You want me to understand how decent Philip can be. Often you wonder what's wrong with you that you cannot bring that Philip back. What you loved was his self-assurance, his calm in the face of turmoil. Back then, you were attractive, and—you wonder whether I can believe this—accustomed to avid responses from men. In

"The only distinctive thing I know about ending enslavement in a relationship is that sometimes you get a gift—an act by your partner that crystalizes what you should do."

Philip, you met a man who made you want to earn his admiration. You gladly merged your consulting business into his, and moved from a business relationship to courtship.

When you discovered you were pregnant by Philip, you were secretly thrilled. You had believed you were infertile, because in years of unprotected sex with an old boyfriend, you had never conceived. But Philip turned icy cold—how could you do this to him? He would marry you, but on the condition that you abort the pregnancy. You aborted, which was more horrible for you than Philip could know, or that you would let him know, since you wanted to enter the marriage as the sort of woman he demanded, a happy one. What was funny was that you loved him all the more, loved his little boy squeamishness about intimacy.

After the marriage you started falling apart, failing him in small but important ways. At the office, you might fail to pass on a phone message, or in the middle of a meeting make a comment that infuriated him. He began to demand—with every reason—that you stay in the office and do grunt work.

When Philip was finally ready to have children, you failed to give him any. There has been unspoken resentment about that, you suspect. And now you sometimes wonder if he is turning his attention elsewhere. You came across a document that seems to show he co-owns a condominium with a woman. He yells at you so much over little things, you can't image what would happen if you asked him about the condo.

What put you up to asking for advice was a word in Philip's diatribe at the party—he called you a dried-up prune. You know what he meant: infertile. That one epithet seemed to step over the line. You realized, in a confused moment, that some of what has kept you in the marriage is loyalty to your lost pregnancy—your lost unborn child. After what you sacrificed, the marriage *has* to work. You feel foolish asking whether you should leave a man you love and who has put up with so much from you.

If I thought I could get away with it, if you were not too skittish, I would advise you to leave. But I am afraid that if I give you advice in full measure you will bolt. My first goal is not to lose you; my second is to make you less isolated within your fearful perspective. The only rhetoric at my service is the look on my face when you say "prune." Not horror or astonishment, just your expression plus a little extra. I want to underline what you have said.

Sometimes I think of enslavement in relationships as a hypnotic phenomenon: The enslavers induce a substitution of their will for the subject's. They are vampires, gaining strength as their victim wastes away; the commanding and decisive executive by day flourishes on the blood of the wife he drains by night. Lesser degrees of possession are the root of many ordinary relationship troubles. The demanding impose expectations, while the loyal are exploited for their loyalty.

After 20-odd years in the field, the only distinctive thing I know about ending enslavement is that sometimes you get a gift—an act by your partner that crystalizes what you should do—and if you receive such a gift you had better recognize and accept it. Usually I hear about these gifts in retrospect. A woman who is now doing well tells me about an incredible act of overstepping by her former possessor: He knocked up a single mother with four kids and wanted to move them in. Or the act may seem indistinguishable from the person's habitual behavior, as with Philip's shockingly unreasonable diatribe at the party.

I take your response to the gift Philip offers as an important part of our transaction because it is your own. If you have filled your life with authoritative others who tell you what to do, I will not want to validate that behavior. In highlighting this gift, I hope to instead validate what remains of your perspective. I offer the self-help bromide "listen to your own voice," with this difference: I point to one of your voices and say this one, and not the others. The voice that says: No human being should be asked to give what that man demands nor accept what he imposes.

MY MISGIVINGS ABOUT GIVING ADVICE

Despite the psych jockeys on the radio, despite the widespread acceptance under managed care of therapies that entail little more than the quick proffering of an opinion, despite my own enduring curiosity about advice, I find the prospect of advising slightly illicit. I am suspicious of books of advice: When I read a self-help precept, I think that the opposite advice might be equally apt, for someone. The advice that I have valued in my own life has never turned on fixed maxims or canned metaphors. More crucially, lists of precepts don't work like targeted advice because lists contain inherently constraining messages. They seem to say that complex mat-

> *"I am suspicious of advice books: When I read a self-help precept, I think that the opposite advice might be equally apt. The advice I have valued has never turned on fixed maxims."*

ters are knowable, that a given process leads to foreseeable results. It implies a thin and predictable world, whereas the sort of advice that has mattered to me bespeaks a quite tentative optimism, the optimism of the quest of whose outcome is finally unknowable.

Thus, even after an extended interview, as we have had, you might remain unknown to me in important ways. This, then, is the advisor's dilemma: Like a partner in a troubled relationship, an advisor faces an other who is at once transparent and opaque. I will offer a perspective, you will add it to those you already entertain, and you will stay, or leave, or remain in limbo.

NOW & FOREVER

'It' Doesn't Just Happen

A lifetime prescription for sizzling sex

by Clifford L. Penner and Joyce J. Penner

Do you remember the anticipation of going on a date with your future spouse and how desperately you desired one another? And how the sexual tension seemed to mount as you moved toward marriage? Today you may be wondering, "Where's our energy and desire for sex now?"

After 20 years as sex therapists, we're convinced that good sex in marriage doesn't "just happen." Couples who keep the sexual spark glowing through the changing stages of marriage are those who are deliberate about their sexual relationship.

Early Years

Setting the Stage

Vibrant married sex depends in part on getting off to a good start. Newlyweds must compare and work through their conflicting expectations. The most common surprises couples face are differences regarding how often they have sex and who initiates it. If couples discuss and negotiate their differences, they can avoid a good deal of frustration and confusion.

A few possible solutions to differences in desire are: compromise on frequency; the husband brings his wife pleasure with or without release, even if he doesn't feel the need himself; the two can cuddle while the husband or wife bring him release; increase the amount of nonerotic cuddling; or enjoying sexual intimacy without intercourse or orgasm.

Surprisingly, couples often think they are arguing about frequency when the real issue relates to who

initiates sex. In therapy, when we ask spouses how often each of them initiates sex, a common response is that the husband initiates sex 90 percent of the time and the wife 10 percent. And yet when we ask the same couple how often they each desire sex, he answers three to four times a week, and she says two to three times a week. Frequency isn't the issue, so what's going on?

Men and women differ in how they initiate sex. The wife, for example, might snuggle with her husband and give him a few kisses. If he takes her overture one step further, he seems like the one who is initiating sex since he has become more direct. Over time, this pattern leads a couple to believe the husband is always the pursuer and the wife is never the initiator. Better communication and reversal of roles

can help break this negative pattern, as was the case with Jim and Jenny.

Jim feared that if he left it up to Jenny, they would never have sex. However, he was surprised to learn that she actually enjoyed preparing for and initiating time with him once she gave herself permission to overtly express her desire and he gave her the space to do so.

For some couples, expectations aren't the problem area. Instead, they must work through past sexual experiences that have a way of creeping into their relationship and destroying the joy of new discoveries and unique experiences, as Tony and Beverly learned.

Naturally shy, Tony didn't date much in college. The few relationships he did have involved limited physical contact because of his Christian values. Then he met Beverly. She was everything he wanted in a wife—except she wasn't a virgin. Knowing that Beverly had been sexually active with several serious boyfriends left Tony caught between his attraction to her and his desire to enter marriage as a virgin and marry a virgin.

The intensity of his dismay over Beverly's past didn't hit Tony until a month after he proposed to her. After they married, he continually let her know how disgusted he was with her. He asked detailed questions about her previous boyfriends, then used that information to shame her. Their sex life continued to deteriorate, and finally they sought help.

The first step we recommended was for both Tony and Beverly to experience God's forgiveness. We helped Tony realize that Beverly's actions were not an intentional violation of him as her current husband. He needed to acknowledge that she had been spiritually washed clean before God and could now be considered his virginal bride.

Next, he had to stop asking questions about his wife's past and then learn to distract his mind from any mental images of her previous involvements. We further recommended that they temporarily stop having intercourse and learn to delight in each other by working through a step-by-step retraining program. This process would eventually lead them to re-consummate their marriage based on a foundation of mutual trust and desire.

Finally, many couples have difficulty transferring their premarital passion into their marriages because they have false assumptions about married sex. Jamie had been raised in a warm, nurturing home, but much of her knowledge about sex came from movies and television—especially daytime soap operas. Curtis, on the other hand, had grown up seeing playful flirting and open physical affection between his father and stepmother. Jamie was devastated when Curtis would come up behind her and start fondling her. She was convinced that a satisfying and delightful sex life should be like what is portrayed on the "soaps."

She envisioned the powerful pull of desire and the wooing of a new or "illicit" sexual relationship. Her tears of disappointment left Curtis befuddled, and eventually his frustration over not being able to please her led to outbursts of anger.

To develop a mutually satisfying and delightful love life, couples have to make the shift from the newness of passion to the intimacy of deeply sharing themselves with each other for the joy of companionship and the pleasure of each other's bodies. Jamie needed to counter her myth that passion just happens with the knowledge that she and Curtis were responsible for making great sex happen.

The Middle Years
Making Time, Finding Energy

During marriage's middle years, you may feel as though you are merely surviving sexually. The demands of life use up your energy, and your primary desire is often for sleep, not sex.

> Couples who keep the sexual spark glowing are those who are deliberate about their sexual relationship.

Jerry and Elaine, married for 13 years, know firsthand that with three kids, two careers and other commitments, finding the time and energy for sex is a challenge. However, another issue complicates their love life. Jerry clings to the false assumption that Elaine should be available to him sexually whenever he desires. The reality is that marriage is a license to freedom without demand; not a license to possess and control a spouse.

Couples in the second stage of marriage will find their sex life stymied if they continue to believe certain myths about sex. For instance, if Jerry believes that sex has to be spontaneous to be wonderful, he and Elaine won't be having a whole lot of sex. And when they do have sex, it will come at the end of the day when they are both fatigued—something neither of them would prefer.

Another common myth is that spouses must wait for sexual desire before they initiate lovemaking. If they follow that principle, couples can expect to do a lot of waiting and not much acting. Activities and jobs are not the only distractions. At this stage, the privacy necessary for sexual freedom must be protected. For the sexual relationship to survive the challenges of these middle years, private, uninterrupted time for the two of you must be planned into your schedule.

You must keep the pilot light of your sexual relationship lit—even if you don't have the time and energy to turn the flames up as high as you used to. But how do you do that?

- *Keep kissing, passionately, every day.* Kissing is the barometer of the state of your sexual relationship.
- *Keep open by sharing every day.* Also, plan regular times to talk about sex. Talk about what you like and don't like. Share your dreams and desires. Negotiate your differences. Don't give up.
- *Keep committed to sex, in spite of all the distractions.* Your marriage and sexual relationship must continue to be high priorities. Be cautious of commitments that rob you of time for one another.
- *Keep physically fit.* Rather than watch TV, take a walk together or go bicycle riding. In fact, the best thing you can do for your sex life is to put the TV in the garage!
- *Keep well-groomed.* Maintaining proper care of your body and practicing good hygiene show that you care about and respect your spouse.
- *Keep your sexual feelings turned toward home.* Fantasize being with each other. If sexual feelings are triggered in response to someone other than your mate, immediately put your spouse in the picture and bring the spark home!
- *Keep scheduled.* Just as you need to schedule quality time with your family or individual time with a child, you need to schedule time for your sexual relationship.
- *Keep sex positive.* Your sexual times will be most satisfying if they are free of demand and anxiety and full of care, warmth, physical pleasure and fun.
- *Keep learning about your own body and your mate's body.* Read books on sexual enhancement out loud together. Experiment with new ideas.
- *Keep coming up with surprises to keep sex from becoming boring.* Leave a love note on your spouse's pillow, light a candle, buy new sheets or change your position in bed.

The Later Years
Saving the Best for Last
With children out on their own, personal distractions reduced and work pressures lessened, marriage's later years can be the most delightful, relaxed years of a couples' sexual life. When our last child left for college three years ago, she wondered if we'd get bored.

Far from it! We can spontaneously have a candlelight dinner by the fireplace and make love anytime, anywhere. We're once again enjoying the freedom we had in the early years of our marriage, a freedom that we gladly relinquished during the 26 years we had children at home.

In a society that worships youth and disregards the elderly, it is not uncommon to encounter the attitude that sexual activity among the "older set" is suspect or strange. Since sex is so highly connected with the virility of youth, it is no wonder that some people assume sexuality disappears as the skin wrinkles and the hair turns gray. But couples who remain sexually

Past sexual experiences have a way of creeping into a marriage and destroying the joy of new discoveries.

active to the end are likely to be healthier and happier as well as more agile and virile. In fact, the oldest couple we've ever counseled was an 85-year-old man and his 84-year-old wife. They just needed a few sessions for some "mid-course" adaptation!

Certain physical changes are to be expected as the body ages, and those changes naturally affect sexual functioning. However, knowing what to expect can eliminate some of the stress you may experience as you adjust to the changes.

The production of estrogen and progesterone decrease when a woman reaches menopause. Physical and emotional symptoms accompany the hormonal changes. Hot flashes, general aches and pains and weight gain are common. Emotional reactions such as depression, anxiety or erratic mood swings can affect the sexual relationship. The physical changes that most affect sex are a thinning of the vaginal wall, a lessening of vaginal lubrication and a sluggishness of the vaginal muscle. Hormonal replacement therapy, a vaginal lubricant, regular exercise, exercise of the vaginal muscle and good nutrition with a vitamin-mineral supplement can increase a woman's sense of well-being and sexual pleasure.

Men must also adapt to the changes that come as a result of lower testosterone levels. A husband may experience less urgent, and possibly less frequent, sexual desire. He will likely require direct penile stimulation to get aroused rather than responding to visual stimulation. His erections may not be as firm as they once were, but will still be sufficient for entry. He may not need to ejaculate with each experience, and his ejaculations will be less intense. But neither of these changes should detract from his satisfaction.

At any stage of life, an illness or accident may interfere with typical sexual patterns, but this is more likely true with aging. Touch and the intimacy of closeness are even more important when dealing with physical limitations. Pleasure does not need to stop; it may only need to change. New positions, such as lying side by side, may actually add a new spark. Sex in the morning or after a nap when both of you are well rested may be better.

There is something beautiful about two people enjoying physical intimacy in their fading years just as they did in their blooming years. Older couples can do most anything the young can do—it just may take them longer.

A married life of greater love, passion and intimacy begins with a husband who adores and affirms his wife, and a wife who invites her husband to share in all her sexual intensity. And that can only happen when couples commit time and energy to creating a rewarding, healthy sex life—from the honeymoon night right through to their golden years.

Clinical psychologist Clifford Penner, Ph.D., and Joyce Penner, a clinical nurse specialist, practice in Pasadena. California. They are co-authors of Getting Your Sex Life Off to a Great Start *(Word),* Restoring the Pleasure *(Word) and* Men and Sex *(Thomas Nelson).*

Celibate Passion

The hidden rewards of quitting sex

Kathleen Norris
The Christian Century

Kathleen Norris is the author of Dakota *(Ticknor & Fields, 1993).*

Celibacy is a field day for ideologues. Conservative Catholics tend to speak of celibacy as if it were an idealized, angelic state, while feminist theologians such as Uta Ranke-Heinemann say, angrily, that celibate hatred of sex is hatred of women. That celibacy constitutes the hatred of sex seems to be a given in popular mythology, and we need only look at newspaper accounts of sex abuse by priests to see evidence of celibacy that isn't working. One could well assume that this is celibacy, impure and simple. And this is unfortunate, because celibacy practiced rightly is not at all a hatred of sex; in fact it has the potential to address the troubling sexual idolatry of our culture.

One benefit of the nearly ten years that I've been affiliated with the Benedictines as an oblate, or associate, has been the development of deep friendships with celibate men and women. This has led me to ponder celibacy that works, practiced by people who are fully aware of themselves as sexual beings but who express their sexuality in a celibate way. That is, they manage to sublimate their sexual energies toward another purpose than sexual intercourse and procreation. Are they perverse, their lives necessarily stunted? Cultural prejudice would say yes, but I have my doubts. I've seen too many wise old monks and nuns whose celibate practice has allowed them to incarnate hospitality in the deepest sense. In them, the constraints of celibacy have somehow been transformed into an openness. They exude a sense of freedom.

The younger celibates are more edgy. Still contending mightily with what one friend calls "the raging orchestra of my hormones," they are more obviously struggling to contain their desire for intimacy and physical touch within the bounds of celibacy. Often they find their loneliness intensified by the incomprehension of others. In a culture that denies the value of their striving, they are made to feel like fools, or worse.

Americans are remarkably tone-deaf when it comes to the expression of sexuality. The sexual formation that many of us receive is like the refrain of an old Fugs song: "Why do ya like boobs a lot—ya gotta like boobs a lot." The jiggle of tits and ass, penis and pectorals assaults us everywhere—billboards, magazines, television, movies. Orgasm becomes just another goal; we undress for success. It's no wonder that in all this powerful noise, the quiet tones of celibacy are lost.

But celibate people have taught me that celibacy, practiced rightly, does indeed have something valuable to say to the rest of us. Specifically, they have helped me better appreciate both the nature of friendship and what it means to be married. They have also helped me recognize that celibacy, like monogamy, is not a matter of the will disdaining and conquering the desires of the flesh, but a discipline requiring what many people think of as undesirable, if not impossible—a conscious form of sublimation. Like many people who came into adulthood during the sexually permissive 1960s, I've tended to equate sublimation with repression. But my celibate friends have made me see the light; accepting sublimation as a normal part of adulthood makes me more realistic about human sexual capacities and expression. It helps me better respect the bonds and boundaries of marriage.

Any marriage has times of separation, ill health, or just plain crankiness in which sexual intercourse is ill advised. And it is precisely the skills of celibate friendship—fostering intimacy through letters, conversation,

From *Utne Reader,* September/October 1996, pp. 51–53. Originally from *The Christian Century,* March 20, 1996. Adapted from *The Cloister Walk* by Kathleen Norris. © 1996 by Kathleen Norris. Reprinted by permission of Riverhead Books, a division of The Putnam Publishing Group.

performing mundane tasks together (thus rendering them pleasurable), savoring the holy simplicity of a shared meal or a walk together at dusk—that help a marriage survive the rough spots. When you can't make love physically, you figure out other ways to do it.

The celibate impulse in monasticism runs deep and has an interfaith dimension. It is the Dalai Lama who has said, "If you're a monk, you're celibate. If you're not celibate, you're not a monk." Monastic people are celibate for a very practical reason: The kind of community life to which they aspire can't be sustained if people are pairing off. Even in churches in which the clergy are often married—Episcopal and Russian Orthodox, for example—their monks and nuns are celibate. And while monastic novices may be carried along for a time on the swells of communal spirit, when that blissful period inevitably comes to an end the loneliness is profound. One gregarious monk in his early 30s told me that just as he thought he'd settled into the monastery, he woke up in a panic one morning, wondering if he'd wake up lonely for the rest of his life.

Another monk I know regards celibacy as the expression of an essential human loneliness, a perspective that helps him as a hospital chaplain when he is called upon to minister to the dying. I knew him when he was still resisting his celibate call. The resistance usually came out as anger directed toward his abbot and community, more rarely as misogyny. I was fascinated to observe the process by which he came to accept the sacrifices that a celibate, monastic life requires. He's easier to be with now; he's a better friend.

This is not irony so much as grace: In learning to be faithful to his vow of celibacy, the monk developed his talent for relationship. It's a common story. I've seen the demands of Benedictine hospitality—the requirement that all visitors be received as Christ—convert shy young men who fear women into monks who can enjoy their company.

Celibates tend to value friendship very highly. And my friendships with celibate men, both gay and straight, give me some hope that men and women don't live in alternate universes. In 1990s America, this sometimes feels like a countercultural perspective. Male celibacy, in particular, can become radically countercultural insofar as it rejects the consumerist model of sexuality that reduces a woman to the sum of her parts. I have never had a monk friend make an insinuating remark along the lines of "You have beautiful eyes" (or legs, breasts, knees, elbows, nostrils), the kind of remark women grow accustomed to deflecting. A monk is supposed to give up the idea of possessing anything, including women.

Ideally, in giving up the sexual pursuit of women (whether as demons or as idealized vessels of purity) the male celibate learns to relate to them as human beings. That many fail to do so, that the power structures of the Catholic Church all but dictate failure in this regard, comes as no surprise. What is a surprise is what happens when it works. For when men have truly given up the idea of possessing women, a healing thing occurs. I once met a woman in a monastery guest house who had come there because she was pulling herself together after being raped, and she needed to feel safe around men again. I've seen young monks astonish an obese and homely college student by listening to her with as much interest and respect as to her conventionally pretty roommate. On my 40th birthday, as I happily blew out four candles on a cupcake ("one for each decade," a monk in his 20s cheerfully proclaimed), I realized that I could enjoy growing old with these guys.

As celibacy takes hold in a person, as monastic values supersede the values of the culture outside the monastery, celibates become people who can radically affect those of us out "in the world," if only because they've learned how to listen without possessiveness, without imposing themselves. In talking to someone who is practicing celibacy well, we may sense that we're being listened to in a refreshingly deep way. And this is the purpose of celibacy, not to attain some impossibly cerebral goal mistakenly conceived as "holiness," but to make oneself available to others, body and soul. Celibacy, simply put, is a form of ministry—not an achievement one can put on a résumé but a subtle form of service. In theological terms, one dedicates one's sexuality to God through Jesus Christ, a concept and a terminology I find extremely hard to grasp. All I can do is catch a glimpse of people who are doing it, incarnating celibacy in a mysterious, pleasing, and gracious way.

The attractiveness of the celibate is that he or she can make us feel appreciated, enlarged, no matter who we are. I have two nun friends who invariably have this effect on me, no matter what the circumstances of our lives on those occasions when we meet. The thoughtful way in which they converse, listening and responding with complete attention, is a marvel. And when I first met a man I'll call Tom, I wrote in my notebook, "Such tenderness in a man . . . and a surprising, gentle, kindly grasp of who I am."

I realized that I had found a remarkable friend. I was also aware that Tom and I were fast approaching the rocky shoals of infatuation—a man and a woman, both decidedly heterosexual, responding to each other in unmistakably sexual ways. We laughed a lot; we had playful conversations as well as serious ones; we took delight in each other. At times we were alarmingly responsive to one another, and it was all too easy to fantasize about expressing that responsiveness in physical ways.

The danger was real but not insurmountable; I sensed that if our infatuation were to develop into love, that is, to ground itself in grace rather than utility, our respect for each other's commitments—his to celibacy, mine to monogamy—would make the boundaries of behavior very clear. We had few regrets, and yet for both of us there was an underlying sadness, the pain of something incomplete. Suddenly, the difference between celibate friendship and celibate passion had become a reality; at times the pain was excruciating.

Tom and I each faced a crisis the year we met—his mother died, I suffered a disastrous betrayal—and it was the intensity of those unexpected, unwelcome experiences that helped me to understand that in the realm of the sacred, what seems incomplete or unattainable may be abundance after all. Human relationships are by their nature incomplete—after 21 years my husband remains a mystery to me, and I to him, and that is as it should be. Only hope allows us to know and enjoy the depth of our intimacy.

Appreciating Tom's presence in my life as a miraculous, unmerited gift helped me to place our relationship in its proper, religious context, and also to understand why it was that when I'd seek him out to pray with me, I'd always leave feeling so much better than when I came. This was celibacy at its best—a man's sexual energies so devoted to the care of others that a few words could lift me out of despair, give me the strength to reclaim my life. Celibate love was at the heart of it, although I can't fully comprehend the mystery of why this should be so. Celibate passion—elusive, tensile, holy.

Unit 4

Key Points to Consider

❖ In your opinion, what are the most important characteristics of a contraceptive? Why?

❖ What personal feelings or expectations make you more likely to use contraception regularly?

❖ Under what circumstances might a person not use contraception and risk an unintentional pregnancy?

❖ Should contraceptive responsibilities be assigned to one gender or shared between men and women? Defend your answer.

❖ Have you found a fairly comfortable way to talk about contraception and/or pregnancy risk and prevention with your partner? If so, what is it? If not, what do you do?

❖ In the situation of an unplanned pregnancy, what should be the role of the female and the male with respect to decision making? What if they do not agree?

❖ Should there be some kind of proficiency test or license required in order to be a parent? Why or why not? If you had the responsibility for setting forth the requirements—age, marital status, knowledge of child development, emotional stability, income level, or anything you choose—what would they be and why?

 **Links**   # www.dushkin.com/online/

These sites are annotated on pages 4 and 5.

While human reproduction is as old as humanity, many aspects of it are changing in today's society. Not only have new technologies of conception and childbirth affected the *how* of reproduction, but personal, social, and cultural forces have also affected the *who*, the *when*, and the *when not*. Abortion remains a fiercely debated topic, and legislative efforts for and against it abound. Unplanned pregnancies and parenthood in the United States and worldwide continue to present significant, sometimes devastating, problems for parents, children, families, and society.

In light of the change of attitude toward sex for pleasure, birth control has become a matter of prime importance. Even in our age of sexual enlightenment, some individuals, possibly in the height of passion, fail to correlate "having sex" with pregnancy. In addition, even in our age of astounding medical technology, there is no 100 percent effective, safe, or aesthetically acceptable method of birth control. Before sex can become safe, as well as enjoyable, people must receive thorough and accurate information regarding conception and contraception, birth, and birth control. However, we have learned that information about, or even access to, birth control is not enough. We still have some distance to go to make every child one who is planned for and wanted.

Despite the relative simplicity of the above assertion, abortion and birth control remain emotionally charged issues in American society. While opinion surveys indicate that most of the public supports family planning and abortion, at least in some circumstances, there are certain individuals and groups strongly opposed to some forms of birth control and to abortion. Within the past few years, voices for and against birth control and abortion have grown louder, and, on a growing number of occasions, overt behaviors, including protests and violence, have occurred. Some Supreme Court and legislative efforts have added restrictions to the right to abortion. Others have mandated freer access to abortion and

reproductive choice and have restricted the activities of antiabortion demonstrators. Voices on both sides are raised in emotional and political debate between "we must never go back to the old days" (of illegal and unsafe back-alley abortions) and "the baby has no choice."

The nature and scope of the questions raised about the new technologies of reproduction from contraception and abortion through treatments for infertility or what has become known as "assisted reproduction" have become very complex and far-reaching. Medical, religious, political, and legal experts, as well as concerned everyday people, are debating basic definitions of human life, as well as the rights and responsibilities not only of men, women, and society, but of eggs, sperm donors, and surrogates. The very foundations of our pluralistic society are being challenged. We will have to await the outcome.

The articles in the *Birth Control and Abortion* subsection are designed to inform and update readers on available birth control methods as well as on the myriad of factors that go into individuals' and couples' choices and uses of them. The subsection's two articles demystify the broad range of prescriptions and guidelines for choices of primary and back-up contraceptive methods as well as times and situations where method changes may be indicated. In the fact-filled and comprehensive style that is well known to its readers, *Consumer Reports* asks and answers the question, "How Reliable Are Condoms?" both for birth control and disease prevention.

The first two of the three articles in the second subsection of this reproduction unit focus on pregnancy experiences, especially as they relate to sexuality, and the impact on relationships (see "Six Dads Dish" and "Pregnant Pleasures"). The final article "The Cost of Children" is an eye-opening explanation and calculation of the costs of raising a child from birth to age 21.

Because of the magnitude of recent and current changes occurring in the field of infertility and its treatment, coverage of these topics has been moved to unit six's *Legal and Ethical Issues Related to Sex* subsection.

Protecting Against
Unintended Pregnancy
A Guide To Contraceptive Choices

by Tamar Nordenberg

I am 20 and have never gone to see a doctor about birth control.
My boyfriend and I have been going together for a couple of years and have
been using condoms. So far, everything is fine. Are condoms alone safe enough,
or is something else safe besides the Pill? I do not want to go on the Pill.
—Letter to the Kinsey Institute for Research in Sex, Gender, and Reproduction

This young woman is not alone in her uncertainty about contraceptive options. A 1995 report by the National Academy of Sciences' Institute of Medicine, *The Best Intentions: Unintended Pregnancy and the Well-being of Children and Families,* attributed the high rate of unintended pregnancies in the United States, in part, to Americans' lack of knowledge about contraception. About 6 of every 10 pregnancies in the United States are unplanned, according to the report.

Being informed about the pros and cons of various contraceptives is important not only for preventing unintended pregnancies but also for reducing the risk of illness or death from sexually transmitted diseases (STDs), including AIDS.

The Food and Drug Administration has approved a number of birth control methods, ranging from over-the-counter male and female condoms and vaginal spermicides to doctor-pre-

From *FDA Consumer,* April 1997, pp. 20-26. Reprinted by permission of *FDA Consumer,* the magazine of the U.S. Food and Drug Administration.

scribed birth control pills, diaphragms, intrauterine devices (IUDs), injected hormones, and hormonal implants. Other contraceptive options include fertility awareness and voluntary surgical sterilization.

"On the whole, the contraceptive choices that Americans have are very safe and effective," says Dennis Barbour, president of the Association of Reproductive Health Professionals, "but a method that is very good for one woman may be lousy for another."

The choice of birth control depends on factors such as a person's health, frequency of sexual activity, number of partners, and desire to have children in the future. Effectiveness rates, based on statistical estimates, are another key consideration (see "Birth Control Guide"). FDA is developing a more consumer-friendly table to be added to the labeling of all contraceptive drugs and devices.

Barrier Methods

• *Male condom.* The male condom is a sheath placed over the erect penis before penetration, preventing pregnancy by blocking the passage of sperm.

A condom can be used only once. Some have spermicide added, usually nonoxynol-9 in the United States, to kill sperm. Spermicide has not been scientifically shown to provide additional contraceptive protection over

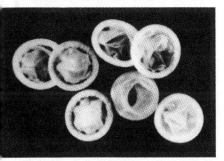

the condom alone. Because they act as a mechanical barrier, condoms prevent direct vaginal contact with semen, infectious genital secretions, and genital lesions and discharges.

Most condoms are made from latex rubber, while a small percentage

are made from lamb intestines (sometimes called "lambskin" condoms). Condoms made from polyurethane have been marketed in the United States since 1994.

Except for abstinence, latex condoms are the most effective method for reducing the risk of infection from the viruses that cause AIDS, other HIV-related illnesses, and other STDs.

Some condoms are prelubricated. These lubricants don't provide more birth control or STD protection. Non-oil-based lubricants, such as water or KY jelly, can be used with latex or lambskin condoms, but oil-based lubricants, such as petroleum jelly (Vaseline), lotions, or massage or baby oil, should not be used because they can weaken the material.

• *Female condom.* The Reality Female Condom, approved by FDA in April 1993, consists of a lubricated polyurethane sheath shaped similarly to the male condom. The closed end, which has a flexible ring, is inserted

into the vagina, while the open end remains outside, partially covering the labia.

The female condom, like the male condom, is available without a prescription and is intended for one-time use. It should not be used together with a male condom because they may not both stay in place.

• *Diaphragm.* Available by prescription only and sized by a health professional to achieve a proper fit, the diaphragm has a dual mechanism to prevent pregnancy. A dome-shaped rubber disk with a flexible rim covers the cervix so sperm can't reach the uterus, while a spermicide applied to the diaphragm before insertion kills sperm.

The diaphragm protects for six hours. For intercourse after the six-hour period, or for repeated intercourse within this period, fresh spermicide should be placed in the vagina with the diaphragm still in place. The diaphragm should be left in place for at least six hours after the last intercourse but not for longer than a total of 24 hours because of the risk of toxic shock syndrome (TSS), a rare but potentially fatal infection. Symptoms of TSS include sudden fever, stomach upset, sunburn-like rash, and a drop in blood pressure.

• *Cervical cap.* The cap is a soft rubber cup with a round rim, sized by a health professional to fit snugly around the cervix. It is available by prescription only and, like the diaphragm, is used with spermicide.

It protects for 48 hours and for multiple acts of intercourse within this time. Wearing it for more than 48 hours is not recommended because of the risk, though low, of TSS. Also, with prolonged use of two or more days, the cap may cause an unpleasant vaginal odor or discharge in some women.

• *Sponge.* The vaginal contraceptive sponge has not been available since the sole manufacturer, Whitehall Laboratories of Madison, N.J., voluntarily stopped selling it in 1995. It remains an approved product and could be marketed again.

The sponge, a donut-shaped polyurethane device containing the spermicide nonoxynol-9, is inserted into the vagina to cover the cervix. A woven polyester loop is designed to ease removal.

The sponge protects for up to 24 hours and for multiple acts of intercourse within this time. It should be left in place for at least six hours after intercourse but should be removed no more than 30 hours after insertion because of the risk, though low, of TSS.

Vaginal Spermicides Alone

Vaginal spermicides are available in foam, cream, jelly, film, suppository, or tablet forms. All types contain a sperm-killing chemical.

Studies have not produced definitive data on the efficacy of spermicides alone, but according to the authors of *Contraceptive Technology,* a leading resource for contraceptive information, the failure rate for typical users may be 21 percent per year.

Package instructions must be carefully followed because some spermicide products require the couple to wait 10 minutes or more after inserting the spermicide before having sex. One dose of spermicide is usually effective for one hour. For repeated intercourse, additional spermicide must be applied. And after intercourse, the spermicide has to remain in place for at least six to eight hours to ensure that all sperm are killed. The woman should not douche or rinse the vagina during this time.

Hormonal Methods

• *Combined oral contraceptives.* Typically called "the pill," combined oral contraceptives have been on the market for more than 35 years and are the most popular form of reversible birth control in the United States. This form of birth control suppresses ovulation (the monthly release of an egg from the ovaries) by the combined actions of the hormones estrogen and progestin.

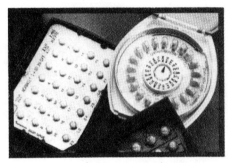

If a woman remembers to take the pill every day as directed, she has an extremely low chance of becoming pregnant in a year. But the pill's effectiveness may be reduced if the woman is taking some medications, such as certain antibiotics.

Besides preventing pregnancy, the pill offers additional benefits. As stated in the labeling, the pill can make periods more regular. It also has a protective effect against pelvic inflammatory disease, an infection of the fallopian tubes or uterus that is a major cause of infertility in women, and against ovarian and endometrial cancers.

The decision whether to take the pill should be made in consultation with a health professional. Birth control pills are safe for most women—safer even than delivering a baby—but they carry some risks.

Current low-dose pills have fewer risks associated with them than earlier versions. But women who smoke—especially those over 35—and women with certain medical conditions, such as a history of blood clots or breast or endometrial cancer, may be advised against taking the pill. The pill may contribute to cardiovascular disease, including high blood pressure,

blood clots, and blockage of the arteries.

One of the biggest questions has been whether the pill increases the risk of breast cancer in past and current pill users. An international study published in the September 1996 journal *Contraception* concluded that women's risk of breast cancer 10 years after going off birth control pills was no higher than that of women who had never used the pill. During pill use and for the first 10 years after stopping the pill, women's risk of breast cancer was only slightly higher in pill users than non-pill users.

Side effects of the pill, which often subside after a few months' use, include nausea, headache, breast tenderness, weight gain, irregular bleeding, and depression.

Doctors sometimes prescribe higher doses of combined oral contraceptives for use as "morning after" pills to be taken within 72 hours of unprotected intercourse to prevent the possibly fertilized egg from reaching the uterus. In a Feb. 25, 1997, *Federal Register* notice, FDA stated its conclusion that, on the basis of current scientific evidence, certain oral contraceptives are safe and effective for this use.

• *Minipills.* Although taken daily like combined oral contraceptives, minipills contain only the hormone progestin and no estrogen. They work by reducing and thickening cervical mucus to prevent sperm from reaching the egg. They also keep the uterine lining from thickening, which prevents a fertilized egg from implanting in the uterus. These pills are generally less effective than combined oral contraceptives.

Minipills can decrease menstrual bleeding and cramps, as well as the risk of endometrial and ovarian cancer and pelvic inflammatory disease. Because they contain no estrogen, minipills don't present the risk of blood clots associated with estrogen in combined pills. They are a good option for women who can't take estrogen because they are breast-feeding or because estrogen-containing products cause them to have severe headaches or high blood pressure.

Side effects of minipills include menstrual cycle changes, weight gain, and breast tenderness.

• *Injectable progestins.* Depo-Provera, approved by FDA in 1992, is injected by a health professional into the buttocks or arm muscle every three months. Depo-Provera prevents pregnancy in three ways: It inhibits ovulation, changes the cervical mucus to help prevent sperm from reaching the egg, and changes the uterine lining to prevent the fertilized egg from implanting in the uterus. The progestin injection is extremely effective in preventing pregnancy, in large part because it requires little effort for the woman to comply: She simply has to get an injection by a doctor once every three months.

The benefits are similar to those of the minipill and another progestin-only contraceptive, Norplant. Side effects are also similar and can include irregular or missed periods, weight gain, and breast tenderness.

(See "Depo-Provera: The Quarterly Contraceptive" in the March 1993 *FDA Consumer.*)

• *Implantable progestins.* Norplant, approved by FDA in 1990, and the newer Norplant 2, approved in 1996, are the third type of progestin-only contraceptive. Made up of matchstick-sized rubber rods, this contraceptive is surgically implanted under the skin of the upper arm, where it steadily releases the contraceptive steroid levonorgestrel.

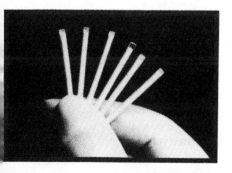

The six-rod Norplant provides protection for up to five years (or until it is removed), while the two-rod Norplant 2 protects for up to three years.

Norplant failures are rare, but are higher with increased body weight.

Some women may experience inflammation or infection at the site of the implant. Other side effects include menstrual cycle changes, weight gain, and breast tenderness.

Intrauterine Devices

An IUD is a T-shaped device inserted into the uterus by a health-care professional. Two types of IUDs are available in the United States: the Paragard CopperT 380A and the Progestasert Progesterone T. The Paragard IUD can remain in place for 10 years, while the Progestasert IUD must be replaced every year.

It's not entirely clear how IUDs prevent pregnancy. They seem to prevent sperm and eggs from meeting by either immobilizing the sperm on their way to the fallopian tubes or changing the uterine lining so the fertilized egg cannot implant in it.

IUDs have one of the lowest failure rates of any contraceptive method. "In the population for which the IUD is appropriate—for those in a mutually monogamous, stable relationship who aren't at a high risk of infection—the IUD is a very safe and very effective method of contraception," says Lisa Rarick, M.D., director of FDA's division of reproductive and urologic drug products.

The IUD's image suffered when the Dalkon Shield IUD was taken off the market in 1975. This IUD was associated with a high incidence of pelvic infections and infertility, and some deaths. Today, serious complications from IUDs are rare, although IUD users may be at increased risk of developing pelvic inflammatory disease. Other side effects can include perforation of the uterus, abnormal bleeding, and cramps. Complications occur most often during and immediately after insertion.

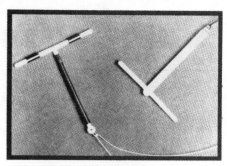

Traditional Methods

• *Fertility awareness.* Also known as natural family planning or periodic abstinence, fertility awareness entails not having sexual intercourse on the days of a woman's menstrual cycle when she could become pregnant or using a barrier method of birth control on those days.

Because a sperm may live in the female's reproductive tract for up to seven days and the egg remains fertile for about 24 hours, a woman can get pregnant within a substantial window of time—from seven days before ovulation to three days after. Methods

to approximate when a woman is fertile are usually based on the menstrual cycle, changes in cervical mucus, or changes in body temperature.

"Natural family planning can work," Rarick says, "but it takes an extremely motivated couple to use the method effectively."

• *Withdrawal.* In this method, also called *coitus interruptus,* the man withdraws his penis from the vagina before ejaculation. Fertilization is prevented because the sperm don't enter the vagina.

Effectiveness depends on the male's ability to withdraw before ejaculation. Also, withdrawal doesn't provide protection from STDs, including HIV.

Birth Control Guide

Efficacy rates in this chart are based on *Contraceptive Technology* (16th edition, 1994). They are yearly estimates of effectiveness in typical use, which refers to a method's reliability in real life, when people don't always use a method properly. For comparison, about 85 percent of sexually active women using no contraception would be expected to become pregnant in a year.

This chart is a summary; it is not intended to be used alone. All product labeling should be followed carefully, and a health-care professional should be consulted for some methods.

Type	Male Condom	Female Condom	Diaphragm with Spermicide	Cervical Cap with Spermicide	Sponge with Spermicide (not currently marketed)	Spermicides Alone
Estimated Effectiveness	88%[a]	79%	82%	64–82%[b]	64–82%[b]	79%
Some Risks[d]	Irritation and allergic reactions (less likely with polyurethane)	Irritation and allergic reactions	Irritation and allergic reactions, urinary tract infection	Irritation and allergic reactions, abnormal Pap test	Irritation and allergic reactions, difficulty in removal	Irritation and allergic reactions
Protection from Sexually Transmitted Diseases (STDs)	Except for abstinence, latex condoms are the best protection against STDs, including herpes and AIDS.	May give some STD protection; not as effective as latex condom.	Protects against cervical infection; spermicide may give some protection against chlamydia and gonorrhea; otherwise unknown.	Spermicide may give some protection against chlamydia and gonorrhea; otherwise unknown.	Spermicide may give some protection against chlamydia and gonorrhea; otherwise unknown.	May give some protection against chlamydia and gonorrhea; otherwise unknown.
Convenience	Applied immediately before intercourse; used only once and discarded.	Applied immediately before intercourse; used only once and discarded.	Inserted before intercourse and left in place at least six hours after; can be left in place for 24 hours, with additional spermicide for repeated intercourse.	May be difficult to insert; can remain in place for 48 hours without reapplying spermicide for repeated intercourse.	Inserted before intercourse and protects for 24 hours without additional spermicide; must be left in place for at least six hours after intercourse; must be removed within 30 hours of insertion; used only once and discarded.	Instructions vary; usually applied no more than one hour before intercourse and left in place at least six to eight hours after.
Availability	Nonprescription	Nonprescription	Prescription	Prescription	Nonprescription; not currently marketed.	Nonprescription

a   Effectiveness rate for polyurethane condoms has not been established.
b   Less effective for women who have had a baby because the birth process stretches the vagina and cervix, making it more difficult to achieve a proper fit.
c   Based on perfect use, when the woman takes the pill every day as directed.
d   Serious medical risks from contraceptives are rare.

Oral Contraceptives—combined pill	Oral Contraceptives—progestin-only minipill	Injection (Depo-Provera)	Implant (Norplant)	IUD (Intrauterine Device)	Periodic Abstinence	Surgical Sterilization—female or male
Over 99%[c]	Over 99%[c]	Over 99%	Over 99%	98–99%	About 80% (varies, based on method)	Over 99%
Dizziness; nausea; changes in menstruation, mood, and weight; rarely, cardiovascular disease, including high blood pressure, blood clots, heart attack, and strokes	Ectopic pregnancy, irregular bleeding, weight gain, breast tenderness	Irregular bleeding, weight gain, breast tenderness, headaches	Irregular bleeding, weight gain, breast tenderness, headaches, difficulty in removal	Cramps, bleeding, pelvic inflammatory disease, infertility, perforation of uterus	None	Pain, bleeding, infection, other minor postsurgical complications
None, except some protection against pelvic inflammatory disease.	None, except some protection against pelvic inflammatory disease.	None	None	None	None	None
Must be taken on daily schedule, regardless of frequency of intercourse.	Must be taken on daily schedule, regardless of frequency of intercourse.	One injection every three months	Implanted by health-care provider—minor outpatient surgical procedure; effective for up to five years.	After insertion by physician, can remain in place for up to one or 10 years, depending on type.	Requires frequent monitoring of body functions (for example, body temperature for one method).	One-time surgical procedure
Prescription	Prescription	Prescription	Prescription	Prescription	Instructions from health-care provider	Surgery

Birth Control In the Body

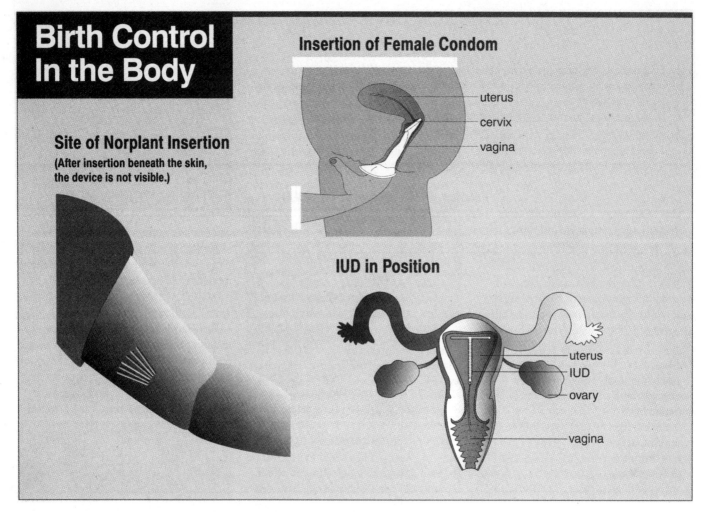

Site of Norplant Insertion
(After insertion beneath the skin, the device is not visible.)

Insertion of Female Condom

uterus
cervix
vagina

IUD in Position

uterus
IUD
ovary
vagina

Infectious diseases can be transmitted by direct contact with surface lesions and by pre-ejaculatory fluid.

Surgical Sterilization

Surgical sterilization is a contraceptive option intended for people who don't want children in the future. It is considered permanent because reversal requires major surgery that is often unsuccessful.

• *Female sterilization.* Female sterilization blocks the fallopian tubes so the egg can't travel to the uterus. Sterilization is done by various surgical techniques performed under general anesthesia.

Complications from these operations are rare and can include infection, hemorrhage, and problems related to the use of general anesthesia.

• *Male sterilization.* This procedure, called a vasectomy, involves sealing, tying or cutting a man's vas deferens, which otherwise would carry the sperm from the testicle to the penis.

Vasectomy involves a quick operation, usually under 30 minutes, with possible minor postsurgical complications, such as bleeding or infection.

Research continues on effective contraceptives that minimize side effects. One important research focus, according to FDA's Rarick, is the development of birth control methods that are both spermicidal and microbicidal to prevent not only pregnancy but also transmission of HIV and other STDs.

Tamar Nordenberg is a staff writer for FDA Consumer.

HOW RELIABLE ARE CONDOMS?

They're the best protection against sexually transmitted diseases. But several popular varieties failed our tests.

Every day some 6000 people around the world become infected with HW, most of them through sex. In the U.S., more than a million people carry the virus that causes AIDS, and the count rises by one every 13 minutes. Nearly everyone knows how AIDS is spread—and how to stop it. Three out of four Americans now know that latex condoms, used correctly and consistently, will block AIDS and other sexually transmitted diseases, says Melissa Shepherd, who heads AIDS education efforts at the Federal Centers for Disease Control and Prevention.

Condom sales, driven by the fear of AIDS, have climbed to 450 million a year in the U.S. Once only whispered about, condoms are now routinely advertised on cable TV and in magazines, are sold in supermarkets, and come in a dizzying variety of styles. (One brand alone promotes nine variations: lubricated, mint-scented, spermicidal, studded, sensitive, ribbed, colored, black, and snug.)

Yet many people who should use condoms still don't, apparently put off by the inconvenience or the feel. A recent survey of people with multiple sex partners, for instance, found that those who never use condoms, or use them inconsistently, outnumbered those who always use them by 11 to 1.

Now there's more bad news: Couples who do use condoms may not be getting all the protection they think they are. How well a condom works is in good part up to the use—some people are more likely than others to break condoms through misuse. But some break-age may be due to real differences among the brands and varieties.

To assess their reliability, we bought and tested 6500 latex condoms—37 different kinds. Among our findings:

■ A half-dozen types of *Trojans*, the best-selling brand, too often flunked an air-inflation test. Long part of many other countries' condom standards, that test was adopted by U.S. inspectors last year after we bought our condoms. Had such guidelines been in place when these condoms were made, and had Government inspectors checked production lots as we did, some lots of those *Trojans* probably would not have made it out the factory door. (One variety of *LifeStyles* condoms failed the same test.)

■ Several condoms promoted as stronger" did not do as well as others in our inflation tests. Inflating condoms checks their elasticity, which experts say is the quality that tends to keep a condom intact during intercourse.

■ Several condoms promoted as "thin" are not especially so, according to our measurements. And the condoms that really are thinnest, although they passed the basic inflation test, tended to break more easily than did the other condoms we tested. They may not provide as much protection as their thicker counterparts.

FOR PREVENTION OF DISEASE

Condoms are considered crucial for slowing the spread of sexually transmitted diseases, because the odds of transmission are cut nearly to zero if condoms are used consistently and correctly. If they're not used, here is the estimated chance that microbes will be transmitted from one infected partner to the other during a single act of intercourse.

Microbe for:	male-to-female	female-to-male
Gonorrhea	50 to 90 %	20 %
Genital herpes	0.2	0.05
AIDS	0.1 to 20	0.01 to 10

Source: K.M. Stone, HIV, STDs, and Other Barriers. In Barrier Contraceptives, Current Status and Future Prospects, 1994.

From *Consumer Reports*, May 1995, pp. 320–325. © by Consumers Union of U.S., Inc., Yonkers, NY 10703-1057. Reprinted by permission.

A protective barrier

It may not be obvious from the packaging, but all condoms are pretty much the same. They're nearly all made of latex, in the same basic shape, according to industry standards for size and thickness.

Latex condoms are produced by dipping a cylindrical form in liquid latex and heating it. Machines shape and trim the condom's ring; then the new condoms are washed and aged for a number of days, a "curing" that lets the rubber complete the chemical reactions that strengthen the latex. The final steps: rolling and wrapping individual condoms. The basic process hasn't changed much in 50 years.

The industry standards say a condom's width should be no greater than 54 millimeters—about 2⅛ inches—to prevent slippage; "snugger" condoms are about 10 percent narrower. The minimum length is 160 millimeters, roughly 6 ½ inches, but some products are up to 2 inches longer.

Condoms for contraception

As a contraceptive, condoms are cheap and easy to obtain, and usually cause no side effects. (A very small number of people are allergic to latex—see box "Two Ways to Avoid Latex.")

They are not, however, perfect. The condom's reliability in preventing pregnancies depends on how it's measured. Researchers don't count the number of individual condoms that fail; instead they define contraceptive failure as the percentage of women who use a given method but nonetheless become pregnant over a year's time. For condoms, the typical rate is about 12 percent, somewhat worse than birth control pills but better than the diaphragm (see graph below). But researchers know that, as with other methods, the failure figures include many couples who don't use contraception every time.

If couples used condoms consistently and correctly, researchers estimate, the condom's failure rate would plummet to 2 or 3 percent, or perhaps even less. One way some couples might further reduce the failure rate—to an estimated one tenth of a percent, if used consistently—is to use condoms in combination with a vaginal spermicide.

Stopping germs

As a means of preventing the transfer of disease causing microbes between sex partners, condoms have no equal. The condom shields the penis from cervical, vaginal, oral, or rectal secretions. At the same time, the partner is protected from potentially infectious semen and any lesions on the penis.

The need for such protection is apparently greater than many people realize: Every year, 12 million Americans—one-fourth of them teenagers—come down with sexually transmitted diseases. Chlamydia the most common such disease but often unrecognized, can lead to tubal scarring that experts believe is a key factor in the quadrupling of ectopic pregnancies in the last 10 years. And AIDS is still increasing in the U.S., particularly among women. (Gay men still account for the largest number of AIDS cases; there's concern that condom use is falling among younger gay men.)

Chlamydia, gonorrhea, and AIDS—as well as other sexually transmitted diseases—are virtually 100 percent preventable with proper con-

dom use. So well do latex condoms block germs that, since 1987 the U.S. Food and Drug Administration has allowed condom boxes to list all the diseases condoms help avert. More recently, the FDA told companies that the disease prevention message was so crucial, they should also print it on the wrappers of individual condoms. Condom boxes warn that the product is intended for vaginal sex, but health officials say it's crucial to use condoms in anal and oral sex, too.

Preventing sexually transmitted disease is in some ways a more rigorous test of condoms than is preventing pregnancy. While conception is a concern only a few days a month, diseases can be caught all the time. Over the decades since the latex condom's introduction, epidemiologists have amassed considerable evidence that it does cut disease rates, but not quite to zero. A 1992 review in the American Journal of Public Health, summing up the results of many varied studies found that condoms on average cut the risk of infection in half. But the authors said the studies included many couples who failed to use condoms properly or consistently.

When couples are strongly motivated to use condoms every single time, the score greatly improves. Herbert Peterson, chief of the CDC's women's health and fertility branch, cited two recent "block-buster" studies on condoms' use against HIV. Both focused on heterosexual couples, with one partner carrying HIV at the start of the study, who continued to have sex regularly for two years or more.

In the first study, Italian researchers followed more than 300 healthy women in stable, monogamous relationships with HIV-positive men, questioning the women closely about condom use and testing them periodically for HIV. Among women whose partners never or inconsistently used condoms, 12 percent eventually were infected with HIV. By contrast, fewer than 2 percent of the women whose partners always used condoms became infected.

The second report, from the European Study Group, showed even better results for some 250 uninfected men and women with HIV-positive partners. Among the half who used condoms inconsistently, 10 percent of the previously uninfected partners acquired HIV. When condoms were used all the time, however, HIV was never passed on to the healthy partner—even though the average couple had sex about 120 times over the course of the study.

"If everyone used condoms correctly and consistently, we could break the

FOR BIRTH CONTROL

As a contraceptive, condoms are more effective than the diaphragm, less so than the Pill. Below are percentages of women relying on each method who nonetheless become pregnant over a year's time. If birth control is used perfectly—consistently and correctly—failures can be cut dramatically. If no birth control method is used, 85 percent become pregnant.

METHOD	PERCENTAGE WHO BECOME ACCIDENTALLY PREGNANT IN A YEAR
Spermicide	
Rhythm (calendar)	
Withdrawal	
Diaphragm and spermicide	
Condom	
Condom and spermicide	Not available
Pill	
Male sterilization	
Female sterilization	

■ TYPICAL USE
■ PERFECT USE *

0   5   10   15   20   25

Source: "Contraceptive Technology," Irvington Press; and "Family Planning Perspectives" journal.

* Estimated

back of the AIDS epidemic," Peterson told us.

When they fail

An estimated 2 to 5 percent of condoms tear during use. Most of those failures are thought to stem from misuse, not inherent product flaws. (And misuse is common: When the British Consumers' Association asked some 300 Englishmen to demonstrate putting a condom on a model penis, nearly one in five got it wrong—they tried to unroll the condom from the inside out.) Bruce Burlington, who heads the FDA's Center for Devices and Radiological Health, which is responsible for condoms, told a CU reporter that the difference in quality between the best and worst condoms on the market is "tiny compared with the problems that users introduce."

When condoms do break despite being used correctly, it's probably caused by hidden weaknesses in the rubber. Both manufacturers and the Government take steps to catch flawed condoms before they can leave the factory.

Manufacturers test each lot of condoms for leaks and for strength, according to voluntary guidelines set by the American Society for Testing and Materials, the major U.S. standard-setting organization. Those tests, however, which destroy the condoms being examined, can be used only to spot-check a batch of condoms, not to check individual condoms before packaging and sale.

Companies can test every condom for leaks, with a gentler but telling electrical procedure. In one variant of the test, each condom is placed on a charged metal form and swept over by a soft, conductive brush. Minute holes in the condoms trip circuitry that shunts many "leakers" aside. Sometimes this test finds thin spots as well.

The FDA, which regulates condoms as medical devices, sends inspectors to factories unannounced. They review production records and examine stock at random, checking for cracked, moldy, dry, or sticky rubber. The inspectors also test the condoms—until now primarily with a water-leakage test. In this protocol, they pour 10 ounces of water into a condom, then press and roll it along blotter paper. Should leaks turn up in the equivalent of more than 4 per 1000 condoms in a run, the manufacturer must scrap the entire lot, perhaps tens of thousands of condoms.

In 1993, the latest year for which we could obtain data, the FDA rejected 2 of the 44 lots of domestic condoms it checked for leakage. The FDA tests every batch of imported condoms as well, though imports account for very few condoms used in this country.

Although the smallest hole the water test can find is 100 times bigger than the HIV virus, officials believe the test is sufficient. The laboratory and clinical studies of HIV persuade them that smaller holes are rare or possibly even nonexistent. Such minute holes are a problem for "skin" condoms, however (see box on next page).

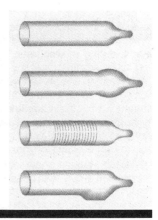

Shapes vary The brands we tested included plain condoms (Ramses), contoured (Saxon Gold), textured (Trojans Ribbed), and an unusual pouch (Pleasure Plus).

How we tested condoms

When we last tested condoms, in 1989, none of the brands we checked failed the water test. This time, we concentrated on air-burst testing, which we think better predicts breakage in use. Condoms are locked onto an apparatus that slowly inflates them until they're bigger than a watermelon and finally burst with the bang of a gunshot. Meters record the volume of air and amount of pressure the condom withstand.

Unlike tests of tensile strength—done by stretching a band cut from the condom—air-burst testing stresses the entire condom. Last year, the FDA added the air-burst test to its inspectors' repertoire, and asked the companies to include it in their internal quality-control regimens. The testing guidelines are expected to be adopted shortly as the industry standard.

Published research has linked a condom's air-burst volume to its resistance

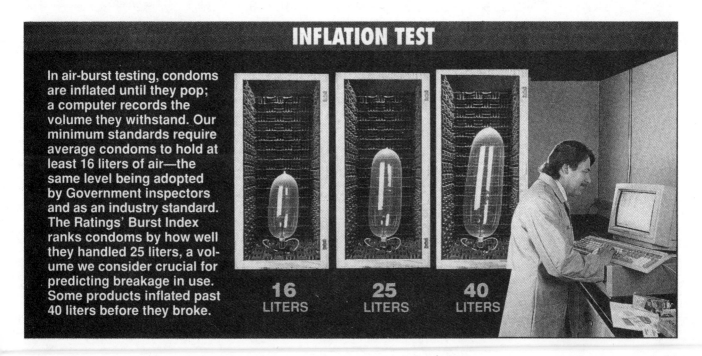

INFLATION TEST

In air-burst testing, condoms are inflated until they pop; a computer records the volume they withstand. Our minimum standards require average condoms to hold at least 16 liters of air—the same level being adopted by Government inspectors and as an industry standard. The Ratings' Burst Index ranks condoms by how well they handled 25 liters, a volume we consider crucial for predicting breakage in use. Some products inflated past 40 liters before they broke.

16 LITERS   **25** LITERS   **40** LITERS

to breakage during use. Scientists believe that a condom's "extensibility"—its stretchiness—is what helps keep it whole during intercourse. The air-burst test assesses that vital quality.

We tested about 120 individual condoms for each of the 37 styles we bought. To see as many lots as possible for each product, we generally combined samples from five different lots, identifiable by date codes on boxes.

As the Ratings show, our tests were designed to answer two questions: whether a condom passes a minimal standard and, if so, how well it performs on a tougher test, a measure of a product's tendency to break in use. To make the first cut, our combined lots of each product had to pass the new Government air-burst requirement. That rule allows no more than 1 ½ percent of condoms in a lot to fall short of the required pressure and volume limits. Average-sized condoms, for instance, are supposed to inflate to at least about 16 liters (it varies with condom width) before breaking. Using statistical techniques, inspectors can sample a production run and project a failure rate for the entire lot.

Seven products we tested did not meet that minimal requirement. In each case, at least 4 out of 120 condoms broke too soon during inflation. Based on statistical projections, we believe that more than 1 ½ percent of condoms in at least some of those products' manufacturing lots would not have inflated to the required minimum volume of air. The products include six styles of Trojans—

Other Condom Options
TWO WAYS TO AVOID LATEX

If latex condoms irritate your skin, the culprit may be the lubricant, the spermicide, or the materials used in processing; try switching brands. If that doesn't work, you may be among the small percentage of people whose skin is sensitive to latex itself. You have two other choices in condoms, each with pluses and minuses.

'Skin' condoms

Made from a natural pouch in lambs' intestines, these condoms cost several times as much as latex ones. The membrane is especially strong and may enhance sensitivity. The downside: They have small holes.

The microscopic pores can be up to 1.5 microns across. Since sperm cells are twice as wide as that, skin condoms still make an effective contraceptive. But viruses and some bacteria are far smaller than these pores (see diagram). Lab work has shown that HIV and the herpes and hepatitis-B viruses can pass through skin condoms. So these condoms must bear a warning that they are not intended for disease prevention.

We examined *Fourex* and *Kling-Tite Naturalamb* brands. *Fourex* condoms come folded, not rolled, inside plastic capsules (the condom is pulled on, like a glove). We found the capsules surprisingly hard to open. *Kling-Tite* may be easier to don because it's rolled, like a latex condom. Skin condoms might slip off some men during intercourse because both *Fourex* and *Kling-Tite* are significantly wider than the latex condoms we tested: 78 and 68 millimeters, respectively (latex condoms average 52 millimeters). The *Fourex* has a rubber band rolled onto the base of the condom to prevent slippage. The *Kling-Tite's* elastic band is sewn on more securely.

Polyurethane condoms

Last year, on the basis of limited testing, the FDA gave Schmid Laboratories approval to sell its new *Avanti* brand, a clear condom made of polyurethane. The agency justified approving the product because it felt a pressing public-health need to offer latex-sensitive people an alternative that could prevent disease as well as pregnancy. The *Avanti* condoms first appeared in Western states and should be available elsewhere by summer. But it's unclear just how much protection they offer. A label on the foil packet declares it "effective" against pregnancy and sexually transmitted diseases, while the label on the box warns that "the risks of pregnancy and STDs . . . are not known for this condom." The FDA says it has noted the discrepancy; the packet label will be changed to match the box.

The manufacturer says it has demonstrated to the FDA that *Avanti* does block viruses and neither slips nor breaks more often than latex. Studies of its contraceptive value are under way.

We bought *Avanti* and *Avanti Super Thin,* which cost us $1.75 each, more than the most expensive latex condoms. Both products are in fact the same condom; the *Super Thins* come with more lubricant.

In the lab, we found the condoms thinner than any conventional condoms tested—roughly 0.04 millimeters. They are also among the shortest of condoms but wider than even larger-size latex brands (60 millimeters versus 55 or 56). That's probably because polyurethane doesn't stretch as much as latex. Despite the com-

pany's statements to the contrary, we suspect some men might have slippage problems. When we placed the *Avanti* on a model of an average-sized penis, we found we could pull the condom off quite easily.

Since *Avanti* isn't latex, the label claims that any lubricant may be used safely. We cannot comment on the *Avanti's* strength. Because synthetic condoms are so new, researchers don't know how to compare their performance in standard tests against that of latex condoms.

Mixed messages

The box and packets of this new polyurethane condom bear conflicting messages about users' risks of disease or pregnancy. The correct answer, the FDA says: The risks are unknown.

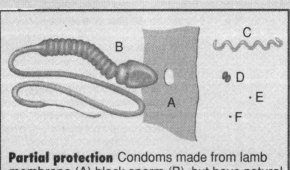

Partial protection Condoms made from lamb membrane (A) block sperm (B), but have natural pores that may be large enough to let through the syphilis (C) and gonorrhea (D) bacteria, and the herpes (E) and AIDS (F) viruses.

Highly ranked condoms
Products that did especially well in our air-burst tests were Excita Extra Ultra Ribbed, the domestic version of Sheik Elite, and Ramses Extra Ribbed. We judged Touch from Protex, which costs less than 35 cents each, A Best Buy.

including, ironically, Trojans Extra Strength—and LifeStyles Ultra *Sensitive*. We downrated all seven in the Ratings.

For the 30 products that passed that initial screening, we then ranked condoms by a "burst index"—the percentage of samples that withstood at least 25 liters of air. This volume is much greater than the standards specify, but we consider it a crucial measure. In a key study in the journal Contraception—which relied on 260 couples who used 4600 condoms—breakage was more likely among

products from manufacturing lots whose condoms typically could not hold 25 liters of air before rupturing.

Condoms with higher scores on this index should offer greater protection. Three products turned in perfect scores in our tests: *Excita Extra Ultra-Ribbed Spermicidally Lubricated*, *Ramses Extra Ribbed Spermicidally Lubricated*, and the U.S.-made version of *Sheik Elite Lubricated* (distinguished from the Japanese-made version by a label on the box). The other high-scoring condoms

include a mix of *LifeStyles, Ramses, Sheik*, and *Trojans* brands with varied lubricants, both straight and contoured.

Recommendations

Latex condoms work well—both to prevent pregnancy and to avoid sexually transmitted diseases. Unless you know your partner is uninfected, the CDC recommends—for disease prevention—that you use condoms, start to finish, for all sex—vaginal, anal, and oral.

Here are important factors to consider when selecting a condom:

Strength. Among the 30 products that passed our initial screening, those with a higher Burst Index should minimize the possibility of breakage during sex. Our findings don't match the claims on several packages, however. Five condoms we tested claim to be strong (or stronger than some other brand), but only one of those products—*Ramses Extra Ribbed Spermicidally Lubricated*—earned a top score on our Burst Index.

Sensitivity. When researchers asked a national sample of men in their 20s and 30s about condoms, the biggest gripe concerned sensitivity: Three out of four complained that condoms reduce sensation.

Some brands claim to enhance sensitivity, but it's not clear how they do. Some makers say a snug condom helps, but others say it's a looser fit (*Pleasure Plus* has a floppy pouch near the head, for instance). As a group, condoms promising sensitivity aren't especially thin, by our measurements.

What's more, even if a thin condom does heighten sensitivity, thin is not necessarily desirable. The thinnest products—*Beyond Seven*, a Japanese import; and *Sheik Super Thin* and *Ramses Ultra Thin*, both American—had some of the lowest burst scores; they passed our minimum standards,

USING CONDOMS WISELY

Most of the products we tested provide adequate instructions, often including pictures. But some print the information on the inside surface of the box, which must be torn apart before the instructions can be read. That's unfortunate—good instructions are key for people unaccustomed to using condoms.

Here are the most important points to remember:

■ Open an individual packet only when ready to use the condom—and open it gently, to avoid tearing the contents. If the rubber feels brittle or sticky or looks discolored, discard the condom—it's spoiled.
■ Don the condom when the penis is erect but before sexual contact. Place the tip of the rolled-up condom over the penis. It there is a reservoir tip, first squeeze out the air. If there is no tip, leave a half-inch space at the end for semen, and squeeze the air out.
■ Unroll the condom down the entire length of the penis (uncircumcised men should first pull back the foreskin).

■ Right after ejaculation, grasp the condom firmly at the ring and withdraw before losing the erection, to prevent spillage.
■ Use a new condom for each act of intercourse—never reuse condoms.
■ Store condoms in a cool, dry place. Heat, light, and air pollution can all hasten deterioration.
■ If you want additional lubrication, use only water-based lubricants, such as surgical jelly. Petroleum jelly and mineral-oil products (baby oil, cold cream, many hand lotions) all rapidly weaken latex. Even some lotions that easily wash off with water may contain oils; check the label.
■ If a condom does fail, both partners should wash their genitals with soap and water. Urinating may also help to avoid infections. If the breakage is discovered after ejaculation, having a separate spermicide handy to apply quickly may help. Or a doctor can prescribe an intense dose of birth-control pills, which will block most pregnancies if used within 72 hours of intercourse.

RATINGS Latex condoms

Listed in order of air-burst performance [5]

Product	Cost PER CONDOM	Burst Index	Lubricant feel	Spermicide	Size (LENGTH X WIDTH)	Thickness	Comments
Excita Extra Ultra-Ribbed, spermicide	$1.00		glycerine	8%	193 x 53 mm	0.07 mm	Textured. Product renamed Sheik Excita Extra Ribbed.
Ramses Extra Ribbed, spermicide	0.99		glycerine	5	187 x 52	0.07	Textured.
Sheik Elite [1]	0.53		oily	—	187 x 52	0.07	Renamed Sheik Classic.
LifeStyles Vibra-Ribbed	0.44		glycerine	—	188 x 54	0.08	Wider than most. Textured.
Ramses Extra, spermicide	0.75		glycerine	15	200 x 51	0.07	Spermicide now 5%.
Ramses Sensitol	0.83		oily	—	192 x 52	0.07	—
Sheik Elite Ribbed, spermicide	0.68		oily	8	190 x 51	0.07	Textured. Renamed Sheik Classic.
Sheik Elite, spermicide	0.59		oily	8	190 x 51	0.07	Renamed Sheik Classic.
Trojan-Enz Large	0.75		jelly	—	214 x 56	0.07	Wider, longer than most.
Trojan-Enz Nonlubricated	0.47		—	—	191 x 53	0.07	
LifeStyles	0.46		glycerine	—	186 x 54	0.07	Wider than most.
Touch from Protex, **A BEST BUY**	0.31[2]		oily	—	193 x 52	0.07	—
Trojan-Enz, spermicide	0.64		jelly	5	202 x 51	0.07	Heavier lubrication than most.
Saxon Gold Ultra Lube	0.43		jelly	—	191 x 51	0.08	Contoured.
Trojan Magnum	0.69		oily	—	205 x 55	0.07	Wider, longer than most. Heavier lubrication than most.
Trojan Very Sensitive	0.62		oily	—	206 x 50	0.07	Longer but narrower than most.
LifeStyles, spermicide	0.45		glycerine	7	189 x 54	0.06	Wider than most. Heavier lubrication than most.
Trojan Ribbed	0.64		oily	—	199 x 53	0.07	Textured.
Rough Rider Studded	1.04[3]		glycerine	—	186 x 53	0.10	Textured. Heavier lubrication than most.
LifeStyles Extra Strength, spermicide	0.65		oily	7	191 x 53	0.09	—
Gold Circle Coin Nonlubricated	0.60[4]		—	—	184 x 52	0.09	Shorter than most.
Sheik Elite [1]	0.53		oily	—	188 x 51	0.06	Discontinued.
Trojan Naturalube Ribbed	0.66		jelly	—	205 x 53	0.07	Longer than most. Textured.
Class Act Ultra Thin & Sensitive	0.33[2]		oily	—	193 x 53	0.06	Wider than most.
Kimono	0.39		glycerine	—	193 x 52	0.07	Contoured. Lighter lubrication.
Pleasure Plus	0.98		glycerine	—	197 x 51	0.09	Textured, with floppy pouch.
Beyond Seven	0.50		oily	—	194 x 50	0.05	Narrower than most. Lighter lubrication than most
Gold Circle Rainbow Coin Nonlubricated	0.67[4]		—	—	180 x 51	0.08	Various colors, contoured.
Sheik Super Thin	0.62		glycerine	—	193 x 51	0.05	—
Ramses Ultra Thin	0.88		glycerine	—	190 x 51	0.05	—
The following products, listed alphabetically, had an overall burst volume defect rate that exceeded 1.5%.							
LifeStyles Ultra Sensitive	0.46	—	glycerine	—	187 x 53	0.06	—
Trojan Extra Strength	0.78	—	oily	—	198 x 53	0.07	—
Trojan Mentor	*1.08[4]	—	glycerine	—	181 x 52	0.07	Contoured. Has applicator and adhesive band.
Trojan Plus	0.66	—	oily	—	196 x 52	0.07	Contoured.
Trojan Very Thin	0.64	—	oily	—	195 x 53	0.06	Lighter lubrication than most.
Trojan-Enz	0.58	—	jelly	—	201 x 54	0.07	Wider than most.
Trojans Nonlubricated	0.49	—	—	—	200 x 53	0.06	No reservoir tip.

[1] *Higher-rated product made in U.S.; lower-rated, in Japan (box flaps are marked).*
[2] *Purchased in boxes of 13.*   [3] *Purchased in boxes of three.*   [4] *Purchased in boxes of six.*
[5] *Products tested were manufactured prior to the FDA's air-burst test requirements, which should reduce the defect rate.*

Notes on the table

Cost is the estimated average, based on a national survey. An * indicates the price we paid. Except where noted, we purchased boxes of 12.
Burst Index is the percentage of condoms that inflated to at least 25 liters in air-burst testing. Products with higher scores should offer greater assurance against breakage in use.

Lubricant feel indicates which substances feel like oil, glycerine, or surgical jelly.
Spermicide in the lubricant may offer some extra safety against disease and pregnancy if a condom breaks; the extent of this protection is unknown. Figure given is the concentration of nonoxynol-9.
Size was measured on unrolled, flattened condoms and are averages of several samples. Proper fit affects comfort and may help avoid breakage or slippage.

Thickness is the average of three measurements along the length of the condom. The typical condom we tested is about 0.07 millimeters thick.
Comments identify textured condoms—which have raised bumps or rings—and contoured condoms—which generally flare out near the head of the condom.

but may not always hold up as well as higher-ranked condoms. When inflated, one-fourth to one-third of those thinner condoms did not reach the crucial 25-liter mark before bursting.

If sensitivity is an issue for you, be aware that this is a poorly defined term. If you want to try some "sensitive" products, it's safest to start with the higher-scoring condoms that make this claim—such as the top rated *Excita Extra Ultra*-Ribbed—before trying thinner ones.

Size. Size does matter. If a condom is too tight, it can be both uncomfortable and more likely to break; too loose, and it is more likely to slip off. We measured the condoms: Width varied by 12 percent, product to product; length, by almost 20 percent. (The two types we tested that claim to be larger than aver-

age—*Trojan-Enz Large* and *Trojan Magnum* were in fact longer and wider.) The Ratings give the details.

Lubricant. Many condoms come coated with various preparations that feel like oil, glycerine, or surgical jelly. Using a lubricated condom is largely a matter of preference. If couples wish to add their own lubricant, they should be certain not to use petroleum- or mineral oil-based products, which rapidly weaken latex. (See "Using Condoms Wisely")

Spermicide. Many condoms' lubricants include a small amount of nonoxynol-9, a spermicide that promises extra protection. It's a promise without much proof behind it. In the test tube, the chemical does kill sperm and inactivate a range of microbes, including HIV. But

no one knows if it works as well in real use and if there's enough of it to make a difference if the condom breaks. (The CDC says it's optional, that the latex barrier alone should offer sufficient protection.)

Age. As condoms age, the rubber in them may weaken, so it's a good idea to avoid packages that are more than a few years old. (We found no sign of aging among the condoms we tested, which were all less than three years old.) Unfortunately, different brands date products differently. Bear this in mind when you're checking the label: Products containing spermicide are given a shelf life of roughly two or three years (to assure that the spermicide still works), while other condoms are allowed as many as five years on the shelf.

Pregnant *pleasures*

Your sex life will change . . . maybe for the better.

By Caren Osten Gerszberg

The question of whether a woman is sexy during pregnancy was never debated on CNN—until actress Hunter Tylo sued the makers of *Melrose Place* for pregnancy discrimination last year. The actress had been fired after becoming pregnant; the producers felt that she couldn't realistically play the role of a seductress (even if her belly was hidden from view). A jury of ten women and two men sided with Tylo, awarding her almost $5 million.

Although Tylo felt confident about the fact that she was as alluring as ever, it's hard for most pregnant women to feel like sex symbols. Plagued by fatigue and morning sickness in her first trimester, Trish Ratliff, of Fort Eustis, Virginia, for example, says that making love was the last thing on her mind. She also had visible stretch marks on her breasts, hips, and thighs, which made her feel self-conscious about her body. On the other hand, Laurie Greenberg, of New York City, was surprised to find that she constantly seemed to be in the mood. Everything seems to take on a new shape during pregnancy—your body, your future, and, inevitably, your sex drive.

It would be remarkable, in fact, if pregnancy had no effect on sexual desire, because your libido is linked to both the physical and emotional changes you're experiencing, notes Christiane Northrup, M.D, assistant clinical professor of obstetrics and gynecology at the University of Vermont, in Burlington. In a normal pregnancy, sexual intercourse is safe and healthy right until the very end, even in a slightly modified version of the man on top. Many women actually find that it's the most enjoyable sex

they've ever had, according to Northrup, who is the author of *Women's Bodies, Women's Wisdom* (Bantam).

For many expectant mothers, pregnancy is a rare opportunity to have spontaneous sex. "It's very exciting not having to worry about birth control or trying to get pregnant," says Lee Dannay, of New York City. "Without either concern, I can just relax and enjoy the moment."

When your partner takes delight in your changing appearance, it can help alleviate anxiety you may feel about your burgeoning body. Once her morning sickness subsided, Trish Ratliff liked the way her husband watched her as she dressed or undressed. "He wanted to make love as much as he always had, and he particularly loved touching my breasts, because they were twice as big as they used to be."

Laurie Greenberg's husband, Ira, however, admitted that he was less turned on, even though he responded whenever she initiated lovemaking. "It didn't really bother me," says Laurie, "because the thought of a beautiful baby growing inside of me made me feel very good about my body."

Of course, in addition to raising emotional issues in bed, your changing shape also poses physical ones. Nausea can make any sexual position uncomfortable if pressure is placed on your abdomen. And your size may keep you from feeling either agile or alluring.

However, sexual desire returns to normal for most women during the middle trimester, when their bodies have adjusted to pregnancy and size isn't a major obstacle. In fact, increased blood flow to the pelvic area caused by hormonal changes can produce a heightened sensitivity, explains Northrup, allowing

some pregnant women to experience orgasm more easily and more frequently—or maybe even for the first time in their life.

Don't worry—you won't hurt the baby

Both of you may be concerned that intercourse could harm the baby, but it is well protected by the amniotic sac and the mucous plug, which blocks the cervix and guards against infection. Some couples even have the irrational notion that the baby seems to be "watching" them.

As your pregnancy progresses, you may have to experiment with different positions. Some doctors suggest having vaginal intercourse facing each other side by side, or in the spooning position, in which your partner lies behind you; this prevents excess pressure from being placed on your belly.

"Positions that might be dangerous are going to be very uncomfortable," says Linda Hughey Holt, M.D., director of the Institute for Women's Health at Evanston Northwestern Healthcare, in Evanston, Illinois, and coauthor of *The Pregnancy Book* (Little, Brown & Co.). "A woman in her ninth month, for example, shouldn't lie with her full weight on her belly, but she wouldn't be able to anyway." Similarly, a man should use his arms to support himself when he's lying on top.

Sex has been shown to speed up labor only when a woman is at term or past her due date. In normal pregnancies, there is no direct link between intercourse earlier on and the start of labor. Sometimes, however, a doctor may rec-

Reprinted with permission from *Parents* magazine, April 1998, pp. 89-90, a publication of Gruner & Jahr USA Publishing. © 1998 by Caren Osten Gerszberg.

Too embarrassed to ask your doctor?

Q: Sometimes urine trickles out during sex. Is this normal?
A: Yes. This can happen during intercourse if there's pressure put on your belly. The muscles in the bladder also tend to relax during pregnancy, causing small amounts of urine to leak in some women when they laugh, cough, or sneeze.

Q: Is it okay for my partner to perform oral sex on me?
A: Generally, yes. In very rare instances, forcefully blowing air into the vagina can cause an amniotic fluid embolism—air enters the uterus and forces amniotic fluid into the mother's circulatory system—which could be fatal to both mother and baby.

Q: Why do my breasts leak when my husband touches them?

A: When the nipples are stimulated during the last weeks of pregnancy, they may leak colostrum, a protein-filled liquid produced for the baby before the milk comes in. (Nipple stimulation also can cause the uterus to contract, but there's no reason to avoid it in a healthy pregnancy.)

Q: In my last pregnancy, I was overdue, and having sex finally started my labor. I'm worried that sex may cause me to go into labor early this time. Is that possible?
A: Although sexual intercourse can trigger uterine contractions that may lead to labor, it's not a cause of premature labor. However, if you are at risk for preterm labor because of a prior history, if you're carrying twins, or if your cervix has started to dilate, your doctor may suggest that you abstain.

ommend limiting or abstaining from sex after a certain point if you have a prior history of early contractions or preterm labor, since nipple stimulation and orgasm may trigger contractions. Sex also should be avoided by women who have placenta previa, a condition in which the placenta covers the cervix.

If you've had a prior miscarriage, your doctor may suggest abstaining from sex during the first trimester, just to be on the safe side. Although there is no causal connection between intercourse and miscarriage, it's possible that your uterus may be especially sensitive. Lynn Gallop, of Wilmington, North Carolina, had six first-trimester miscarriages before getting pregnant with her son, Jack. "My doctor told us we could start having sex after four months, but I was always too scared," she says. If you notice any spotting or bleeding, have pain during intercourse, or if your water breaks, stop having sex immediately and call your doctor.

This is also the perfect time to experiment with alternative ways to express your affection, from foot rubs to taking baths together. Your comfort level—both physical and emotional—should determine how often you have sex and when. Whether it's a question of general anxiety or a specific technique, communication is the best way for you and your partner to maintain a healthy sex life. "Once I explained to my husband that my nipples were very sensitive but I still enjoyed it when he touched the rest of my breast, he changed his technique, and it felt good," says Ratliff. And if the two of you can talk openly about your sex life now, you'll also feel more comfortable discussing it after the baby arrives.

Caren Oslen Gerszberg is a freelance writer in Larchmont, New York.

six
dads
dish

So, what's it like to be a brand-new dad? Six first-timers tell the surprising truth about pregnant sex, labor and delivery, and more.   by Armin Brott

i **recently sat down with six first-time fathers** in the San Francisco Bay Area to discuss everything from their roles during their wife's pregnancy to their feelings about new fatherhood. Five men had become new dads within the four months just prior to our meeting, and one was expecting his baby to arrive any moment. Participants included Dave, a physical therapist; Jeffrey, a writer; Steve, a special-education teacher; Nick, a sculptor; Kurt, a student and hotel worker; and David, a social worker.

At what point did you really start getting into your wife's pregnancy?

DAVE: I guess you could say I'd been into the pregnancy for years. My wife and I are sort of old and we'd been trying for a long time and we'd already had one miscarriage. But then one night—I know this is going to sound weird—but right after sex I knew she was pregnant.

KURT: I didn't really realize the gravity of what was happening until I actually felt the baby kick. In those sonograms the baby just looked like something out of *The X-Files*, and I was like "I think that's a UFO," so I really wasn't in tune with it. But when the baby started kicking, I thought "This is really something."

STEVE: I spent a lot of time in denial. [The pregnancy] was really hard for my wife, and I was always worried she would have a miscarriage. I think I was

afraid to get too attached, just to set myself up for something bad.

JEFFREY: When we heard that first heartbeat, that was pretty real to me. Later, after the sonogram, when you could see it was fully formed—after that I couldn't stop talking about it.

NICK: We weren't married when she got pregnant. We'd been living together for two years. Finding out she was pregnant was like a slap in the face. It really hit me at the birth.

DAVE: I'm a little younger than my wife, and I had fears I wasn't ready. It's like all her maternal instincts were instantly downloaded: Her womanhood, her femininity were all on-line, but it was a huge and slow adjustment for me. It helped a lot when her tummy got bigger. I felt a little stupid about that at the time, as though I needed physical evidence to validate that this was happening. At a certain point I remember thinking, "Oh, my God, I have a mammal for a wife!"

What were the worst fears that you had about the pregnancy?

DAVE: I had a lot of fears about my wife's dying in childbirth. I work in healthcare and know that things can go wrong.

NICK: I was really afraid that the child would come out deformed.

DAVID: I remember I stopped running yellow lights. I was terrified that something would happen to me, and

then my wife would be left all alone with the kid.

DAVE: Oh, yeah—I completely stopped riding my motorcycle.

JEFFREY *(laughing):* We sold our two-door compact and bought a four-door Saab.

KURT: I was mostly afraid of the old stereotypes . . . I was afraid my wife was going to turn into this irrational person that was sick all the time, but she didn't really change. Actually, as it got closer, she became the more levelheaded one.

JEFFREY: My biggest fear was that my life was over—that I'd trash my career and I'd never have time for myself. After we were pregnant, I stopped some guy pushing a stroller in the park and said, "We're going to have a baby and I'm freaking out" and he told me not to worry, that it was the most amazing thing, and after that I felt better. Then I started worrying about money, mostly. Like, was I going to be able to make enough money to support everybody? *(Groans of agreement.)*

DAVID: Oh, yeah, the money.

NICK: That was a biggie. I mean, if you're out earning money, you can't be at home. One pulls against the other.

KURT: We *still* don't know what we're going to do about the money.

Was it hard to give your wife the support she needed during pregnancy?

STEVE: During the last trimester I felt like, emotionally, I wasn't doing enough for my wife, but I felt like I needed to be at work to make some more money.

DAVE: I was in school, so it was hard to be there as much as I wanted. There were some ways in which she wanted more support than I was capable or giving or understanding enough to give. She wanted a lot of attention, and we had some tension around that—she wanted perfect support. But I was more limited in what I could offer.

KURT: Sometimes I felt like maybe I was getting more support than she was. On top of the classes we went to together, I took these fatherhood classes where we all talked about our angst and worries. But she never had a class without me. I'm not sure she had a place to unload—you know, "My husband's doing this" or "I'm worried about that."

DAVE: I was extremely supportive of my wife, but sometimes I feel like it was hard for her to accept that support. We both do equal things in our marriage and in our life together, and my wife felt sort of guilty when she wasn't able to do a lot of those things, especially later in the pregnancy when she was very tired and not feeling great. I had to say to her on numerous occasions, "You're growing a baby. You're doing this for us, so it's only right that I do the dishes two nights in a row."

What was the most helpful preparation for the birth of your child?

KURT: We took Lamaze, but I still had a lot of anxiety. I mean, you learn how to be there for her during the actual labor, and the breathing and the massage and saying all the right things, but I still didn't feel like I knew what to expect. I kept hearing horror stories . . .

DAVE: I actually found it sort of therapeutic to hear other people's horror stories. These men from a previous fathering class would bring in their babies and tell you the most god-awful stories about the birth of the child, the worst stories imaginable. . . . But then you'd see how utterly cute the kids were. . . . Those stories were especially helpful in our case because we had a really bad birth.

I think that it would help everybody if they'd stop using that term *due date* and change it to *due month. (Loud agreement from everyone.)* No matter what

they tell you, you still sort of expect the kid to be born when you hit that date.

JEFFREY: Something that helped me was that I'd spent a lot of time bonding with the baby before she was born. Anytime anyone came over and Jacqui wanted the baby to kick for them, all I had to do was talk to the baby for a second, and she'd start kicking because she recognized my voice. I loved knowing that when my baby was born she'd have something to recognize me by.

And what exactly happened to your sex life during this time?

DAVE: Actually, there wasn't a huge change in our sex life. I know my wife didn't feel as attractive, but I was as attracted to her as ever. It just got a little weird sometimes because suddenly there was this third person there we were both really aware of.

NICK: Yeah, sometimes the baby would be moving, then when we started having sex he would go to sleep. It felt almost like a rejection.

STEVE: During the pregnancy we had sex up until the last month and a half. Then the amount of sex decreased, but the amount of just holding each other increased so the sense of intimacy and support was the same.

DAVID: I remember sex diminishing for a period, and there got to be a little pressure around it. We have some tension in our relationship, and sex sometimes helps eliminate it for her but it doesn't for me. She's saying, "Let's connect, let's have sex," but I want to connect with someone first, then have sex. When we did have sex, though, it was better than before—her body was very beautiful as she grew. It made me feel more connected to her.

NICK: We had sex right up to the very end. What's the difference between that and having sex during menstruation? It's the closeness of it.

I find that sex does bring me a lot closer to my wife. We argue a lot, and sex brings us a lot closer together.

JEFFREY: Toward the end, the nurse practitioner advised us to stop having sex. That was fine with me, not a big burden. I didn't want anything to happen to the baby. We haven't had sex since Ariane was born, though. We're planning to go to this hot-spring hotel when the baby gets to be a little bit older, and we're planning to have sex again there. Jacqui really likes going to fancy hotels, and we've always had really amazing sex in fancy hotels—so that's how we're going to start having sex again.

DAVE: Afterward, my wife had a significant tear that didn't heal properly. She also had a lot of dryness that has really delayed things. If you redefine what sex is—not just in and out, but closeness and lots of touching—you can get back to sex a lot earlier.

When the big day finally came, were you as prepared as you'd imagined?

NICK: No way! I'd really geared up for the birth. But during labor my wife didn't even want me to talk, so I couldn't say all the things I was supposed to say. I could hold her hand, but that was it. I'd have banged my head against the wall if it would have helped, but there was absolutely nothing I could do, really. I felt guilty about that. I kept apologizing, but everything I said annoyed her.

DAVID: There's only so much from those classes you can digest. You can't imagine what labor's going to be like. You're supposed to focus on the woman's need the whole time, but I remember in the last half-hour of pushing I was really freaking out, wondering if the baby was really coming, and I stopped focusing completely on her. I still feel a little guilty about that.

JEFFREY: Ariane was born blue, and that was pretty hairy. In the 30th hour of labor they offered my wife an epidural so that she could go to sleep, then [wake up and] start pushing. Suddenly, she was at six centimeters. We probably could have had the baby right there, but they gave her the epidural anyway and we both fell asleep. Then the lights came on and I heard, "We need to put in an internal monitor!" I didn't know the heart rate had dropped to 90 beats per minute. I don't know if I'd ever want to relive that, but I would not want to have missed it, either. It was pretty intense.

NICK: Mostly, I wasn't really prepared for what he'd look like. I'm white and my wife is black, and he came out

---

"Money was a biggie. I mean, if you're out earning money, you can't be home."—Nick

really white, except for his penis and testicles, which were really dark. He's gotten darker, though, and they're lighter.

What's been the hardest part about the first couple of months of parenthood?

NICK: I didn't expect that my wife would be so tired—it's a big problem. She can't do a lot. She went through a period when every time she woke up she'd wake me up, too, but now she's figured out that letting me sleep can actually help her out, too.

DAVID: I feel like I could have used more help after the birth. My wife had a really hard time breastfeeding. Breastfeeding is a complex thing, and everybody has their own philosophy. My mother-in-law had 30-year-old information, and we needed up-to-date information. We were just so insecure.

JEFFREY: Thankfully, we got four home visits from the nurse. It was an amazing relief to have a nurse come to the house to help you bathe the baby, change the baby, check out how your wife is breastfeeding, and tell you what that weird acne is on the baby's skin.

"If you redefine sex as closeness and touching, you can get back to it a lot earlier."—Dave

NICK: I never thought I'd get jealous of the baby, but I find that I do get jealous that he gets all the attention, especially in terms of breastfeeding. He gets more time with my wife than I do.

So far, are you as good a father as you wanted to be?
STEVE: It's a lot easier than I thought it would be, actually. At first I had a lot of anxieties about being able to do the right things, but a lot of it is just common sense. Being there for Ariel, playing with Ariel, changing Ariel.
DAVE: On a day-to-day basis, sometimes I'm a little less involved

than I projected since I'm back at work and Mary Ann is not. Then, when I come home, I have to figure out whether to spend the rest of my time with Sage or do other things that are also supportive, like cooking and cleaning. I'm still struggling to find that balance.

JEFFREY: When we first came home, Ariane started crying and I picked her up and she immediately stopped. Jacqui was thrilled at how quickly I could comfort her. When she said that, I realized that's all I had to do—my minimum responsibility—and even if I just did that, my wife would be completely happy that I could do that. Now I'm as involved as I could possibly be. Since my wife's gotta do the breastfeeding, I change the baby and carry her around when she's crying and keep her stimulated. I think I could take care of her if Jacqui got a full-time job and I had to stay home. I don't want that to happen, but I could handle it.

Armin Brott's latest book is The New Father: A Dad's Guide to the Toddler Years *(Abbeville Press).*

THE COST OF CHILDREN

Of course they're cute. But have you any idea how much one will set you back? A hardheaded inquiry

BY PHILLIP J. LONGMAN

To examine in coldly economic terms a parent's decision to have children is widely thought to be in bad taste. A child, after all, isn't precisely akin to a consumer product such as a dishwasher, a house, a car, or a personal computer–any one of which, of course, is cheaper to acquire and usually easier to return. A child is a font of love, hope for the future, continuation of one's bloodline, and various other intangible pleasures, and it is these sentimental considerations (along with some earthier imperatives) that prevail when parents bring a child into this world.

But let's face it: Children don't come free. Indeed, their cost is rising. According to one government calculation, the direct cost of raising a child to age 18 has risen by 20 percent since 1960 (adjusted for inflation and changes in family size). And this calculation doesn't take into account the forgone wages that result from a parent taking time off to raise children–an economic cost that has skyrocketed during the last generation as women have entered the work force in unprecedented numbers. "It's become much more expensive to raise children while the economic returns to parents have diminished," notes feminist economist Shirley Burggraf. "The family can't survive on romance."

Knowing the real cost of children is critical to a host of financial questions, such as how much house one can afford, how much one should be saving for college tuition, and how much one must earn to have a larger family. To help answer such questions, *U.S. News* has undertaken to identify and add up as best it can all the costs of raising a child from birth to college graduation. (For the purposes of this calculation, we're assuming these children will pay for any advanced degrees they may want out of their own pockets.)

Our starting point is data from the United States Department of Agriculture, which every year publishes estimates of how much families in different income brackets spend on raising children to age 18. To these calculations we have added the cost of a college education and wages forgone because of the rigors of child-rearing. (There's plenty we haven't counted: soccer camp, cello lessons, SAT prep., and other extra-cost options.) What we've found is that the typical child in a middle-income family requires a 22-year investment of just over $1.45 million. That's a pretty steep price tag in a country where the median income for families with children is just $41,000. The child's unit cost rises to $2.78 million for the top-third income bracket and drops to $761,871 for the bottom-third income bracket.

Tut tut, you say. Surely this is another case of newsmagazine hyperbole. All right, then, let's take it from the top:

■ **Acquisition costs.** In most cases, conceiving a child biologically is gloriously cost free. But not for all: An estimated 6.1 percent of women ages 15–24, and 11.2 percent of women ages 25–34, suffer from what health statisticians refer to as "impaired fecundity." Serving this huge market are some 300 infertility clinics nationwide that performed 59,142 treatment "cycles" in 1995, according to a recently released study by the Centers for Disease Control and Prevention. The cost of treatments–only 19 percent of which actually produced a take-home baby–averaged around $8,000 a try. It's not uncommon for infertile couples to spend $50,000 or more in pursuit of pregnancy. Though most insurance policies will pay for some form of infertility treatment, insurers are cutting back rapidly in the total bills they'll cover. For the purposes of our tally, we'll ignore fertility treatments, but this can be a significant cost.

For most people, the meter starts running with pregnancy. Costs vary dramatically from hospital to hospital, from region to region, and according to how complicated the pregnancy is. Out-of-pocket costs, obviously, will also vary depending on how much health insurance you have. But here's an idea of what your bills might be.

For an uneventful normal pregnancy, 12 prenatal care visits are usually recommended–the cost of which varies according to one's insurance plan. According to HCIA Inc., a Baltimore health care information company, the cost to insured patients of a normal delivery in a hospital averages about $2,800. (Twins are cheaper on a per-head basis: typical total delivery cost: $4,115.)

For parents without insurance, direct costs are clearly much higher. According to a 1994 study, the cost of an uncomplicated "normal" delivery averages $6,400 nationally. Caesarean delivery costs an average of $11,000, and more complicated births may range up to $400,000. Premature babies requiring neonatal intensive care will cost $1,000 to $2,500 for every day they stay in the hospital. Though most people can count on insurance to cover a majority of such costs, there are many people who can't. According to a report issued in March by the U.S. government's Agency for Health Care Policy and Research, 17 percent of Hispanic children, 12.6 percent of black children, and 6 percent of white ones lack any health in-

surance coverage whatsoever, including coverage by Medicaid or other public programs.

An alternative path to acquiring a child is through adoption. Of the roughly 30,000 adoptions of healthy infants in the United States each year, most involve expenses of $10,000 to $15,000. These include the cost of paying for a social worker to perform a "home study" to vouchsafe the adoptive parents' suitability, agency fees, travel expenses (many adoptions these days cross national boundaries), medical and sometimes living expenses for the birth mother, and legal fees. Offsetting these costs for parents who adopt is a new $5,000 federal tax credit. Since most people don't adopt, these costs, too, are excluded from *U.S. News*'s tally.

THREADS.
To clothe a child to age 18 costs **$22,063.** And yes, girls cost 18 percent more than boys.

■ **Child care.** The Department of Agriculture calculates that the middle-class parents of a 3-to-5-year-old spend just over $1,260 a year on average for child care. (According to the Census Bureau, fully 56 percent of American families with children use paid child care.) Wealthier families are more likely to opt for the pricier nanny. Irish Nanny Services of Dublin advertises Irish nannies "with good moral standards" who are "renowned for their expertise with children." The price for U.S. parents begins at $250 per week; plus 1.5 paid holidays for every month

worked; plus a nonrefundable finder's fee equal to 10 percent of the yearly salary payable upfront.

The average cost for all families using child care is $74.15 a week, or about 7.5 percent of average pretax family income, which is roughly equal to most workers' employee-contribution rate for Social Security. The rate is much steeper, of course, at the low end of the income scale; families making less than $1,200 a month who use day care spend an average 25.1 percent of their income on day-care expenses.

■ **Food.** Middle-class families spend an average $990 a year feeding a child under 2. (Breast-feeding helps: One serving of infant formula can cost as much as $3.29.) As kids get bigger, so do their appetites: Feeding a middle-class 15-year-old currently costs $1,920 a year on average. A middle-class only child born in 1997 can be expected to consume a total of $54,795 in food by age 18.

■ **Housing.** The bigger your family, the bigger the house you need. Families with children also often pay a premium to live in safe, leafy neighborhoods with good schools. USDA estimates that the average middle-class, husband-wife family with one child will spend, on a per capita basis, an additional $97,549 to provide the child with shelter.

■ **Transportation.** Priced a minivan lately? The added transportation cost of having one middle-class child totals $46,345, according to the USDA. This does not include the cost of commuting to jobs parents must hold in order to support their children. Predictably, as children get older, the cost of driving them around grows. Parents with teenagers spend over 70 percent more on transportation than families with infants. Just the cost of providing teenage drivers with auto insurance can run into the thousands.

■ **Health care.** Obviously, this cost varies tremendously, depending largely on the health of the child. The lifetime health costs of a child born with cerebral palsy, for instance, average $503,000; with Down's syndrome, $451,000; and with spina bifida,

$294,000, according to the March of Dimes.

Again, out-of-pocket costs for health care will depend largely on whether the parents have good (or any) health insurance. In 1996, nearly 11 million American children, or 15.4 percent of the population under 18, had none. Deductibles, copayments, and specific coverages also vary widely even among those with insurance. Taking all these variables into account, and including the cost of insurance, the USDA estimates that the average cost of keeping a middle-class child born in 1997 healthy to age 18 will be more than $20,757.

■ **Clothing.** Even after allowing for hand-me-downs and gifts from doting grandparents, keeping an only child properly dressed to age 18 will cost an average total of $22,063, according to the USDA. Predictably, in this realm, daughters cost more than sons: According to the Bureau of Labor Statistics, husband-wife families with children spend nearly 18 percent more on girls' clothes than on those for boys.

■ **Primary and secondary education.** Fully 89 percent of all school-age kids in the United States attend public schools. Public education costs American society more than $293 billion per year, but for the purposes of this tally, we'll exclude taxes (which, after all, are paid by parents and non-parents alike) and consider public education to be free.

For the roughly 5 million grade-school students now enrolled in private schools, costs vary widely. About 50 percent of these students attend parochial schools, where tuition averaged $1,934 in 1993–94, the last school year for which data are available. By contrast, parents earning over $125,000 a year who send a child to the elite Deerfield Academy in Deerfield, Mass., and who manage to qualify for financial aid, are expected to contribute $10,600 a year in tuition. Overall, the U.S. Department of Education reports, private-school tuition in 1993–94 averaged $2,200 a year in elementary schools and $5,500 in secondary schools, with

schools for children who are handicapped or have "special needs" charging an average $15,189. These costs have been rising quickly. Reflecting increasing demand, the average tuition of private schools increased by more than double the overall rate of inflation between 1990 and 1996.

■ **Toys and other miscellaneous expenses.** The USDA doesn't break out spending on toys by income group or the age of children. But for all husband-and-wife families with children, the average amount spent on pets, toys, and playground equipment in 1995 was $485.

> # TUMBLES.
> Children are usually quite healthy, but they'll still run you **$20,757** to keep fit till age 18.

What do all these bills come to? USDA calculates that a typical middle-class, husband-wife family will spend a total of $301,183 to raise an only child born in 1997 to age 18 (table, "Cost of children born in 1997). More affluent parents (with income over $59,700 a year) will spend an average of $437,869 on an only child. The average figure for lower-income families (with income between $35,500 a year) is $221,750.

Certain economies of scale are available to larger families. As family size increases, food costs per person go down the most. (Just feed everyone stew.) Per capita housing and transportation costs also decrease, but not by as much. All told, for middle-class families, the marginal cost of raising a second child will be approximately 24

percent less than the cost of a single child. The marginal unit cost continues to drop for each successive child.

Now let's consider two costs the USDA calculation leaves out. The first is college. From the start of the 1990s through September of 1997, average tuition at the nation's colleges increased by more than 75 percent, while overall prices in the economy inflated by little more than 26 percent. Common sense would suggest that this rate of tuition inflation cannot possibly sustain itself over the long term, especially if real family income remains flat or grows only slowly. Sooner or later, some combination of new technology and organizational reform will surely render higher education less costly. Still, who would have imagined that the price of a college education would ever have risen to where it is today? With an undergraduate education becoming ever more necessary to guarantee a middle-class lifestyle, perhaps its price will rise even faster in the future. Given these imponderables, we'll assume college costs will continue to rise at the average annual rate of the 1990s, or 7.45 percent, and that the cost of room, board, and books grows at 5 percent, which is the annual inflation rate of the past 20 years.

Now, let's do some illustrative arithmetic. Say you had a child in September 1997. Let's forget straight off about sending him to Harvard or Princeton, or any other private college, and aim for a top state school, the University of Michigan–Ann Arbor. Tuition, fees, plus room and board for in-state students there currently amount to $11,694 a year. Under the inflation assumptions described above, it turns out you'll need a total of $157,831 to see a child born last year through graduation at Ann Arbor (assuming you are a Michigan resident; tuition is more than three times higher for out-of-state residents).

Ok, now let's figure out how to pay for that tuition. Assuming an average annual 7 percent total return on savings, you'll have put away more than $319 each month, starting on your child's date

Cost of children born in 1997

Higher income (one-child family; 1997 before-tax family income: more than $59,700)

Age	Housing	Food	Transportation	Clothing	Health care	Day care and education	Misc.	College (Princeton)	Forgone wages	Total for year
0	$5,915	$1,624	$1,885	$719	$744	$2,120	$1,860		$44,650	$59,518
1	$6,211	$1,706	$1,979	$755	$781	$2,226	$1,953		$48,669	$64,279
2	$6,521	$1,791	$2,078	$793	$820	$2,338	$2,051		$53,049	$69,440
3	$6,804	$2,124	$2,139	$818	$833	$2,670	$2,168		$57,823	$75,379
4	$7,144	$2,231	$2,246	$859	$874	$2,803	$2,276		$63,027	$81,461
5	$7,501	$2,342	$2,358	$902	$918	$2,944	$2,390		$41,047	$60,402
6	$7,760	$2,974	$2,675	$1,030	$1,097	$2,127	$2,576		$45,847	$66,087
7	$8,148	$3,123	$2,809	$1,082	$1,152	$2,233	$2,704		$52,033	$73,285
8	$8,556	$3,279	$2,950	$1,136	$1,209	$2,345	$2,840		$57,900	$80,214
9	$8,599	$4,001	$3,232	$1,308	$1,366	$1,712	$3,039		$65,315	$88,572
10	$9,029	$4,201	$3,393	$1,373	$1,434	$1,798	$3,191		$72,460	$96,880
11	$9,480	$4,411	$3,563	$1,442	$1,506	$1,888	$3,351		$64,402	$90,042
12	$10,444	$4,855	$3,986	$2,494	$1,581	$1,537	$3,897		$72,230	$101,024
13	$10,966	$5,097	$4,185	$2,619	$1,660	$1,613	$4,092		$82,517	$112,750
14	$11,514	$5,352	$4,395	$2,750	$1,743	$1,694	$4,296		$92,118	$123,863
15	$11,008	$5,929	$5,620	$2,629	$1,933	$3,119	$3,944		$104,460	$138,642
16	$11,558	$6,226	$5,901	$2,761	$2,030	$3,275	$4,141		$116,188	$152,080
17	$12,136	$6,537	$6,196	$2,899	$2,132	$3,439	$4,348		$130,979	$168,665
18								$103,574	$145,257	$248,831
19								$110,831	$140,766	$251,597
20								$118,605	$156,987	$275,592
21								$126,935	$177,732	$304,667
Total	$159,294	$67,805	$61,589	$28,370	$23,813	$41,881	$55,117	$459,945	$1,885,454	$2,783,268

Middle income (one child family; 1997 before-tax family income: $35,500 to $59,700)

Age	Housing	Food	Transportation	Clothing	Health care	Day care and education	Misc.	College (Univ. of Michigan)	Forgone wages	Total for year
0	$3,720	$1,228	$1,352	$546	$645	$1,401	$1,104		$23,600	$33,594
1	$3,906	$1,289	$1,419	$573	$677	$1,471	$1,159		$25,724	$36,218
2	$4,101	$1,353	$1,490	$602	$711	$1,545	$1,217		$28,039	$39,058
3	$4,263	$1,636	$1,522	$617	$718	$1,809	$1,306		$30,563	$42,434
4	$4,476	$1,718	$1,598	$648	$754	$1,899	$1,372		$33,313	$45,778
5	$4,700	$1,804	$1,678	$681	$791	$1,994	$1,440		$21,695	$34,783
6	$4,819	$2,426	$1,961	$798	$947	$1,346	$1,579	.	$24,233	$38,108
7	$5,060	$2,547	$2,059	$838	$995	$1,413	$1,658		$27,502	$42,072
8	$5,313	$2,675	$2,162	$879	$1,044	$1,484	$1,740		$30,603	$45,901
9	$5,194	$3,289	$2,405	$1,020	$1,193	$1,020	$1,885		$34,523	$50,527

(continued on next page)

of birth, to have enough money on hand to pay for four years of college as each semester's tuition bill comes due. If you wait until the child is in kindergarten to start saving, your monthly savings requirement will jump to $524. If you wait until the child reaches freshman year of high school, the number will jump to $1,957 a month.

Or here's another way to look at the challenge. Take a middle-class fam-

Age	Housing	Food	Transportation	Clothing	Health care	Day care and education	Misc.	College (Florida A&M)	Forgone wages	Total for year
10	$5,454	$3,454	$2,525	$1,071	$1,252	$1,071	$1,979		$38,299	$55,104
11	$5,726	$3,627	$2,651	$1,124	$1,315	$1,124	$2,078		$34,040	$51,685
12	$6,502	$3,852	$3,029	$1,982	$1,381	$868	$2,539		$38,178	$58,331
13	$6,828	$4,045	$3,180	$2,081	$1,450	$912	$2,666		$43,615	$64,776
14	$7,169	$4,247	$3,339	$2,185	$1,522	$957	$2,799		$48,690	$70,908
15	$6,445	$4,950	$4,434	$2,037	$1,701	$1,701	$2,372		$55,213	$78,852
16	$6,767	$5,197	$4,656	$2,138	$1,786	$1,786	$2,490		$61,412	$86,233
17	$7,105	$5,457	$4,888	$2,245	$1,876	$1,876	$2,615		$69,230	$95,292
18								$35,821	$76,777	$112,598
19								$38,140	$74,402	$112,543
20								$40,614	$82,976	$123,591
21								$43,255	$93,941	$137,196
Total	$97,549	$54,795	$46,345	$22,063	$20,757	$25,678	$33,996	$157,832	$996,567	$1,455,581

Lower income (one-child family; 1997 before tax family income: less than $35,500)

Age	Housing	Food	Transportation	Clothing	Health care	Day care and education	Misc.	College (Florida A&M)	Forgone wages	Total for year
0	$2,753	$1,029	$905	$459	$496	$856	$719		$11,050	$18,267
1	$2,890	$1,081	$950	$482	$521	$898	$755		$12,045	$19,622
2	$3,035	$1,135	$998	$506	$547	$943	$793		$13,129	$21,085
3	$3,144	$1,321	$1,005	$517	$545	$1,120	$847		$14,310	$22,808
4	$3,301	$1,387	$1,055	$543	$573	$1,176	$889		$15,598	$24,521
5	$3,466	$1,456	$1,108	$570	$601	$1,234	$934		$10,158	$19,527
6	$3,523	$1,977	$1,363	$681	$731	$764	$1,047		$11,346	$21,433
7	$3,699	$2,076	$1,431	$715	$768	$803	$1,099		$12,877	$23,468
8	$3,884	$2,180	$1,502	$751	$806	$843	$1,154		$14,329	$25,450
9	$3,674	$2,732	$1,712	$866	$923	$539	$1,270		$16,164	$27,879
10	$3,858	$2,868	$1,798	$909	$970	$566	$1,333		$17,932	$30,233
11	$4,051	$3,012	$1,888	$954	$1,018	$594	$1,400		$15,938	$28,854
12	$4,743	$3,318	$2,227	$1,692	$1,069	$445	$1,826		$17,876	$33,196
13	$4,980	$3,484	$2,338	$1,777	$1,122	$468	$1,917		$20,421	$36,508
14	$5,229	$3,658	$2,455	$1,866	$1,178	$491	$2,013		$22,797	$39,689
15	$4,434	$4,150	$3,480	$1,727	$1,315	$851	$1,547		$25,852	$43,355
16	$4,656	$4,358	$3,654	$1,814	$1,380	$893	$1,624		$28,754	$47,133
17	$4,888	$4,576	$3,837	$1,904	$1,449	$938	$1,705		$32,415	$51,713
18								$16,783	$35,948	$52,731
19								$17,802	$34,837	$52,639
20								$18,886	$38,851	$57,737
21								$20,038	$43,985	$64,023
Total	$70,208	$45,797	$33,705	$18,732	$61,013	$14,421	$22,873	$73,508	$466,613	$761,871

Note: Numbers may not add up because of rounding

ily earning, say, $47,200 in 1998. Assume that inflation will average 5 percent over the next 18 years and that this family's income will grow 4 percent above inflation. Assume finally that this family will earn a 7 percent annual average return on its savings. Now suppose this family had a new child last year, and the parents want to prefund the likely cost of sending this child to a top-rank state school. What percent of family income do they need to put away each year toward the child's college expenses? Answer: about 4 percent.

So far, this accounting puts the cost of raising and educating a middle-class, only child at roughly $459,014 ($301,183 in direct expenditures to age 18 plus $157,831 for college costs). Now suppose you're considering having a child and want to have enough money in the bank by the day the child is born to be able to cover all of his or her direct future costs to you. No one actually does this, of course, but as any chief financial officer knows, this is a useful way to calculate the real burden of long-term liabilities. Assume you can earn 7 percent on your investments after your child is born. In that case, you'll need to build a nest egg of $204,470 by delivery day. Assuming you want to raise your child with a middle-class standard of living, this is the approximate present value of your liabilities for future expenses related to that child.

Or, suppose you want to have a child 10 years from now and want to start a regular savings plan that will allow you just enough money by the child's date of birth to cover all future child-related expenses as they occur. What you need to start saving today is $1,181 a month. Again, nobody actually does this, but amortizing the cost of children in this way provides a useful benchmark in figuring how "affordable" children are. Could you "afford" to pay an extra $1,181 every month for the next 10 years servicing your credit-card debt? Failing to prefund future liabilities, such as the future cost of a child, is financially equivalent to borrowing. If your family income goes up substantially in the future, you may be able to afford your child-related "unfunded liabilities," but if it remains stagnant or grows only slowly, as real family income has for decades, then these unfunded liabilities will hurt.

A final expenditure to add to our tally is a bit more abstract but no less real: forgone family income. People who have children tend to have less time on their hands to make money.

Consider first the forgone income for an unwed teenage mother who rears her child alone. Researchers at the University of Michigan have compared the earning power, over 20 years, of women who did and did not have children out of wedlock as teenagers. Interestingly, at ages 19 and 20, women who had given birth to illegitimate children actually had slightly higher incomes on average than women who remained childless during their teenage years; this presumably reflected the effect of welfare payments, which can boost short-term income above what the average childless full-time student earns. But by age 21, unmarried women who refrained from having become pregnant as teenagers, or who had abortions, began to pull well ahead of those who did not. By age 29, women who did not have the burden of raising a child alone as teenagers could expect to have earned a total of $72,191 more than women who did carry this burden.

What does it cost a married woman to have children? The answer depends crucially on her opportunities. Obviously, a woman who gives up a career as a nurse's aide to have a baby does not forgo as much income as a woman who gives up a law partnership. But for both there is an "opportunity cost," which can be roughly estimated. As economist Burggraf points out in her recent book, *The Feminine Economy and Economic Man,* people tend to take marriage partners of similar educational backgrounds and aspirations (social scientists label this "assortive mating"). For example, college-educated men are 15 times more likely to marry college-educated women than are men who never completed high school. This means that the opportunity cost of either spouse taking time off to raise a child is often 50 percent of a family's potential income.

That's exactly the trade-off faced by Colette Hochstein and her husband, Michael Lingenfelter. Both are librarians who work extensively with computer-information retrieval systems. Her position is with the National Institutes of Health in Bethesda,

Md.; he works in the White House library. Together, they spend more money on day care for their 2-year-old daughter, Miranda—about 17 percent of their household income—than on any other expense except their mortgage. Yet since they both earn roughly the same salary, the only way to avoid paying for day care would be to sacrifice half their household income. If either of them were to quit work to take care of Miranda full time, says Hochstein, the economic cost would extend beyond Miranda's childhood years: "In this rapidly changing, high-tech time, there are few professions in which one could take even a year's leave of absence without falling seriously behind."

Given the career opportunities now available to women, virtually all parents face some opportunity cost in having children, and it usually adds up to serious money. Consider this hypothetical middle-class, husband-wife family. They met in college and soon after married. Two years into their marriage, they each were earning $23,600, but then came Junior. She immediately quit her job to stay home with the baby, causing their family income to fall by half. After their child reaches kindergarten, she hopes to begin working half time; by the time the child reaches age 11, she hopes to be able to boost her work hours to 30 a week. But remembering her own escapades while home alone during high school, she does not plan to return to full-time work until the child goes off to college.

What's the opportunity cost of these life choices? Assume, as the USDA does, that inflation averages 5 percent over her working life. Further assume that, because of her "mommy track," her average annual real wage increases come to 2 percent instead of a possible 4 percent she could have earned as a childless and fully committed full-time professional. In that event, she'll sacrifice $996,567 in forgone income over just the next 21 years. Adjusting for inflation, that's equal in today's dollars to roughly $548,563.

Where does this leave the total bill? Combine $996,567 in forgone wages with the USDA's estimates of a typical middle-class family's direct child-related expenses for an only child ($301,183); add in the likely cost of sending a child born last year to a first-rank, in-state public university ($157,831), and the total cost of one typical middle-class child born in 1997 comes in at $1,445,581. Even after adjusting for inflation, the cost of a middle-class child born last year is still $799,913 in today's dollars.

To be sure, parents also receive some direct subsidies for their child-care costs. Being able to claim a dependent is worth $2,650 in federal taxes due this year, for example. And under current law, families are eligible to take a tax credit for child-care expenses, with a maximum credit of $720 for one child in a low-income family and up to $1,440 for two or more children. President Clinton recently proposed making this credit more generous, so that a family of four making $35,000 and saddled with high child-care bills would no longer owe any federal income taxes. But even if Clinton's plan is approved, parents who stay home with their kids will continue to receive no compensation for their lost income, and even those taking the credits will find themselves far worse off financially, in most cases, than if they had decided to remain childless.

Given current economic incentives, it is hardly surprising that the "smartest" people in our society end up being those least likely to have children. Middle-aged women with graduate degrees are more than three times more likely to be childless than those who dropped out of high school. Similarly, two-income married-couple families earning over $75,000 are 70 percent more likely to be childless than those earning between $10,000 and $19,999. You don't have to be an economic materialist to see the financial reality behind these numbers. Highly educated, high-income people have a higher opportu-

nity cost, in the form of lost income, if they decide to have children.

Government policy makers are forever talking about the need for society to "invest" in today's youth, if for no other reason than to pay for the huge, largely socialized cost of supporting the growing ranks of the elderly. It's a noble goal, but at the individual family level, a child, financially speaking, looks more like a high-priced consumer item with no warranty. It's the decision to remain childless that offers the real investment opportunity.

> **TUMMIES.** Feeding a middle-class 15-year-old costs **$1,920** a year on average. Hide the Cheez-Its!

Imagine a middle-class, college-age, sexually active woman who is contemplating whether to spend $5,000 to have her tubes tied so she'll never have to worry about getting pregnant. We've already seen how the cost of giving birth to just one child could easily exceed $1.4 million over the next 22 years. Even though many of those costs could be well down the road, a typical middle-class young woman paying $5,000 for such an operation could expect that "investment" to compound at a rate of fully 680 percent over the next 22 years alone. (The return on a vasectomy, which is even cheaper, would be much high-

er.) It will be a long time before anyone finds a deal that lucrative on Wall Street.

But wait a minute. Isn't this an absurd conclusion? Children aren't just a bundle of liabilities. If they were, the way for society to become richer would be for everyone to stop having kids, but of course that wouldn't work. Without a rising new generation of workers, there will be nobody around to assume our debts, and before long, even the store shelves will be empty. So why does our accounting suggest the opposite?

Because society's economic interests and those of parents as individuals don't perfectly coincide. The financial sacrifice a parent makes to have and raise children creates enormous wealth for society as a whole. But the modern reality is that everyone shares in much of that wealth regardless of what role he or she played in creating it. If, for example, you don't choose to have children, or you treat your children badly, you still won't have to give up any of your Social Security pension.

Historically, support in old age did depend, almost entirely, on how many children you had, and on how well your investment in them turned out. Even before parents grew old, they could usually count on their children to perform economically useful tasks around the farm or shop. This made children economic assets–from the point of view of both society at large and parents.

Now the economic returns of parenting mostly bypass parents, and a proper accounting has to reflect that. For economic man in the late 20th century, child-rearing has become a crummy financial bargain. Fortunately, as Mom always said, there's more to life than money.

Amy Graham contributed to this article.

Unit Selections

Key Points to Consider

❖ Do you remember trying to get answers about your body, sex, or similar topics as a young child? How did your parents respond? How did you feel?

❖ As an adolescent, where did you get answers to your questions about sex? Are you still embarrassed at any lack of information you have? Why or why not?

❖ Would you like to be a junior or senior high school-aged young person today? Why or why not? In what ways is being a young teen easier than when you were that age? How is it more difficult? In what ways is being a young male different? A young female? A young person discovering that she or he is not heterosexual?

❖ How do you view sex and sexuality at your age? In what ways is it different from when you were younger? How do you perceive the changes—positively, negatively, not sure—and to what do you attribute them? Are there things you feel you have missed? What are they?

❖ Close your eyes and imagine a couple having a pleasurable sexual interlude. When you are finished, open your eyes. How old were they? If they were younger than middle age, can you replay your vision with middle-aged or older people? Why or why not? How does this relate to your expectations regarding your own romantic and/or sexual life a few decades from now?

❖ Do you ever think about your parents as sexual people? Your grandparents? Was considering these two questions upsetting for you? Embarrassing? Explain your answers as best you can.

 **Links** | # www.dushkin.com/online/

22. **American Association of Retired Persons (AARP)**
http://www.aarp.org
23. **National Institute on Aging (NIA)**
http://www.nih.gov/nia/
24. **Teacher Talk**
http://education.indiana.edu/cas/tt/tthmpg.html
25. **World Association for Sexology**
http://www.tc.umn.edu/nlhome/m201/colem001/was/wasindex.htm

These sites are annotated on pages 4 and 5.

Individual sexual development is a lifelong process that begins at birth and terminates at death. Contrary to popular notions of this process, there are no latent periods during which the individual is nonsexual or noncognizant of sexuality. The growing process of a sexual being does, however, reveal qualitative differences through various life stages. This section devotes attention to these stages of the life cycle and their relation to sexuality.

As children gain self-awareness, they naturally explore their own bodies, masturbate, display curiosity about the bodies of the opposite sex, and show interest in the bodies of mature individuals such as their parents. Exploration and curiosity are important and healthy aspects of human development. Yet it is often difficult for adults (who live in a society that is not comfortable with sexuality in general) to avoid making their children feel ashamed of being sexual or showing interest in sexuality. When adults impose their ambivalence upon a child's innocuous explorations into sexuality, fail to communicate with children about this real and important aspect of human life, or behave toward children in sexually inappropriate ways, distortion of an indispensable and formative stage of development occurs. This often leaves profound emotional scars that hinder full acceptance of self and sexuality later in the child's life.

Adolescence, the social stage accompanying puberty and the transition to adulthood, proves to be a very stressful period of life for many individuals as they attempt to develop an adult identity and forge relationships with others. Because of the physiological capacity of adolescents for reproduction, sexuality tends to be heavily censured by parents and society at this stage of life. Societal messages, however, are powerful, conflicting, and confusing: Just Say No . . . Just Do It; billboards and magazine ads using adolescent bodies provocatively and partially undressed; "romance" novels, television shows, movies with torrid sex scenes, and Internet chat rooms. In addition, individual and societal attitudes place tremendous emphasis on sexual attractiveness (especially for females) and sexual competency (especially for males). These physical, emotional, and cultural pressures combine to create confusion and anxiety in adolescents and young adults about whether they are okay and normal. Information and assurances from adults can alleviate these stresses and facilitate positive and responsible sexual maturity if there is mutual trust and willingness in both generations.

Sexuality finally becomes socially acceptable in adulthood, at least within marriage. Yet routine, boredom, stress, pressures, the pace of life, work or parenting responsibilities, and/or lack of communication can exact heavy tolls on the quantity and quality of sexual interaction. Sexual misinformation, myths, and unanswered questions, especially about emotional and/or physiological changes in sexual arousal/response or functioning, can also undermine or hinder intimacy and sexual interaction in the middle years.

Sexuality in the later years of life has also been socially and culturally stigmatized because of the prevailing misconception that only young, attractive, or married people are sexual. Such an attitude has contributed significantly to the apparent decline in sexual interest and activity as one grows older. As population demographics have shifted and the baby boomer generation has aged, these beliefs and attitudes have begun to change. Physiological changes in the aging process are not, in and of themselves, detrimental to sexual expression. A life history of experiences, good health, and growth can make sexual expression in the later years a most rewarding and fulfilling experience, and today's aging population is becoming more vocal in letting their children and grandchildren know that *old can be sexy!*

The articles chosen for the *Youth and Their Sexuality* subsection address several difficult and somewhat controversial issues related to sexuality, society, and children. The opening article, "Where'd You Learn That?" dramatically illustrates that today's younger generation appears to know more facts and to be less embarrassed about talking about sex than their parents. The next two articles provide expert and practical assistance for parents who do want to be effective sex educators for their children. "Age-by-Age Guide to Nudity" dramatically shows that children are born as sensual and sexual people, and that adults' verbal and nonverbal messages about nudity and bodies can have powerful effects. "Raising Sexually Healthy Kids" emphasizes that "the talk" about sex is not the only crucial role parents play in their child(ren)'s sexual development. The final article in the subsection addresses an often-neglected minority in our adolescent population that many would, it seems, prefer to believe does not exist. "Breaking through the Wall of Silence: Gay, Lesbian, and Bisexual Issues for Middle Level Educators" details the lonely, confusing, stigmatized, and, sometimes tragic experience of growing up gay, lesbian, or bisexual and includes the recommendations of the National Middle School Association for helping these young people.

The *Sexuality in the Adult Years* subsection deals with a variety of issues for individuals and couples who are 20-something, 30-something, or 90-something. The opening article's title, "The Three Kinds of Sex Happy Couples Need" is enticing and explains how couples can arrive at a balance of sexual intimacy that will nurture their relationship. The next article not only challenges readers to replace their old-is-dried-up or over-the-hill perceptions of aging; it tells readers how to have full, healthy, and satisfying sex no matter what their age.

Sexuality through the Life Cycle

WHERE'D YOU LEARN THAT?

American kids are in the midst of their own sexual revolution, one leaving many parents feeling confused and virtually powerless

By RON STODGHILL II

THE CUTE LITTLE COUPLE LOOKED AS if they should be sauntering through Great Adventure or waiting in line for tokens at the local arcade. Instead, the 14-year-olds walked purposefully into the Teen Center in suburban Salt Lake City, Utah. They didn't mince words about their reason for stopping in. For quite some time, usually after school and on weekends, the boy and girl had tried to heighten their arousal during sex. Flustered yet determined, the pair wanted advice on the necessary steps that might lead them to a more fulfilling orgasm. His face showing all the desperation of a lost tourist, the boy spoke for both of them when he asked frankly, "How do we get to the G-spot?"

Whoa. Teen Center nurse Patti Towle admits she was taken aback by the inquiry. She couldn't exactly provide a road map. Even more, the destination was a bit scandalous for a couple of ninth-graders in the heart of Mormon country. But these kids had clearly already gone further sexually than many adults, so Towle didn't waste time preaching the gospel of abstinence. She gave her young adventurers some reading material on the subject, including the classic women's health book *Our Bodies, Ourselves,* to help bring them closer in bed. She also brought up the question of whether a G-spot even exists. As her visitors were leaving, Towle offered them more freebies: "I sent them out the door with a billion condoms."

G-spots. Orgasms. Condoms. We all know kids say and do the darndest things, but how they have changed! One teacher recalls a 10-year-old raising his hand to ask her to define oral sex. He was quickly followed by an 8-year-old girl behind him who asked, "Oh, yeah, and what's anal sex?" These are the easy questions. Rhonda Sheared, who teaches sex education in Pinellas County, Fla., was asked by middle school students about the sound *kweif,* which the kids say is the noise a vagina makes during or after sex. "And how do you keep it from making this noise?"

There is more troubling behavior in Denver. School officials were forced to institute a sexual-harassment policy owing to a sharp rise in lewd language, groping, pinching and bra-snapping incidents among sixth-, seventh- and eighth-graders. Sex among kids in Pensacola, Fla., became so pervasive that students of a private Christian junior high school are now asked to sign cards vowing not to have sex until they marry. But the cards don't mean anything, says a 14-year-old boy at the school. "It's broken promises."

It's easy enough to blame everything on television and entertainment, even the news. At a Denver middle school, boys rationalize their actions this way: "If the President can do it, why can't we?" White House sex scandals are one thing, but how can anyone avoid Viagra and virility? Or public discussions of sexually transmitted diseases like AIDS and herpes? Young girls have lip-synched often enough to Alanis Morissette's big hit of a couple of years ago, *You Oughta Know,* to have found the sex nestled in the lyric. But it's more than just movies and television and news. Adolescent curiosity about sex is fed by a pandemic openness about it—in the schoolyard, on the bus, at home when no adult is watching. Just eavesdrop at the mall one afternoon, and you'll hear enough pubescent sexcapades to pen the next few episodes of *Dawson's Creek,* the most explicit show on teen sexuality, on the WB network. Parents, always the last to keep up, are now almost totally pre-empted. Chris (not his real name), 13, says his parents talked to him about sex when he was 12 but he had been indoctrinated earlier by a 17-year-old cousin. In any case, he gets his full share of information from the tube. "You name the show,

"If you're feeling steamy and hot, there's only one thing you want to do."

—STEPHANIE, WHO LOST HER VIRGINITY AT 14

and I've heard about it, *Jerry Springer,* MTV, *Dawson's Creek,* HBO *After Midnight . . ."* Stephanie (not her real name), 16, of North Lauderdale, Fla., who first had sex when she was 14, claims to have slept with five boyfriends and is considered a sex expert by her friends. She says, "You can learn a lot about sex from cable. It's all mad-sex stuff." She sees nothing to condemn. "If you're feeling steamy and hot, there's only one thing you want to do. As long as you're using a condom, what's wrong with it? Kids have hormones too."

In these steamy times, it is becoming largely irrelevant whether adults approve of kids' sowing their oats—or knowing so much about the technicalities of the dissemination. American adolescents are in the midst of their own kind of sexual revolution—one that has left many parents feeling confused, frightened and almost powerless. Parents can search all they want for common ground with today's kids, trying to draw parallels between contemporary carnal knowledge and an earlier generation's free-love crusades, but the two movements are quite different. A desire to break out of the old-fashioned strictures fueled the '60s movement, and its participants made sexual freedom a kind of new religion. That sort of reverence has been replaced by a more consumerist attitude. In a 1972 cover story, TIME declared, "Teenagers generally are woefully ignorant about sex." Ignorance is no longer the rule. As a weary junior high counselor in Salt Lake City puts it, "Teens today are almost nonchalant about sex. It's like we've been to the moon too many times."

The good news about their precocious knowledge of the mechanics of sex is that a growing number of teens know how to protect themselves, at least physically. But what about their emotional health and social behavior? That's a more troublesome picture. Many parents and teachers—as well as some thoughtful teenagers—worry about the desecration of love and the subversion of mature relationships. Says Debra Haffner, president of the Sexuality Information and Education Council of the United States: "We should not confuse kids' pseudo-sophistication about sexuality and their ability to use the language with their understanding of who they are as sexual young people or their ability to make good decisions."

One ugly side effect is a presumption among many adolescent boys that sex is an entitlement—an attitude that fosters a breakdown of respect for oneself and others. Says a seventh-grade girl: "The guy will ask you up front. If you turn him down, you're a bitch. But if you do it, you're a ho. The guys

are after us all the time, in the halls, everywhere. You scream, 'Don't touch me!' but it doesn't do any good." A Rhode Island Rape Center study of 1,700 sixth- and ninth-graders found 65% of boys and 57% of girls believing it acceptable for a male to force a female to have sex if they've been dating for six months.

Parents who are aware of this cultural revolution seem mostly torn between two approaches: preaching abstinence or suggesting prophylactics—and thus condoning sex. Says Cory Hollis, 37, a father of three in the Salt Lake City area: "I don't want to see my teenage son ruin his life. But if he's going to do it, I told him that I'd go out and get him the condoms myself." Most parents seem too squeamish to get into the subtleties of instilling sexual ethics. Nor are schools up to the job of moralizing. Kids say they accept their teachers' admonitions to have safe sex but tune out other stuff. "The personal-development classes are a joke," says Sarah, 16, of Pensacola. "Even the teacher looks uncomfortable. There is no way anybody is going to ask a serious question." Says Shana, a 13-year-old from Denver: "A lot of it is old and boring. They'll talk about not having sex before marriage, but no one listens. I use that class for study hall."

Shana says she is glad "sex isn't so taboo now, I mean with all the teenage pregnancies." But she also says that "it's creepy and kind of scary that it seems to be happening so early, and all this talk about it." She adds, "Girls are jumping too quickly. They figure if they can fall in love in a month, then they can have sex in a month too." When she tried discouraging a classmate from having sex for the first time, the friend turned to her and said, "My God, Shana. It's just sex."

Three powerful forces have shaped today's child prodigies: a prosperous informa-

tion age that increasingly promotes products and entertains audiences by titillation; aggressive public-policy initiatives that loudly preach sexual responsibility, further desensitizing kids to the subject; and the decline of two-parent households, which leaves adolescents with little supervision. Thus kids are not only bombarded with messages about sex—many of them contradictory—but also have more private time to engage in it than did previous generations. Today more than half of the females and three-quarters of the males ages 15 to 19 have experienced sexual intercourse, according to the Commission on Adolescent Sexual Health. And while the average age at first intercourse has come down only a year since 1970 (currently it's 17 for girls and 16 for boys), speed is of the essence for the new generation. Says Haffner: "If kids today are going to do more than kiss, they tend to move very quickly toward sexual intercourse."

The remarkable—and in ways lamentable—product of youthful promiscuity and higher sexual IQ is the degree to which kids learn to navigate the complex hypersexual world that reaches out seductively to them at every turn. One of the most positive results: the incidence of sexually transmitted diseases and of teenage pregnancy is declining. Over the past few years, kids have managed to chip away at the teenage birthrate, which in 1991 peaked at 62.1 births per 1,000 females. Since then the birthrate has dropped 12% to 54.7. Surveys suggest that as many as two-thirds of teenagers now use condoms, a proportion that is three times as high as reported in the 1970s. "We're clearly starting to make progress," says Dr. John Santelli, a physician with the Centers for Disease Control and Prevention's division of adolescent and school health. "And the key statistics bear that out." Even if they've had sex, many kids are learning to put off having more till later; they are also making condom use during intercourse nonnegotiable; and, remarkably, the fleeting pleasures of lust may even be wising up some of them to a greater appreciation of love.

For better or worse, sex-filled television helps shape your opinion. In Chicago, Ryan, an 11-year-old girl, intently watches a scene from one of her favorite TV dramas, *Dawson's Creek.* She listens as the character Jen, who lost her virginity at 12 while drunk, confesses to her new love, Dawson, "Sex doesn't equal happiness. I can't apologize for my past." Ryan is quick to defend Jen. "I think she was young, but if I were Dawson, I would believe she had changed. She acts totally different now." But Ryan is shocked by an episode of her other favorite

---

From what sources do teenagers today mainly learn about sex?	1986	1998
Friends	43%	45%
Television	11%	29%
Parents	8%	7%
Sex Ed	18%	3%

From a telephone poll of 1,011 adult Americans taken for TIME/CNN on April 8–9 by Yankelovich Partners Inc. Sampling error is 3.1%

"If the President can do it, why can't we?"

—A MALE STUDENT, REASONING AT A DENVER MIDDLE SCHOOL

show, *Buffy the Vampire Slayer,* in which Angel, a male vampire, "turned bad" after having sex with the 17-year-old Buffy. "That kinda annoyed me," says Ryan. "What would have happened if she had had a baby? Her whole life would have been thrown out the window." As for the fallen Angel: "I am so mad! I'm going to take all my pictures of him down now."

Pressed by critics and lobbies, television has begun to include more realistic story lines about sex and its possible consequences. TV writers and producers are turning to groups like the Kaiser Family Foundation, an independent health-policy think tank, for help in adding more depth and accuracy to stories involving sex. Kaiser has consulted on daytime soaps *General Hospital* and *One Life to Live* as well as the prime-time drama *ER* on subjects ranging from teen pregnancy to coming to terms with a gay high school athlete. Says Matt James, a Kaiser senior vice president: "We're trying to work with them to improve the public-health content of their shows."

And then there's real-life television. MTV's *Loveline,* an hour-long Q.-and-A. show featuring sex guru Drew Pinsky (*see accompanying story*), is drawing raves among teens for its informative sexual content. Pinsky seems to be almost idolized by some youths. "Dr. Drew has some excellent advice," says Keri, an eighth-grader in Denver. "It's not just sex, it's real life. Society makes you say you've got to look at shows like *Baywatch,* but I'm sick of blond bimbos. They're so fake. Screenwriters ought to get a life."

With so much talk of sex in the air, the extinction of the hapless, sexually naive kid seems an inevitability. Indeed, kids today as young as seven to 10 are picking up the first details of sex even in Saturday-morning cartoons. Brett, a 14-year-old in Denver, says it doesn't matter to him whether his parents chat with him about sex or not because he gets so much from TV. Whenever he's curious about something sexual, he channel-surfs his way to certainty. "If you watch TV, they've got everything you want to know," he says. "That's how I learned to kiss, when I was eight. And the girl told me, 'Oh, you sure know how to do it.' "

Even if kids don't watch certain television shows, they know the programs exist and are bedazzled by the forbidden. From schoolyard word of mouth, eight-year-old Jeff in Chicago has heard all about the foul-mouthed kids in the raunchily plotted *South Park,* and even though he has never seen the show, he can describe certain episodes in detail. (He is also familiar with the AIDS theme

of the musical *Rent* because he's heard the CD over and over.) Argentina, 16, in Detroit, says, "TV makes sex look like this big game." Her friend Michael, 17, adds, "They make sex look like Monopoly or something. You have to do it in order to get to the next level."

Child experts say that by the time many kids hit adolescence, they have reached a point where they aren't particularly obsessed with sex but have grown to accept the notion that solid courtships—or at least strong physical attractions—potentially lead to sexual intercourse. Instead of denying it, they get an early start preparing for it—and playing and perceiving the roles prescribed for them. In Nashville, 10-year-old Brantley whispers about a classmate, "There's this girl I know, she's nine years old, and she already shaves her legs and plucks her eyebrows, and I've heard she's had sex. She even has bigger boobs than my mom!"

The playacting can eventually lead to discipline problems at school. Alan Skriloff, assistant superintendent of personnel and curriculum for New Jersey's North Brunswick school system, notes that there has been an increase in mock-sexual behavior in buses carrying students to school. He insists there have been no incidents of sexual assault but, he says, "we've dealt with kids simulating sexual intercourse and simulating masturbation. It's very disturbing to the other children and to the parents, obviously." Though Skriloff says that girls are often the initiators of such conduct, in most school districts the aggressors are usually boys.

Nan Stein, a senior researcher at the Wesley College Center for Research on Women, believes sexual violence and harassment is on the rise in schools, and she says, "It's happening between kids who are dating or want to be dating or used to date." Linda Osmundson, executive director of the Center Against Spouse Abuse in St. Petersburg, Fla., notes that "it seems to be coming down to younger and younger girls who feel that if they don't pair up with these guys, they'll have no position in their lives. They are pressured into lots of sexual activity." In this process of socialization, "no" is becoming less and less an option.

In such a world, schools focus on teaching scientific realism rather than virginity. Sex-ed teachers tread lightly on the moral questions of sexual intimacy while going heavy on the risk of pregnancy or a sexually transmitted disease. Indeed, health educators in some school districts complain that teaching abstinence to kids today is getting to be a futile exercise. Using less final terms like "postpone" or "delay" helps draw some kids

in, but semantics often isn't the problem. In a Florida survey, the state found that 75% of kids had experienced sexual intercourse by the time they reached 12th grade, with some 20% of the kids having had six or more sexual partners. Rick Colonno, father of a 16-year-old son and 14-year-old daughter in Arvada, Colo., views sex ed in schools as a necessary evil to fill the void that exists in many homes. Still, he's bothered by what he sees as a subliminal endorsement of sex by authorities. "What they're doing," he says, "is preparing you for sex and then saying, 'But don't have it.' "

With breathtaking pragmatism, kids look for ways to pursue their sex life while avoiding pregnancy or disease. Rhonda Sheared, the Florida sex-ed teacher, says a growing number of kids are asking questions about oral and anal sex because they've discovered that it allows them to be sexually active without risking pregnancy. As part of the Pinellas County program, students in middle and high school write questions anonymously, and, as Sheared says, "they're always looking for the loophole."

A verbatim sampling of some questions:

- "Can you get AIDS from fingering a girl if you have no cuts? Through your fingernails?"
- "Can you get AIDS from '69'?"
- "If you shave your vagina or penis, can that get rid of crabs?"
- "If yellowish stuff comes out of a girl, does it mean you have herpes, or can it just happen if your period is due, along with abdominal pains?"
- "When sperm hits the air, does it die or stay alive for 10 days?"

Ideally, most kids say, they would prefer their parents do the tutoring, but they realize that's unlikely. For years psychologists and sociologists have warned about a new generation gap, one created not so much by different morals and social outlooks as by career-driven parents, the economic necessity of two incomes leaving parents little time for talks with their children. Recent studies indicate that many teens think parents are the most accurate source of information and would like to talk to them more about sex and sexual ethics but can't get their attention long enough. Shana sees the conundrum this way: "Parents haven't set boundaries, but they are expecting them."

Yet some parents are working harder to counsel their kids on sex. Cathy Wolf, 29, of North Wales, Pa., says she grew up learning about sex largely from her friends and from reading controversial books. Open-

"Teens today are almost nonchalant about sex."

—JUNIOR HIGH SCHOOL COUNSELOR IN SALT LAKE CITY, UTAH

minded and proactive, she says she has returned to a book she once sought out for advice, Judy Blume's novel *Are You There God? It's Me, Margaret,* and is reading it to her two boys, 8 and 11. The novel discusses the awkwardness of adolescence, including sexual stirrings. "That book was forbidden to me as a kid," Wolf says. "I'm hoping to give them a different perspective about sex, to expose them to this kind of subject matter before they find out about it themselves." Movies and television are a prod and a challenge to Wolf. In *Grease,* which is rated PG and was recently re-released, the character Rizzo "says something about 'sloppy seconds,' you know, the fact that a guy wouldn't want to do it with a girl who had just done it with another guy. There's also another point where they talk about condoms. Both Jacob and Joel wanted an explanation, so I provided it for them."

Most kids, though, lament that their parents aren't much help at all on sexual matters. They either avoid the subject, miss the mark by starting the discussion too long before or after the sexual encounter, or just plain stonewall them. "I was nine when I asked my mother the Big Question," says Michael, in Detroit. "I'll never forget. She took out her driver's license and pointed to the line about male or female. 'That is sex,' she said." Laurel, a 17-year-old in Murfreesboro, Tenn., wishes her parents had taken more time with her to shed light on the subject. When she was six and her sister was nine, "my mom sat us down, and we had the sex talk," Laurel says. "But when I was 10, we moved in with my dad, and he never talked about it. He would leave the room if a commercial for a feminine product came on TV." And when her sister finally had sex, at 16, even her mother's vaunted openness crumbled. "She talked to my mom about it and ended up feeling like a whore because even though my mom always said we could talk to her about anything, she didn't want to hear that her daughter had slept with a boy."

Part of the problem for many adults is that they aren't quite sure how they feel about teenage sex. A third of adults think adolescent sexual activity is wrong, while a majority of adults think it's O.K. and, under certain conditions, normal, healthy behavior, according to the Alan Guttmacher Institute, a nonprofit, reproductive-health research group. In one breath, parents say they perceive it as a public-health issue and want more information about sexual behavior and its consequences, easier access to contraceptives and more material in the media about responsible human and sexual interaction. And in the next breath, they claim it's a moral issue to be resolved through preaching abstinence and the virtues of virginity and getting the trash off TV. "You start out talk-

---

LISTENING IN ON *BOY TALK*

THE THREE BOYS, ALL 12, HAVE REQUESTED THAT THEIR MOMS NOT BE ALLOWED IN THE room. W. takes pains to close all the doors to the dining room where the discussion is going to take place. At one point, he gets up to chase away his little brother. W.'s friends H. and P. are twins, but H. quickly points out, "Trust us. We have completely different views on the subject." The subject is sex.

Do the boys think about sex?

"Do we ever," giggles W.

"Yes is the short answer," says H. "We think about when we will have sex and who it will be with. We've seen nudity—on TV, in *Playboys.*"

"He took them from my dad last year," P. interrupts. "My dad is a writer, and he was using them to research an article."

Why did H. take the *Playboys*? "Put yourself in our shoes," he explains. "You're 12 years old, and you're alone in the house. What would you do?"

The three boys have checked out *Beverly Hills 90210,* which, says H., "definitely had enough sex going down." The Internet is tempting and accessible but, says W., "you never really use it because it takes so much time and money." They say the movie that really got their juices flowing was the vintage frat-boy flick *Animal House.* W. saw it at a sleepover, and the twins say their older brother brought it home one night. Says W.: "It really opened me up to sex."

Do the three hang out with girls much?

"I have no shortage of time with girls," says H.

"He certainly doesn't," says his twin.

"What I mean is, I have a lot of friends who are girls," says H., stressing that the conversations don't get much into sex. "I'm really careful how I talk to girls. You have to have personal limits. Sex is not something I go around blabbing about." But girls are enough on their minds so that P. taped a phone conversation his brother was having with a classmate about girls.

The three have attended school dances where they've seen people "grinding" and getting "frisky and stuff." At the ice-skating rink, P. saw a seventh-grade couple tightly embracing and passionately kissing. "It was pretty scary," he says.

The subject turns to other classmates. "I think he likes boys," says H. about one. He and W. start to imitate the classmate, talking in high voices and with their hands. What makes them so suspicious? "He went out for five months with a girl and didn't kiss," says H. "I went out with someone for five days, and we did kiss."

"Maybe he's bisexual," says W.

"The vibe here is overhomophobic," says P. with a look of disapproval.

"We really try not to be homophobes," says his chastened brother.

How much sex goes on among the other kids in their grade? Says H. "There are some who do make out; they do hang out on the couch at parties. I think they go as far as kids our age should. They can't go beyond the makeout stage because somebody will find out."

But, says W., "the only reason they don't go further is because they're afraid rumors will be spread."

The three devise a makeshift formula to measure appropriate sixth-grade sexual activity. On a scale of 1 to 10, level 2 is hand holding, 4 is hugging, 6 is kissing and 7 is tongue-kissing. "If they're feeling each other up with their clothes on," says H., "then one thing leads to another. They're 12 years old. You know what I mean? Before you know it, you'll have kids our age having sex." Says W.: "The frenching thing is the edge." For now.

—*By Charlotte Faltermayer*

"If you watch TV, they've got everything you want to know."

—BRETT, 14, IN DENVER

Since 1991, the teenage birth rate has dropped 12%

ing about condoms in this country, and you end up fighting about the future of the American family," says Sarah Brown, director of the Campaign Against Teen Pregnancy. "Teens just end up frozen like a deer in headlights."

Not all kids are happy with television's usurping the role of village griot. Many say they've become bored by—and even resent—sexual themes that seem pointless and even a distraction from the information or entertainment they're seeking. "It's like everywhere," says Ryan, a 13-year-old seventh-grader in Denver, "even in *Skateboarding* [magazine]. It's become so normal it doesn't even affect you. On TV, out of nowhere, they'll begin talking about masturbation." Another Ryan, 13, in the eighth grade at the same school, agrees: "There's sex in the cartoons and messed-up people on the talk shows—'My lover sleeping with my best friend.' I can remember the jumping-condom ads. There's just too much of it all."

Many kids are torn between living up to a moral code espoused by their church and parents and trying to stay true to the swirling laissez-faire. Experience is making many sadder but wiser. The shame, anger or even indifference stirred by early sex can lead to prolonged abstinence. Chandra, a 17-year-old in Detroit, says she had sex with a boyfriend of two years for the first time at 15 despite her mother's constant pleas against it. She says she wishes she had heeded her mother's advice. "One day I just decided to do it," she says. "Afterward, I was kind of mad that I let it happen. And I was sad because I knew my mother wouldn't have approved." Chandra stopped dating the boy more than a year ago and hasn't had sex since. "It would have to be someone I really cared about," she says. "I've had sex before, but I'm not a slut."

With little guidance from grownups, teens have had to discover for themselves that the ubiquitous sexual messages must be tempered with caution and responsibility. It is quite clear, even to the most sexually experienced youngsters, just how dangerous a little information can be. Stephanie in North Lauderdale, who lost her virginity two years

DR. DREW, *AFTER-HOURS* GURU

KIDS AREN'T SUPPOSED TO BE TUNING IN TO DR. DREW PINSKY ON *Loveline,* MTV's popular nightly call-in show on relationships. The program is aimed at young adults, and, Pinsky says, younger teens shouldn't watch it without a parent nearby. But they manage to. Sometimes because of a technicality: the show airs at 10 p.m. in the Central time zone instead of 11 p.m., as it does on the East and West coasts. But mainly because the subject is sex. And if sex is on the tube, adolescents are sure to find a way of getting to it—and talking about it.

And what do kids see? This scene, for example: Dr. Drew listening closely to an embarrassed 21-year-old whose girlfriend has been joking to his friends about the size of his penis. Pinsky handles this painful subject with a quick, matter-of-fact suggestion: Take a closer, more informed look at your abusive girlfriend. After a crass joke from Pinsky's partner, comedian Adam Carolla—there to provide levity—*Loveline's* newest co-host, Diane Farr, affirms that size, despite what the ads for *Godzilla* say, is not all it's cracked up to be. Pinsky's message, both educational and reassuring, is one that permeates his show: Respect yourself.

"I suppose I'm a healthier role model than, say, Slash of *Guns N' Roses,*" concedes the practicing internist of his idol status among the scores of adolescents and young adults comforted by his gently informative, utterly genuine approach. But what motivates him is his ability to reach a population in desperate need of information—a skill he first discovered 15 years ago as a medical student in California. When two disc-jockey acquaintances were starting a new show on relationships, they asked him to be the medical consultant. Pinsky, now a happily married parent of triplets, had sensed that young people were not receiving much sex education from their parents—a result of what he calls the 1970s "abdication of parenting" ethos. But he was stunned by the response to the first few shows. "It was an epiphany. The most important health issues for younger people were being presented to FM disc jockeys!"

A full-fledged convert, Pinsky signed on as "Dr. Drew" to what quickly became *Loveline,* the hit Los Angeles-based radio show he still plays host on (and which MTV's version is based on). His growing medical practice confirmed his suspicions about kids: "Behind closed doors, they wouldn't talk at all. In my white coat, I was an authority figure. I was Dad, their worst nightmare." In a medium in which kids were comfortable, he could "demystify" difficult issues surrounding sexuality and "maybe make adolescence less painful."

What may make *Loveline* a particularly compelling alternative to, say, daytime TV's *Jerry Springer,* is its underlying "mission." Pinsky is obsessed with changing what he views as a culture of "broken-down interpersonal relationships" that lack intimacy. He calls the show a "sheep in wolf's clothing that discourages sexual activity and encourages responsibility and connection in a hip, relatable context. Of particular concern to him is the rest of the media, which often portray sex as a simple physical act with no emotional consequences. Is he troubled about young teens having sex? Pinsky says a significant percentage may be reacting to having been sexually abused. He also suggests, though, that as a whole this group tends to be healthier, more inquisitive and "more realistic" than the older generation. That bodes well for Pinsky's aim to change the world. "We're not glamourizing sex; we are confronting behavior," he says emphatically. "The idea is to climb into their culture. I'll take any punch. I'm just grateful I'm welcomed."
—*By Harriet Barovick*

ago, watches with concern as her seven-year-old sister moves beyond fuzzy thoughts of romance inspired by *Cinderella* or *Aladdin* into sexual curiosity. "She's always talking about pee-pees, and she sees somebody on TV kissing and hugging or something, and she says, 'Oh, they had sex.' I think she's

going to find out about this stuff before I did." She pauses. "We don't tell my sister anything," she says, "but she's not a naive child." —*With reporting by Julie Grace/Salt Lake City, Richard Woodbury/Denver, Charlotte Faltermayer/New York, Timothy Roche/Fort Lauderdale and other bureaus*

age-by-age guide to nudity

Families differ when it comes to modesty, but how much privacy do kids (and parents) really need?

Anthony E. Wolf, Ph.D., with Ellen H. Parlapiano

Contributing editor Anthony E. Wolf, Ph.D., is the author of "It Isn't Fair" ... A Guide to the Tougher Parts of Parenting. Ellen H. Parlapiano is a writer and mother of two.

Three-year-old Malcolm stripped off his swimming trunks and began to romp in the nude at the crowded beach he was visiting with his parents. "Look, Mommy, now everybody can see my weeny!" he declared with pride. Of course, we want our kids to feel good about their bodies. We want them to be proud of how they look—but maybe not quite that proud! How do we help them become confident and comfortable with nudity, yet at the same time teach them that their bodies are private and not for public show? And how do our own attitudes and reactions to nakedness affect our children's physical confidence? The following guide to body-baring behaviors, from infancy through the grade-school years, reveals what you can expect and how best to handle nudity—your kids' and your own.

Birth to 18 months

Bare-All Babies

"Where's Amy's nose?" Dad asked his 13-month-old as he bathed her. But Amy couldn't have cared less about her nose right then—she was investigating the territory between her legs instead.

Being naked helps infants learn about their bodies by giving them the opportunity to see and touch their various parts. Even if it's embarrassing to you as an onlooker, you shouldn't underestimate the value of this type of exploration. A child's gaining a clear sense of her physique is an integral part of good emotional and intellectual development.

The learning process is gradual. Newborns don't even know they have a body. But as they grow, so does their self-awareness. Their tactile and visual senses increase, and their muscle control strengthens. Little by little, babies realize that their body parts belong to them. They can reach out and touch things, experience what it feels like to be touched back, and learn about themselves and how they are connected to the world around them.

How can you help your baby learn about her body? The bathtub and the changing table are the most logical places to provide your little one total access to her body. There, she can regularly see and touch herself all over while she interacts with you. Let her explore herself freely, and don't take her hands away from her private areas.

Don't be afraid to let your baby be naked at other times, too. As long as she's in a place that's safe and warm, she'll be fine. Let her go diaperless in the crib or on the playmat. Allow her to learn what it feels like to be bare-bellied on a flannel sheet or bare-bottomed on the smooth kitchen floor. At this stage, the big issues about nakedness are that your child gets to experience it at least some of the time and that she learns to recognize and point to most of her body parts.

18 months to 3 years

Should Toddlers Run Naked?

Two-year-old Kenny was playing in the front yard with his mother. As soon as she turned her back to say hello to an

From *Child* magazine, June/July 1996, pp. 36-38, 40. © 1996 by Anthony E. Wolf and Ellen H. Parlapiano. Reprinted by permission.

Toddlers love taking their clothes off. Being naked gives them a sense of freedom and helps them feel independent.

elderly couple strolling by, Kenny whipped off his clothes and streaked across the lawn exuberantly—giving the senior citizens quite a surprise. "I just can't seem to keep his clothes on lately!" Kenny's mother explained with a sheepish grin.

Toddlers love taking off their clothes. Wearing clothes can feel confining and uncomfortable, while being naked gives them a sense of freedom and helps them feel independent. But since it's too early to teach toddlers rules about nudity, the responsibility of deciding whether they can be naked or not falls to you. No matter how much children enjoy being nude, there are simply some times and places where you have to see to it that they keep their clothes on.

First, determine when and where nudity is appropriate, according to what you are most comfortable with: Some parents allow their toddlers to be nude in the front yard, for example, while others do not. Of course, your personal policy should be in keeping with the norms of society. Allowing a nude toddler to romp in the front yard may be no big deal, but bringing a na-

get into a power struggle about it, as this can easily escalate into a battle of wills in other areas besides dressing.

Do designate some places —such as the backyard— where your toddler can bare all. Many parents find this is a great time to play "name that body part." Romps in the nude can also be helpful during these accident-prone toilet-training years. When they cavort in the nude, keep the potty nearby. Then, when the urge strikes, they can get to it quickly and easily with-out having to fumble with clothing.

3 to 6 years

Becoming Body Conscious

Denise's father was taking a shower when she came into the bathroom to chat. In the past, he hadn't worried if his daughter, now 4, saw him naked.

Words That Hurt

A negative reaction to your child's nudity can have a big impact on how comfortable she'll be with her body.

Never make statements that express:

Shame "It's not nice for little girls to run around naked."

Shock "I can't believe you're doing that in front of your Aunt Louise! Put some clothes on!"

Insensitivity "I don't understand why you're so nervous about undressing in gym class."

Good-natured teasing "Too bad. You've got thunder thighs just like your mom."

Negative comparisons "Your brother was much more muscular at this age."

It all depends on your personal philosophy and style. What's most important is that you convey a sense of confidence, not uneasiness, about your body. So do what makes you feel the most comfortable. If you're the uninhibited type who often walks around in the buff, you needn't stop. But do tune into your child's feelings about it. If she seems bothered by your nudity, you'll want to start limiting her exposure to it.

On the other hand, if you feel uncomfortable about your child's seeing you nude, now is the time to establish some privacy boundaries. Show her that in some places—specifically bathrooms and bedrooms—you want privacy. But teach this lesson in a low-key way. Denise's dad might say something like, "We'll talk as soon as I get out of the shower, honey." He shouldn't get anxious or angry, and he certainly shouldn't ban Denise from the room. Eventually, preschoolers will learn to respect the boundaries on their own.

Still, it's natural for children this age to be curious and make comments about what they observe. Be prepared for questions like, "What are those big bumps on your chest, Mommy?" or "How come you're so hairy there?" The best response is always a matter-of-fact one. You don't have to go into great detail, but you should acknowledge and answer questions like these with simple, straightforward responses. For example, you could say, "They're called breasts," and, "Because grown-ups have hair there."

"Mommy, what are those big bumps on your chest?" It's natural for preschoolers to ask questions about what they see.

ked tot to the supermarket would surely raise some eyebrows! Be respectful of other people's sensibilities and avoid practices that would be considered shocking by most people. It's not fair to your children to impose countercultural rules upon them.

Your next job is clothes management. If Kenny's mother doesn't want him to be nude in the front yard, she has to matter-of-factly say, "When we're in the front yard, we need to wear our clothes." If he refuses to put his clothes on, she should calmly do it for him. Avoid saying things that imply that nudity is bad. And certainly don't

But lately he'd been finding himself increasingly uncomfortable. What's more, Denise had begun asking him lots of questions about his private parts. Should he be more discreet?

In the preschool years, children are not only more aware of the differences in people's bodies but more inquisitive about them. That may leave you wondering just how much of your own body to bare, particularly if your child is of the opposite sex. Should you cover up when preschoolers see you naked in the bathroom or bedroom? Should you discourage them from entering a room when you're getting dressed?

6 to 9 years

Modesty and Manners

Seven-year-old Joseph was changing in his room when his mom appeared in the doorway with clean socks. "Don't come in! I'm naked!" he screamed, jumping up to close the door.

To feel good about their bodies, school-age kids need some control over who sees them naked. Parents need to respect that.

Joseph's mom was surprised. He'd never been self-conscious about his body before. Why the sudden desire for privacy?

Modesty emerges in the early grade-school years. In order to feel good about their bodies, kids this age need to know that they have some control over who sees them naked. As a parent, you need to respect that. Clue in to your child's feelings, and be sensitive to his growing need for privacy. If he doesn't want you or his siblings to see him nude, go along whenever it's practical. It's important that grade-school kids have a place where they can undress without interruptions. Simple gestures, like knocking before entering the bedroom or bathroom,

will show your child that you value his feelings.

If grade-schoolers are being bothered by siblings who insist on barging in on them, set some family rules. Tell the sibling, "Your brother doesn't want you coming into his room when he's dressing. I need you to respect that." But don't get too involved in enforcing this. It's best for siblings to resolve such issues on their own.

Be aware, too, that grade-schoolers are likely to become increasingly uneasy about seeing you in the nude. Start being more discreet when you dress and undress—especially with kids of the opposite sex—but don't get so obsessed with covering up that you become aloof or send the message that nudity is bad.

And never tease or judge kids about their modesty or self-consciousness. A positive, nurturing attitude that re-

When Mom and Dad Disagree

You're always careful to cover up in front of your kids, but your spouse parades around stark naked. You think he's an exhibitionist, and he wonders why you're such a prude. How should parents with differing philosophies handle nudity? Here are some secrets to minimizing conflict and conveying a healthy message.

Respect each other's styles. Don't be judgmental about your partner's beliefs. No one is right or wrong on this issue. You simply have different comfort levels, and it's important to recognize that.

Don't worry about having different points of view. It's all right for kids to see that their parents have opposing opinions on an issue, as long as the two of you remain calm and matter-of-fact about your differences. Your children will learn that, in this world, people don't always agree on things.

Don't criticize your spouse in front of the kids. Not only will it put a negative spin on nudity, but children will feel that they have to take sides.

flects supportiveness and sensitivity will help your child develop a healthy body image that will last a lifetime.

Playing Doctor and Other Dicey Issues

Is it proper to undress in front of your kids? Up to what age can you take your son into the ladies' room with you? A good rule of thumb is to do whatever you feel most comfortable with, keeping in mind what's considered acceptable by society, and being sensitive to your child's feelings.

Should you:	Allow children to play doctor?	Let kids touch themselves?	Bathe siblings of the opposite sex together?	Take a child of the opposite sex into a public restroom with you?	Undress in front of your kids?
Things to think about:	This is normal for preschoolers. But if kids are playing this game excessively, stop the activity in a calm and nonjudgmental way. Be particularly vigilant if grade-school kids are playing with their younger siblings.	Teach kids that this behavior is okay and that it's something they can do at home when they're in a private place, but that they shouldn't do it in public. If your child is doing it excessively, mention it to your pediatrician.	Take into account the children's ages and awareness levels. It's fine when they're really young, but as they approach school age, it's best to bathe them separately.	Consider the child's age and competency levels. Kids are generally able to go into public restrooms alone by age 5 or 6. If you're worried about your child's ability or safety, though, bring him in with you.	Take stock of your kids' gender, awareness level, and feelings. Be more discreet as your kids reach the grade-school and preteen years, particularly if they're of the opposite sex.

Kids' Behavior | sexuality

Raising **sexually** healthy kids

Everything from **bathtime** to how often you **kiss your husband** shapes your child's future **relationships.**

BY JENNIFER CADOFF

Talking about sex makes most parents—even the chatty ones—very nervous. How much do kids need to know? When should the topic be introduced? How can we help our children grow up prepared to form happy, healthy sexual relationships?

Too often, when we do attempt to broach the topic, we find ourselves fumbling through awkward explanations of the mechanics of sex or "how babies grow," all the while sensing that we are, somehow, missing the real point—that sex is an expression of love. It's not about sperm swimming up vaginas; it's about tenderness, the desire to please someone we care about. It's about being completely at ease with another person—and feeling good about that.

Children certainly do need to learn the "facts of life," but experts say that even more important is raising them to be confident, compassionate, and kind, which will teach them more about how to behave in their adult relationships than any discussion of anatomy.

"Good values are good values," says Karen Shanor, Ph.D., a Washington, D.C.-based clinical psychologist who has written several books on human sexuality. Teaching thoughtfulness and courtesy in any situation will eventually translate into how kids behave in future relationships. "If, for example, you don't teach your children to be respectful of others when you take them out for dinner, it generalizes itself later in many ways, including that child's future approach to sexual situations."

Some of the most important things we teach our children—about love and trust and physical pleasures—we do naturally, starting the day they're born. When your baby cries, you pick her up gently and speak softly. You feed her if she's hungry, tuck an extra blanket around her when it's chilly. All this teaches your baby a profound lesson: That people who care about her will respond to her needs.

Sex Ed starts at birth

For the sheer sensual delight of it, we sniff and nuzzle a powdery neck, stroke a delicious, peachy cheek, smooth the downy fuzz on a tiny head. And as we do, we are also teaching our newborns about the pleasures of another person's touch.

At the same time, you need to be aware of your baby's responses to your ministrations. "Each child, from infancy, is his own human being, with his own temperament," says Martin J. Drell, M.D., head of infant, child, and adolescent psychiatry at Louisiana State University Medical School, in New Orleans. "Some babies don't want to cuddle."

But all infants do have reflexive, sexual responses from day one. "Little boys have erections from infancy. The physical response in both girls and boys is in place very early on," notes Shanor. They frequently explore their genitals, for instance, and by the age of 10 months can deliberately fondle themselves.

And from infancy, they observe our own attitudes. "Babies understand what you're saying before they can talk, and they are exquisitely sensitive to non-verbal communication. When you scrunch up your face at a stinky diaper, it conveys clearly to your baby what you feel about a very natural process," says Drell.

By the time kids do start to talk, one of the first things we teach them is the names of body parts. What toddler can resist a rousing rendition of "Head and Shoulders, Knees and Toes"? To that lineup, experts agree, we need to add the correct terminology for a child's sexual parts. It's not likely your little boy hasn't noticed that he has a penis or your daughter that she has a clitoris. Not giving them names implies that they are forbidden.

Marty Klein, Ph.D., a Palo Alto-based sex therapist and lecturer, enjoins his audiences to repeat "vagina," loud and clear. "They think I'm kidding, at first," he admits. "But we have a responsibility for the education of our children. I'm sympathetic to parents who find talking about sex embarrassing. But instead of avoiding the topic, we need to become comfortable with it."

Learning about boundaries and privacy

Two- and 3-year-olds are often exuberantly physical. They are likely to be enthusiastic huggers, cuddlers, and masturbators, and they love to parade around buck naked.

"By age 3, you can start introducing the concept of public versus private behavior," says E. Mimi Schrader, Ph.D., a psychologist and sex therapist in Boulder, Colorado. "You might talk about using some words discreetly, or when it's okay for them to touch their private parts. If you're irritated with a child this age barging into your bathroom, you can also let her know that you need a little privacy every once in a while."

"One of the biggest jobs parents have is teaching children what's appropriate under what circumstances," says Klein, who is also the author of *Ask Me Anything: A Sex Therapist Answers the Most Important Questions for the '90s* (Pacifica). "Just as there are rules about when and what we eat and names for the body parts connected with eating, there are rules about sex, too. Playing on the floor is okay; eating on the floor is not okay. Rubbing between your legs is okay in your room but not okay in line at the grocery store."

But rub they will: Preschoolers, freed from diapers, will often touch, hold, or massage themselves, sometimes as a way to unwind. It soothes them much the same way rocking or cuddling does. Children this young can even have very pleasurable sensations—a feeling of physical release. Some children actually say, "I'm finished" when they're ready to stop.

Besides setting privacy limits, parents should allow their children to have more independence and more decision-making power as they get older.

Raising sexually healthy **boys**

Discomfort with intimacy and an inability to express affection in nonsexual ways are top problems sex therapists see in the adult men they treat. The following can help young boys grow up to be more comfortable with physical and emotional closeness. **Foster empathy in boys** by encouraging them to think about how others might feel in various situations, particularly in response to their own actions. **Praise boys when they are kind,** gentle, and considerate of others. **Teach boys that girls have a right to say no . . .** and that boys, too, can decline the advances of girls. **Allow boys to express their full range of feelings,** including pain, fear, and timidity. "When little boys fall down, we tend to tell them not to cry, that it doesn't hurt. That teaches them from very early on to deny their feelings, even to themselves," says Karen Shanor, Ph.D., a Washington, D.C.— based clinical psychologist. Instead, acknowledge the hurt, then reassure the child it will feel better soon.

Jamie Wasserman, a New York City psychoanalyst. "By your respecting their boundaries, they learn to respect their own boundaries. They learn it's else to move in and overwhelm them." Similarly, parents should respect a child's desire for privacy, letting him use the bathroom and get dressed on

Two-year-olds are enthusiastic **cuddlers** and **huggers,** and they love to **parade around naked.**

"If a child doesn't want to cuddle and doesn't want a kiss, you need to respect that and not force them," says okay to say no to people. They learn to pay attention to their own needs and desires, instead of allowing someone his own, if he wishes, as early as they can.

Raising sexually healthy **girls**

There's no mystery to what prevents most adult women from fully enjoying sex: Therapists say it's most often low self-esteem and body-image problems. The following are ways parents can help girls to grow up feeling good about themselves. **Talk to little girls about how** healthy, strong, and capable their body is. As they grow, encourage athletics so their sense of physical prowess develops. **Let them wear overalls,** get dirty, "play rough." **Try not to focus too much on a girl's weight** or appearance. Instead, applaud school and other accomplishments so she learns to value who she is and what she can do above what she looks like. **Appreciate girls when they are outgoing,** determined, and spirited. **Teach girls that they have a right to say** no to unwanted advances—even yours. A little girl who is taught always to submit to your hugs and kisses could grow up to be a woman who doesn't believe she has the right to say no.

Teach by example

Children learn how to form happy, loving relationships by growing up in a happy, loving home. "From their parents' hugs, passing kisses, and friendly pats, a child sees love in operation," explains Schrader. "I see so many adults whose families never expressed affection. They just don't know how."

If warmhearted squeezes and smooches "in front of the kids" don't come naturally at your house, remember that the practice is likely to benefit your children as much as your marriage. And if your child wants to turn it into a group squeeze, let her join in and be assured there's plenty of love to go around.

"Affection is always the best context for sexuality," Shanor says. "If the father doesn't usually greet his wife with a kiss or ignores her, or the mother constantly complains that he's never home, those are sexual lessons. If, on

"From their parents' **hugs,** passing **kisses,** and friendly **pats,** a child sees **love in operation.**"

the other hand, children see their parents trying to be kind, that, too, is a lesson."

Help children handle our sex-permeated society

"This is a much more sexually stimulating culture than the one we were raised in," says Drell. "It's almost impossible to protect children from it." What parents can do is set standards for what we believe is appropriate for children at what age—in terms of television and movies—and to at least occasionally sit down and watch together. "The world," says Drell, "is not going to convey your values. That's something you have to do."

As children get older, they will need help handling the social aspects of sex. "If you want kids to make sexually responsible decisions, you have to teach them good decision-making skills," says Klein. "We gradually give children more responsibility for crossing streets as they get older, and we need to do the exact same thing with sex. If a 12-year-old girl is worried about kissing a boy, you can't just say, 'It's bad, don't do it.' Talk to her about whether she likes the way that person treats his friends. Does she like the way he talks about them? If he brags, she can count on the whole school finding out if she makes out with him," Klein says. Without such decision-making skills, he says, your child is left to her own devices.

In very fundamental ways, Shanor concludes, "teaching healthy sexuality works in the same format as raising healthy children in general. You teach them about love and respect and empathy by treating them with love, respect, and empathy. You're not afraid to create structure and rules that make them feel safe. If you help your children develop a strong sense of themselves and respect of themselves and respect for their own bodies, then your children, in turn, will respect other people, their bodies, and their feelings."

*Health writer **Jennifer Cadoff** has a 6-year-old son and a 9-year-old daughter.*

Breaking Through the Wall of Silence: Gay, Lesbian, and Bisexual Issues for Middle Level Educators

Norma J. Bailey and Tracy Phariss

Norma J. Bailey is a doctoral student at the University of Northern Colorado, Greeley.
Tracy Phariss teaches at Creighton Middle School in Lakewood, Colorado.

When I was in the Pearl River Middle School from sixth to eighth grade ... I did not know I was gay. I did have a feeling I was different from everyone else. These three years were my worst years in school. I was constantly called a faggot. I did not have many friends. I was very lonely and insecure. The worst part was that I could not talk to teachers ... about my feelings" (Whitlock, 1989, p. 3).

"During junior high and in my freshman year of high school, I was very depressed. Feeling alone and isolated from the rest of the world, I managed to fail three of my five majors that year Matthew, 18 (Governors Commission, 1993, p. 17).

"I felt as though I was the only gay person my age in the world. I felt as though I had nowhere to go to talk to anybody. Throughout eighth grade, I went to bed every night praying that I would not be able to wake up in the morning, and every morning waking up and being disappointed. And so finally I decided that if I was going to die, it would have to be at my own hands" Steven, 18 (Governors Commission, 1993, p. 12).

On November 6, 1993, at the Annual Business Meeting of the National Middle School Association in Portland, Oregon, the membership adopted a resolution that encouraged middle level schools to gather information on school policies and programs addressing the needs and problems of gay, lesbian, and bisexual youth so that these schools could "organize and conduct staff development initiatives designed to elevate staff awareness and sensitivity in order to ensure safe and equitable school environments for youth of every sexual orientation."

The question raised at the Open Resolutions Hearing the previous day and at the Annual Business Meeting was "Why?" Why is it necessary for NMSA to include a resolution regarding gay, lesbian, and bisexual youth in its list of resolutions which serve to focus the Association's efforts during the coming years? This may be a question that you raised as you read that this resolution was passed. Why does my *middle school* association have to deal with this issue? Surely, homosexuality is not a big concern for young adolescents. And besides, should the middle school be dealing with such an issue anyway? And, if it should, in what ways can it do that? To answer these questions is the purpose of this article.

Current Problems Regarding Gay and Lesbian Youth

In 1972 Kinsey reported that an estimated 10% of the population "has more than incidental homosexual experiences" and identifies as a gay male or lesbian in their lifetime. Although there is controversy related to sexual identity, cause and effect, most of the available evidence indicates early determination of sexual orientation, but not necessarily early recognition or acknowledgment by the individual. Nevertheless, researchers have generally accepted consistently that 10% of the population is gay or lesbian and that this portion represents every race, creed, class, ability, and disability (Grayson, 1987).

Suicide is the leading cause of death among gay male and lesbian youth . . . they are five times more likely to attempt suicide than their heterosexual peers.

This means, therefore, that a significant proportion of the educational population throughout the nation, teachers and students included, is also gay or lesbian. Leaving teachers aside, it is estimated that there are 2.9 million gay or lesbian adolescents in the United States (Colorado Department of Health, 1992; Dunham, 1989). These students, again from every race, creed, class, ability, and disability, found in urban, suburban, and rural schools, have for the most part sat passively through years of school education where their identities as gay and lesbian people have been ignored or even denied. They have done this because of their own fears and isolation and because of the failure of a society full of cultural taboos and fear of controversy, to take up their cause (Rofes, 1989). This has resulted in an "invisible" minority within our schools whose needs are just now beginning to be addressed.

The growth of gay activism in the 1980s and 1990s has yielded a new assertiveness on the part of gay and lesbian youth that has forced individual schools and sometimes entire school systems, particularly in large cities, to grapple with the reality that gay and lesbian youth are in the schools and are not going to go away (Rofes, 1989). More importantly,

however, and more widespread in its impact, is the fact that helping professionals are beginning to realize that these "invisible" students are becoming more visible each day through increased numbers of referrals to school counselors, school social workers, substance abuse personnel, and various other support staff. Individual reasons for these referrals are diverse, but among the most common concerns are efforts to clarify sexual orientation, anxiety, attempted suicide, substance abuse, low self-esteem, family conflict, and emotional isolation (Dunham, 1989). In other words, these students are finally being recognized as among our most "at risk" populations.

The normal trials of growing up as an adolescent in today's society are trying enough, but it is particularly trying for young people who experience difficulties in understanding what may be a developing homosexual orientation, in part because of the stigma attached to homosexuality in contemporary American society. These youth face problems in accepting themselves due to internalization of a negative self-image and the lack of accurate information about homosexuality and the lack of positive role models. They often face physical and verbal abuse, rejection, and isolation from family and peers. They often feel totally alone and socially withdrawn out of fear of adverse consequences. As a result of these pressures, lesbian and gay youth are more vulnerable than other adolescents to psychosocial problems including substance abuse, chronic depression, school failure, early relationship conflicts, and being forced to leave their families prematurely (Dunham, 1989).

Suicide

Each of these problems presents a risk factor for suicidal feelings and behavior for any adolescent. However, the 1989 Department of Health and Human Services Report on the Secretary's Task Force on Youth Suicide reported that suicide is the leading cause of death among gay male and lesbian youth. Furthermore, it was estimated that gay and lesbian youth are five times more likely to attempt suicide than their heterosexual peers. A majority of the suicide attempts by homosexual youth took place at age 20 or younger, with nearly one third occurring before age 17 (Gibson, 1989). It is also estimated that of the more than 5,000 annual suicides committed by young adults in the United States, about 30% are committed by gay or lesbian youth or youth dealing with issues of sexual orientation and sexual identity (Gibson, 1989; Harbeck, 1992; Hunt, 1986; Rofes, 1989; Russell, 1989; Sears, 1989; Whitlock, 1989).

Substance abuse

Even if gay or lesbian adolescents do not choose suicide as an avenue of escape (or a cry for help), they face many other problems which put them at high risk. If they are closed about who they are, they may be able to pass as "straights" in their schools and communities, but they face a tremendous internal struggle to understand and accept themselves, especially in that they feel "different" from their peers. With little or no access to information which portrays the homosexual in a positive light, they often buy in to society's stereotypic negative views of the homosexual, and thus begins the internal erosion of self-worth which ultimately leads to a sense of inferiority, disregard for personal self and loss of identity (Dunham, 1989). In response to these negative self-images, many gay and lesbian youth become involved in substance abuse to reduce the pain and anxiety of the internal conflicts (Dennis & Harlow, 1986; Dunham, 1989; Gibson, 1989; Harbeck, 1992; Lenskyj, 1990; Russell, 1989; Sears, 1991). In the Report of the Secretary's Task Force on Youth Suicide, it is estimated that gay and lesbian youth are three times more likely to abuse substances and that 58% of the adolescent gay males studied suffered from substance abuse disorder (Gibson, 1989).

Sexual activity

Young adolescents who suspect they may be gay or lesbian often engage in frequent sexual involvements in order to either deny their homosexuality or to experiment to affirm it. Although both male and female adolescents will engage in opposite-sex relationships to deny their homosexuality, some (lesbians) purposely get pregnant in order to "disprove it" (Dunham, 1989; Gibson, 1989; Harbeck, 1992; Lenskyj, 1990; Rofes, 1989).

Because a high percentage of gay and lesbian youth experiment sexually in a search for their identity, this increases their risk of infection from STDs and of the transmission of HIV (Rofes, 1989; Russell, 1989; Whitlock, 1989). Although the vast majority of all adolescents have the "can't happen to me" atti-

tude regarding HIV infection, gay and lesbian youth give even less attention to prophylactics because the fear of pregnancy is not present with same-sex sexual activity (Colorado Department of Health, 1992).

Family and homelessness

If young gays or lesbians are "out," there are additional problems which may occur. Although they may feel some sense of internal integrity and security within themselves, they may face tremendous external conflicts with family and peers.

The loss of family support is a tremendous blow to a young gay or lesbian, but it happens quite frequently because many families are

---

The shame of ridicule and the fear of attack make school a fearful place, resulting in frequent absences and sometimes academic failure.

---

unable to reconcile their child's sexual identity with moral and religious values. Because of this, many are often forced to leave their homes as "pushaways" or "throwaways" rather than running away on their own (Gibson, 1989). Thus, the incidence of homelessness among gay and lesbian youth is very high (Andrews, 1990; Dennis & Harlow, 1986; Grayson, 1987; Rofes, 1989; Whitlock, 1989), with some estimates as high as 50% of homeless youth being gay or lesbian (Colorado Department of Health, 1992).

When gay youth are forced out of their homes, they often flee to large cities, hoping to find families and friends to replace the ones that did not want them or could not accept them. Here, however, they become street kids and enter a world that presents serious dangers and often an even greater risk of suicide. Without adequate education, many are forced to become involved in prostitution in order to survive. Thus they face physical and sexual assaults on a daily basis and constant exposure to sexually transmitted diseases including AIDS (Dennis & Harlow, 1986; Dunham, 1989; Gibson, 1989; Russell, 1989).

The education of gay and lesbian youth: harassment and violence issues

Besides the home, school is the other primary social institution where all young people should be able to feel safe. For openly gay or lesbian youth, or those "suspected" or "accused" of being so, however, this is not in any way the case. For these students, middle school, junior high school, and high school most often mean cruel harassment from fellow students, ridicule from teachers, and refusal from school personnel to punish verbal and physical attacks upon them. The shame of ridicule and the fear of attack make school a fearful place, resulting in frequent absences and sometimes academic failure. These and other school practices undermine the ability of gay students to learn in school and frequently cause them to forfeit an education altogether (Dennis & Harlow, 1986; Gibson, 1989).

In schools across the country, even very young children learn those words which are sure to deliver an insult or to keep someone in line—*queer, lezzy, faggot,* or *sissy.* Children may not always know what these words mean, but they know the demeaning power of this language (Whitlock, 1989). By the time students are in the secondary schools, this kind of name calling, while still directed indiscriminately at times to any student one dislikes, becomes a virulent form of verbal harassment when directed against gay and lesbian youth, and it is often accompanied by physical assaults such as shoving, into lockers and beatings. (Colorado Department of Health, 1992). In a recent national survey done by the National Gay Task Force, approximately 20% of lesbians and 50% of gay males reported that they had been harassed, threatened, or physically assaulted in secondary schools (Gibson, 1989; Lenskyj, 1990).

While some teachers and administrators harass, ridicule, and unfairly punish gay students, the predominant feature of the discriminatory school environment or gay youth is the failure of school officials to provide protection from peer harassment and violence (Dennis & Harlow, 1986; Grayson, 1987). By far the most common form of this failure is when teachers, who would most often confront instances of racist or sexist name calling or jokes, make no effort to intervene when they hear homophobic name calling or jokes. Non-gay students have reported that teachers have observed verbal or physical harassment and done nothing to intervene on behalf of gay or lesbian students (Lenskyj, 1990). When school personnel fail to protect gay students from verbal or physical harassment, for whatever reason, they fail in their duty to provide for the welfare of *all* students.

Counseling issues

Since the school guidance counselor may often be the first person within the educational community with whom the gay or lesbian adolescents choose to disclose (or at least explore) their sexual orientation, these educators are in important positions to provide confidential and supportive personal counseling to gay and lesbian youth. However, for a variety of reasons, this is not what often occurs. Unfortunately, counselors are often engaged in too many administrative duties that leave little time for personal counseling and that convey a message of unapproachability to all students, especially to gay students who are already extremely hesitant to approach any adult with issues of sexuality (Sears, 1989). Second, because in most schools and communities homosexuality is still a forbidden subject so that the presence of homosexuals among the student population is tacitly denied or because the school population and the general public are still rather hostile toward homosexuals, most school counselors are often uncomfortable with discussing homosexuality (Powell, 1987). Third, many counselors are not trained by the counselor education programs of their colleges and universities around the needs of the gay and lesbian population, especially in terms of the coming-out process. Neither are there sufficient inservice programs available to allow school counselors to upgrade their knowledge to provide quality services to gay youth (Powell, 1987).

Fourth, because most counselor training programs have not dealt with these issues, most counselors have not thoroughly examined their own knowledge, beliefs, values, prejudices, and biases about homosexuality. Therefore, they are not comfortable when dealing with these students (Krysiak, 1987). Worse yet, some counselors further undermine conditions for these youth because they are unwilling to acknowledge or support an adolescent's homosexual identity exploration, instead giving students inaccurate information, reinforcing the myths, encouraging them to "change" their identities, or forcing them into therapy and mental hospitals under be guise of "treatment" (Gibson, 1989).

Table 1

Mean Age of Coming Out

	Males	Females
1971	19.3	—
1980	16.3	—
1982	15	20
1987	14	—
1993	13.1	15.2

Curriculum issues

Another school practice which needs to be addressed in order to provide a more equitable education for gay and lesbian youth is the "conspiracy of silence" which envelops most schools (Sears, 1991). In most schools neither curriculum content, including sex education classes, nor library resources provide students, gay or non-gay, with accurate and positive information about homosexuality.

If homosexuality were to be discussed anywhere in the curriculum, one would expect to find it in the health or sex education curriculum. However, in reviews of representative textbooks used in these kinds of classes, researchers found few references to the subject of homosexuality and many of those references had a homophobic bias. Even those texts that treated homosexuality in at least a neutral manner tended to "ghettoize" it by discussing the topic in a condensed section or by switching from a personalized "you" voice to a detached "they" format, thus implying the inferiority of homosexuality as a form of human sexuality (Sears, 1989; Whitlock & DiLapi, in Gordon 1983). This assumption only serves to reinforce the sense of isolation experienced by many lesbian and gay adolescents. Also, because of the initial, and often yet believed, image of AIDS as a "gay disease," as well as a the attitude of a society which does not want "these" issues discussed in schools, access to straightforward and clear information about AIDS, HIV, and safe sex practices, which is essential for the survival of all youth, is truly limited (Whitlock, 1989).

Given these attitudes and beliefs, it is little wonder that other subjects taught in the curriculum are devoid of references to gays or lesbians or the topic of homosexuality. Just as with the experience of blacks 30 years ago, the experiences and contributions of lesbian and gay men are not acknowledged in the curriculum, thus depriving gay and lesbian youth of positive role models from history. Although some might argue that homosexuality is not relevant to the accomplishments of these men and women, the argument does not hold up when these biographies are examined nor when compared to the relevance of race, gender, or religion in other biographies (Sears, 1989).

A school library or media center is very important to support the curriculum and to meet the individual needs of students in a school. Based on Kinsey's 10% figure, a school of one thousand students might have approximately one hundred students needing information about their own homosexuality. However, finding books that present accurate information about homosexuality or a positive view of gay and lesbian life can be very difficult for adolescents, even in large cities (Whitlock, 1989). In the first place, holdings on homosexuality may be very limited. In a study designed to examine the holdings of school libraries on sensitive topics such as child abuse, incest, and homosexuality, the responding schools reported the fewest holdings on homosexuality regardless of format (fiction, non-fiction, vertical files, or professional titles) (VanMeter, 1991). Second, access to gay and lesbian library materials is difficult because the standard cataloging classifications do not fully nor easily identify these materials by means of contemporary subject headings which would make it easier for young people to find these materials (Berman, in Gordon, 1983). Third, even encyclopedias, which adolescents questioning and assessing their own sexual identity often consider to be a safe (i.e., private) resource, tend to have inaccurate, misleading, and often biased information about homosexuality and gay and lesbian people, especially considering the fact that most school libraries tend to maintain outdated editions of encyclopedias in their collections (Burke, in Gordon, 1983).

Middle school connection

Maturation of all young people has been occurring earlier in successive generations due to several factors. "As a result of earlier maturation, sexual relations, pregnancy and sexu-

Figure 1

Resource Guide

Organizations

The Gay, Lesbian, and Straight Teachers Network (GLSTN). GLSTN is a national organization that brings together gay and straight teaches in order to combat homophobia in their schools as well as to support gay teachers. For information, contact GLSTN, 2124 Broadway, Box 160, New York, NY 10023, (212) 387-2098.

Parents and Friends of Lesbians and Gays (P-FLAG). P-FLAG offers support to family members of gay people. Its national office can refer you to local chapters: PO Box 27605, Washington,DC 20038, (202) 638-4200.

The Hetrick-Martin Institute, a New York–based social service agency, has long been a leader in providing services for gay youth. They also publish *You Are Not Alone: The National Lesbian, Gay, and Bisexual Youth Directory,* which is available for a $5 fee. Address: 2 Astor Place, New York, NY 10003-6998, (212) 674-2400.

The Bridges Project of the American Friends Service Committee facilitates communication among gay youth service providers through its newsletter and other activities. Address: c/o AFSC, 1501 Cherry St., Philadelphia, PA 19102, (215) 241-7133.

Project 10 is an on-campus counseling program in the Los Angeles Unified School District which responds to the needs of adolescent lesbians/gays in the educational system. It also produces a resource directory for teachers, guidance counselors, parents, and school-based adolescent care providers. For information, contact

Virginia Uribe, Fairfax High School, 7850 Melrose Avenue, Los Angeles, CA 90046, (213) 651-5200.

Publications

Looking at Gay and Lesbian Life by Warren Blumenfeld and Diane Raymond is a good general introduction.

Is It a Choice?: Answers to Three Hundred of the Most Frequently Asked Questions about Gay Men and Lesbians by Eric Marcus is a good starting point as well.

Making Schools Safe for Gay and Lesbian Youth, the Education Committee Report of the Massachusetts Governor's Commission on Gay and Lesbian Youth surveys the needs of gay youth and presents detailed recommendations for action by schools to meet those needs. Its recommendations were adopted as state educational policy by the Massachusetts Board of Education in May 1993. Write the Commission at State House Room 111, Boston, MA 02133, to receive a copy.

Understanding Sexual Identity: A Book for Gay Teens and Their Friends by Janice E. Rench is geared for grades 6–12.

Two Teenagers in Twenty: Writings by Lesbian and Gay Youth edited by Ann Heron are the writings of youth, ages 12 to 14 years old.

Gay Men and Women Who Enriched the World by Thomas Cowan consists of biographies of positive role models throughout history.

---

ally transmitted diseases are now issues of concern at the middle school, whether or not educators and parents prefer it" (George & Alexander, 1993, p. 5).

This is true for the lesbian and gay population as well. Although the problem of sexual minority youth engaging in high-risk behaviors and the failures of schools to address these problems are more acute later in adolescence, they are becoming more prevalent and relevant at the middle level. Studies have shown that the mean age of coming out of sexual minority youth is declining, at least in urban areas (Table 1).

Other studies also show that homosexuality or the struggle with sexual identity is a

middle level issue. Most gay and lesbian youth report having experienced the feeling of being "different" long before the onset of puberty, some as early as first grade (Herdt & Boxer, 1993). In a comprehensive national study in which the researchers interviewed over 4400 gay men and lesbians, Jay and Young (1979) reported significant evidence concerning the incidence of adolescent homosexuality. Their findings revealed that the majority of gay and lesbian adults reported knowing about their homosexuality prior to the age of 18, with approximately 30% reporting knowing prior to the age of 13.

Many studies have shown that gay and lesbian youth are self-identified (recognize their same-sex attraction and have same-sex fantasies) before they have had a same-sex experience (Herdt & Boxer, 1993; Remafedi, 1987), just as heterosexual youth could identify themselves as heterosexual before engaging in opposite-sex activity. In a Chicago study of a sample of lesbian, bisexual, and gay male youths done by Boxer, Cook, and Herdt (1989), they reported that first homosexual attraction occurred at average age 9.6 for males and 10.1 for females, with first homosexual fantasy occurring at average age 11.2 for males and 11.9 for females. It is clear "that

---

Professional educators, regardless of their moral or political convictions, are duty bound to protect and promote the human and civil rights of all people within the classroom.

---

gay and lesbian youth exist during childhood and early adolescence with or without homosexual behavior and/or homosexual identity" (Savin-Williams, 1990, p. 204).

That homosexuality, or the struggle with sexual identity, is a middle level issue is also strongly supported by the results of a 1992 large-scale study of adolescent sexual orientation surveying nearly 35,000 junior and senior high school students from diverse ethnic, geographic, and socioeconomic strata in Minnesota (Remafedi, Resnick, Blum, & Harris, 1995). They reported that at 12 years old, 25.9% of the students were "unsure" about their orientation; at 13 years old, 17.4%; at 14 years old, 12.2%; and at 15 years old, 7.0% (declining to 5% in 18-year-olds). It seems clear that this is an issue that educators avoid to the detriment of their young adolescent students.

The middle school philosophy is based on the principle that middle schools accept the responsibility to try to meet the needs of all the young adolescents in their care (National Middle School Association, 1995). This responsibility should be interpreted to include the needs of those youth who are struggling with their sexual identity, as well at all youth who have the right to have accurate information about one of the human diversities, sexual orientation. Since early adolescence is a time of searching for personal identity; of questioning and testing; of building beliefs, attitudes, and values; of building, consolidating, confirming, and affirming identity and self-concept; and of building social skills, it is right for middle level schools to address the issues of homosexuality and the existence of gay and lesbian youth.

Recommendations

So what should be an appropriate response to meeting the needs of gay and lesbian youth? What can school officials do to improve the atmosphere in our schools so that all our students can receive a safe and equitable education?

There seem to be several factors which serve as barriers to making changes which would allow for the development of services to meet the needs of gay and lesbian youth, including a lack of courage from adults, both gay and non-gay; a lack of information available about the needs of these young people; and the failure of school systems to confront controversial matters, especially in the area of youth sexuality. Rofes (1989) outlines several things that will need to change if schools are truly going to meet the needs of the gay and lesbian student population. He contends that schools are going to have to focus on the needs of young people rather than on the demands of parents or the larger community. In light of STDs and HIV, issues of sexuality must move from the taboo into a public forum. Teachers will need to be helped to become comfortable with gay and lesbian issues through sensitive training, including exploring their own beliefs about sexuality and sexual orientation. School curricula will need to be integrated to include the historical contributions of gay men and lesbians in order to provide positive messages and role models to our sexual minority youth. Finally educators must abandon the myth that by discussing homosexuality in a positive way they will cause young people to grow up to be gay or lesbian.

Sears (1987) approached the task of making these changes occur by listing several steps that he believed socially responsible educators must take in order to have a positive impact upon the quality of life in school for all students, especially for gay and lesbian youth. As a first step, educators must examine their own attitudes toward homosexuality. When people become comfortable with their feelings, they more easily educate themselves about this subject. The second step is educating others about homosexuality with particular emphasis on replacing myths with accurate information. This means communicating with the school board, parents, and community groups, as well as with students. As a third step, concerned educators must be responsive to the needs of gay and lesbian youth. This means providing young people with a nonjudgmental atmosphere in which they can process their feelings and come to terms with their sexuality and know that they are "okay" as well as providing a curriculum and educational resources which should include information about sexual orientation and people who are gay and lesbian.

Fourth, Sears believes that professional educators, regardless of their moral or political convictions, are duty bound to protect and promote the human and civil rights of all people within the classroom. This implies enforcing responsible standards of professional and student conduct in terms of verbal and physical harassment of gay and lesbian students, as well as combating the ignorance and fear engendered by the AIDS health crisis. The fifth step that educators can take is to encourage the hiring of and to provide support for gay and lesbian educators who will be healthy role models for such students. Finally Sears (1987) contends that educators, as articulate citizens of the community, must speak out in favor of legislation that bars discrimination against homosexual men and women. He believes, "The struggle for social change must begin with a critical examination of arbitrary narrow and socially constructed categories in our lives as well as an assessment of how those categories affect the lives of those around us. Only when human beings accept themselves and respect the dignity of others can a genuine commitment to social justice be possible" (p. 96).

Jennings (1995), executive director of the Gay, Lesbian, and Straight Teachers Network, a national organization based in New York City, describes several specific steps that he believes teachers and schools can take to provide safe and inviting learning environments in schools. They are:

1. *Guarantee Equality.* Schools should add "sexual orientation" to their non-discrimination statements in all school publications as a way to communicate their commitment to equal treatment for all.

2. *Create a Safe Environment.* Schools must make it clear that neither physical violence nor harassing language like "faggot" and "dyke" will be tolerated, just as they are not for any other group. Clear harassment policies, which include sexual orientation, must be developed and then publicized to the entire school community so that the consequences of and procedures for dealing with such behavior are clear to all.

3. *Provide Role Models* Studies consistently show that personal acquaintance with gay and lesbian people is the most effective means for developing positive attitudes toward acceptance. Both gay and straight students benefit from having role models such as openly gay and lesbian teachers, coaches, and administrators. Straight students are offered an alternative to the stereotypes with which they have often been raised. Gay and lesbian students get the chance, often for the first time, to see healthy gay and lesbian adults, which gives them hope for their own future. Schools need to create the conditions necessary for gay and lesbian faculty to feel safe in "coming out." If no role models are available from within the school community, the school can bring in presenters from a local gay and lesbian speakers bureau or from a college gay and lesbian student association.

4. *Provide Support for Students.* Peer support and acceptance is the key to any student's feelings that he or she "belongs" in the school. "Gay Straight Alliances," groups which welcome membership from any student interested in understanding issues of sexual identity, regardless of sexual orientation, have been the key to creating such an atmosphere in many schools. Counselors must also be specifically trained in the needs of gay and lesbian youth in order to provide the support that students struggling with their sexual identity so desperately need.

5. *Provide Training for Faculty and Staff.* School staff need to be equipped to serve all the students with whom they work, including gay and lesbian ones. Understanding the needs of gay and lesbian youth, and developing the skills to meet those needs, should be expected of all

staff members. Schools must provide the ongoing training necessary for the staff to fulfill this expectation (Figure 1).

6. *Reassess the Curriculum.* Teachers need to incorporate gay and lesbian issues throughout the curriculum—not just in classes such as health education, where students would learn about the continuum of sexual orientation, but in other classes taught in the school. For example, when discussing hate crimes or civil rights issues in a social studies class, include examples related to gays and lesbians. If you would address the fact that Langston Hughes is a Black author because of the impact of his race on his work, then also address the fact that Walt Whitman was a gay author because of the impact of his sexual identity on his work. This identification also provides positive role models from history for our gay and lesbian youth. Teachers can also work to undo the "hidden heterosexism" of the curriculum, such as the exclusive use of opposite-sex couples in math word problems and foreign language exercises.

7. *Provide Appropriate Health Care and Education.* While being gay is not a "health issue" (any more than being heterosexual is), health education on sexuality and sexually transmitted diseases should sensitively address the particular issues of gay and lesbian people.

8. *Diversify Library and Media Holdings.* Often the school or classroom library is the first place students turn to for accurate sexuality information. Yet, too often, few or no works on gay and lesbian issues are found there. It is important that library holdings are up to date, present accurate information about homosexuality and a positive view of gay and lesbian life, and are catalogued so that students can easily access the materials (Figure 1).

Conclusion

Although the National Middle School Association took a courageous stance in passing Resolution 93–4 in Portland, NMSA is not promoting homosexuality It is simply stating that if the middle school's mission is to meet the needs of all young adolescents, then the needs of sexuality minority youth must also be met. There is a great deal we all have to learn in order to meet these needs. NMSA, by adopting this resolution, is simply acknowledging these needs and encouraging us to get started. May we, teacher by teacher and middle school by middle school, have the courage to continue this process "in order to ensure safe and equitable school environments for youth of every sexual orientation."

References

Andrews, J. (1990). Don't pass us by: Keeping lesbian and gay issues on the agenda. *Gender and Education, 2,* 351–355.

Boxer, A. M., Cook, J. A., & Herdt, G., (1989, August). *First homosexual and heterosexual experiences reported by gay and lesbian youth in an urban community.* Paper presented at the Annual Meeting of the American Sociological Association. San Francisco, California.

Boxer, A., Levenson, R., & Peterson, A. C. (1990). Adolescent sexuality. In J. Worrell & F. Danner (Eds.), *The adolescent as decision-maker* (pp. 93–124). New York Academic Press.

Colorado Department of Health. (1992). *Adolescent health in Colorado: Statistics, implications and strategies for action* (Report and Recommendations of the Advisory Council on Adolescent Health). Denver, CO: Author.

Dennis, D. I., & Harlow, R. E. (1986). Gay youth and the right to education. *Yale Law and Policy Review, 4,* 445–455.

Dunham, K. L. (1989). *Educated to be invisible: The gay and lesbian adolescent.* University of Southern Maine: U.S. Department of Education.

George, P. S., & Alexander, W. M. (1993). *The exemplary middle school* (2nd ed.). Fort Worth, TX: Holt, Rinehart and Winston.

Gibson, P. (1989). *Gay male and lesbian youth suicide. In Report of the secretary's task force on youth suicide. Volume 3: Preventions and interventions in youth suicide.* (DHHS Pub. No. ADM 89–1623). Washington, DC: U.S. Government Printing Office.

Gordon, L. (Ed.). (1983). Homophobia and education (Special double issue). *Interracial Books for Children Bulletin, 14,* (3/4).

The Governor's Commission on Gay and Lesbian Youth. (1993). *Making schools safe for gay and lesbian youth: Breaking the silence in schools and in families.* (Publication No. 17296-60-50-2/93-C. R.). Boston, MA: Author.

Grayson, D. A. (1987). Emerging equity issues related to homosexuality in education. *Peabody Journal of Education, 64,* 132–145.

Harbeck, K. M. (Ed.). (1992). *Coming out of the classroom closet: Gay and lesbian students, teachers, and curricula.* Binghamton, NY: Harrington Park Press.

Herdt, G. (1989). Introduction: Gay and lesbian youth, emergent identities, and cultural scenes at home and abroad. In G. Herdt (Ed.), *Gay and lesbian youth* (pp. 1–42). New York Harrington Park Press.

Herdt, G., & Boxer, A. (1993). *Children of horizons: How gay and lesbian teens are leading a new way out of the closet.* Boston, MA: Beacon Press.

Hunt, C. Y. (1986). Adolescents at risk: Homosexuality. In C. Y. Hunt, (Ed.). *The tree of life: A response to teen suicide* (pp. 41–46). Wayne, MI: Wayne County Intermediate School District.

Jay, K., & Young, A. (1979). *The gay report: Lesbians and gay men speak out about sexual experiences.* New York: Washington Square Press (Simon & Schuster).

Jennings, K. (1995, January). What you can do: Ten steps toward ending homophobia in your school. (Available from Kevin Jennings, GLSTN, 2124 Broadway, Box 160, New York, NY 10023).

Krysiak, G. J. (1987): A very silent and gay minority. *The School Counselor 34,* 304–307.

Lenskyj, H. (2990). Beyond plumbing and prevention: Feminist approaches to sex education. *Gender and Education, 2,* 217–230.

National Middle School Association. (1995). *This we believe* (3rd ed.). Columbus, OH: Author.

Powell, R. E. (1987). Homosexual behavior and the school counselor. *The School Counselor 34,* 202–208.

Ramafedi, G. (1987). Male homosexuality: The adolescent perspective. *Pediatrics, 79,* 326–330.

Remafedi, G., Resnick, M., Blum, R., & Harris, L. (1992). Demography of sexual orientation in adolescents. *Pediatrics, 89*(4),]714–721.

Rofes, E. (1989). Opening up the classroom closet: Responding to the educational needs of gay and lesbian youth. *Harvard Educational Review, 59,* 444–453.

Russell, T. G. (1989). AIDS education, homosexuality and the counselor's role. *The School Counselor 36,* 333–337.

Savin-Williams, R. C. (1990). Gay and lesbian adolescence. In F. W. Bozell & M. B. Sussman (Eds.). *Homosexuality and female relations* (pp. 197–216). New York: Harrington Park Press.

Sears, J. T. (1987). Peering into the well of loneliness: The responsibility of educators to gay and lesbian youth. In A. Molnar (Ed.). *Social issues and education: Challenge and responsibility* (pp. 79–100). Alexandria, VA: Association for Supervision and Curriculum Development.

Sears, J. T. (1989, March). *Personal feelings and professional attitudes of prospective teachers toward homosexuality and homosexual students: Research findings and curriculum recommendations.* Revision of a paper presented at the Annual Meeting of the American Educational Research Association, San Francisco, CA.

Sears, J. T. (1991). Helping students understand and accept sexual diversity. *Educational Leadership, 49*(1), 54–56.

Troiden, R. R. (1993). The formation of homosexual identities. In L. D. Garnets & D. C. Kimmel (Eds.), *Psychological perspectives on lesbian and gay male experiences* (pp. 191–217). New York: Columbia University Press.

VanMeter, V. L. (1991). Sensitive materials in U.S. public schools. *School Library Media Quarterly, 29,* 223–227.

Whitlock, K (1989). *Bridge of respect: Creating support for lesbian and gay youth* (2nd ed.). Philadelphia, PA: American Friends Sevice Committee.

The 3 Kinds of Sex Happy Couples Need

Spouses locked into one style of making love ultimately feel trapped. Free yourselves (and firm up those vows) by getting these essentials into your bedroom repertoire.
by Julie Taylor

NOT ALL SEX IS CREATED EQUAL. THAT MUCH YOU KNOW. What you may not realize is that when it comes to lovemaking, marriages *need* a little variety. *No* married coupled is having lengthy, adventurous, tantric-orgasm encounters every time they climb into bed, and according to sex experts, no married couple should. The most satisfied husbands and wives find a loose balance among the three basic food groups of lovemaking: quickies, "comfort sex" (we'll explain later), and spectacular sex.

"In its own unique way, each of the three types is absolutely essential to a happy marriage," says Sharyn Hillyer, a Beverly Hills-based marriage and family therapist. "The recipe for a great marriage is having an equal balance of the three."

Does this mean that every third encounter needs to be a quickie? Hardly. While maintaining a healthy ratio will keep your sex life humming, starting a mental scorecard is going to strike some sour notes. "Keeping score will put you on edge and kill all the spontaneity," says Sari Locker, a New York-based sex educator and author of *Mindblowing Sex in the Real World.* Instead, listen to the signals your libidos are sending you, and take things from there.

Here, everything you need to know about the essential types of sex, why you need each, and what to do if you're getting too little—or too much—of one of the big three:

Quickies

"Right after my son was born, my husband and I were exhausted most of the time," recalls Traci, 35, an accountant in Oklahoma City. "We couldn't exactly spend Sunday mornings in bed anymore like we did in the old days. Fitting in a quickie right before we went to sleep meant we connected but still had enough energy to wake up for those 3 A.M. feedings. It kept the fires burning even when we felt burnt out."

Quickies are a handy time-management tool in a busy life, but they offer a lot more, as well. They're tailor-made for those marriages in which the man has a higher sex-per-week requirement than the woman. And approached with the right attitude, they can bring with them an element of illicit excitement. "That initial urgency and thrill you feel about sex tends to wane over the years," says Kathleen Mojas, Ph.D., a Beverly Hills-based clinical psychologist. "A good quickie can inject that passion back into your relationship."

To wit: "The best quickie I ever had was in this really swanky hotel at my cousin's wedding," says Leslie, 34, a graphic designer from Dayton. "Since my kids were the flower girl and ring bearer, they were at the head table and we were sitting off to the side. My husband asked me to dance, and as we were slow dancing he whispered for me to follow him. I was confused, but trailed after him anyway. Before I knew it, he had pulled me into a broom closet, and we did it right there. We could hear the music and the guests' laughter the whole time. It was such a thrill. When we sat back down, my cousin came over and asked if we were having fun. If she only knew!"

As a relationship enhancer, quickies can't be topped; men love them, so proposing one is likely to meet a warm reception and engender some positive overall sexual and romantic vibes in your marriage. Explains Hillyer, "Guys like quickies. Smart women are good sports about that."

• **The trouble with too many.** Bear in mind, however, that if you tip the scales too far in favor of the quickie, problems are likely to crop up–especially for you. "When my husband and I started our own business, the *only* sex we were having was quickies," says Robyn, 31, a retailer in Newark, New Jersey. "For a while, I had a 'better than nothing' attitude, but then I became very resentful, because while I was maybe having an orgasm one out of three times, he was batting a thousand. I felt cheated and mad, and our relationship suffered as a result." Robyn was smart. She talked with her husband, who quite happily agreed that the business could afford to hire a manager. The couple used the windfall of free time to focus on their relationship, which improved quickly.

If too many quickies are spoiling your fun, but you're not prepared to use Robyn's straight-up approach, try this: "Plan a slow seduction scene," advises Dr. Mojas. "Light some candles, run a bubble bath–really set the mood." This way, your husband will feel pampered rather than criticized. If you go on and on about how great it was afterward, Dr. Mojas suggests, he'll be more apt to set the mood next time.

If he still doesn't get it, you're going to have to be frank. Try to be nice about it. Says Hillyer, "At the right moment–not in the middle of sex–say, 'We've been having a lot of fun with these quickies, sweetie, but I need some more time.'" Tell him a longer session makes you feel sexier and more turned on–code for, "Hey, there's something in this for you, too." Comments Locker, "If you're more into it, it's obviously going to be more enjoyable for both of you. You both win."

• **Getting too few?** "If you have kids and a full-time job, you won't always have the time or the inclination to make sex a big production, even

if your husband wants you to," says Hillyer. If he craves a marathon and you're only game for a 50-yard dash, say so. "Tell him you're too exhausted to go all night, but a quickie is just fine," advises Locker. That way, you can feel close without collapsing from exhaustion.

Comfort sex
It's one of the great perks of monogamy. Comfort sex is lovemaking that can only be enjoyed by two people who know each other, and each other's bodies, extremely well. You rub him here, he nibbles you there, and you both leave the table extremely satisfied.

"Comfort sex is the glue that keeps you connected," says Dr. Mojas. "It doesn't hold many surprises, but that's part of its appeal." And just because it's comfortable doesn't mean it isn't exciting; sometimes merely knowing the nooks and crannies and hot spots of each other's bodies so completely can be a big turn-on. Says Hillyer, "This sex is loving rather than crazy-in-love." It's not about athletic prowess or number of orgasms, but rather about the bonds of time, experience, and intimacy you and your husband share.

"Comfort sex is the best thing about being married," confirms Leslie, 34. "It's a no-fail orgasm every time. There's none of that experimental fumbling around that comes with a new partner."

Adds Traci, "Since I've been married for 14 years, my husband and I just know what the other wants. It feels good to just sit back, have a glass of wine, and go with the flow. It's like watching a *Seinfeld* rerun. Sure, you've seen it already, but that doesn't mean you won't enjoy seeing it again. And again."

• **When comfort sex gets too comfy.** After one too many reruns, however, you might get the urge to change channels. "Too much comfort sex can get boring," Mr. Mojas warns–and boredom is anathema to sexual bliss. "If you're having mostly comfort sex, plan a date for after the children are in bed," advises Hillyer. "Wear something you feel sexy in and

light some incense. Eat dinner on the floor in front of the fireplace, then make love on the kitchen table." The change in circumstances inevitably leads to a change in sexual experience.

Locker further suggests you buy a book on sexuality and experiment with different techniques and positions. "Tell him you heard about the book on TV and thought it might be fun to check it out," she says. This lets him know you bought it out of curiosity, not because you think he needs lessons.

• **A lack of comfort.** "With my husband, it's either a quickie or an all-out sex romp," complains Kimberly, 25, a St. Louis-based retail sales manager. "I'd love to have average, run-of-the-mill sex, but he's just not into it. I wish he could loosen up."

Performance pressure is a common culprit among men who can't relax into easygoing sex, says Locker. "Tell him you sometimes need a hug more than sex, and that predictable sex can make you feel both secure and satisfied," she says. "Let him know it doesn't always take a big production for you to see fireworks." But if speaking with him doesn't work, she suggests you let your fingers do the talking: Give him a massage, a way of achieving intimacy without intercourse. "Comfort sex is as much about connecting emotionally as it is about connecting physically," she says. A back rub or a long, slow dance can demonstrate to him that closeness can be expressed in many ways other than world-rocking sex.

Mind-blowing sex
"The other night my husband and I were talking about what a stressful day it had been," recalls Jenni, 27, an advertising sales representative in Las Vegas. "We were both exhausted and had agreed sex was out of the question. I rolled over away from him and he put his hand on the small of my back. Just his touch made my body tingle. I turned over and looked into his eyes. We started kissing, something we don't do too much of usually, and then proceeded to have some of the deepest sex we'd ever

had. It wasn't premeditated or con-trived. It was just right."

Every once in a while, you get lucky and fall into an erotic encounter that reminds you all over again that you are one hot couple. Usually, though, it's circumstances—often con-trived just for this purpose—that send sex into "Oh my God" territory: The kids are away, it's your anniversary, or you're on vacation. "Special-occa-sion sex is the thing that breaks up the monotony and gives you the chance to fall in love again," says Dr. Mojas. "I see a lot of couples who go on vacation solely to have vacation sex. Their vacation is the time their marriage comes back together."

Other times, mind-blowing sex is the simple result of trying something new that works. Explains Hillyer, "In exploring and experimenting, you might discover something that really feels wonderful, and suddenly the sex is elevated from everyday to spec-tacular." Maybe it's a new position or some sensual music that pushes you over the edge. The only way to find out what turns both of you on is through trial and error.

• **When sensational sex is some-thing that only happens to other people.** "When I watch movies that portray people in amazing lingerie performing these acrobatic acts, I have to laugh," comments Robyn. "With two kids, a career, and a mil-lion errands to run, who has the time or energy?"

True, daily life can make incredible sex seem like the impossible dream—until you make up your mind to get some. And you do have to make up your mind. "People have this errone-ous idea that you don't have to put effort into amazing sex, that it should just be there," says Dr. Mojas. "But when you're juggling children and work and a marriage, you have to put in extra energy to create that spark."

What to try? Says Locker, "Make love in a different room of the house or tell your husband that you're not wearing any underwear when you're in public." Any small stimulus can do the trick.

Sharing fantasies is another time-honored way to rev up your sex life. "Ask him what his top five fantasies are, and share yours with him," ad-vises Locker. "Then choose a few you would feel comfortable acting out to-gether." (If you feel uneasy about do-ing something, Hillyer advises, don't do it. Refusing to act out a fantasy doesn't mean you're uptight; it simply means you know your limits and aren't willing to cross them.)

• **Too much of a good thing:** "No one can have a sex life that is 100 percent earth-shattering," says Hillyer. "It would become a burden to think of something new to do night after night, and your body would grow tired. A relationship just can't sustain that sort of sexual level. And who'd want it to?"

If you've been striving to be a ma-jor sex kitten, it should come as a re-lief to give yourself a break. Try initiating a quickie. Try, another night, simply concentrating on the feeling of his body inside of you rather than on reaching orgasm. Pretty soon, you'll realize that variety really is the spice of a great sex life, and that out-of-this-world sex is much more so when you're not trying to reach some inter-nal quota. "No matter how many creative sexual tricks you add to your repertoire, you still have to make your sex life your own," says Locker. "That means having the kind of sex you want rather than having the type of sex you think you should be hav-ing." And that in itself is the secret to a satisfying sex life.

Julie Taylor is the author of *Franco American Dreams,* a novel.

A SPECIAL *AMERICAN HEALTH* SURVEY

THE JOY OF MIDLIFE SEX

We made love, not war; defied the double standard; and redefined female sexuality. Now the daughters of the sexual revolution are marching through midlife—and changing the way America thinks about what it means to be women of "a certain age." > According to an exclusive new *American Health* survey of 500 women between ages 35 and 55, boomer babes are still sexy after all these years, with the healthiest women reporting the happiest sex lives of all. Among the eye-opening findings from our peek into the bedrooms of women in their prime:

BY DIANNE HALES

HEALTHY ATTITUDES + HEALTHY HABITS = HOT SEX More than half of you say sex is better now than at age 25. Why? "Practice, practice, practice," quips one respondent. But seriously, "you're more comfortable with your body, your sexuality, your partner," says San Francisco psychotherapist Lonnie Barbach, Ph.D., author of *The Pause.* "It's like learning to drive. First you're nervous. Then it becomes second nature."

Your health is also a factor: 54% of you exercise regularly, and 81% watch what you eat, although you don't obsess about every calorie. You also make healthy communication a priority: 55% discuss sexual issues with your partner; 40% talk things over with close women friends.

The payoff? A whopping 30% of you make love three to six times a week. "This frequency absolutely shocked me," says Beverly Whipple, Ph.D., of Newark, NJ, president-elect of the American Association of Sex Education Counselors and

RATING *Your Mates*

Women whose partners are in good shape are more likely to report that sex is better than it was at age 25. Here's what you said about *his* physique:

14% *EXCELLENT* HE'S THE NEXT JAMES BOND
55% *GOOD* HE COULD GO JOGGING WITH PRESIDENT CLINTON
19% *NOT SO HOT* HARVEY KEITEL HAS NOTHING TO FEAR
 4% *LOUSY* HOMER SIMPSON HAS HIM BEAT

Therapists. "It's extremely high compared to past studies." The 44% of you who report having sex three to six times a month is more in line with previous reports. Of those who describe their health as good, 37% make love three to six times a week. By comparison, only 19% of those in poor health have sex three to six times a week.

Yet sometimes even the liveliest sex lives run out of steam. Seven in 10 of you have felt too tired for sex at some time in the past year, while half have felt too stressed.

Unfortunately, help can be hard to find—at least in doctors' offices. When it comes to sex, physicians don't ask and women don't tell. About eight in 10 of you have never discussed sex with your doctors. "It's sad that even though so much has changed from a generation ago, physicians and patients still aren't comfortable talking about sex," says Fran Kaiser, M.D.,

GETTING PHYSICAL

44% of those who don't exercise, versus only **30%** of those who work out regularly, report they've felt too fat or undesirable for sex. Among those eating high-fat diets, **69%** have felt that way, vs. just **33%** of healthy eaters.

rector of women's health at Canyon Ranch Health and Fitness Resort in Tucson, AZ. "For the short amount of time that sex

"WHY GIVE UP ON SEX?" SAYS ONE WOMAN. "AS A GOOD BABY BOOMER, I WANT IT ALL."

a specialist in geriatrics, endocrinology and sexuality at St. Louis University.

But this too may change. "The baby boom generation has demanded more for itself all the way through the life cycle, and that's not going to stop now," observes psychologist Michael A. Perelman, Ph.D., acting codirector of the sex therapy program at New York Hospital–Cornell Medical Center in New York City. As an unmarried survey respondent, age 50, puts it, "Why should I give up on sex? As a good baby boomer, I still want it all."

PRIME-TIME SEX

How does what's going on in your bedroom compare to what you see on TV? The ratings look like this:

MAD ABOUT YOU	**65%**	(warm, friendly sex)
SEINFELD	**13%**	(all talk, not much action)
THE SINGLE GUY	**12%**	(sex life? What sex life?)
E.R.	**7%**	(fast-paced, short-lived sex)

SECRETS OF SEXUAL VITALITY Asked to rate your sex lives, 32% of you say things are "smoking!" What accounts for all this sizzle? "It may well be a function of being in better health in mind and body," says Dr. Perelman. About six in 10 of those with X-rated sex lives work out regularly.

"If you're feeling good, you're more aware of your body, and that spills over into sex," says Lana Holstein, M.D., di-

takes, we get so much out of it," she says. "We sleep better. We feel better. Loving sex with a trusted partner may be the best thing you can do for your body."

Women in good physical condition are also more comfortable during pelvic exams and Pap smears and less prone to health problems such as high blood pressure, which can sabotage sexual pleasure. But life's fast pace is taking a toll on even the healthiest, wealthiest and wisest (or, at least, best educated) of you. "Fatigue has become the most common cause of sexual problems," says Dr. Perelman. "Busy people put sex last on their priority list, and then they're just too tired to do it." His advice: Make time for dating (each other). "A date can be very romantic. Even if half the time you just have a good time together and don't have sex, your marriage and sex life will definitely improve," he says.

SEXY IS AS SEXY DOES How-to sex manuals and videotapes. Sex-related Websites. Vibrators. Masturbation. A generation ago, middle-aged women might never have acknowledged that such titillating things existed, let alone admitted to trying them. But the veterans of sexual liberation are much more open-minded. "I'm impressed with their self-help efforts," says Dr. Perelman, "and they've tried a lot."

Six in 10 of you dress up in sexy clothes. More than four in 10 (42%) masturbate, while 44% read sex self-help books and 38% surf into sex info Websites or watch sex videos. About 40% use vaginal lubricants or do Kegel exercises to strengthen vaginal muscles; 21% have tried a vibrator.

But some of you still struggle with inhibitions: 23% have felt too fat for sex at some time in the previous year, while

13% have felt physically undesirable for other reasons. "This whole idea of equating feeling pretty or thin with being sexy is one of the few remaining differences between the sexes," notes Dr. Perelman. "Men are much less likely to say, 'Gee, I put on two pounds; I just don't feel like sex tonight.'"

THE SCREEN TEST *Mad About You,* TV's top-rated show about a pair of nicely neurotic New Yorkers, may not seem like the stuff sexual fantasy is made of. But when we asked you to compare your sex life to a sitcom, 65% chose its warm, friendly, lighthearted brand of sex.

"My husband and I are definitely like *Mad About You,* " says a 54-year-old survey respondent married for 25 years. "Sex is a connection we feel all day long. I'll put a note in my husband's lunch—something like 'Think of me when you're eating this.' He'll leave me a sexy message on the answering machine. It's that kind of back-and-forth that makes sex fun."

"The quality of a relationship has a lot more to do with how satisfied women are than with whether their orgasm was a '10' or an '8,' " says psychologist Norma McCoy, Ph.D., a professor of psychology at San Francisco State University. "As women get older, sex remains very, very gratifying even if they do it less, because it's a symbol of the relationship."

In our survey the women with smoking-hot sex lives were likeliest to give credit to a longtime, comfortable relationship with a loving partner. "If they're lucky, couples who've been together awhile move into a phase of lovemaking where they still play around and tease, but where there's also a deeper kind of bonding taking place because they've shared a lot. Most people really treasure this," says Dr. Holstein.

Other factors also contribute to the joys of midlife sex. "In the past there was always the fear of pregnancy," notes a 46-year-old respondent who has been married for 23 years. "The spontaneity wasn't there. Now we're comfortable with each other, and I've come to value not just the sex, but

HEALTHY SEX 62%

of women who describe their health as good say sex has improved with age, and **37%** of them make love three to six times a week. By comparison, just **45%** of those in poor health think sex has gotten better, and only about half as many— **19%**—have sex that often.

having someone to go through life with. That makes everything better as you get older."

HOW MATES RATE Who are the men sharing the beds of the sexiest midlife women? Not baby-faced boy-toys (Cher, take note), but thoroughly grown-up guys. Of the women who rate sex as better now than at 25, two-thirds have partners between 40 and 54. These fellows aren't sexual Olympians either. In the past year 52% of your partners have felt too tired or stressed to have sex, 21% were occasionally impotent and 17% were premature ejaculators. Four percent of you have partners with persistent impotence; after age 45 this percentage doubles.

Most of you (63%) don't worry about a partner's less-than-impressive sexual performance. Dr. Perelman finds that fact encouraging. "Men need reassurance that they are more than their penises," he says, adding that when imperfect sex persists, remedies are available. "Women who feel angry or frustrated because of a partner's sexual difficulties [as do 8% of survey respondents] need to know this."

THE LAST TABOO Sexual dysfunction doesn't discriminate against women. In the past year, 41% of you experienced a temporary loss of interest in sex. Dr. Barbach isn't surprised.

BETTER THAN SEX
(Well, Almost)
Your top five sources of sensual pleasure—outside of intercourse, that is:

1 MASSAGE
2 EXERCISE
3 MASTURBATION
4 CHOCOLATE
5 SHOPPING

CAN WE TALK?

(Maybe). When it comes to confessing your concerns about sex to your doctor, menopause may be the catalyst for more open, honest communication. Twenty-three percent of postmenopausal women, vs. only 12% of premenopausal ones, say they have discussed sexual issues with their physicians.

"For many midlife women, it's difficult just fitting sex into a busy schedule," she says. Twenty-one percent of you have lacked desire for your partner, 15% have a problem with vaginal dryness and 10% have difficulty achieving orgasm. Women who are ages 35 to 44 and who are juggling the demands of little kids and careers are likeliest to feel too stressed or tired for sex, to report other sexual problems and to avoid bringing up sexual concerns with their partners.

And what of the 80% of you who *never* talk about sex with your doctors, regardless of whether the physician is male or female? Why are you far likelier to report an ingrown toenail than a lack of sexual desire? "Those of us who grew up in the '50s and '60s never heard sex discussed," says a married 52-year-old respondent. "We may feel freer and be more sexually active than our parents were—or than we think they were—but that doesn't mean it's easy to talk to our doctors." Like 75% of survey respondents, she'd talk if her doctor asked. But our survey shows that when conversations do take place, women are the instigators 67% of the time. Why don't doctors ask? "Their education doesn't include enough information on sexuality," notes Dr. Whipple. "Health professionals need more than one lecture on sex—which is all they get if they're lucky."

Of the women who did ask about sexual concerns, 28% were told to relax, go home and keep trying. "That is truly unfortunate, because so much more can be done to help," says Dr. Perelman. Dr. Kaiser agrees. "It would be sad for women to think that sexual pain or problems have to be part of aging, because they don't," she says. "A lot can be done so women can continue to enjoy sex throughout their lives."

For many respondents that's exactly what's happening. "Our children may not believe it, but sex goes on," says a 53-year-old who has been married for 30 years. "I had a stroke nine years ago; my husband has had prostate cancer. But we're not dead yet. And the love we have for each other after all we've been through makes sex more beautiful than ever."

"Such feelings aren't unusual," says Dr. Barbach. "Sex truly is wasted on the young. They may have the equipment and the energy, but they don't have the experience. Couples who have a really good, caring relationship over a long period talk about sex in a way that a 25-year-old couldn't begin to understand."

Dianne Hales writes extensively on women's issues and is co-author of Caring for the Mind.

Unit Selections

Key Points to Consider

❖ What does your college or community do about date or acquaintance rape or child sexual abuse? Are there any education or prevention efforts? What do you think of them?

❖ Have you participated in formal or informal discussions about potential or real sexual harassment at your job or school? How do you, your classmates, or coworkers feel about it? How would you rate your school or employer regarding awareness, prevention programming, and response to complaints?

❖ How do you feel about laws restricting sexual behaviors (for example, age limits, marital requirements for engaging in sex, or laws making specific sexual behaviors illegal)? Where do you believe "personal freedom" or "choice" about sexually related behaviors begins to collide with the "greater good" of society?

❖ What is your response to radio or television talk shows on sexual topics? Be honest: Do you watch them? Why? Do you think the media should report on the sexual activities of public figures? Why or why not?

❖ Which of the following two statements do you most closely agree with and why? (1) Available Internet networks provide an important, private way to obtain accurate, discreet information that can enhance intimate relationships. (2) Sex online is simply pornography.

 **Links**   # www.dushkin.com/online/

These sites are annotated on pages 4 and 5.

This final unit deals with several topics that are of interest or concern for different reasons. Also, as the title suggests, it combines "old" or ongoing topics and concerns with "new" or emerging ones. In one respect, however, these topics have a common denominator—they have all taken positions of prominence in the public's awareness as social issues.

Tragically, sexual abuse and violence are long-standing occurrences in society and in some relationships. For centuries, a strong code of silence surrounded these occurrences and, many now agree, increased not only the likelihood of sexual abuse and violence, but the harm to victims of these acts. Beginning in the middle of this century, two societal movements helped to begin eroding this code of silence. The child welfare/child rights movement exposed child abuse and mistreatment and sought to improve the lives of children and families. Soon after, and to a large extent fueled by the emerging women's movement, primarily "grass-roots" organizations that became known as "rape crisis" groups or centers became catalysts for altering the way we looked at (or avoided looking at) rape and sexual abuse.

Research today suggests that these movements have accomplished many of their initial goals and brought about significant social change. The existence and prevalence of rape and other sexual abuse is much more accurately known. Many of the myths previously believed (rapists are strangers that jump out of bushes, sexual abuse only occurs in poor families, all rapists are male and all victims are female, and so on) have been replaced with more accurate information. The code of silence has been recognized for the harm it can cause, and millions of friends, parents, teachers, counselors, and others have learned how to be approachable, supportive listeners to victims disclosing their abuse experiences. Finally, we have come to recognize the role that power, especially unequal power, plays in rape, sexual abuse, sexual violence, and, a term coined more recently, sexual harassment.

The first two articles in the first subsection, *Sexual Abuse and Harassment*, seek to highlight several ongoing and emerging issues with respect to sexual abuse, violence, and harassment. Despite some progress, such abuse still occurs, and the damage to victims can be compounded when they are not believed or, worse yet, are blamed. At the same time, these and the remaining articles identify emerging complexities surrounding sexual abuse, and, in turn, all sexual behavior. As we as a society have sought to expose and reduce abusive sex, it has become increasingly clear that all of society and each of us as individuals/potential partners must grapple with the broader issue of what constitutes consent: What is non-abusive sexual interaction? How can people communicate interest, arousal, desire and/or propose sexual interaction when remnants of unequal power, ignorance, misinformation, fear, adversarial sex roles, and inadequate communication skills still exist? Finally, another layer of perplexing questions: What is, or should be, the role of employers, school personnel, or simply any of us who may be seen as contributing on some level due to awareness or complicity to an environment allowing uncomfortable, abusive, or inappropriate sexual interaction?

The second subsection, *Legal and Ethical Issues Related to Sex*, delves into some current legal and ethical dilemmas associated with sexuality and sexual behavior. All societies have struggled with the apparent dichotomy of freedom versus protection when it comes to enacting laws about human behavior. In addition, the pace of technological advances (infertility treatment, AIDS, and nonsurgical abortion methods, to name just a few) has far outstripped society's attempts to grapple with the legal, ethical, and moral issues involved. At the present time, a variety of laws about sexual behaviors exist. Some are outdated, apparently in conflict with evolving social norms, even majority behaviors. Some laws are permissive, seeking to protect individual freedoms. Others are restrictive, seeking to protect society and allowing the intrusion of legal representatives into the private, even consensual, sexual behaviors of otherwise law-abiding citizens. The first article in this subsection addresses the very perplexing legal and ethical issues involved with the technologies of infertility treatment, assisted reproduction, and the specter of human cloning within this century. The next three articles address long-standing and very polarized controversies associated with sex and sexual behavior: sexual orientation, especially attitudes about the legitimacy of "equal rights" for nonheterosexuals, and reproductive health services, especially "morning-after" medication and abortion. The question posed by the final article "Is Sex a Necessity?" is a fitting one to bridge the second and third subsections. Although its basic focus is the question of whether insurance companies should cover Viagra, its consideration easily flows into thinking about the role and place of sexuality in our lives as we approach the new millennium.

The final subsection, Focus: *Sexuality in the New Century . . . Better or Worse?* refers to some very broad questions, reactions, and predictions of a wide variety of people, from political and religious leaders to sexuality experts to everyday men and women. Even thoughtful "big picture" views of the sociocultural trends related to sexuality seem to create some puzzling dichotomies. Have we come too far or not far enough? Has the crippling antisex ethic of the past been transformed to an equally crippling antiresponsibility or antimeaning standard of today? Have the social changes we have witnessed, especially in the second half of this century, helped or hurt humankind's quest for joyful, healthy, fulfilling sex? The final three articles present differing views on trends and advocate or predict different desired directions for the future. Although the focus question was "better or worse?" we challenge readers to confront the questions and issues raised and to conceptualize a future that finds a balance between complete freedom for the individual and subjugation or homogenization of human diversity to a narrow definition of the common good. For after all, you are the people of the twenty-first century.

Healing the
SCARS

SEXUAL VIOLENCE IN THE BLACK COMMUNITY

PRODUCES TRAUMA THAT TEARS AT

SELF-WORTH, FAMILY AND GENDER ISSUES

BY LOTTIE L. JOINER

According to a 1992 study by the National Victim Center, of Arlington, Va., 84 percent of rape survivors do not report their rape and, consequently, many do not get the professional help that can aid in the healing process. Sexual assault is a serious problem in the African-American community. Though Black women are 7 percent of the population, they are 27 percent of rape victims, according to federal statistics. Two African-American counselors discussed the consequences of rape and how it can be overcome.

Rhonda Brinkley-Kennedy is the clinical director of the Rosa Parks Sexual Assault Crisis Center in South Central Los Angeles. Brinkley-Kennedy, 41, received her master's degree in clinical psychology in 1986 from Pepperdine University and her doctorate of psychology from the California School of Professional Psychology in 1992. She has been counseling victims of sexual assault for more than 10 years and continues to train future psychologists on the issue of sexual assault in the African-American community.

Andrea Thompson Adam, 44, is the Crisis Intervention Direct Services Volunteer Coordinator at the Los Angeles Commission on Assaults Against Women. She earned her bachelor's of arts degree in theater in 1975 from Fontbonne College in St. Louis, with a minor in sociology and psychology. Adam has been counseling sexual assault victims for more than six years.

From *Emerge*, May 1997, pp. 34-35, 39, 40-41.

EMERGE: According to the U.S. Department of Justice, a woman is raped every two minutes. Why do some men rape?

THOMPSON ADAM: The first thing about rape is that it's not about sex. Rape is actually about power and control. And people who perpetrate this kind of crime have issues of their own that are driving them to do these things. It's all about having some loss of control within their own lives. This is another way for them to get this control, to dominate someone else in this manner . . . and compensate for what they don't have in their own lives.

BRINKLEY-KENNEDY: Consensual sex means that two adults have agreed to engage in a mutual encounter that's pleasurable to both people, I think men and women are often confused in that understanding. People do not understand the difference between sex, love, consent, power. Our society, in general, doesn't teach us these things. So there lies part of our dilemma.

it does not go away. It will impact your children. It will impact all relationships. It will impact how you see the world and especially how you see yourself.

We have women who are walking around, especially African-American women, with so much pain they don't even know they have because we have carried the weight of the world for so long that our attitude is "get over it." The women come in and they feel ashamed for feeling pain. We don't know how to say, "I hurt." We don't know how to say, "You hurt me." We know how to say, "You piss me off," which is just a mask for pain anyway. But we do not know how to say, "I'm hurting." And we have been hurting for a long time.

THOMPSON ADAM: And one of the things that we also have to address is the fact that for so many of us, talking about things that happened that are considered personal is so taboo. You don't go outside the family. You don't go outside and

Rape will impact all relationships. It will impact how you see the world and especially how you see yourself.

THOMPSON ADAM: In terms of the way law enforcement looks at it and the judicial system looks at it, rape is, as is stated in most of the penal codes, the act of sex forced on another person without their consent. There has to be an actual yes given, and if there is no yes given, her not saying yes . . . leaves room for them to prosecute on a rape charge.

I think there are men who really don't understand what rape is. I mean really don't understand that forcing your wife to have sex, forcing their girl friend to have sex, forcing somebody that they meet . . . they don't understand that that is wrong. They don't understand that because society has allowed people to get away with this without any repercussions. So it's been an allowed tradition that a man can take what he wants and a woman simply must deal with that.

When a person says no, regardless of what you may think that person feels about you, the answer is no.

EMERGE: Why is it important for a woman who has been raped to get counseling?

BRINKLEY-KENNEDY: The reason people, especially African-Americans, need to deal with the trauma of sexual assault in one's history is because

tell people your business. You don't share this kind of information. . . . Trying to get our people into counseling is a major struggle. It's a major struggle because they can't feel the freedom to unburden themselves to somebody that they don't know. Being a professional doesn't make any difference. You can have the 26-letter alphabet behind your name and have all the credentials and schooling in the world, but if that person cannot relate to you on a very personal level, the chance of your doing any type of treatment with them is out the door.

Another thing that we have to address within our own communities is the fact that sometimes the best person to tell is not somebody in your family. Sometimes the best person to talk to about this is an objective third party who has nothing vested except your well-being.

EMERGE: You don't hear much about male rape, but it does occur. What does rape do to a man's psychological and emotional well-being and how does he deal with this?

BRINKLEY-KENNEDY: We really have increased our male client population, believe it or not. I understand that this whole issue is often a childhood issue and the boys are taught not to talk about these things. All I have to do is go into the drug treatment facility and ask the right question about when a big brother or big uncle did the wrong thing or did the thing that wasn't quite right. They didn't know what to do with it at the time and never dealt with it. We have so many men now from our recovery system who are knocking at our doors. Men are now understanding that if they're going to move forward in their lives, they have to deal with the traumas in their lives. They're very cautious. They just don't call up and say, "I was sexually assaulted." . . . They do handle it differently.

One of those ways is . . . feeling out of control. If you ask the rapist, they are going to tell you that they come from a history of sexual assault, the majority of them. One way is to act out against another [person]. Another way is substance abuse. Another way is to mistreat others in different kinds of ways, maybe, that might be to abandon their own children, and then do some other things. So yes, men do have that history. Yes, they must come to terms with it if we are going to ever feel safe. We must help men deal with that history and let them know that it's okay to talk about these issues.

EMERGE: When a high-profile person in the community is accused of rape, how does that affect gender relationships? What about the sense of loyalty to race?

BRINKLEY-KENNEDY: We would be happy to support all of our men if they were all doing right. But you know what? Black, White, Latino, Asian, there is no race where they're all doing right or they're all doing wrong. So we have to take each one of them on individual merit. What we have to do is be willing to look at the fact that some of these people are not the saints we want them to be. On the issue of these young girls making accusations against these men and people saying, "Well why was she doing this, and why was she doing that?" I'm sorry, but regardless of what she did, she may be guilty of making a stupid choice, she may be guilty of dressing inappropriately, that does not mean that she deserves to have whatever happens happen to her. We have got to get away from that [mindset].

EMERGE: What is more common in the African-American community, rape by a stranger or someone that the victim knows?

THOMPSON ADAM: It doesn't make any difference whether it's an African-American community or any community. The majority of rapes occur with people who you either know or are acquainted with or even have a passing relationship with. Most of the time, the people who rape are people who have watched you for a day or two,

a week, or something. They know something about your behavior, something about your habits, because what happens is that a lot of these petty people pick prey and they acquaint themselves with behavior. So it's almost like they're stalking their prey before they commit the act. There is a very small percentage of people who are raped by onetime strangers who absolutely have no connection to them whatsoever.

EMERGE: What are some of the ways the African-American community handles rape?

BRINKLEY-KENNEDY: Well, first of all, we want to say it doesn't happen. That's the first problem and I think that's one of our biggest denial issues. The other issue is that the majority of rapes happen by someone you know, and to add to that, in the home. Also, the rapist picks people who they feel they can overpower, because it's about power and control. That's why men don't rape men unless they are gang-raping men, because the issue is I don't pick someone that I think I'm going to lose to. They take the woman who looks confused, who looks distracted, the vulnerable. But the biggest piece we have in our community is denial. In the Black community, and I think all communities, they assume that rapists have these neon lights on that say, "I am a rapist." When rapists are people who are living next door to you. This is a scary thought for us. We want to feel safe. So we have the myth that it has to be somebody that is somewhere else. And the other thing, too, with the Black community is that we don't understand the impact, even if we believed it happened. We also believe that it's not a big deal. We do not understand the connections between something—someone assaulting you today—having an impact in your life tomorrow. So part of it is just even if I can say, "yes it happened, I'm sorry it happened," we still don't understand the importance. But because we don't see blood, we just sweep it under the rug and say, "Okay, you know, get over it, you're going to be okay," and that's part of the problem.

EMERGE: Why do some men who may spend a large amount of money on their dates assume that the woman is obligated to have sex with them?

BRINKLEY-KENNEDY: Our society has taught them that. They're grown up on thinking that, first of all, they should be able to have sex on demand, period. They've also been taught that that's all women think about and that's all they really want but they're saying no because they have to play coy. It's like an "I do this for you so you're going to do this for me" kind of belief system. Unfortunately, women believe it, too. It's really the way we raise our children. It's the way we pretty much are as a society.

EMERGE: What are some safety measures that women should practice to avoid or prevent being raped?

THOMPSON ADAM: For our organization, when we talk about self-defense, we don't talk about women simply learning how to do physical exercises and defense movements to protect themselves. We talk about a woman using her mind . . . all of her senses to take care of herself. You want to be aware. You want to be alert. You want to think before you put yourself in any situation. So we have to be cognizant of every little thing. That's part of what our self-defense program teaches women. It's not all about getting in there and learning how to kick butt. This is a good thing, but that's not enough. We have to be aware on all levels and no one is saying that you can't make mistakes, that's fine, just learn from whatever mistakes you do make. It's going to take a lot of time and energy to make women believe that they have the right to say no.

EMERGE: Justice Department figures indicate that a large number of rapes occur among children. Is that true for African-Americans and how do we protect our children?

BRINKLEY-KENNEDY: Yes, it is true, and there are many ways we can protect our children. One is to be more involved with our children. Two is to understand what the signs might be of any kind of abuse going on. Sometimes we don't look at our children when their behavior changes and so we don't know what the signs are. Teachers don't know what the signs are. We don't know the impact of it so, therefore, we're not even looking for it, we're not even understanding that it could possibly happen. So yes it's higher for our children, and it's really clear to me when I talk to women.

EMERGE: What can we teach our children to combat the problem of rape?

THOMPSON ADAM: One of the things is we not only have to educate our children, we have to educate the parents. But the other thing, too, is that we can't just do this with women. We have to do this with the men. The men have to take as active a part as the women. Because who are the people who rape? And how can a woman make a man understand it?

You have to be willing to teach your boys and girls the same thing. You have to be able—be willing—to teach your son, just as you would teach your daughter, what it is to respect another human being. If you do not touch that child and love that child and hug that child, then that child is not going to know to touch, hug, or love anybody else. That's where it comes from. One of the most important things is that we have got to make our children understand that they are worth something. They are worth something, and you can't put a dollar figure on it.

BRINKLEY-KENNEDY: We have to sensitize ourselves to dealing with this issue. It's a hard thing because it means a shift for everybody, not just for women or just for the people dealing with this, but for everybody, for an entire community.

THESE WOMEN UNCOVERED SEXUAL SLAVERY IN AMERICA

Two women risked their safety to gather evidence of **forced prostitution** in New York. Daniel Jeffreys reports on the continuing fight to get the authorities to take action

THE NAKED GIRL making her way offstage at the Brooklyn club was exhausted, but her shift was only beginning: For the rest of the night, she would be expected to service a string of clients supplied by her employers, members of a Russian organized-crime syndicate known as the *mafiya*. She wasn't turning tricks for the money—the Russian club owner would be pocketing 90 percent of her earnings. The tired young dancer began to cry, and the owner warned her she had "one last chance" before he issued orders to have her parents in Kiev beaten, "maybe to death."

This exchange was overheard recently by an undercover investigator for the Global Survival Network, a Washington-based nonprofit organization that has spent the past two years conducting an investigation into forced prostitution. GSN was first created to monitor illegal trade in endangered species, but three years ago, their mission was expanded.

In the spring of 1995, Steven Galster, a GSN operative, was in Russia posing as a businessman trying to purchase contraband Siberian leopard skins. The salesman asked him if he would also like to buy some young women, promising reasonable prices, "even for virgins."

That was Galster's first inkling that Russian organized-crime groups had begun running international prostitution

> ## "WE HOPE THE LAW WILL TREAT THESE CASES AS EXAMPLES OF SLAVERY, NOT ILLEGAL IMMIGRATION."
>
> —GILLIAN CALDWELL

rings. These groups entice impoverished Eastern European women to leave their homes with promises of lucrative jobs overseas. Once such a woman arrives in a foreign country, her passport is confiscated and she is imprisoned in a brothel, where she is then forced to service between eight and 10 "johns" every day.

On his return, Galster told this story to his friend Gillian Caldwell, a high-flying Washington, D.C. attorney. She was so horrified she resigned from her job and became the codirector of GSN.

In February 1996, Caldwell and Galster set up a dummy corporation and traveled undercover to Moscow, St. Petersburg and Vladivostok, claiming they were buying women to staff an escort business. They were offered dozens of

girls and were told, "Compliance is guaranteed." As a result of their investigative work, GSN became the first organization to document an emerging slave trade in Eastern Europe.

GSN's report "Crime and Servitude," published last November, included personal testimony from women who had been held captive and forced to sell their bodies in Germany, Hong Kong, Macau and Japan. But as Caldwell soon learned, the problem is not confined to these countries.

In the spring of 1997, a tip from a Moscow contact led Caldwell and Galster to the Russian community of Brighton Beach, Brooklyn. Working undercover in nightclubs and restaurants, they saw activities which supported claims they had heard from other human rights groups: Organizations that trade in women who have been made to prostitute themselves against their will are operating in the United States on a substantial scale.

Ukrainian-born Rima Kotov, a former strip club manager in Queens, has witnessed several examples of women forced into prostitution. In January 1997, Rima met Irina* and Katrin*, two Eastern European girls who were working with her daughter in a New York strip club. When Irina and Katrin were on stage, they were constantly observed by representatives of the mafiya, who would invite audience members to make "dates" with the girls for later in the evening. The two girls were also made to hand over any money they had been given when they came offstage.

Beaten into submission

"Irina and Katrin came from a small Ukrainian village where people were close to starvation," says Rima. "They answered an ad for mail-order brides,

Irina barely speaks English. Her passport has been confiscated. If she runs away, the mafiya has told her, she will be found, beaten and maybe killed.

Gillian Caldwell admires Rima Kotov's courage in coming forward with her knowledge. Her testimony will be used by Global Survival in their campaign to persuade law enforcement officials and the U.S. government to become more active in prosecuting cases of forced prostitution.

Rima Kotov is an especially valuable witness because she is a member of the Russian community and can provide direct evidence of a problem some law enforcement officials deny exists. "Often the police would rather arrest the prostitutes than the gangsters, making the women victims twice over," says Caldwell. "With testimony from people like Rima Kotov, we can hope law enforcement will begin to treat these cases as examples of slavery and fundamental human rights abuses, instead of pretending the issue is prostitution or illegal immigration."

who had shipped girls to Tokyo. Natasha said it would be easy to provide them with women—even girls aged 14 or 15: She could arrange fake passports for underage girls, giving their age as 18. These documents would come from mafiya contacts working for the Ministry of Foreign Affairs.

A matter of greed

The Diplomatic Security Service of the State Department has been investigating the Russian slave trade since 1995. One agent confirms that "the Russian mafiya has experts who fraudulently obtain B1 and B2 tourist visas." Evidence further suggests that "because of a more open policy toward the former Soviet Union since the collapse of communism, it has been easier for the mafiya to get girls in through basic visa fraud."

Forced prostitution and the use of visa fraud to get potential sex slaves into the United States has become a hot topic in the State Department, reflecting the growing evidence that the practice is now widespread in the Russian-American community. The State Department acknowledges that knowing the problem exists is quite different from being able to solve it. But it believes an opportunity may come soon, because the mafiya is getting greedy.

Up to now, Russian mafiya bosses have had advantages that made it very difficult for the FBI and the New York Police Department to infiltrate their clandestine operations. They've known that the prevention of drug trafficking is a much bigger priority and will always attract greater resources. They have enforced the silence of victims and witnesses with aggressive threats and, in some cases, vicious punishments. And they once opened their Brooklyn brothels only to Russian customers, which made their activities almost impossible to investigate, given existing FBI resources. But business has been too lucrative for the "Russian only" rule to last. At the rate the women are forced to work, 10 of them in one small brothel can earn mafiya bosses more than $200,000 a month. With these numbers, expansion to non-Russian customers was inevitable.

That's how Robert* met Olga*.

Robert and Olga are key witnesses living under police protection. Although their identities must be concealed, their stories have been verified by the private

> "IRINA ANSWERED AN AD FOR **MAIL-ORDER BRIDES,** BUT ONCE IN NEW YORK WAS TOLD SHE HAD TO BECOME A PROSTITUTE."

but once they arrived in New York, they were told they had to become prostitutes. Both of them refused and both were raped. Irina was beaten night and day for a week."

Rima says Irina lives under tight security. She must be available for work from 8 p.m. to 4 a.m. every day. She stays with five to eight other girls in a one-room apartment with a view of Coney Island. Their apartment shares a door with a neighboring house, which is how the girls will be forced to flee, should there be a police raid.

Irina is never allowed to leave the brothel with money in her pocket. All her clothes and food are provided by the mafiya, who also have the girls checked every week by a Russian émigré doctor.

Names have been changed.

Peter Grinenko is a supervising investigator with the Brooklyn District Attorney's office. He was one of the first Russian-speaking officers to work on mafiya cases. Grinenko doubts the veracity of these claims of sexual slavery. He does not believe Russian women are naïve enough to answer fake advertisements for maids and nannies, and says, "I don't know of any Russian women who have been forced into prostitution in the United States."

GSN has a powerful rebuttal: In the course of their undercover work, they were given contracts drawn up by traffickers that gave overseas employers of Russian girls the right to enslave an employee who broke any rule on a long list of vague regulations. They also spoke at length with a Moscow trafficker, Natasha,

WHAT THE GOVERNMENT IS DOING

The trafficking of women and girls has become one of the fastest-growing criminal enterprises in the world. The U.S. Department estimates that between 1 and 2 million women around the world are caught in these trafficking rings each year, generally for the purpose of forced labor, domestic servitude or sexual exploitation. President Clinton is committed to combating this abuse, and has directed the Secretary of State, the Interagency Council on Women and the Attorney General to develop strategies for protecting and assisting victims of trafficking.

WHAT YOU CAN DO

More and more often, North America is a destination point for victims. Senators Wellstone (MN) and Feinstein (CA) are cosponsoring a Sense of Congress Resolution on International Trafficking. Visit the Marie Claire website (www.marieclaire.com) to add your name to our petition, or call your senators and ask them to cosponsor the Wellstone-Feinstein International Trafficking Resolution.

A RUSSIAN TRAFFICKER TOLD INVESTIGATORS SHE COULD EASILY PROVIDE THEM WITH GIRLS AS **YOUNG AS 14.**

regular girlfriend, because he has no time for commitments. At least he didn't until he met Olga.

Robert is the kind of customer the Russian mafiya wants to cultivate. He thinks nothing of paying $500 for the right girl. Mafiya groups have been marketing their girls aggressively to men like Robert, giving out business cards at upscale New York bars—cards with names of escort agencies like "Elegant Evenings" and "Park Avenue Pride." Robert received a card for "Elegant Evenings" in March. He had been using one escort service regularly for six months and felt like a change. The "Elegant Evenings" switch-board directed him to a studio apartment on East 74th Street. There he found Olga, a beautiful 19-year-old. Robert was shocked to see the deplorable condition of the apartment and the emaciated state of the girl. He pressed her for details of her employment, but she had a limited grasp of English. All Robert could tell for sure was that Olga had been made to turn tricks against her will.

The next day, Robert returned to East 74th Street with a Russian translator and got Olga's full story. She had come from Kiev, where the monthly wage is $30, after answering an advertisement which promised domestic work in the U.S. as part of a "pay-as-you-learn" educational project. Olga agreed to pay $3000 for a passport and visa processed by her new employer, the sum to be deducted from her U.S. earnings. These documents were taken from her within minutes of her arrival in New York, and she was brought to a house near JFK airport.

Here she was beaten and threatened with death if she didn't pay $5000 immediately. Her captors accused her of lying about her qualifications—she hadn't—and demanded reimbursement of her fare and accommodation expenses. That figure soon doubled, and she was given a week to pay. This demand was coupled with threats against her family back in Kiev. After three

more days, Olga, a virgin, was given the opportunity to discharge her debts by working as a prostitute. She was told the money was good, $400 a night, and she was assured her debts would quickly be cleared. She soon learned that she had been lied to again. Almost all her clients paid in advance with credit cards. She was told to hand any cash to her "supervisor" at the end of each night, and in return she was given a daily stipend of between $10 and $20. Olga was warned the apartment was under video surveillance. She was also told any attempt to escape would be met with punishment, for her and her family.

Threats against family members back home normally enable the ruthless Russian organized crime syndicate to control girls from a distance. However, when Robert met Olga she was so demoralized that escape had become her paramount concern. Robert believed that Olga was days away from a mental collapse. After an intense three hours of persuasion, she became convinced that Robert could keep her safe if she ran away from the mafiya. She left with him for a series of apartments that he had arranged through friends.

"Arrests will follow"

Within days, Olga's parents were harassed and Robert received a threatening phone call. He had used his credit card when booking his "date" with Olga, and assumes that was how the mafiya found his address. He was told to return Olga or suffer dire consequences. Instead, he hired a private investigator, who gave the couple personal protection for five weeks and then turned the case over to the NYPD when the threats intensified.

Olga's case is now under active investigation. Dennis Hawkins, a Brooklyn district attorney for Rackets and Organized Crime, confirms that the case "will lead to a significant breakthrough, from which a series of arrests and prosecutions will follow."

investigator called in to protect Robert and the NYPD officer who took over Olga's case.

One woman's escape

Robert is a wealthy money manager whose business obliges him to travel constantly. He is single and has a luxurious apartment in Manhattan, but spends even less time there than he does in the two new Porsches he keeps in a garage on the Upper East Side. He has no time for dating, so he frequently uses prostitutes. He is not proud of this, nor is he especially ashamed. He says it would be dishonest of him to bed a

WHEN PREACHERS
PREY

A minister's wife speaks candidly about the currents
of sex and power that flow between the men in the pulpit
and the women in the pews and the dangerous liaisons they can spark

By Marcia L. Dyson

I REMEMBER HOW BAD I FELT LAST SUMMER when I first saw the news photos of Sister Deborah Lyons, the wife of the Reverend Henry J. Lyons, the leader of the nation's largest and most influential Black Church organization, the National Baptist Convention (NBC), U.S.A. Arrested, fingerprinted and charged with burglary and arson, Deborah Lyons was accused last July of breaking in and setting fire to a $700,000 Florida home her husband apparently co-owned with his business partner, the convention's corporate public-relations executive, Bernice V. Edwards.

I, too, am a minister's wife. My husband of seven years, Michael Eric Dyson, is not only ordained in the Baptist church but is also a prominent professor, author and media commentator. The fact that he is as handsome as he is charismatic is something that is rarely lost on the sisters who hear his sermons or attend his lectures. But it's not the threat of women who are perennially attracted to my husband that kept me on edge during the Lyons controversy.

What I was reminded of by the Lyons melodrama as it unfolded last summer was the many other similar scenarios I've witnessed over my decades in the church. They always seemed to me to be signs of the undeniable power that the men in our pulpits have over the women in the pews. And too many times I've seen preachers exploit this power and even take it for granted, as if it were an entitlement—sometimes preying on vulnerable and lonely women,

at other times seeking out accomplices in sexual misconduct who are quite willing or, at best, self-deceived.

The fact is, long before I ever met my husband, I found myself in the position of the preacher's prey. More than 20 years ago, I was in an unhappy first marriage to an abusive man. At the end of my rope in that relationship, though committed to my faith and still praying for God's wisdom to show me the way to heal and grow within my marriage, I sought counseling from my minister. As far as I knew, I had no reason not to trust this man. Yet he betrayed me by seizing this vulnerable moment in the life of a naive and distressed woman as an opportunity for a sexual come-on.

This minister showed up at my home—calculating the very time he would find me alone—and tried to seduce me. While I managed to get loose from his embrace and get him out of my house, I was stunned and hurt. I couldn't imagine what I had done to encourage his advances. Nor could I bring myself to return to worship in his congregation. I said nothing to anyone and just stopped going to services. Only two months after this incident, I learned from a friend in my old congregation that the offending minister had just been asked to leave the church by the executive board because his wife had caught him in an affair with another church member.

It took me two years to find another church home. By then I had gone through a painful divorce, and I was relieved to be able to spend more of my leisure hours at my new church as a healing distraction. Still emotionally vulnerable, though, I yielded to the seductive charms of a married minister who visited my new congregation. He pursued me, but instead of firmly turning him away, this time I let my need for male companionship compromise my relationship with God. I indulged in the same corrupt delusion I've since seen many of my sisters use to justify an illicit relationship—that God Himself had sent this man to me.

But it proved to be the Devil's work after all. Our tryst failed to fill the void I felt in my life and led instead to an abyss of guilt and shame. It was a romance I certainly couldn't share with the world. I felt I had to protect the minister's reputation, although I later learned that his philandering was well known. Of course, the rumors already circulating about him didn't stop other sisters from stepping up and filling in as new links in his chain of fools.

So it was that I became familiar with the distorted perspective of the preacher's woman, just as I now live with the challenges of being a preacher's wife. I know what it is to be innocent prey to a predatory man, but I also know what it is to be complicit in predatory behavior.

It is well acknowledged that Black women are the very foundation of the Black church. We make up more than 70 percent of the membership, according to documentation cited by C. Eric Lincoln and Lawrence H. Mamiya in their valuable reference *The Black Church in the African-American Experience.* Despite our being such a key church constituency, women "are generally excluded from the church's central station of power, the pulpit," as my husband has written in *Between God and Gangsta Rap.* He terms this state of affairs "ecclesiastical apartheid." So while male ministers give plenty of lip service to the

church's reliance on Black women, that recognition does not spur them to envision a church where justice for women prevails.

Yes, male clergy who abuse their power and engage in sexual misconduct are unfortunately as pervasive in our churches as they are in White churches or in mosques and temples. Indeed, many powerful men, in God's house or the White House, have been subjected to temptation *and* have succumbed to it. But what disturbs me more are those who consider it a way of life or their right. Anthony L. Mitchell—a 26-year-old Harvard medical student who's also working toward a degree in theology at Boston University—recounts how he was once exhorted by his minister to look into the

'For many women, getting attention from the man in the pulpit is like receiving it from God. We may even view the minister as we would a glamorous entertainer or professional sports star. I've seen sisters rush for those seats in the first three rows in the sanctuary—to be close to the preacher.'

choir stand, which was full of women. "Many sisters are waiting for a man like you," Mitchell recalls him saying. "Just take your pick, boy. That's why they're there." Mitchell later understood that he was being initiated into the power dynamics between pulpit and pew, between male and female.

"The power one has in the pulpit is extraordinary," notes the Reverend Dr. Prathia Hall, a Princeton Theological Seminary–trained religious scholar and pastor of Philadelphia's Mount Sharon Baptist Church. (She was also recently cited by *Ebony* magazine as one of the nation's most distinguished women preachers.) "Men can believe that the power is their own, that it is a sign of God's favor. . . . There-

fore they believe that nothing they desire can be denied. And many women are attracted to this power."

For many women, getting attention from the man in the pulpit is roughly equivalent to receiving it from God. "It is difficult for women to separate this voice of authority, this messenger of God, who prays for you, who soothes you," says Dr. Evelyn Brooks Higginbotham, Harvard professor and author of *Righteous Discontent,* the groundbreaking religious history of Black Baptist women. "He has magnetism that a woman can never have. For women, the pastor can become a husband figure, a lover figure, not necessarily acted out but desired."

We may even view the minister as we would a glamorous entertainer or celebrated professional sports star. I have witnessed sisters who rush for those seats in the first three rows in the sanctuary—to be close to the preacher. We become sanctuary cheerleaders, rooting the minister on. Later we swell the reception line, wanting our Sunday best acknowledged by a hug from the man of God. "You're sure lookin' good there, sistah" is the admiring refrain many of us look for from the minister. Often women press notes into his palm: "Call me tonight, please. I can only confide in you."

The troubles we may take to the pastor have probably already been shared with a mother, a sister or an aunt. But while we may easily confide in other women, many of us still maintain a fairy-tale vision of a Black knight in shining armor who will deliver us and project that fantasy onto the minister. That's certainly an ironic setup for a downfall, because our most acute heartaches are often male-related. And we never seem to notice the other women who are engaging in the same wistful self-deception.

I am often reminded of my own moral failing when I see women who are attracted to my husband. Some of them are more brazen than I could ever be. "You know how blessed you are, girl, to have this man?" a woman once asked me while adjusting her cleavage to make certain that her ample bosom caught my husband's eye. "You better keep an eye on him and me."

But scores of others simply make long-distance phone calls to Michael for his advice—their pastors aren't as "sensitive" as he is, they tell him. They send him long letters, photos of themselves and gifts that have nothing to do with seeking spiritual guidance. Michael and I have had many conversations on how we deal with these women. Although it is very difficult, we have found it best to ignore them. I have to admit, though, I do get angry; then I often pray for these sisters because I see the ghost of my former self in them—haunted by the demons of loneliness and need. But my knowing their problems can't justify their actions, any more than it can excuse my own poor judgment in the past.

When Michael and I first met nine years ago, I talked with him frankly about my past experiences with so-called men of God. He also felt it was important in our relationship that I know and love him simply as a man with human failings like any other. When we decided to marry, we also decided I would always travel with him, as we foresaw that his very active preaching and teaching schedule would mean a lot of time on the road. It is now well known on his circuit that if you want to have Dyson as your guest preacher or speaker, you have to be prepared to send *two* tickets—the second one for his wife, Marcia. People often applaud the way we travel together, apparently taking pleasure in the sight of a Black couple obviously united in love and respect. But others, even some among the clergy, sometimes ridicule our keeping such close company with each other. One minister even had the nerve to warn Michael that he might "miss some good opportunities" by always having his wife by his side.

Let's face it: The bravado and machismo of many male ministers link them to their secular brethen. "You know all she needs is a good f—" echoes not just on the streets, around the watercooler or in the army barracks—it's heard even in the pastor's study. And a bigoted clergy also painfully interferes with God's healing for lesbian sisters. "In my late teens I struggled with my sexuality and confided in my minister," recalls Carrietta Jackson, a lesbian student at Union Theological Seminary. "The minister did not pray with me or console me as a child of God," she says. Instead, he told her she needed "straightening out" and said, "I'm the man to do it." Jackson recalls, "I was in shock. He was offering himself as a 'sacrificial lamb' to right the wrong [that he felt was] in my body."

Black women are so often called upon to appear strong, independent and self-confident. Church is the one place we feel safe enough to wear our vulnerability on the sleeves of our designer dresses. We feel secure in stitching our neediness into the hems of our softly tailored suits. When we share our tears and fears with our male ministers, we forge one of the most intimate relationships possible between two human beings. If we're the least bit careless about our principles and prayers, it becomes easy to confuse spiritual and emotional needs with erotic desires and to act on them inappropriately.

Most women who have been ensnared in such dangerous liaisons never speak up about their spiritual warfare, and they are wary of exposing themselves for a couple of reasons. First, they don't want to be shamed. Second, they don't want to be demonized as the woman who brings a brother down. Some sisters go to extraordinary lengths to defend the clergymen who become their lovers. "He has integrity," says a woman I'll call Kelly, who maintains a relationship with a married minister. "Our church grew substantially while he was pastor. He knows he can trust me. I wouldn't do anything to make people think badly of him."

Of course, imperfect men and women sometimes stumble, but when they earnestly repent sinful behavior and seek God's forgiveness, they should also find reconciliation in the Christian community. Still, we should never fail to censure ministers who employ their powerful positions to exploit, abuse or corrupt naive or vulnerable women. No less accountable are ministers who may presume to use their clerical authority to violate their own marriage vows with not-so-innocent partners. Such scandals don't simply hurt individual congregations. They distort the meaning and message of our Black faith to the wider community.

The status of Rev. Henry J. Lyons as a religious leader certainly did not exempt him from critical scrutiny, but it did seem at first to protect him from the complete public humiliation his wife endured. When allegations of questionable financial dealings on his part as well as the appearance of unseemly irregularities in his personal life prompted a small but distinguished group in the NBC to call for Lyons's resignation, Deborah Lyons tried to assume the full responsibility for her husband's problems. She made a public statement before the entire convention during its annual meeting in September, confessing that she was a recovering alcoholic, that her problems had added to her husband's burdens, that she had been mistaken about her husband's having an affair and had caused a good man unnecessary pain and embarrassment. She claimed the fire was an accident, though she subsequently pleaded guilty to arson.

Meanwhile, amid revelations of Edward's previous record of embezzlement in another organization and her own hand in NBC financial improprieties, the suspected "other woman" was fired from the NBC corporate public-relations position for which Lyons had originally hired her. She dropped from sight until she was arrested in Milwaukee a few months ago on Florida state charges connected with her alleged NBC financial schemes. Lyons was also arrested in February on theft and racketeering charges. But it looked as if he would be the only one given a break in this sad story. At last year's annual meeting, the convention delegation voted to let him keep his leadership role; so far, even his arrest seems to have changed nothing.

Black churches will suffer as long as a double standard prevails for males and females. For instance, in our loving churches teenage girls are condemned for out-of-wedlock pregnancies. They are often required to confess their sins and ask for forgiveness in front of the entire congregation, and they may be expelled from the choir or kept from participating in other public church functions. But the (usually older) men who impregnate them are overlooked and hence implicitly excused. Sometimes the father of the child sits on the deacons' row or in the pulpit. Then, too, Black men's lives are often given a higher premium than women's. "I was once told that one man standing up for God is greater than ten women standing up for God," says Anthony Mitchell, the Harvard medical and Boston University divinity student.

This point came home to me with thunderous clarity at a church baptism of year-old twins, a boy and a girl. The female was sprinkled with holy water. Few words were spoken over her tiny head. By contrast, the male was given a *Roots*-like baptism. His small body was held high near the cross. Charges of masculine protection were pronounced. Hands were laid on his head.

"There is neither male nor female: for you are one in Christ Jesus," writes the apostle Paul in the book of Galatians. We can no longer embrace a theology that reflects and reinforces our nation's sexism, patriarchy and misogyny. Ministers must look to

Christ's example of "feed[ing] my sheep" rather than aping disobedient biblical icons like David and Solomon, polygamous patriarchs of old.

I encourage sisters to face their needs honestly within the church, but also outside it. "It will take a conscientious coalition to openly discuss the particular needs of women in our houses of worship," says the Reverend Dr. Cheryl Townsend Gilkes, a Colby College professor and ordained Baptist minister. As much as we refer to an independent incorruptible moral will among women, we're human, too, and it takes a united spiritual community to keep us making the right choices and sticking with them.

How can imperfect humans avoid dangerous liaisons and unholy alliances? First, over the years I've learned to trust the wisdom and direction of sisters for my personal and spiritual needs. Sensitive male ministers should help direct sisters to strong women ministries, even if outside their own congregations. Of course, we must encourage each congregation to develop a thriving female ministry within its own walls.

Second, women must stop playing house in God's House, transferring real longings for a husband or lover onto the married minister. If Sunday church service is the one chance in the week you have to seek male attention, make sure you direct your attention to a man who is more appropriate and available. Or find an available partner in the world and bring him to church with you. Flirting on Sunday morning may feel like fun and look harmless, but it's never your prerogative to violate borders of sanctity and trust. As Reverend Carmen Lattimore, copastor of Victory Church International in Fort Washington, Maryland, says, "Love and re-

spect for one another, oneself and especially for God are key."

Third, churches must establish reasonable guidelines to address sexual misconduct by pastors and other members. The challenge will be to acknowledge unseemly behavior and deal with it quickly without encouraging sexual suspicion and repression. We must also take care to ensure the psychological well-being of our ministers. Some pastors are suffering from unknown hurts, unacknowledged pain and unresolved sexual conflicts. Often we expect them to function as superhumans without need for rest or repair. Such misplaced expectations only reinforce some ministers' resorting to sexual sin and abusive power. We must provide ministers with outlets—both spiritual and therapeutic—to vent their anger, cleanse their hearts and heal their hurts.

In many ways, ministers are cocooned inside a punishing, sanctified silence. As the New Living Translation of a Galatian passage reminds us: "Dear Friends, if a Christian is overcome by some sin, you who are godly should gently and humbly help that person back onto the right path. And be careful not to fall into the same temptation yourself."

Finally, those of us who claim to be Christians should, as the powerful words from the Old Testament book of Micah direct us, "do justice, love mercy and walk humbly with our God."

Marcia L. Dyson has published personal essays on spiritual growth and personal relationships among African-Americans. Most recently, her work has been anthologized in Men We Cherish: African American Women Praise the Men in Their Lives, *edited by Brooke Stephens (Doubleday). She and her husband live in New York City.*

SEX @ WORK

What are the rules?
Confused by the Rules

By Gloria Jacobs with Angela Bonavoglia

Ruby S. was working late one night when the supervisor of her department at a large banking firm came up behind her and started massaging her back. She hadn't been working for the company long; didn't know the guy very well; and didn't particularly like him: "He was a little too slick for my taste." She turned to him and said, "Thanks for the back rub, but I have to go; I'm meeting someone in a few minutes." He laughed, let go of her shoulder, and asked, "Who's the lucky guy?" As he helped her on with her coat, he brushed his hand over her hair, tucking a strand behind her ear. She grabbed her things and got out of there, even though she still had a lot of work to do on an important project that was due the following week. "He gave me the creeps," she says, "but I never felt like I could be more firm about telling him to leave me alone, because it had taken a long time to find that job, and I really liked it except for him. I didn't

want to risk losing it." After about six months, she switched to another department with another supervisor. Her ex-boss stayed right where he was.

What exactly was going on in Ruby's office? Was it sexual harassment? Was it illegal? Was it someone trying to be friendly who just wasn't Ruby's type? And who gets to decide? Ruby? Her boss? Her company? A judge?

If you asked ten different people those questions, you'd probably get ten different answers. The truth is that just as the United States has become mired in media overkill on the topic of sexual harassment—was it or wasn't it? did he or didn't he?—many people of perfectly good intentions have absolutely no idea what such harassment really is. Short of the most egregious cases, we still don't "get it."

The lack of clarity at all levels has left corporate counsels shaking in their boots, haunted by visions of financial ruin

HARASSMENT OR HANKY-PANKY? These days, a lot of people, faced with a confusing and sometimes contradictory array of state and federal laws and individual company policies, are unable to tell the difference. Is offensive behavior automatically harassment? What about harassment that isn't sexual? Confusion about questions like these, along with a deliberate distortion of the meaning of the law, has plunged the nation into a rancorous, passionate debate about what is—and is not—sexual harassment. In the meantime, the President of the United States stands accused of sexual harassment (as well as other questionable sexual behavior).

We decided it was time to sort out the issues. What follows are factual articles, deeply felt opinions, and the voices of the best experts: women who have been harassed and who, in the process, learned something about themselves and their rights in the workplace.

—The Editors

(sales of employment practices insurance, which covers sexual harassment settlements, more than doubled in the last 18 months, from $100 million to over $200 million, according to *U.S. News & World Report*). Government employees and workers in companies and universities all across the country, private and public, large and small, are completely confused—many are convinced that the new rules forbid everything from flirting to joking to falling in love with your cubicle-mate.

Confusion may be inevitable when it comes to personal relations: so much of it is based on nuance, anyway. But it's also true that sexual harassment law, perhaps more than most, is constantly evolving as each new case comes before the courts and establishes new precedents. Thus, what today would be a perfectly obvious (and winnable) case of harassment—a woman loses her job because she won't sleep with her boss—was far from obvious to judges in the early 1970s.

Discrimination based on race, color, religion, national origin, or sex was outlawed in 1964 by Title VII of the Civil Rights Act. But over the next decade more than one sexual harassment case was lost when judges ruled that being punished for refusing to have sex with your boss had nothing to do with discrimination per se—these were "personal" relationships—and therefore did not fall under Title VII. Eventually several cases were successfully argued—by lawyers who claimed that because of the sexual stereotyping of women, an unwanted sexual advance by a person with supervisory power did amount to discrimination. In 1980, the Equal Employment Opportunity Commission (EEOC), which enforces federal antidiscrimination laws (some states have their own laws, in addition), issued specific guidelines on sexual harassment. Title VII covered nonsexual harassment as well, the kind used to keep women from competing with men for jobs—such as tampering with their work or equipment, threatening them, or deliberately jeopardizing their safety. But the EEOC emphasized sexual relations—the guidelines focused only on harassment between members of the opposite sex, and so have the courts over the years. It was not until March 4, 1998, that the Supreme Court declared same-sex harassment (whether against gays or straights) illegal.

The EEOC's guidelines identified two types of harassment: quid pro quo and hostile environment. As more and more cases were won using these categories, legal precedents were established, and expectations of what was acceptable behavior began ponderously but steadily shifting, like tectonic plates lumbering under the earth. As with many of the changes feminism has brought about, the idea that men—and some women—would have to question male prerogatives has elicited hostility and hosannas, as well as bewilderment and confusion. This discomfort, along with fear of litigation, has frequently led employers to overreact: if they don't know for sure where the line is, they'll draw it far enough back so hardly anyone can claim they didn't know they were stepping over it. Often companies end up with policies that don't make distinctions between office romances (given all the hours we spend at work, where else are we going to find a date or a mate?) and harassment.

Quid pro quo is Latin for "this for that"—it involves a boss demanding sexual favors in exchange for things like a job, a promotion, a raise, or benefits. Sexual favoritism is an offshoot of quid pro quo: it postulates that if a boss has sex with an employee and gives her promotions, better hours, and other benefits in return, the other women on the job can argue that they're being penalized for not sleeping with the boss.

It took 12 years for quid pro quo to be recognized by the courts. In 1976 in *Williams v. Saxbe*, a district court in Washington, D.C., finally ruled that sexual harassment is a form of unlawful sex discrimination. A year later, a higher court, the D.C. court of appeals, one of the most influential courts in the country, concurred. In *Barnes v. Costle*, the court ruled that having a job be "conditioned upon submission to sexual relations" was illegal. In response to *Barnes* and several big settlements that followed it, many employers took drastic steps, banning all romantic involvement between supervisors and their subordinates. The same thing happened in universities that created policies forbidding teachers from having a sexual relationship with students.

Employers develop exhaustive lists of all the behaviors that won't be tolerated, which they generally post and distribute.

Not surprisingly, there's a lot of disagreement about the effect of such sweeping policies. Some people believe they are essential, others say they rob us of the ability to make personal decisions. Last year, the president and chief operating officer of Staples, the office supply giant, resigned after it was revealed that he had had a consensual affair with his secretary. Staples' policy was that anyone in a close reporting relationship with another employee is prohibited from sexual relations with that person. That resignation received a great deal of media attention and set off a lot of second-guessing—the man was considered a top-notch leader, and if the woman consented, and he didn't show her any favoritism at work, who was harmed?

What is surprising in all the debate about no-dating's pros and cons is that, despite backlash rantings in the media against puritanical feminists, few feminists involved in workplace issues actually support policies like Staples'. "A no-dating policy is a quick-fix solution," insists Ellen Bravo, codirector of 9to5, a working women's advocacy group, "and a foolish policy." Carol Sanger, who teaches sexual harassment law at Columbia University in New York City, says these policies simply set women up as victims. "What women don't need is for the law to say, 'Guess what, you thought you were consenting to have sex, but we say you couldn't possibly have, because you're in an inferior power position, you're only a secretary.' Women's sexuality has been repressed too long. Let them consent." On the other hand, warns Sanger, if the initiator of an unwanted sexual advance is the person with more power, they must be willing to pay the price, if necessary: "If you fuck around with your young employees or your students, and they decide they're injured, then the risk should be on your head."

The Supreme Court first addressed the issue of sexual harassment in a 1986 ruling that set precedent by recognizing "hostile environment" harassment. In *Meritor Savings Bank v. Vinson*, the Court ruled that harassment could occur even if the victim hadn't lost any job benefits. In this case, the plaintiff had slept with her boss, but the justices said that he had sexualized the workplace to such an extent that it amounted to a hostile environment—which, according to the EEOC guidelines, consists of "unwelcome sexual advances, requests for sexual favors, and other verbal or physical conduct of a sexual nature" when it affects employment, interferes with work performance, or creates "an intimidating, hostile, or offensive working environment."

Since *Meritor*, the largest number of legal cases brought to the courts involve hostile environment. It is also the murkiest area of the law. What type of sexual conduct are we talking about exactly? When does harmless workplace behavior morph into a potentially hostile environment? When a guy e-mailing "The 50 Worst Things About Women" to several of his buddies hits the "all" key by mistake? When a man asks a female coworker for a date by e-mail, then voice mail, then sends a fax, then goes back to e-mail again, even though she has said no each time? When a male manager insists on checking a problem with a female coworker's computer and leans over her shoulder and whispers compliments in her ear? When the guys in the mail room begin the day with the latest raunchy joke, within obvious earshot of an older woman worker? When a male professor uses *Hustler* to teach female anatomy despite students' concerns? When a female administrator whose office brims with posters and cartoons that rag on men is assigned a male office mate?

With the exception of the e-mail of the "50 Worst Things" (assuming it was a one-time mistake, and recognizing the risk of using company e-mail for personal communiqués), all of the other examples may amount to sexual harassment. "Sexual harassment is deliberate, repeated, unwelcome, not asked for, and not returned," says Susan Webb the author of *Shades of Gray*, a guide on sexual harassment in the workplace. Her Seattle-based consulting firm that advises corporations on preventing harassment was one of the first to enter the field.

Firms like Webb's are multiplying because most companies feel they're on shaky ground when it comes to figuring out what a hostile environment is. "Sexual harassment is not black and white," says Webb. "You've got to take the whole thing in the context in which it occurred." It's not surprising that some of the examples given above could leave people scratching their heads. And many companies have established guidelines that go beyond the EEOC or their state laws. So you could lose your job for having violated company rules, but not have committed an illegal act. Companies are creating these policies because they are legally liable if they knew or should have known that harassment existed and failed to act. So far,

VO!CES   *"I was more angry than frightened."*

DEBORAH WITHERSPOON, 43 • CURRENT JOB AND JOB WHEN HARASSED: SECURITY GUARD IN BANKING INDUSTRY I work midnight to 8 A.M. I'm one of only two females on that shift. I started being sexually harassed last year when one of my bosses started making little innuendoes, flirting with me, and from there it just escalated. He became more aggressive because I was ignoring him. He started coming out to where I lived and would watch me come and go. I became very hostile and I kept telling him to leave me alone. But he took it like a joke—he paid it no mind.

Then he began to use his power as my boss to threaten me. He would say: "You're going to be transferred!" If I came in five or ten minutes late, he would record it. He told me the company wasn't satisfied with my performance.

One night, I was the only guard posted when he came in and closed the door and started talking some trash—telling me, "Now we can get it on." I became very frightened. I thought maybe he was going to attack me. I told him to get away from me and that the cleaning man was nearby. When I said that he left.

I'm not the type of person who likes to start problems or cause anyone to lose their job, but after that incident, I grew concerned. A girlfriend told me, "Look, it's not going to stop," so I took the situation to his boss, the vice president.

He seemed concerned and immediately rushed me over to human resources, where I gave them a statement. But the human resources person told me it was my word against his, and that he had said he didn't want to transfer. She asked me if I wanted to transfer. I told her I thought it was very unfair that she suggest I transfer when I wasn't the one who did anything wrong. What did she mean it was my word against his? Did she think I just picked him out of a crowd?

I stayed at my job. I'm not going to give up a good job for something someone else did to me. For a while the man who was harassing me stayed away from me. But recently he's started to come over to where I work. He hasn't said anything out of order yet, but I think he's getting more comfortable. Whenever he's around, I'm on my guard.

I surprised people by speaking out the way I did. And I think, at first, I got more respect from the other men because of it. People saw that I wasn't somebody you could push over. I will stand my ground for what I believe is right.

Overall, this situation made me more angry than frightened—until I was cornered that night. But even then I was angry. I don't like people to treat me like they can do what they want to me, as if I have no say. And what makes me angrier is how human resources dealt with the situation. Harassment is very serious.

I think that this type of behavior is wrong, and women should stand up against it even though there are consequences when you do. I should be respected just like the next person, regardless of the fact that I'm a female. I do my work, and I respect people. I demand that that same respect be given to me.

—ALL "VOICES" INTERVIEWED BY KATIE MONAGLE

the courts have said that the company is somewhat less liable for a hostile environment than for quid pro quo harassment, but most employers are trying to avoid as much risk as possible. With the sheer potential for liability—there are 137.6 million people working in the U.S.—and the damage that can be done to a carefully honed corporate image by one sensational suit, many employers have gone off the deep end in their efforts to control personal behavior.

Often, they've turned to what are known as "zero tolerance" policies. These say, in effect, one wrong move and you're out the door. But how to interpret that wrong move? Employers develop exhaustive lists of all the behaviors that won't be tolerated, which they generally post and distribute. Some behaviors on the lists are understandable: no unwelcome physical contact; and some are unrealistic: absolutely no touching. "One of my favorite examples of the stupidity of these lists," says Freada Klein, a longtime consultant on corporate policy, "is when some corporation did the typical thing after a lawsuit. They overreacted and put in a policy that said no touching ever. One of the first complaints came from someone who had observed a manager embracing his secretary—well, she had just found out her mother had died and he came out and consoled her."

When it comes to the people who truly use these behaviors to harass, the lists don't do much good, insists Klein. "Do you really think that someone who would engage in that kind of behavior, if they had a laminated card in their pocket with dos and don'ts, would decide not to act that way?" This rigid approach is "bizarre, insulting, infantalizing, and ineffective." She adds: "For every other workplace issue, we're talking about driving decision-making down. On this one, we say, 'You can't think for yourself, you're not a grown-up, you will only do as you're told.'"

Schools are another place where a "dos and don'ts" approach to harassment can melt down into the ludicrous. In 1996, two little boys, ages 6 and 7, were accused of sexual harassment for stealing kisses (and, in one case, the button of a dress) from female classmates. Each was briefly suspended from his school. The impetus was fear of liability by the schools involved: families have been successfully suing school districts for sexual harassment involving kids. And plenty of awful cases abound. A study by the American Association of University Women has shown that harassment of teenage girls in middle and high schools is pervasive and has devastating effects.

Based on its own studies, as well as reports like the AAUW's, and complaints received by the agency, in 1997 the U.S. Department of Education issued guidelines for stopping student-to-student harassment, as well as harassment between students and teachers, that hold schools responsible for their implementation. Unfortunately, despite the fact that the guidelines made distinctions according to age, cases like the ones involving the two little boys indicate, as in corporate America, a tendency to overreact, to see discipline problems involving children of different genders as harassment, and to disregard what any good educator should know: moral standards develop with age. "A 12-year-old's understanding of what is right and wrong on this subject can be very different from what a 7-

At the core of sexual harassment law lies a concept that the "victim" gets to decide if she has been victimized.

VO!CES *"He got away with it, that's the long and the short of it."*

ANONYMOUS, 34 • CURRENT JOB AND JOB WHEN HARASSED: UNION TECHNICIAN IN ENTERTAINMENT INDUSTRY I'm an apprentice technician. Before I was sexually harassed, I was a rising star. I was using cutting-edge technology and had achieved a lot of prestige and recognition in my field.

One day, I was working alone in a room with my boss on a particular job, and he pushed me over, sat in the chair with me and kissed me on the head. The next day I was in a warehouse, alone again, and he came up from behind me and wrapped his arms around me and kissed me. I squirmed. I didn't say anything. I was scared to the point of paralysis. That night I couldn't sleep at all. So the next day I call him up at home and say, "Your behavior yesterday and the day before was inappropriate, and I want to have a strictly professional relationship." He says, "You're absolutely right, I was out of line and I should stop—but I want to talk to you about it." So on a coffee break the next day he tells me, "I have been totally infatuated with you ever since I met you. The main reason why I hired you is because I'm attracted to you."

I documented the entire incident in a memo—including all the specific details, like dates, places, the number of times. I went to the union business agent, who's the head of the union. I wanted him to tell this guy to leave me alone. I didn't want him brought up on charges because I didn't want anyone else to know about this. In my field it can be very hard to get people to take me seriously because I'm a woman, and women doing what I do is very unusual. I already have to work twice as hard for respect. This would make things worse. Also, I was ashamed that this had happened to me at all.

The agent talked to him and he apologized for his actions. Shortly after, there was a three-month break on that job, so I took another assignment. I wasn't in touch with him at all until it was time to return. I called him to check in, and he said, "Oh, by the way, I've changed your rate of pay." Basically, he cut my pay.

Again, I went straight to the union business agent, who controls what jobs I get and who is ultimately responsible for my pay. But I could not convince the agent that the reason my boss had cut my pay was because I had busted him on sexual harassment. The business agent saw a legal loophole to explain my pay cut, and that's the story he stuck with. So there was nothing I could do. The business agent was totally against bringing this guy up on charges, and without the agent's support, I could never win in a grievance procedure in the union, because he had been there 30 years and was rarely challenged. I agreed to take another job with the union at the same location but doing something different, for less money, and in a different department from my harasser.

Recently, a new, younger business agent and president took over the union. They found work for me at different locations because the guy continued to harass me. I'm happy with this work, but not with how things turned out. If justice was ultimately what I wanted, I should have brought him up on charges right away. But the price for justice would have been so high, that in hindsight I don't have regrets. I just wish the world were different. He got away with it, that's the long and the short of it. I would have had to sacrifice my whole career to make him pay.

year-old thinks," Gwendolyn Gregory, who was the deputy general counsel for the National School Boards Association at the time of the incidents, told the Washington *Post*.

The cases involving these young boys were exceptional, but they received an enormous amount of derogatory press, some of it implying that sexual harassment as a concept was so off the wall, it made these kinds of cases inevitable. "By playing up the ridiculous, the exaggerations, or the aberrations, what the right wing tries to do is make it seem that that's the main thing that's going on, and it isn't," argues Ellen Bravo. "The main thing going on in the schools is not a 6-year-old being kicked out for kissing a girl on the cheek, but grabbing, groping, and sexual assault that borders on criminal behavior. By trivializing sexual harassment that way, they can dismiss it."

VO!CES   *"Was it all in my head?"*

ANONYMOUS, 22 • HIGH SCHOOL STUDENT WHEN HARASSED; CURRENTLY A COLLEGE STUDENT I was an easy target—I had "victim" written all over me. I was a junior in high school and I wasn't doing great academically. I had just moved to a new school and wasn't close with a lot of people there. Plus, I was going through a lot of emotional stuff at home. He was my U.S. history teacher and he always chose one girl to pick on every year. That year it was me.

In class he would try to make me look stupid, try to provoke me into arguing with him. I was really quiet and I tried to be almost invisible. The last thing I wanted was someone pointing me out, always being after me. Outside of class he would make comments about my appearance and proposition me. One time he cornered me and said, "I just need to know—do you want to have a teacher-student relationship, or do you want something more?"

There would be these really intense periods in which he'd make comments, touch my hair, grab my hand, things like that. Then it would be followed by a week when he wouldn't talk to me or acknowledge me in the classroom, even if I were to try to ask a question, or hand in a test. I got to a point where I had no idea what was real. It made me think I was going crazy because I would think maybe it wasn't really going on, maybe it was all in my head. At the same time, I was afraid that he would attack me. I thought it probably wouldn't happen at school, but I just didn't know. I also feared that my grade could be affected.

For a long time, I thought it wasn't such a big deal. But now I see that it had a huge impact on how I perceived myself. I became less confident. I started to wear baggy sweaters so that I would appear less sexual. By the end of that year I wouldn't even wear a skirt or anything that could have been seen by him as suggestive.

To me, there weren't any options in dealing with this. I didn't feel that there was anyone I could go to. I wasn't close enough to my mom to say anything to her, and my best friend was actually having an affair with one of her high school teachers. I didn't think that people would believe me or take me seriously. I figured they would think I was leading him on or encouraging him in some way. How else could this happen? It just seemed implausible that a high school teacher was saying these things to his student.

Later I realized that having "victim" written all over me didn't mean that it was my fault or that I necessarily deserved how he victimized me. I'm glad I never have to be 16 again. My only regret is that I didn't do anything about the harassment because he's probably still doing it to other students.

At the core of sexual harassment law lies a concept that the "victim" gets to decide if she has been victimized. (This strikes fear in the hearts of many—and may have contributed to employer overreaction.) If a coworker tells dirty jokes in your presence, and they don't bother you—you laugh along with everyone else—that's not harassment. If a coworker tells those same jokes as part of a pattern of hostility that makes you so uncomfortable it's hard to do your job, it's harassment. To those who have to implement the law, this can seem like a fairly subjective standard. Especially when it comes to trying to win a case in court. Recognizing that, the courts have ruled that the standard must be that of the so-called reasonable person. Because most plaintiffs in sexual harassment cases have been women, the standard is often referred to as that of a "reasonable woman."

This woman is a kind of Jane Doe/Everywoman: not too sensitive, not too idiosyncratic, sort of "just right," like Goldilocks' porridge. It would seem like an impossible task to figure out what's "reasonable" under such an amorphous standard. But the point, many lawyers insist, is that women do have a certain experience of the world that the courts should take into account. "We realize there's a broad range of viewpoints among women as a group," says Carol Sanger, "but we believe many women share common concerns which men do not necessarily share. For example, because women are disproportionately victims of rape and sexual assault, women have a stronger incentive to be concerned with sexual behavior. If a man gets a note from a female coworker who's been making sexual overtures, he's not afraid she's going to come up behind him in the parking lot one night."

But this attempt to give some flexibility to the law and prevent frivolous lawsuits has led to endless legal debates about just what is "reasonable" in a multicultural society, anyway. One of the biggest areas of contention involves the issue of speaking up. Because the law gives the victim the power to define the offense, many lawyers feel strongly that, when possible and safe, women ought to let the potential harasser know that his behavior is offensive. One law professor describes an incident when she served as ombudsman for her students. "A girl comes in and tells me that a guy says to her, 'I'd love to see you naked.' I say to her, what did you do? And she says, 'Well, I giggled and ran into my room.' That wasn't good enough. All you have to do is say, 'Don't do that to me again.' " A few days later, the woman came back, furious that she was expected to confront her fellow student. The professor eventually convinced her to write a letter, if for no other reason than to document his behavior should he repeat it. In this case, says the professor: "He really didn't know it was wrong. This is a guy who lives in a completely sexualized culture and he's a complete nerd and he's trying to be cool."

Others argue that men should know by now when their behavior is unacceptable, it shouldn't be up to women to teach them, and it isn't always possible to speak to a harasser. "In principle, it makes sense," says Katherine Franke, a professor of law at New York City's Fordham University, who specializes in sexual harassment. "But as a practical matter, a lot of women don't feel in a position to say to their boss, cut that out. What the law requires is often very different from what people feel empowered to do."

Topping off the debate on what's reasonable is the question of bigotry. Is someone's homophobia, for example, reasonable because a lot of people might share it? Vicki Schultz, a professor at Yale Law School in New Haven, Connecticut, describes a case in which a gay man was sued by a female coworker for sex harassment because he talked about his sex life at work. Although the woman lost, Schultz cautions, "I can see this being a very punitive measure in the hands of socially conservative people who don't want to hear people they perceive to be sexually deviant talk about their lives at all."

So here we are, women at the turn of the century who have transformed the workplace and the rules that govern it, by our presence. The good that has come from that transformation is now inevitably bogged down in the messy, complicated task of trying to make sure all the pieces of this particular puzzle fit together. It's a task that makes many people uncomfortable, and feminists have taken the brunt of the backlash. "The accusation lies there: you're just a frigid feminist, all you want to do is regulate sexuality," says Sanger. "But what kind of lives have people led that they don't know what awaits women?"

Ellen Bravo makes the point that "people have described in a trivializing, minimizing, and parodying way those of us who fight sex harassment, as if what we want is a repressive workplace where no one can tell a joke, no one can flirt, no one can date. This is not what we want. We want an end to unwelcome, offensive behavior of a sexual nature."

That is what we want, but nevertheless, the question remains—and it's a huge one—how can the average well-intentioned person figure out what behavior is acceptable in the workplace, especially when the damage is always in the eye of the beholder? The answer, say those who help devise the corporate rules, is deceptively simple: respect. Nearly everyone agrees that you can't just teach people a set of rules, expect them to memorize them, and that's it. It takes communication and discussion over a period of time. Not a one-day training session. Not handing people a manual and saying, "Read this." It takes a willingness to listen, respect for the concerns and fears of others, and an ability to honor differences, in order to reach some common ground. "Boilerplate policies are preposterous," says Freada Klein. "You have to respect the culture of the organization. Many of us are not in the same businesses, and even when we are, one company may be much looser than another." So the company has to set the tone and the standard.

Several companies are starting to do just that. DuPont, for example, has created a sexual harassment training program called A Matter of Respect. It consists of several workshops, some lasting several hours, some several days. The workshops use role playing, videos, and group discussions to help all levels of employees understand harassment. According to the company, about 75 percent of its 60,000 workers have attended some part of the program. Dupont diversity consultant Bob Hamilton says the goal is to "get people to build relationships so that they can talk freely, and so that if someone does something that bothers them, they can feel comfortable knowing they have the support of management and the organization to say something."

DuPont is one of the leaders in the attempt to create policies that rely on judgment and communication rather than specific rules. Even those who are most in favor of such policies say the effort is not easy. It demands that people do some second-guessing of themselves. One female executive says she now controls her impulse to touch her staff. "All of a sudden I realized I can't go out there and stand behind one of my employees and put my hand on his shoulder. That may be offensive to him and may be misinterpreted by him. So I've had to change my behavior."

Other executives say it's possible to get to a point where the decision-making about what's acceptable is more couched in the moment and the context. Burke Stinson, a spokesman for AT&T, which has an antiharassment program based on individual judgment, says women and men are definitely more comfortable about where to draw the line now. "If colleagues from different offices run into each other, there will be a hug, a 'God-it's-good-to-see-you' exchange that is nonsexual, nonthreatening, nongroping, based on one human being to another. Five or six years ago, I would say each party would have thought three times about it, and then just shaken hands."

People are more relaxed, Stinson believes, because they know the company will support them if there is a problem. "Employees who grew up in the work environment of the seventies and eighties feel that corporate America's hallways are not as threatening, are more secure, that there is recourse if there is some nasty business with words, deeds, or actions, a policy to fall back on. We're beginning to see a new sense of confidence."

Let's hope he's right. And that, along with that sense of confidence, there is a willingness to continue to struggle to figure out what's right, rather than resorting to inflexibility and archaic notions of women's "protected" status.

Gloria Jacobs is the editor of "Ms." Angela Bonavoglia, the author of "The Choices We Made: 25 Women and Men Speak Out About Abortion" (Random House), conducted research for, and helped to develop, this article.

The New Fertility

The promise—and perils—of human reproductive technologies.

by Harbour Fraser Hodder

WHEN SARA BENNETT LEARNED AT THE AGE OF 42 that she had breast cancer, she faced not one potential death but two—her own and that of the child she might never have. A few years ago, her only medical options would have been radiation and chemotherapy, treatments that destroy a woman's ovarian function along with her cancer. Today, as a single woman, she could undergo IVF (in vitro fertilization) with donor sperm. Before starting her cancer therapy, she would receive fertility drugs and have anywhere from 10 to 20 eggs surgically removed. After being mixed with sperm in a coaster-size petri dish, her fertilized eggs would be frozen until she regained her health or enlisted another woman to be the gestational surrogate for her embryos. The latest advances in reproductive medicine could provide her with the opportunity to salvage her genetic legacy while she was fighting for her life.

But Bennett (a pseudonym) quickly discovered that a fertile woman with a life-threatening malignancy didn't fit the accepted profile of women eligible for infertility treatment. Clinic after clinic turned her away. Then she approached Selwyn Oskowitz, director of Boston IVF, one of three fertility clinics affiliated with Harvard Medical School. (The others are at Brigham and Women's Hospital and Massachusetts General Hospital.) "She expressed eloquently what it meant to her to be able to think that her genealogy could be carried on, and that a child of her own could find new life," recalls Oskowitz, assistant professor of obstetrics, gynecology, and reproductive biology at the medical school. He was moved by

her appeal and brought it before Boston IVF's ethics advisory board.

Oskowitz believes Bennett "had been turned away from other clinics because she did not fit the narrow-minded social mores of who is infertile and who can be treated." Nevertheless, he says, her case "did bring up a whole host of ethical dilemmas. Should we use infertility treatments on someone who is *not* infertile? Should we freeze embryos for someone who may be dying, who may not be able to raise her child? Who will have custody of the embryos if she dies? If she wants the embryos to be placed with a surrogate, is it fair to the babies? Is it fair to the surrogate?"

Fertility specialists constantly face a barrage of ethical choices, and most clinics now have at least one advisory board. At Boston IVF, the priest, rabbi, ethicist, social workers, and pediatricians on the board reviewed Bennett's case, concluding that her wish to perpetuate her genetic heritage through IVF in spite of her cancer was ethically sound. They found her arrangements for the loving upbringing of her potential child by her family to be responsible, and she began IVF treatment.

Her eggs were retrieved and fertilized, but by this time Bennett had "personally arranged for a surrogate to carry her baby for her because she was too ill herself," says Oskowitz. The embryos were placed in the surrogate, but she did not conceive. Yet neither Bennett nor her doctors viewed the attempt as a loss. "We still feel, and she felt, that it was very successful in its value to her, to know that she could try to perpetuate her inner soul and all those feelings," reflects Oskowitz. "She felt

From *Harvard Magazine*, November/December 1997, pp. 54-64, 97-99. © 1997 by Harbour Fraser Hodder. Reprinted by permission.

"When you take away being able to have a child biologically, it is like having to face death—almost like having half of you die," says Shanti Fry. "Having kids is the main way that people deal with the fact that they are mortal."

that that gave her enormous strength and courage during her difficult treatments of chemotherapy and radiation. And that it enabled her to deal with the prospect of death in a more wholesome and productive manner." (Sara Bennett died last June, two months after this interview.)

The Soul of Infertility

SARA BENNETT'S CASE ILLUSTRATES HOW FAR ASSISTED reproductive technology, or ART (see "the Science of Assisted Reproduction") has come in the past two decades, how many new applications of these therapies exist, and how vexing are the moral and social issues they entail. It also dramatizes what's at stake.

"When you take away being able to have a child biologically, it is like having to face death—almost like having half of you die," says Shanti Fry '73, M.B.A. '85, a corporate finance director at BancBoston Securities. She speaks from experience, for she tried unsuccessfully for eight years to get pregnant using the full range of infertility options. She and her husband, Jeff Zinsmeyer, are now the proud parents of their daughter Victoria, age 3, whom they adopted in China. Infertility may not be life-threatening in the literal sense, says Fry, "but it does affect people's view of their own mortality, because having kids is the main way that people deal with the fact that they *are* mortal. And it's very hard for people who haven't been through it to understand the magnitude of that."

Understanding and alleviating the psychological impact of infertility has been the decade-long goal of assistant professor of medicine Alice Domar, Ph.D., director of the Mind/Body Center for Women's Health at Beth Israel Deaconess Medical Center. She and her colleagues have demonstrated that women with infertility suffer from significantly more depression than do their fertile counterparts. But their most dramatic finding is that the anxiety and depression scores for infertile women are statistically *equal* to those of women with cancer, heart disease, or HIV.

Although reproductive specialists have long recognized the distressing effects of infertility, the medical profession has not generally accepted it as a condition that stacks up to "real" medical diagnoses. Domar notes that most American health insurance policies exclude infertility evaluation and treatment, suggesting that the country does not perceive infertility to be either a medical diagnosis or a significant life crisis (see "An Infertility Primer").

Yet infertility, whatever its biological cause, creates emotional havoc for those who want children. "Infertility affects *every* aspect of the patient's life," says Domar. While a couple experiences infertility, their siblings and friends are having babies. If their religion disapproves of ART, they may feel even more isolated. And infertility "creates tremendous strain on the couple," she says. "Men can come to feel like they're being used for their sperm," while a woman is "devastated emotionally." Domar once asked Diane Clapp, medical director of the national infertility organization Resolve, about this gender gap. "Men never get pregnant," Clapp answered. "*Not* getting pregnant for a man is the norm, whereas not getting pregnant for a woman is *not* the norm."

Annie Geoghegan, chief social worker for the Center for Reproductive Medicine at Brigham and Women's, looks at the issue developmentally. "We as women expect as a rite of passage to be able to have children when we choose," she says. "And when that gets interrupted, women feel defective." But Ruth Hubbard, professor of biology emerita and a longtime observer of the field, wonders, "How much has to do with the sense that, 'My gosh, I'm a healthy person. If cows can do this, why can't I?' " Shanti Fry, as president of Families with Children from China/New England, says she has observed equal distress in both sexes: "Men suffer just as much and just as deeply as women do."

Although infertility causes levels of depression equal to those associated with cancer, it doesn't elicit equal sympathy. "If you have cancer, you're going to get an outpouring of support," says Domar. "You're not going to hear, 'Just relax and your cancer will go away.' With infertility there's a subtle message that it's all your fault." People have been sensitized about other conditions, but such sensitization hasn't taken place for infertility, says Fry. "They distance themselves from you, as if it were catching. It's *not* catching."

Infertile couples who show up at clinics often feel desperate to have their own baby, and are willing to pay for the chance to do so. Given the costs—and uncertainties—extra care must be taken to counsel prospective patients honestly and appropriately for their particular situation, says Mark Hornstein '77, director of the in vitro fertilization program at Brigham and Women's. He advises infertility patients with extremely low odds not to pursue ART, but on the whole, "the chances that a couple will have a live birth in our program, taking all comers, is about one in four, depending on age." Hornstein, an assistant professor of ob-gyn and reproductive biology

The Science of Assisted Reproduction

IN 1978, LOUISE BROWN, THE FIRST "TEST TUBE BABY," WAS BORN in England. For the first time, a woman with blocked fallopian tubes who could not be helped by conventional surgery could hope to conceive and bear her own child through in vitro fertilization. In IVF, a woman's ovaries are drug-stimulated to produce 10 to 20 eggs, rather than the normal one or two. When mature, these ova are surgically "harvested," or retrieved. Each egg is then combined with 75,000 to 100,000 sperm in a glass petri dish—hence in vitro ("in glass") as opposed to in vivo ("in body"). The next day, two nuclei mean that fertilization has occurred. Forty-eight to 72 hours after retrieval, the embryos are ready for transfer back to a woman's uterus. Then a couple waits to see if implantation "takes" and a pregnancy has begun.

Since 1981, more than 33,000 babies born in the United States have been conceived via assisted reproductive technology (ART). Sperm banks, egg donation, embryo freezing, and surrogacy have been added to the popular lexicon, along with an alphabetic array of high-tech variations on IVF, including GIFT, ZIFT, and ICSI (pronounced ICK-see). GIFT (gamete intrafallopian transfer) involves the same course of fertility drugs and egg retrieval as IVF, but the eggs and sperm are returned to a woman's fallopian tube, the natural site for fertilization. ZIFT (zygote intrafallopian transfer) is like IVF, except that the zygote (the fertilized egg) is returned to the fallopian tube, not to the uterus. Some specialists claim that GIFT and ZIFT may increase the likelihood of implantation—the biggest sticking point in ART—by allowing the fertilized egg to follow its natural course to the uterus. Both require that woman's fallopian tubes be intact.

ICSI (intracytoplasmic sperm injection), discovered by accident in Belgium in 1991, is the most recent addition to the ART family. To cause fertilization, an egg is perforated and a single sperm is injected; any resulting embryo is then transferred to the uterus or the fallopian tubes. ICSI represents "a huge advance for treating male infertility," according to Mark Hornstein '77, director of the in vitro fertilization program at Brigham and Women's Hospital.

The success rates for IVF and other ARTs vary widely from clinic to clinic, depending on screening policies (especially regarding age and type of infertility), available medical protocols, and expertise. The average success rate for standard IVF procedures in 1994, the most recent year for nationwide data, was 21.7 percent deliveries per cycle initiated. At Brigham and Women's, the 1994 delivery rate per IVF cycle for women under 40 was 26.44 percent; for women over 40, it was 5.36 percent. At Boston IVF, for standard IVF in the same year, the delivery rate for women under 40 was 16.5 percent; for women over 40, it was 6.41 percent. (The Boston rates apply to cases where there was no male factor infertility involved.) The nationwide success rates for GIFT and ZIFT are higher, at 28.5 percent and 29.1 percent respectively. The highest overall birth rate—46.8 percent—is found with donor eggs, in which the eggs of a fertile, usually younger woman are fertilized in vitro and transferred to the uterus of an infertile woman.

Since the chances of a fertile couple conceiving in any given month are only about 20 percent, ART raises an infertile couple's odds (per attempt) to fertile odds. But conceiving in vivo and in vitro are two quite different things. "Sex usually feels good, and it's easy, and it's free—not so with assisted reproductive techniques," says Susan Pauker, assistant clinical professor of pediatrics and chief of the genetics department at Harvard Pilgrim Health Plan. The median cost of one cycle of reproductive assistance is $7,800, according to the American Society for Reproductive Medicine. If a couple doesn't succeed at first, they often try three or four times before having a baby or giving up. With little or no insurance coverage available, 85 percent of those fees comes out of patients' pockets.

It is estimated that half the people who suffer infertility never seek a doctor's opinion, and of those who do, approximately 50 percent don't complete the infertility evaluation or the treatment plan. "People think of millions and millions of people getting treatment, when in fact, most people don't go for treatment, and a very, very small percent go for ART," says Alice Domar, director of the Mind/Body Center for Women's Health at Beth Israel Deaconess Medical Center. Many of them hold out hope for a spontaneous cure. Among couples who pursue treatment, some studies show that one third conceive on their own within two to seven years of discontinuing infertility therapy. But Mitchell Rein, assistant professor of ob-gyn and reproductive biology, says, "There's no question that ART is the single most successful treatment for the majority of cases."

at the medical school, emphasizes that "every couple feels that they will get pregnant, regardless of how low their chances are and what they're told. And psychologically, that's a very important thing. To go through invasive, painful, somewhat risky procedures to have a child, you must believe it's going to work for you."

Domar, author of Healing Mind, Healthy Woman, believes psychological factors play an even more important role. "Can psychological symptoms, especially depression, hamper treatment success? I believe the answer is yes," she says. Studies demonstrate a 13 percent success rate if a woman is depressed before an IVF cycle versus a 29 percent success rate for those who are not depressed. Ten years ago, Domar established the first behavioral treatment program for infertility in the country, at Harvard's Mind/Body Medical Institute. In 10 weekly sessions, women (and, for three sessions, their partners) meet in a supportive group environment to learn about relaxation and stress-management techniques, nutrition and exercise, and how to cope with negative emotions. Domar and her colleagues are now in the midst of a five-year study, sponsored by the National Institute of Mental Health, to determine the efficacy of such treatment.

Critics contend that Domar is perpetuating the "relax-and-you'll-get-pregnant myth," but she sees her program as a supplement, not a substitute for traditional medical care. Her brand of treatment, in conjunction with conventional or assisted reproductive therapy, produces im-

When we expose children to these manipulations without any knowledge of the long-range outcome, then we're vulnerable," says clinical geneticist Susan Pauker. "The children absolutely are not giving informed consent."

pressive results—a 37 percent "take-home baby" rate at last count. "I've always said that we consider pregnancy to be a nice side effect," says Domar. "What we do here is teach women skills which they can use to get their lives back. And if they *happen* to get pregnant because they got less depressed, that's great. But if they didn't get pregnant, they're still feeling better."

Superovulatory Risks

APART FROM THE PSYCHOLOGICAL RAMIFICATIONS, THE NEW reproductive therapies involve hormonal and surgical interventions that may cause harm to mother and child. For many who are infertile, the risks of conventional drug therapy and ART may outweigh the potential benefits.

"I don't consider IVF to be a risk-free intervention," says Elizabeth Ginsburg, associate director of the IVF program at Brigham and Women's and an assistant professor of ob-gyn and reproductive biology. She had just performed an emergency procedure for an IVF patient who was hospitalized for severe hyperstimulation of the ovaries, the major potential complication of superovulatory drugs. It involves massive ovarian enlargement due to multiple cysts, among other things, and can cause death if untreated. The woman was not in danger, but "she was extremely uncomfortable and very distended," says Ginsburg. "This happens rarely, and this was our once-a-year."

Inducing ovulation through hormonal drugs has been around since 1938, so the possible side effects from such treatment are well known. In addition to the risk of hyperstimulation, multiple gestations occur in approximately 20 percent of ovulation-induced pregnancies (the formerly infertile couples who have triplets—or quints) and spontaneous abortions occur in 12 to 29 percent. Ectopic pregnancies, when a fertilized egg implants outside the uterus (usually in the fallopian tubes), occur in 3 to 5 percent of IVF pregnancies—or three times as often as they do in natural conceptions.

The long-term effects of infertility therapy are less clear, but some studies show an increased incidence of ovarian cancer. "Women who don't ever conceive are at higher risk for cancer of the ovary and for breast cancer," says Selwyn Oskowitz. "The question is whether fertility medicines enhance that risk or not, and we don't know." For Annie Geoghegan, the potential risk of ovarian cancer raises the specter of diethylstilbestrol (DES). The synthetic hormone, prescribed from the 1940s to the 1970s to prevent miscarriages, was eventually found to cause reproductive problems in the children of women who had used it. "Many of these infertile women are themselves DES daughters, but they're still willing to take the drugs," says Geoghegan. Alice Domar believes that "someone who's so driven to have a baby is willing to undergo anything—no matter what a consent form says."

Susan Pauker, assistant clinical professor of pediatrics and chief of the genetics department at Harvard Pilgrim Health Plan, is also worried about the effects on the children. "When we expose children to these manipulations without any knowledge of the long-range outcome, then we're vulnerable to the same experience as DES," she says. Pauker was a resident at Mass. General when the DES alert came out in the mid 1970s. "We said, 'Never again—like the Holocaust—will we stand by and watch while a drug is being utilized before we know the long-term outcome.' " She also points to a presumably benign element of ART—ultrasound, which electronically converts the echo of a sound wave into an image of the embryo or fetus. "What in the world leads us to think that aiming a high-frequency sound wave at rapidly dividing tissues is a safe thing to do?" she asks. In normal pregnancies, doctors use ultrasound once or twice, but in assisted reproduction, it is often required daily. "What do we do if they all have diminished hearing or diminished reproduction?" Pauker says. "The children absolutely are not giving informed consent." Nonetheless, Oskowitz notes that, "remarkably, the studies thus far are finding very little in abnormalities, both genetically and adaptively."

For Mark Hornstein, "The foremost risk in my mind is the risk of high-order multiple gestation, which means triplets or more." In conventional infertility treatment, multiple gestation is due to superovulation. In ART, it is due to superovulation plus the practice of transferring several embryos at a time to the uterus in order to increase the chances for pregnancy. Because pregnancies of triplets or more endanger both mother and babies, doctors may perform a "multifetal pregnancy reduction." In this procedure, the most accessible gestational sac is injected with potassium. "Unfortunately," says Oskowitz, "a gestational pregnancy fetus has to be lost."

Great Britain and Australia restrict the number of embryos in a single transfer to three. The American Society for Reproductive Medicine (ASRM) condemns the practice of transferring excessive numbers of embryos with the intention of using multifetal reduction for mop-up, but stops short of an all-inclusive limit. Brigham and

An Infertility Primer

"IF YOU ASK A SEVENTH GRADER WHAT IT TAKES TO MAKE A BABY, 90 percent of them could come up with two of the three major ingredients: sperm and eggs," says Mitchell Rein, assistant professor of ob-gyn and reproductive biology at Harvard Medical School and chief of ob-gyn and director of women's services at Salem Hospital / North Shore Medical Center. "The third is a way for them to get together: the tubes."

What causes infertility? Sperm problems are the "most common and will be the major cause in 35 to 50 percent of all cases," he says. Egg or ovulation problems comprise 15 percent and tubal problems 15 to 20 percent of cases. Another 15 percent of couples have "unexplained infertility," and "about 25 percent of infertility cases have more than one factor—so these numbers don't have to add up to exactly 100 percent," he notes. Age also has "a strong impact on a couple's infertility, regardless of the etiology," he adds. Conventional treatments such as fertility drugs (often used in conjunction with IUI—intrauterine or "artificial" insemination) and surgery can help many of these couples, but not all.

Male infertility is easier to detect but more difficult to correct than female infertility. Normal sperm counts range from 20 million to 60 million cells per milliliter (one-fifth of a teaspoon) of semen. Anything below that means a low sperm count, the most common cause of male infertility. About half the cases of low sperm count are caused by varicoceles (varicose veins in the testicle), or blocked sperm ducts, often due to scarring from sexually transmitted diseases (STDs). Microsurgery can be effective for both, and fertility drugs may help the next most common cause: hormonal deficiency. All-out testicular failure can be caused by a range of traumas—including mumps, STDs, and injuries—and is more difficult to treat. Another 10 percent of infertile men have antibodies that destroy their sperm as soon as it's produced. Whatever the cause, IUI and ART are often employed to boost the chances of sperm reaching the egg.

In female infertility, ovulatory or endocrine problems account for about half of all cases. Common causes include failure of the hypothalamus to induce ovulation, polycystic ovarian disease, and premature ovarian failure. In luteal phase dysfunction, there is not enough progesterone after ovulation (the "luteal phase") to support the implantation of a fertilized egg. Oral contraceptives may also render a woman anovulatory after she has stopped taking the Pill. Many of these problems are treated with ovulation-inducing drugs plus IUI.

Obstructions within the reproductive system account for another 40 percent of women's infertility; the leading cause is pelvic inflammatory disease (PID). Twenty years ago, blocked fallopian tubes, pelvic adhesions, and scarring—which can all prevent the egg and sperm from connecting—caused only 25 percent of female infertility. But as men and women have become sexually active earlier and with more partners, the number of pelvic infections caused by sexually transmitted bacteria has multiplied. Barrier contraception protects a woman's reproductive system, but the IUD renders her up to 10 times more likely to contract PID. The second most common cause of obstructions is endometriosis: the blood-rich lining of the uterus escapes and grows on the ovaries or tubes, creating adhesions. Although microsurgery and laser surgery often restore blocked tubes, they do not always restore fertility, at which point couples turn to IVF.

Looming over all these factors is the factor of age. Aging decreases fertility in both sexes, but more dramatically in women. A woman under 30 has a 20 percent chance of becoming pregnant in any given month, but once over 40, her chances plummet to 5 percent. She begins her reproductive life with 300,000 eggs, but only a few thousand remain when she is in her forties. Older eggs do not fertilize as easily, do not respond as well to reproductive hormones, and have a higher number of chromosomal problems. Therefore, the risks of miscarriage, or of bearing a child with genetic disorders such as Down syndrome, increase steadily with age.

Infertility is diagnosed after a woman or a couple has tried to achieve pregnancy for a full year and failed, since it takes, on average, six months to conceive. According to some estimates in the popular press, there are 9 or 10 million infertile couples of child-bearing age in the United States—or 1 in 6 couples—and infertility is reaching "epidemic" proportions. But the National Center for Health Statistics contests this view, reporting that about 4.9 million women between the ages of 15 and 44 were infertile in 1988 (or about 1 in 12). These women represented only 8.4 percent of their age group; in 1965, the percentage of infertile women in the same age group was 11 percent.

The public perception that infertility rates are rising is due, in part, to extensive media coverage of new reproductive technologies and to the proliferation of fertility clinics (from 30 to 300) in the last decade. The huge cohort of baby boomers has also produced "a big bubble of childless women," as one reporter called it. The common practice of delaying child-bearing until couples are in their thirties (20 percent of U.S. women begin their families after age 35) increases the time it takes to conceive naturally, as well as the pressure to conceive quickly. And several international studies have reported dramatic declines in sperm counts, possibly due to environmental causes.

Women's has standard guidelines for how many embryos to transfer. A lot depends on a woman's age and how many IVF cycles she's been through, says Ginsburg, noting that "our upper cut-off" is five. Pauker recommends a different criterion: "I've always said that you should put in only as many eggs as you're willing to raise through college."

What happens to embryos that haven't been transferred? The not-so-good ones are discarded and the good ones are cryopreserved. Freezing has been the answer to quite a few prayers in assisted reproduction. It reduces the need to transfer a number of embryos at once, thereby reducing the need for fetal reduction. It also gives a woman another chance at getting pregnant with-

How many embryos should be transferred? "The foremost risk in my mind," says Mark Hornstein, "is the risk of high-order multiple gestation, which means triplets or more"—which endangers both mother and babies.

out going through fertility drugs and egg retrieval, thereby reducing her risks. But embryo freezing raises its own dilemmas, medical and moral (see "Embryo Banking").

"We make babies from frozen eggs," Pauker says. "Who gives us the right to assume it is safe in the long run to utilize frozen fertilized eggs to make human beings?" As with many elements of ART, the long-term effects of cryopreservation are simply not known. In the interim, freezing allows many couples to take advantage of assisted reproduction without violating their beliefs. "We don't freeze every extra embryo after a transfer, because only embryos of good quality will survive freezing," says Elizabeth Ginsburg. "We check for things like division rate, fragmentation, the appearance of the cell membranes, and symmetry among cells." But for couples who are ethically opposed to discarding embryos, she says, "We'll freeze everything that's left over, even though we don't think that they're going to cause pregnancy in the future. I think you have to, because it's stressful enough without invading people's religious and moral beliefs."

Nuclear Family Meltdown

SARA BENNETT'S DECISION TO HAVE HER EGGS RETRIEVED makes it clear that the advances of reproductive science raise far more than technical and medical issues. Clinical geneticist Susan Pauker empathizes "deeply with people who want to have their own natural child." She also believes that ART "has gone beyond 'assisted' reproduction to manipulations that we certainly didn't dream of 20 years ago. We're getting away from the natural selective process of people being attracted to each other, one of whom had eggs, one of whom had sperm, and the male bearing the sperm to the site of ovulation. Our society is not prepared for the families that will result from these interventions."

When Judith Larkin was pregnant with their son Adam (both pseudonyms), she met with a genetic counselor who asked, "Who's the father?" When Larkin said, "I don't know," the woman stiffened. When she added, "He was an anonymous donor," the counselor let out a sigh of relief.

"My first choice was to be married and get pregnant in a nice, natural, normal way," Larkin says. But when she was 34 she wasn't married and she still wanted a child. She thought about it for a year before she decided, attending workshops held by Single Mothers by Choice. "For women who choose to become parents this way, it's

a very conscious choice," she says. "Women I know agonize over it—How am I going to do this? Am I going to make a good mother? I think *that's* what makes good parents."

Larkin began artificial inseminations with donor sperm when she was 35, assisted by Clomid, the initial drug used to induce ovulation. After five unsuccessful cycles, she advanced to self-administered Pergonal injections. But after four cycles of that, all she had was a blocked tube caused by an earlier infertility procedure. If Larkin wanted to get pregnant, she had no choice but to move on to IVF.

Larkin found IVF to be an even more demanding experience than artificial inseminations with fertility drugs. As a freelance landscape architect, her schedule could accommodate the daily blood tests and ultrasounds. She was also injecting herself with Pergonal twice a day to produce even more eggs—which made her feel like she had "grapefruits for ovaries." Surgery retrieved nine eggs, about average for her age. When none fertilized, she was devastated. Her doctors concluded that there must be a sperm problem, so Larkin went back to the sperm bank to select her third donor. "You get attached to them," she says. "But you reach a point where you're ruthless about it. If he can't cut it, he's out of here."

To counter her increasing depression, Larkin relied on friends from Single Mothers by Choice who were going through ART as well. She also joined Alice Domar's mind/body program before her next try at IVF. "I felt like I could relax for the first time in a year," she recalls. This time her doctors retrieved 12 eggs, which were mixed with the new donor's sperm. Three of them fertilized, but only two survived until the transfer day. Larkin had to lie very still for hours; she thinks she "felt this little twinge" when an embryo implanted. Two weeks later, she was pregnant. "I called everybody I knew that day," she remembers. "It was thrilling. I loved being pregnant even though I was uncomfortable most of the time." She was 37 when her son was born.

Adam is now two and a half. "It's been really hard and really wonderful in all the normal ways," she says. But she admits she hasn't had a "typical single-parent experience." When she was consigned to bed rest during her pregnancy, an old friend she'd once been involved with was looking for a place to live. Jon (not his real name) moved in and took care of her. "He kind of fell in love with Adam and never left. We've gradually started functioning more and more like a family—though that wasn't anyone's intention." Adam had been calling

Embryo Banking

"MEDICALLY, MOST OF US FEEL CONCEPTION OCCURS WHEN AN embryo actually implants in the body of a woman," says Selwyn Oskowitz, assistant professor of ob-gyn and reproductive biology at Harvard Medical School. Some groups believe conception occurs with fertilization or lovemaking, he says, but "if one believes that conception is a phenomenon of a unique union between an embryo and its mother, then that occurs only within the body." In that view, fertilization precedes—and is separate from—conception, whether reproduction is natural or in vitro. Although some people believe that the embryo has no moral status, the view most widely held among ethicists and legal scholars is that the embryo, in the formulation of the American Society for Reproductive Medicine (ASRM), "deserves respect greater than that accorded to human tissue but not the respect accorded to actual persons."

Whether or not human life exists from the moment of conception has "already torn our country apart," says Harvard law professor Elizabeth Bartholet '62, J.D. '65. "I'm an abortion-rights person, and I certainly do not see an embryo as equivalent to a person, but there's an ethical dilemma with a procedure that systematically engages in embryo destruction." She adds that cryopreservation in itself is a social time bomb. "It seems irresponsible not to decide anything and just freeze embryos, because that's what the patient wants and because, for the moment, it gets the doctors off the hook." Great Britain is her case in point. When Parliament passed a law requiring that frozen embryos not used within five years be destroyed, and thousands of embryos were destroyed, "there was a huge public reaction," says Bartholet. "In this country, this is not a problem that's going to go away. We have to decide what we're going to do with these tens of thousands of embryos we're stockpiling. Do you want someone to unfreeze these embryos generations later and have a sibling born when you're a *grandparent*?"

"Most people feel that frozen embryos should *not* outlive the donors," says Kenneth Ryan, M.D. '52, Ladd professor of obstetrics, gynecology, and reproductive biology emeritus, who is co-chair of ASRM's ethics committee. "And when people have embryos frozen, they ought to make a decision as to how they're going to be used and what their disposition is to be." As of late September, the reproductive center at Brigham and Women's Hospital had frozen its 663d embryo for 1997. Altogether, they have 5,118 "freeze-dried" embryos that look like shriveled microscopic raisins. When they're thawed at room temperature for another try at getting pregnant, they swell back up. But once a couple succeeds at pregnancy and has a family of two or three, what should they do with the embryos that are left? Most can't decide.

Jon by name, but "just yesterday he said, 'You're my mommy and you're my daddy.' "

Larkin's own parents have been very supportive of her choice to be a single mother, but her three younger brothers aren't speaking to her. "They said this was a terrible thing to do, and I'd be a terrible mother, and they couldn't have a relationship with me if I was going to do it." Some ethicists are opposed to single women using IVF, as were fertility clinics themselves in the early years of ART. Brigham and Women's was the first Massachusetts program to treat single women, in the mid 1980s. Now, like Boston IVF, they welcome lesbian couples as well.

Most of the gay couples in the Brigham and Women's program use frozen sperm that's donated anonymously, but occasionally there are special requests, says Annie Geoghegan: "Two women want to use the sperm of one of their brothers, so that they're both genetically related to the child." As a social worker, she will help them sort through such questions as, "What's the relationship going to be? How do you tell the child?" Kenneth Ryan, M.D. '52, Ladd professor of obstetrics, gynecology, and reproductive biology emeritus, who is co-chair of ASRM's ethics committee, says his philosophy is, "If no one is exploited in the process, and the child is wanted and loved, there can't be anything wrong with it."

Some lesbian couples choose gestational surrogacy in order to have "a shared experience of a pregnancy," says Elizabeth Ginsburg. "One member of the couple's eggs are used, inseminated with donor sperm, and the other partner carries the pregnancy," she explains. Lesbians, like single women, have had to prove their infertility before participating in IVF. But a controversial protocol eliminating that requirement was recently approved, says Ginsburg, so that the "minority of lesbian couples who feel there's no other way that they can share a pregnancy" may be helped. Patients are screened to determine that the relationship is long-standing and monogamous, and they must have legal, adoption-like documents drawn up.

Ruth Hubbard, who has grandchildren by donor insemination, says her daughter's "partner is certainly as

"For women who choose to become parents this way, it's a very conscious choice," says Judith Larkin. "Women agonize over it—How am I going to do this? Am I going to make a good mother? I think that's what makes good parents."

Ruth Hubbard thinks that exchanging eggs is "pretty darn silly. If it's one person's egg, why shouldn't she have it? What have you done—scrambled eggs, but what else? A lot of intervention for nothing."

much a mother of those children as my daughter, whose biological children they are." But Hubbard thinks that exchanging eggs "is pretty darn silly. That's attaching a significance that's all in the head. If it's one person's egg, why shouldn't *she* have it? What have you done—scrambled eggs, but what else? A lot of intervention for nothing."

Some people may object to "using an elaborate medical technology to get around social convention, personal desire, and biological limitations," says Ryan, but the same questions apply to both heterosexual and gay couples: "What are the driving forces for this? Is the child being brought into the world wanted? How committed to each other are they?"

Procreative Liberty?

"AS A SOCIETY, WE PUSH THE INFERTILE TOWARD EVER MORE elaborate forms of high-tech treatment," writes Elizabeth Bartholet in her book *Family Bonds: Adoption and the Politics of Parenting*. The Wasserstein public interest professor of law at Harvard Law School, Bartholet was herself a pioneer in pursuing assisted reproduction in its formative years. As a single woman with a son from a previous marriage, she wanted to parent again on her own. She wore what she called her "IVF wedding ring" and pretended she was under 40 during her 10-year battle with infertility in three states. Then, one day in 1985, she realized it was time to move on. That fall she adopted Christopher in Peru, returning two years later to adopt Michael.

Bartholet saw herself as bravely exercising her procreative rights. "But what is an obsession and what's freedom, and when is it what you really want to do?" she asks. Now she sees such a quest as "pushing a woman to obsess more and more about her inability to be the woman she's supposed to be in the classical, traditional sense." Such a choice isn't free but conditioned. "What women and couples would be choosing in a world in which we had different attitudes about the significance of biological parenting and different financial structures, and where you had a constitutional right to *adopt* the way you have a constitutional right to procreate—I just think there would be significantly different choices being made if it were a more even playing field," she says.

Bartholet is not out to ban IVF, but she does call for a national commission to discuss the social and ethical issues raised by assisted reproduction. "The fact that

we're not facing these issues as a society is in itself a major ethical issue," says Bartholet. Instead, we're "letting doctors operate in this vacuum and resolve these issues themselves. They are not facing up to the ethical issues, and they are not the ones who should be resolving them."

The ASRM's ethics committee writes that it "is painfully aware that many issues of critical national concern . . . are not being addressed by any effective mechanism for the development of sound public policy," and they, too, call for a national commission. Reproductive biologist Mitchell Rein, an assistant professor at the medical school who is chief of ob-gyn and director of women's services at Salem Hospital/North Shore Medical Center, agrees that "a more formal regulatory board might be helpful" for the ethical issues that challenge infertility specialists, "so that as a field we're somewhat unified in our voice and somewhat consistent in our treatment."

Regulation of the infertility industry is not enough for some opponents. The initial feminist reaction to assisted reproduction in the 1970s was very negative, notes Linda Blum, a sociologist and women's studies specialist at the University of New Hampshire who was a 1996–97 Bunting Fellow. The Boston Women's Health Book Collective, creators of the women's health bible of the '70s, still argues strongly against ART in *The New Our Bodies, Ourselves*. The organization FINRRAGE (Feminist International Network of Resistance to Reproductive and Genetic Engineering) wants to outlaw many forms of the new reproductive technologies completely. They believe that ART is a male-controlled intervention that alienates women from the reproductive process, that commercial surrogacy is a form of slavery and the "sale" of eggs amounts to a "reproductive brothel," that the children produced are then commodities as well—the first step down the slippery slope toward genetic engineering. Ruth Hubbard has long felt that IVF provided experimental biologists with access to human eggs and embryonic development "dressed up as a medical benefit."

Blum, author of a forthcoming book on ideologies of breastfeeding and motherhood, sees a greater diversity of voices now. "There's no 'feminist line,' " she says. "Some women who were infertile—for whatever reasons—felt very insulted that their genuine desires to have a biological child were seen as some sort of patriarchal false consciousness."

For Kenneth Ryan, it's an oversimplification to suggest that the mere existence of assisted reproduction is itself coercive—"Being childless is what is coercive." One of the major distinctions between natural and assisted reproduction, he adds, "is that we know in the infertility case that the couple is actively seeking to have a child. In over half the reproduction that occurs normally, the child is conceived without intent—and that's the height of irresponsibility and poses serious ethical problems."

Arthur Dyck, Ph.D. '66, says we should also ask, "How will others be affected by assisted reproduction, and how will *I* be affected in self-destructive ways?" The professor of population ethics at the Divinity School and the School of Public Health says, "There is such a tendency to make 'autonomy' a moral imperative and to use it as the answer to every difficult question. But choices involving reproductive technologies affect all of us. We are *all* responsible for the children that are born."

The Vatican, the most powerful institutional opponent of ART, condemns it as dehumanizing. The *Instruction on Respect for Human Life in Its Origin and on the Dignity of Procreation (1987)* states that ART denies the "language of the body" for the spousal expression of love. The act of sexual intercourse within marriage "unites body and spirit in the bringing into existence of new life. To create new life without sexual intercourse is thus to fail to accord human reproduction its full dignity." The consequences of disembodied procreation are the objectification and commodification of women and children; therefore, it should be illegal.

But Selwyn Oskowitz has seen the other side of such edicts. "A lot of pain and suffering occurs, including guilt and all its ramifications. Patients agonize and are precluded from having a family because they cannot participate in IVF," he says. It's usually uninvolved bystanders who pass these judgments, he adds. "It's the same old story—there are no atheists on a sinking ship. And the converse is true. It's easy to be religious about certain aspects of life when your life's needs are not threatened."

Ryan has witnessed many people undergo IVF despite the disapproval of their faith. "There's this tremendous drive to have a child," he says. He thinks this drive "looks and feels biological" and suspects it is derived from both culture *and* biology. "But if you've ever seen individuals warm up to a newborn baby, or been on an airplane with a mother and young child, with all of the other passengers eyeing or cooing the child, and the stewardess wanting to hold the child—for lack of a better term, I'd have to say that gets pretty close to human nature."

Help Wanted

WHEN ALL ELSE FAILS, REPRODUCTIVE TECHNOLOGY INCLUDES donor sperm and donor eggs in its arsenal. Elizabeth Bartholet calls these methods, together with surrogacy, "technological adoption," because they involve "the production of children designed to be cut off from their ge-

netic forebears." She feels our society is "completely inconsistent and schizophrenic" regarding the significance of the biological link. Although "adoption regulation is premised on the notion that biology is *everything*," with its focus on the rights of the birth mother (and father), "our tolerance of a free market in the ART realm seems premised on the attitude that biology doesn't matter at all," she says. "Therefore it's OK to induce men to give sperm for money, and have laws set up so that they have no responsibility for the child. Therefore it's perfectly legal, at least so far, for women to be induced to come in and 'sell' their eggs."

The practice of using one man's sperm to rectify another man's infertility is the oldest form of assisted reproduction, going back to the late nineteenth century. In the 1950s and 1960s, universities were the principal repositories of donated sperm. "In the old days, we used to have Harvard medical students come over and donate their sperm and everything was very secretive," Annie Geoghegan recalls. "You probably know some sperm donor children and you don't know that they are—and *they* may very well not know that they are."

In the 1970s, private, for-profit sperm banks arrived on the scene. Susan Pauker, the medical geneticist, was called by one in California: "How many donations did I think a donor should give to a given geographical area before too many people on the street would look like the donor?" This poses another ethical problem, notes Oskowitz—"where there are children born in the community who may mate unknowingly with their half-siblings." In an area the size of greater Boston, he says, statistical models show that the odds of consanguinity are extremely low for up to 10 children from the same mother or father. However, he adds, "if there were a clinic in Hope, Arkansas, they'd have to be very strict on the number of offspring."

In reality, "ovum donors rarely donate that frequently," says Oskowitz. That's because it's much more difficult to donate eggs. "A man can just ejaculate and go on with his day," explains Geoghegan. "A woman who's donating an egg has to go through an IVF cycle, including intramuscular drug injections, daily vaginal ultrasounds, blood tests, and a surgical procedure." Most clinics restrict the number of times a woman may donate eggs to two or three. ASRM is ethically opposed to payment for gametes, recommending compensation only for time, expense, and—for egg donors—risk and inconvenience. That amounts to a generally accepted rate of $35 per semen collection, and $1,500 per egg-retrieval cycle.

Brigham and Women's enlists only "known" egg donors designated by the couples themselves, says Mark Hornstein. "The majority of these tend to be sisters, which is our most common arrangement, or close friends," he says. Other programs, concerned about potential familial problems, may prefer different arrangements. Boston IVF offers an anonymous egg-donor program as well, mostly filled by word-of-mouth recommendations from previous donors. They also advertise in newspapers and elsewhere. Many women who donate for Boston IVF already have children and want to help other people have a family.

Because one-year waiting lists are often the rule for anonymous donation, many couples recruit donors on their own, says Geoghegan. One woman is a Ph.D. candidate at MIT who saw an ad in the Cambridge TAB. "She's smart as can be, needs money, and thought it would be a really cool thing to do," says Geoghegan. Another grad student was recruited by a notice in a Harvard gym—"People think that's a way to get healthy, smart young women," says Geoghegan. "She had to decide that she really wasn't ready to do it. And of course the recipient was heartbroken."

The Politics of Fertility

JANE COHEN, 52, AND LAWRENCE SAGER, 56, ARE THE PARENTS of one-and-a-half-year-old fraternal twins. Their daughters' names are Jemma Marshall Sager and Mariah Mill Sager, after John Marshall, the famous chief justice, and John Stuart Mill, author of On Liberty and The Subjection of Women. Their nominal choices aren't that surprising, for both parents are professors of law: she specializes in family law and bioethics at Boston University, and his area is constitutional theory at New York University. With six previous children between them—Cohen has a 27-year-old daughter from her first marriage, as well as three stepchildren (aged 38, 36, and 34), and Sager has a daughter, 27, and son, 25—neither is new to parenting.

Cohen always wanted to have more children, but her second marriage, to a partner who supported this choice, took place relatively late. When she was 42, she and Sager began their endeavor to start a family together. Her ob-gyn of two decades was "very antitechnology" and urged the couple to stick with conventional treatments. They turned to ART only when Cohen was 45 and still not pregnant. They both found it "fascinating to enter this world at an advanced age," says Cohen, and they have since become champions of reproductive technology.

After four miscarriages, it came time to consider IVF with donor eggs. Jemma and Mariah were conceived at Boston IVF with Sager's sperm, then transferred to Cohen's womb at Brigham and Women's. At 49, she was among the first women of that age to be treated in the hospital's IVF program. Brigham and Women's doesn't generally accept women older than 49; Cohen's understanding is that women who exceed this age "may still be accepted on a case-by-case basis."

For Mark Hornstein, women in their forties are "of advanced reproductive age, but they're still of reproductive age." But the California woman who gave birth at 63 is another story, he notes, pointing out that her "life expectancy is 16 years or so. If her husband is the same age, it is statistically unlikely that both parents will survive long enough to see that child into adulthood. I have a problem with that." Linda Blum views this as just another double standard. "When a man in his sixties—or even older—has children, we admire his attainment of a better moral orientation, since he was too career-oriented before," she says. But now that a woman in her sixties has done the same, there's "a blatant cultural revulsion that a woman who's supposed to be all 'dried up' has the audacity to claim this right." Cohen thinks it's unnecessary to focus on the possibility that women in their sixties are going to be flooding fertility clinics. Choosing to have a child with help of ART—especially in middle age—is, she says, a highly self-selective process.

Cohen considers it much more important to recognize that if having children is a social as well as an individual good, then respecting the values our society shares means that we have to respect this need. "To say, You can change careers, you can change husbands, but you can't change your mind about having children—that empties out one of the great promises of American life, which is that you not only get to choose how to live your life, but you get to make renewed choices if you make mistakes," she says.

Insurance coverage (or the lack of it) is the principal way that society proffers or withholds its support for those who suffer from infertility. Massachusetts is one of only 13 states that mandate insurance coverage for treatment. Surprisingly, President Clinton's national health plan proposal excluded infertility coverage, even though Chelsea Clinton was a "Pergonal baby." Reproductive biologist Mitchell Rein says, "I absolutely believe that people with infertility have just as much right to be treated as patients with kidney failure."

Cohen also envisions a new "vanguard feminism" where "the capacious arms of feminism wrap themselves around the possibility that women get to choose to have, as well as not to have, children." When she teaches about ART and the relevant legal issues, some young women appreciate that "this technology will create great relief later in life, will allow them to sort out career and relationship and then children—will allow them to buy time," she says. Although freezing sperm and embryos is commonly practiced, it will be the "dawn of a new consciousness" when eggs can be "frozen and put on the shelf," she says. When young women can store their eggs until the right time—"That will change people's lives," she says.

Elizabeth Ginsburg has in fact proposed an ovum freezing protocol at Brigham and Women's, for young women with malignancies who will undergo chemotherapy. There have been only three or four pregnancies from frozen eggs reported internationally, "but as the protocols get better, I think we will find fewer and fewer chromosomally abnormal eggs after freezing," she says. "The problem is that once you have a successful therapy, you don't really have control over who offers it," she adds.

She worries that "women might want to freeze their eggs in case they don't meet anyone when they're young, to stave off infertility." She disagrees with this solution. "We already see couples coming in for IVF because it's not a convenient time for them to have kids. But we won't do it because they don't have an infertility diagnosis, and because there are significant risks for these procedures," she says. "Should you use these hi-tech infertility treatments for convenience? Is it just a commodity that you can buy if you have the money? Right now we're uncomfortable with that and we're not offering."

But Cohen takes issue with Ginsburg's argument. "What some people would describe as convenience, I would describe as exactly what society should hope for—the ultimate social dream—creating a technological and social environment in which people have children only if they're ready and when they're ready and not before. It isn't about 'convenience,' it's about social and psychological and financial development," she argues. "Infertility can strike women at *any* age—the likelihood simply increases *with* age. Medical interventionism is not the *only* needed response to the work/family conflicts that pursue women, but it is one of many valuable social options."

Elizabeth Bartholet, on the other hand, does not regard high-tech infertility interventions as a great way to deal with work/family conflict. "A lot of women are infertile because they postpone pregnancy, and there's a lot of pressure on women—particularly professional women—to do that," she says. But instead of assisted reproduction, "what we need is a way of dealing with work/family conflict that enables women to work, earn money, have the power that goes with it, but also get pregnant and have families early enough that they don't have to deal with infertility," she says. "That's what we allow men to do, but we set up the world for women so that they've got to choose—and often choose at the cost of their fertility."

Speaking from experience, Linda Blum, who had her son Saul [Tobin] at 32, recalls that some of her colleagues and friends "thought that was shocking—so *early*." Her husband, Roger Tobin '78, is the same age she is, and his academic colleagues said, "Couldn't you have waited until you had tenure?" He would answer, "I wasn't aware I was supposed to have married a younger women."

Surprising Gifts

WHEN JANET TAFT WAS A NURSE MIDWIFE—DELIVERING 230 babies during her career—she had no idea she would later face difficulties bearing her own children. She and her husband, Renny Merritt, became investment bankers, but Wall Street's pressures didn't help their fertility. They began conventional treatments when Taft was 35. After three years, deciding that having a family was more important than "making a pile of money," they left New York for Massachusetts and began working with Selwyn Oskowitz and ART. They went on to have a total of three miscarriages, becoming more resigned with each one.

They were about to run ads for an open adoption when another pregnancy test came back positive. They didn't expect much, but the first ultrasound found a strong fetal heartbeat and the second found *two*. "It was divine intervention," Merritt likes to say, for this was a spontaneous conception. Their identical twins, Breck and Riley, were born in 1991 when Taft was almost 41. They knew even then that they wanted another child, but at 42, Taft's chances of achieving pregnancy through IVF were only 4 to 6 percent; with the help of an egg donor, they would triple. While they continued to investigate adoption, they signed onto Boston IVF's anonymous egg-donor list.

When their names came up, it appealed to Taft that the donor "did this on her own." They never met, but Taft's and the donor's cycles were synchronized through fertility drugs. The donor's eggs were "harvested," then four were fertilized in vitro with Merritt's sperm and transferred to Taft's uterus. "Three of the four took!" she says. "If I had known how readily it can work with younger eggs, I think I would have done it sooner." During the twin pregnancy (one fetus never developed a heartbeat), Taft marveled at the irony of "capping off seven cumulative years of infertility as a 'gestational surrogate.'"

Now they had to decide what to tell their family and friends. Boston IVF recommends "the value of privacy but not secrecy," says Oskowitz. Taft and Merritt took this one step further, believing "it is healthiest to be born into an atmosphere of complete openness. And if we help even one person by being open, then it's worth it. We're proud of what we've done, and we want everyone to know how we did complete" what they're fond of calling "our industrial strength family."

When Sawyer and Whittaker were born in 1995, when Taft was 44, she remembers feeling, "They're from me but not of me. How do I reconcile this? And yet it seemed like there wasn't any reconciling to do." At about six weeks, "A sense of peace came over me," she says. "I was at peace about the egg donor. How they are like her, how like my husband, what was the significance of this—it all simply evaporated."

Taft and Merritt want their sons to learn about Whittaker and Sawyer's origins with the same instinctive calm. "We don't want to make a big deal about 'telling' them," she says. "It's a fact of their birth. The egg-donor nature of their beginnings is key to who they are, it's central. But in their lives and within our family, it's minimal, it barely matters at all. It's just part of the story of how they came to this family."

Harbour Fraser Hodder, Ph.D. '91, is a frequent contributor to Harvard Magazine. She lives in North Brookfield, Massachusetts.

Battling Backlash

After years of remarkably fast progress, gays are facing a new set of barriers. Where are the lines of tolerance being drawn?

BY MARC PEYSER

The great pool debacle probably won't go down as a major gay-rights setback, but it's shown West Hartford, Conn., how homosexuality can still send people off the deep end. The trouble began in January, when Michael Antisdale, 40, and Mark Melanson, 36, applied for a $395 family pass to the town-owned indoor pool. The couple, who have lived openly in town together for 10 years, knew that some people didn't consider them to be a traditional family. But since West Hartford offers health benefits to the partners of its gay municipal employees, the men assumed they'd also be entitled to the reduced-rate family pass (saving $295). They were wrong. In June, the town council voted 6-3 against them. The men had tripped over a battle line they never imagined existed. "When we were two gay men living quietly in the suburbs and keeping our grass cut, we were perfectly well accepted," says Antisdale, a marking executive. "As soon as we raised our hands and said we want what you get, the response was: *'How dare you even ask'.*"

No one would dispute the fact that homosexuals now enjoy unprecedented freedom—to have children, serve in Congress, even star in a sitcom. But the rapid progress of the last few years has also created a kind of backlash. Some of it has been fairly isolated, like when Irmo High School in South Carolina barred the lesbian folk-rock duo Indigo Girls from performing on campus this May or when Ross Perot revoked domestic-partnership benefits at his Dallas computer-services company in April. Other incidents have national implications, especially Trent Lott and conservative Republicans' attempts to make homosexuality a key issue in the November elections. Few gay-rights leaders think they'll lose their partner benefits or inheritance rights, which have become increasingly commonplace. But the accumulation of setbacks raises the issue of whether straight America has reached some kind of tipping point, a limit to its tolerance for gays. If so, where are the lines being drawn in other West Hartfords across the country? In short, how gay is too gay?

On the national level, the backlash has taken some familiar forms. Perhaps the most glaring is the reported number of anti-gay bias crimes, which rose 7 percent last year while the overall crime rate dropped 4 percent. In the military, gays also face continued resistance. Despite the Clinton administration's "don't ask, don't tell" policy, discharges of gay servicemen and -women increased 67 percent from 1994 to 1997. The hottest issues have been at state level. Before anyone has legalized gay marriage—the Hawaii and Vermont supreme courts are considering it—28 states have rushed to outlaw those unions. And in February, Maine became the first in the nation to reverse a statewide gay-rights law prohibiting housing and employment discrimination.

But it's really on Main Street, U.S.A., where the telltale lines are being drawn. Straight people generally accept what might be called gay civil rights, but they get queasy when they view the issue in terms of morality and taboo sexuality. In a recent NEWSWEEK Poll, the vast majority said gays deserve equal rights in obtaining jobs and housing (83 percent and 75 percent)—52 percent even said gays should be allowed to inherit their partners' Social Security benefits. But 54 percent believe homosexuality is a "sin." That distinction played a major tactical role in overturning the Maine gay-rights law. The conservative forces—led by a group called the Christian Civic League—largely avoided attacking gays for seeking "special rights" like job protections and focused on morality. "They talked much more about how gay people were a threat to their children and were going to take over the Boy Scouts," says Karen Geraghty, a gay-rights lobbyist. The conservatives couldn't agree more. "Technically, it does have to do with special rights," says Michael Heath, president of the Christian Civic League, "but if you scratch the surface, it's a moral concern."

The morality issue may explain why heterosexuals find same-sex marriage to be the most unacceptable item on the gay-rights agenda. The NEWSWEEK Poll found that only 33 percent of people supported legal gay marriage. In part, the fear may flow from straights' belief that marriage is the last arena of public life that sets them apart from gays. "People even think of the actual word—marriage—as a straight institution," says lesbian activist Chastity Bono.

But the often unacknowledged core of the marriage issue is the link with children. Despite studies that show kids of gay parents are no more likely to grow up gay than children of heterosexuals, many people fear that gays will alter a child's sexuality. Joann Flowers, a fortysomething restaurant owner in Myrtle Beach, S.C., counts her gay hairdresser as one of her "favorite people." She was even glad that this year's gay-pride parade moved to her hometown. "To each his own. Plus, it's good for business," she says. Still, she draws the line at gay marriage. "That's taking it too far. They adopt children and then the kids grow up and we've got all this perversion," Flowers says. It's not just marriage that poses a threat. The Boy Scouts recently fought two legal challenges to their ban on gay scoutmasters. "A homosexual is not a role model for traditional family values," says Scout spokesman Gregg Shields.

Not surprisingly, schools have become ground zero in the battle over which kind of gayness is acceptable. Hundreds of high schools nationwide now have Gay/Straight Alliances designed to provide moral support for gay kids and teachers. That openness has

Straight Views, Gay Views: By the Numbers

In two national polls, NEWSWEEK compared the general public's opinions on gay issues with those of the gay community. Though there's more common ground than in recent years, the two groups still disagree strongly about some hotly debated issues.

Overall: 33% say there is 'a lot' of discrimination against gays today, **29%** say the country needs to do more to protect the rights of gays	**Gays: 60%** say there is 'a lot' of discrimination against gays today; **83%** say the country needs to do more to protect the rights of gays	**Overall: 33%** approve of legally sanctioned gay marriage; **36%** say they believe gays should be allowed to adopt children	**Gays: 85%** say legal gay marriage is 'very' or 'somewhat' important; **90%** say adoption rights for gays are important	**Overall: 51%** say they are 'very' bothered by gays kissing in public; **29%** are 'very' bothered by same-sex couples holding hands	**Gays: 64%** think same-sex kissing in public bothers straights 'very much'; **39%** say gays' holding hands bothers straights 'very much'

FOR THIS SPECIAL NEWSWEEK POLL, PRINCETON SURVEY RESEARCH ASSOCIATES CONDUCTED TELEPHONE INTERVIEWS WITH 602 ADULTS JULY 30–31, 1998. THE MARGIN OF ERROR IS +/-4 PERCENTAGE POINTS. FOR THE OPINIONS OF HOMOSEXUALS, PRINCETON SURVEY RESEARCH ASSOCIATES CONDUCTED TELEPHONE INTERVIEWS WITH 502 GAY MEN AND LESBIANS JULY 28–30, 1998. RESPONDENTS WERE RANDOMLY DRAWN FROM LISTS COMPILED BY STRUBCO INC. OF 750,000 WHO ASSOCIATED THEMSELVES WITH GAY OR LESBIAN INTERESTS AND ACTIVITIES. THOSE WHO IDENTIFIED THEMSELVES AS HETEROSEXUAL WERE EXCLUDED FROM THE SURVEY. THE MARGIN OF ERROR IS +/-5 PERCENTAGE POINTS. SOME RESPONSES NOT SHOWN. THE NEWSWEEK POLL © 1998 BY NEWSWEEK, INC.

touched off fierce retaliation. Last October, a lesbian teacher in San Leandro, Calif., came out to her high-school science class during Diversity Week. Parents complained. The teacher became the target of a petition drive and a death threat. When Karl Debro, who is straight, allowed his honors English class to discuss the teacher's situation, he was cited for "unprofessional conduct." "Homosexuality has replaced communism and atheism as the last great threat," says Jerry Underdal, a Gay/Straight Alliance faculty adviser in Fremont, Calif. "People are afraid their sleepy community will turn into San Francisco." (Citing Debro's appeal of the case, San Leandro officials wouldn't comment on specifics.)

But this kind of friction hasn't quelled younger people's tolerance. The NEWSWEEK Poll found that young adults (ages 18 to 29) were significantly more accepting of gay marriage—or even adoption—than people over 30 (and baby boomers were more tolerant than people over 50). That's probably because Gen-X and -Y people also are more likely to have a homosexual friend or acquaintance (65 percent) than 50-plus adults (45 percent). Tony Trueba, 19, of Huntington Beach, Calif., didn't even know what "coming out" meant until his cross-country coach,

Eric Anderson, did just that to the entire team. Five years later, Anderson has become the coach at Saddleback College in Mission Viejo and Trueba, who is straight, has followed him there as an athlete and a friend. Tony's father, Richard, 47, says he no longer worries about his son's being alone with his gay coach. But he's not entirely comfortable with the friendship, either. "Obviously, the coach is not what I'd call an ideal role model for my son, but we've gotten to know him over the years," says Richard. "In most respects, he's an outstanding young man."

It's progress like that, however grudging, that makes gay-rights activists optimistic despite the recent setbacks. "Ellen" may have been pilloried for being too gay, but the past season saw a record 29 openly homosexual characters on network-TV programs. "We've made enough progress so that people feel gays are acceptable, but they'd rather not go behind the bedroom door," says Paul Rudnick, who wrote the screenplay to last summer's hit movie "In & Out," Not surprisingly, NBC's "Will & Grace," the next sitcom with a gay main character won't show any gay kissing when it premières in September. "This is the best of times and the worst of times for the gay community," says Kevin Jennings, executive director of the

Gay, Lesbian, Straight Education Network, a New York-based advocacy group. "We're experiencing unprecedented visibility and success. But in periods of social change, there's always a backlash. In the African-American civil-rights movement, the most violence [by whites] was in the '60s, when things were changing the most."

In West Hartford, the pool-pass defeat has actually made Antisdale and Melanson appreciate their community even more. They received overwhelming support from their straight neighbors, including 450 residents who sent a petition to the town council, to no avail. Doris Uricchio, an 85-year-old churchgoing woman who lives next door to the men, was so angry with the Republicans who voted against them that she left the GOP. "We can't dictate to other people how they lead their lives," says Uricchio. "They're wonderful boys. I don't take kindly to disdain for other human beings." These personal gay/straight alliances—a backlash against the backlash—may ultimately change attitudes once and for all.

With DEBRA ROSENBERG *in Maine,* T. TRENT GEGAX *in Myrtle Beach,* NADINE JOSEPH *in San Francisco and* ANA FIGUEROA *in Los Angeles*

Blocking Women's Health Care

Your hospital may have a policy you don't know about

BY MELANIE CONKLIN

In the parking lot of a hospital in central California, nurses are handing out plastic bags full of drugs to their patients. The nurses are not dispensing illegal substances. They are handing out the morning-after pill. But in the process, they are disobeying hospital policy.

Though emergency contraception is standard medical protocol in treating rape and incest, this hospital forbids prescribing the high dose of birth-control pills that can flush out a fertilized egg shortly after intercourse.

The hospital is Catholic, and the Roman Catholic Church says birth control is morally wrong.

Such instances where medical personnel are having to offer reproductive health care with a wink and a nod are on the rise as religious hospitals and clinics are merging at an accelerated pace with other health-care providers.

In this era of mergers and managed care, the Roman Catholic Church is having more of a say in all sorts of women's reproductive health-care services. Five of the ten largest hospital corporations are Catholic. (These are: Daughters of Charity National Health System, Catholic Health Initiatives, Catholic Healthcare West, Catholic Health Care Network, and Mercy Health Services.) There are more than 600 Catholic hospitals and 200 health-care centers serving some fifty million patients a year. And as the hospitals merge and affiliate with non-religious facilities, they often close off reproductive health care for women.

"We're seeing a huge increase in the number of hospitals and clinics being purchased by religious hospitals that refuse to offer the full range of reproductive care," says Susan Berke Fogel, legal director at the Women's Law Center in Los Angeles. Fogel tells the story of the nurses in the parking lot but declines to name the hospital or location, saying the nurses could lose their jobs for the stance they are taking.

"It's reprehensible at a time when medical trends are toward integrated health care that we are seeing this competing trend to isolate and marginalize women's health care," she says.

Catholic doctrine opposes abortion, contraception, tubal ligations, vasectomies, and fertility treatments. This doctrine applies not just to Catholics, but to any patient treated in a Catholic facility or even at a hospital or clinic affiliated with a Catholic institution that adheres to this doctrine.

And the number of these affiliated facilities is growing. Catholic Health Association estimates there were more than 100 mergers involving Catholic and secular hospitals in 1994 alone. Although other religious denominations, such as Baptists and Adventists, also run health-care facilities that may limit access to abortion, the biggest threat is from Catholic hospitals. A report by the Johns Hopkins School of Hygiene and Public Health found that 18 percent of all hospital affiliations in the past six years have involved a Catholic facility.

"We're seeing religious viewpoints being imposed in an extremely coercive way on people who don't share those views," says Catherine Weiss, director of the American Civil Liberties Union's Reproductive Freedom Project.

Melanie Conklin is a staff writer at Isthmus, the weekly newspaper of Madison, Wisconsin. This article was underwritten in part by a grant from the Fund for Investigative Journalism, Inc.

Often, the patients are the last to know that a hospital merger has restricted their reproductive health-care options.

Only 27 percent of women understood that being part of a Catholic hospital system could limit their reproductive care, according to a 1995 survey by Catholics for a Free Choice.

Catholics for a Free Choice cites the example of Jenni Zehr, who in 1988 went to Sacred Heart General Hospital, a Catholic hospital in Eugene, Oregon, to give birth. She requested to have a tubal ligation. Her doctors not only did not perform the procedure, they neglected to tell her. She found out when she became pregnant again.

Three years ago, according to the *Oregon Register Guard,* the Oregon Supreme Court ruled that Zehr could sue her doctor for the costs of raising that child.

A nineteen-year-old woman from Troy, New York, had one child and was struggling to put herself through community college. One day, she visited her clinic to get her regular birth-control shot. She didn't know that her clinic had merged with a religious facility.

"She was simply told, 'We don't do that anymore,' and was not referred to any other provider," says Lois Uttley, director of MergerWatch, which is funded by Family Planning Advocates. "She did find a Planned Parenthood clinic, but many poor women in those circumstances might not have transportation or even a phone to help them find another clinic." For patients in smaller communities, there may be no other options.

Then there are the added problems that mergers cause.

Judy Stone is an infectious-disease doctor in Cumberland, Maryland. Two years ago, her employer, Memorial Hospital, affiliated with Sacred Heart, the Catholic hospital. This fall, Memorial decided to become a nursing home and planned to transfer all its hospital business over to Sacred Heart.

"I couldn't sleep at night keeping my mouth shut," says Dr. Stone. "The process was covert, and decisions that should have been being made by the community were hidden."

So at an October 28 city council meeting, Stone gave a speech rapping the hospitals.

"This will be particularly detrimental to the women of the community," she said. "Especially those who are poor and unable to seek reproductive care elsewhere." She claimed it could also overrule living wills and prevent the kind of research Stone does into

new antibiotics or treatment for such conditions as blindness or Parkinson's Disease—all of which use fetal tissue. The merger is still pending.

Other communities are in for some post-merger surprises. Not only can Catholic hospitals refuse to perform certain procedures; they often refuse to refer patients to other clinics.

"In many cases, there are gag rules written into these contracts," says the ACLU's Weiss. "Now you've got a patient who needs hormonal contraception because of problems she would experience if she were to bear children—she's a high-risk patient. Well, they don't tell her that, and they don't refer her for that, and they don't provide it. She says to them, 'What should I do?' And they say, 'I'm sorry, I can't discuss that with you.' She says, 'Where should I go?' And they say, 'I'm sorry, I can't refer you.'"

Some secular health-care companies have policies against abortions, too. Earlier this year, Physicians Plus Medical Group in Madison, Wisconsin, was deciding among four potential merger partners. One was the Nashville-based PhyCor, a management company.

In the process of questioning doctors in other markets who are managed by PhyCor, Physicians Plus doctors discovered that PhyCor has an unpublicized policy against allowing abortions in any clinic that it operates. PhyCor confirms that this is company policy: "In the agreements we enter into with physicians groups, we provide that abortions will not be done in any facility PhyCor owns or leases," says Joe Hutts, the company's president and CEO. He says the physicians—who are partners, not employees—are free to perform abortions as long as they don't do so in any hospital or clinic PhyCor owns. Hutts, who helped found PhyCor ten years ago, says his company will not take any of the profits from abortions. But he stresses that PhyCor, which is publicly traded, is not associated with any denomination.

"We're all Christians," says Hutts. "The idea isn't to impose our beliefs on anybody. We just want to be true to what we believe."

On October 29, PhyCor announced its plan to purchase the nation's other largest medical management company, Medpartners. If the shareholders approve the purchase in February, PhyCor will manage 35,000 physicians and have a presence in all fifty states.

Statistics from the ACLU show that 84 percent of U.S. counties have no available abortion services. With the recent spate of mergers, this percentage is likely to grow.

One problem abortion clinics have is guaranteeing backup in case of a medical emergency. Clinics need this guarantee to stay in business and to provide safe treatment for women. But if the local hospitals have merged with facilities that don't do abortions, these clinics may be out of luck.

They may also be easy marks.

"Abortion has been isolated for a very long time from mainstream medical care," says the ACLU's Weiss. "But this further isolates reproductive-health services in a way that endangers them. An isolated service is particularly vulnerable to anti-choice protest. If you force all these services into physically separate buildings, they are much easier to target. Patients going in and out are much easier to identify and harass."

Pro-choice advocates wonder why the government hasn't treated some of the mergers as violations of anti-trust laws. They also wonder why federal and state laws allow church hospitals to have "conscience clauses" that permit them to opt out of procedures on religious or moral grounds.

"What is essentially happening here is that religious doctrines that govern certain religious denominations are being imposed on everybody else," says Weiss. "I think that's wrong in any setting but it is particularly wrong where the government is involved. What of the separation of church and state?"

That separation is narrowing, as the government is signing more and more contracts with religious health-care providers.

States are pushing poor women on Medicaid into managed-care plans. Some of these plans refuse to supply services like birth control. One example is Fidelis Care New York, an HMO formed by eight Catholic Dioceses. Fidelis serves Medicaid recipients. The HMO will not cover services prohibited by the U.S. Catholic Bishops.

Until recently, Fidelis Care had about 20,000 enrollees. But it tripled its enrollment with its purchase last September of Better Health, an HMO that served 40,000 Medicaid recipients and did offer reproductive health services. Federal law mandates that reproductive services must be covered for Medicaid recipients. In New York, even abortions must be covered. But under a conscience clause, Fidelis is allowed to tell women to go to another provider to access those services.

Annie Keating, who researches health-care mergers for the National Abortion and Reproductive Rights Action League in New York, is worried that many women will sign up with Fidelis unaware that it doesn't cover reproductive health care. Once in the plan, women must stay enrolled for one year.

"The government ought not be able to contract with religious-governed health-care providers who have their services driven by religious doctrine and then impose [that doctrine] on recipients of public assistance," Keating says.

In Ulster and Dutchess counties in New York, two nonsectarian hospitals have announced plans to merge with a third, the Catholic-run Benedictine Hospital. The merger requires all three hospitals to stop performing abortions, tubal ligations, vasectomies, and contraceptive counseling. The two nonsectarian hospitals plan to transfer their abortion services to a separate off-premises women's clinic. Currently, the nonsectarian Kingston Hospital performs about 120 abortions a year, mostly for Medicaid recipients.

But last May, when the three hospitals announced, with much fanfare, the plans to unify, the officials weren't prepared for the outcry from the two communities.

"This is part of a stealth war on reproductive rights," says Caryl Towner,

who founded the group Preserve Medical Secularity to fight the merger. "It's being done under the guise of saving our hospitals, but we don't believe for a minute that this has to be done in a way that imposes all these restrictions on reproductive health care."

Towner's group joined forces with others, including twenty-six doctors at Northern Dutchess Hospital (who voted unanimously against the terms of the merger). They held a rally last July that attracted around 800 people. Since then, merger opponents have sent 2,000 postcards to the hospital officials, gathered 7,000 petition signatures, and repeatedly picketed the hospitals.

MergerWatch's Uttley, who is helping organize the opposition, says community involvement frequently makes the difference in preserving reproductive services. Many times, she says, physicians and representatives of non-Catholic churches end up voicing the strongest opposition.

Take the situation in Gloversville, New York. John A. Nelson, pastor of the First Congregational United Church of Christ, is fighting a proposed joint venture between Feldon County's only hospital, Nathan Littauer, and St. Mary's of Amsterdam, a Catholic subsidiary of St. Louis-based Carondolet. He says some of the more conservative pastors from other congregations are joining him in fighting the merger.

Arthur Brelia, a medical doctor at Nathan Littauer, has also proved a powerful opponent. The seventy-one-year-old obstetrician and gynecologist

resigned from his position as medical chief of staff at Nathan Littauer after the two hospitals' governing boards voted to approve the affiliation. He says he resigned partly so he could have the freedom to criticize without violating any confidentiality requirements.

"I took a public stance and put out a position paper," says Brelia. "The loss of our hospital is not going to help our community. In this deal, the church-dominated hospital has ultimate veto power over any decision."

The hospital has announced it will stop performing abortions, even though it is the only local facility offering the procedure. (Brelia estimates forty to fifty abortions are performed annually at Littauer.) But Brelia says his main concern is that pregnant women will be forced to go far out of their way if they want to be sterilized. "Unless a woman travels forty or fifty miles to the closest urban center, she won't be able to have a postpartum tubal ligation," he says. "That's not a very good choice."

The Reverend Nelson believes it is his religious duty to oppose the potential restrictions on health care. He points out that as the only hospital in a county of 55,000, Nathan Littauer Hospital serves people of many faiths. (There's the added irony that its namesake and benefactor was Nathan Littauer, a prominent Jewish citizen.)

"Theologically it's dangerous to make an idol out of doctrine," says Nelson. "When doctrine and care collide, the only faithful and responsible resolution is for doctrine to retire or change."

The Last Abortion

How science could silence the debate

By Elinor Burkett

A b o r t i o n has squeezed the life out of women's politics, and the only way women will regain their political space is for abortion to disappear as a political issue.

Technological advances have long bolstered the cause of anti-abortion advocates, turning fetuses from anonymous creatures into living beings that are photographed, recorded, and loved. Now parents watch sonograms of their children months before birth, making it more difficult for them—and the public—to dismiss fetuses as subhuman parasites.

But the tables are turning, as medical advances allow women to know about their pregnancies days after conception and change the very nature of the act of abortion. For more than two decades, abortion has been a public act involving physicians and clinics and insurance carriers, which is precisely what has given the anti-abortion movement its power.

Imagine, then, an America in which abortion truly becomes a private act. No one would be able to calculate how many pregnancies are terminated each year, and there would be no clinics to be targeted for protests or bombings. No one would keep a list of abortion doctors because there would be no way of knowing which doctors they were. No one could wave lurid photographs of aborted fully formed fetuses because fetuses would be aborted before they bore any resemblance to human life. Can the abortion wars survive a brave new world of nonsurgical abortion?

It seems unlikely—and America is on the cusp of just such a reality. Recent medical advances have revolutionized American women's options for dealing with unwanted pregnancies. Worried about a missed period, a woman no longer has to wait to see her doctor; she can buy an early pregnancy test at her local pharmacy. Unhappy with the results of her test, she doesn't have to brave the protesters at local abortion clinics—if she is lucky enough to have such a clinic in her area. She can go to her own gynecologist and undergo a chemical abortion, a procedure ob-gyns are far more willing to perform than surgical abortions.

Doctors are supposed to report abortions to the Centers for Disease Control, so the government can continue to track the rate of abortion. But if they use the latest abortion procedure—a combination of methotrexate and misoprostol—rather than RU-486 and misoprostol, there is no danger of noncompliance, since no one tracks why a physician writes a specific prescription.

Methotrexate has been on the market for almost half a century as an anti-tumor agent and treatment for arthritis, lupus, and psoriasis, and misoprostol is widely prescribed for patients with ulcers. Fanatics can't root through a doctor's medical waste for telltale signs of an abortion induced by modern chemistry—which must be performed within the first six weeks of pregnancy. The only evidence is a tiny speck that looks like a blood clot. The cost is the price of two prescriptions plus the physician's fee for two office visits.

The anti-abortion crowd hasn't yet figured out how to fight this new breed of abortion, which lacks the images—aborted fetuses with recognizable features, the inherent violence of surgery—that have ignited them. Operation Rescue has sent threatening faxes to and picketed the office of chemical abortion researchers but has found no other clear targets for its wrath. Leaders of more mainstream anti-abortion groups recognize that photographs of minuscule blood clots are unlikely to whip up their followers and that few people are likely to relate to fetuses when they are so underdeveloped that they still look like they have gills. They have begun to switch from calling abortion murder to bemoaning its physical and psychological dangers to women.

These more mainstream abortion opponents have twisted shaky research that might suggest a slight link between abortion and cervical cancer into alarmist headlines. They've warned women about the dangers of hemorrhage and infection from chemically induced abortions, although both are infrequent. When all else fails, they raise the specter of long-term, and still undiscovered, negative side effects from abortions.

"I'm very concerned that the women of this country are going to find . . . in five or ten years that we've opened a Pandora's box as far as complications and damage to women," says Dr. Donna Harrison, a Michigan ob-gyn, though she and her allies offer nothing tangible on which to base the warning.

While over the past two decades technology has undercut the positions of both the pro- and anti-choice forces, the most recent changes, in fact, open a window of opportunity for a truce in the abortion wars—if either side is willing to take advantage of it.

At the moment, all that separates the entrenched enemies is the will to educate women about responsible sexual activity and 10 short days: the 10 days between conception—thus far defined as the moment when a sperm fertilizes an egg—and pregnancy, which is the moment when the fertilized egg finishes its hazardous passage through the fallopian tubes to become implanted in the lining of the uterus—a journey about one zygote in four never completes.

Without implantation, there is no pregnancy, which is how an IUD works: It makes the uterine lining inhospitable to implantation. Stopping implantation through use of the latest medical technology thwarts pregnancy before it occurs. The technology is what physicians call emergency contraception, and it remains a well-kept secret. The most common method is two to four oral contraceptives (depending on the brand and strength) taken within 72 hours of unprotected intercourse, followed 12

From *Utne Reader,* May/June 1998, pp. 80-81, 109-110. Excerpted from *The Right Women* by Elinor Burkett. © 1998 by Elinor Burkett. Reprinted by permission of Simon & Schuster, Inc.

hours later by another equal dosage. Researchers suggest that even the first, single dose might be almost as effective.

Is this abortion? It's clearly not termination, because a pregnancy never occurs. Indeed, the fertilized egg hasn't yet survived its greatest hazard—successful implantation. The most steadfast literalists might argue that this is nonetheless murder, since it occurs after conception. But then those same steadfast literalists also would have to wage war against IUDs. And can the pro-life crowd really argue with a procedure that could dramatically decrease the number of true abortions performed in the nation?

No truce is possible, however, without the cooperation of the pro-choice troops, who would need to put as much time, money, and energy into teaching women about morning-after pills as they've devoted to protecting surgical abortions. But with an opportunity to guarantee women control over their reproductive lives, how could they not? Is it so much to say to women: Look, if you have unprotected sex and don't want to become pregnant, pop some birth control pills and you won't have to worry? Can't we ask grown women to show that modicum of responsibility?

Such a truce is a fantasy, of course—not because the technology does not exist, and not because it poses a significant threat to the belief systems of either side. Neither side really seems to want an end to the abortion wars, which have gone on so long that both sides have lost the ability to envision peace. Resolution seems to have become less important than scoring a win, or at least ensuring that the other side suffers a loss. The stakes are, or have been defined as, too high—morally, politically, and financially.

Pro-choice forces have drawn a line in the sand and dared society to prove its contempt for women by crossing it, thus holding up the existence of unlimited surgical abortion services as the measure of women's liberation. A wealthy and powerful industry of abortion providers—one of the few lobbying groups in the nation to successfully convince the population that its interests are entirely selfless—has reinforced that position. Conservatives have responded by holding up America's abortion policy as the measure of the nation's commitment to life, a position reinforced by a movement that understands full well that abortion, more than any other issue, swells the ranks of conservative activism and thus fuels the engine of the conservative agenda.

Is Sex a Necessity?

The Viagra craze raises some tricky questions—about money. Should health insurance cover sexual satisfaction? If so, how much is enough?

BY GEOFFREY COWLEY

ROBERT POLLYEA JUST GOT A piece of his life back. Until a few years ago, the 66-year-old retired college professor had never complained much about his sex life. But a 1994 prostate operation left him largely impotent, and the penile injections his urologist prescribed were little help. "You have to go to the refrigerator with a syringe, fill it up and inject yourself," he recalls, "all while your wife is there thinking, 'What the hell is going on?'" Everything changed when he started taking Viagra, Pfizer's new potency pill, a few weeks ago. "You use it and have your foreplay," he says. "And when you're ready for intercourse you just do it. It's like when we were first married."

Thousands of older men are now realizing the same dream every day. Urologists are using rubber stamps to keep up with the demand for prescriptions, and Pfizer's stock has soared. But the erection pill's historic takeoff has caught the nation's health insurers off guard. Few of them have decided how to cover the new drug—and as demand explodes, that issue could get large and complicated. Should managed-care plans guarantee their subscribers some sexual pleasure? If so, how much is enough? How should they determine who needs treatment? And how should they pay the tab? Great breakthroughs can have great costs, says Andy Webber of the Consumer Coalition for Quality Health Care. And when health plans cover those costs, we all pay.

No one denies that Viagra can alleviate impotence. Taken an hour before sex, it re-

Drawing the Line

Health plans cover some "quality of life" treatments, but they often impose limits. Some typical policies:

•**Accutane:** Acne medication. Most HMOs cover it, but special approval is often required. COST: about $5 for 20-mg capsule.

•**Caverject:** Injectable impotence drug. Usually covered, but a medical review and prior approval are needed. COST: about $18 for a 10-mcg injection kit.

•**Clomid:** Fertility drug. Not covered unless your employer buys a benefit-rich insurance package; other infertility treatments may be covered. COST: about $8.50 for a 50-mg tablet.

•**Meridia:** Diet drug. Not usually covered. If a patient's obesity is life-threatening, doctors can successfully appeal. COST: about $3 for a 10-mg capsule.

•**Muse:** Penile suppository for impotence. Usually covered, but a medical review and prior approval are required. COST: about $21 for a 250-mcg pellet.

•**Propecia:** Oral remedy for baldness. Not covered; considered purely cosmetic. COST: about $1.50 for a 1-mg tablet.

•**Proscar:** Treatment for benign prostate enlargement. Same drug as Propecia, but with a different name and a lower price. Covered for this use. COST: about $2 for a 5-mg tablet.

•**Protropin:** Recombinant growth hormone for short children. Considered a medical procedure, not a pharmaceutical benefit. Coverage depends on benefits package. COST: $210 for a 5-mg vial.

•**Prozac:** Antidepressant. Usually covered. COST: about $2.50 for a 20-mg capsule.

•**Retin-A:** Topical skin rejuvinator. Covered for acne but not for wrinkles. Some HMOs flag prescriptions to women over 35 to verify they're using it as authorized. COST: about $1.50 for one dose of the cream.

SOURCES: NEWSWEEK RESEARCH; FIRST DATABANK, INC.

laxes the blood vessels feeding the penis, enabling it to respond to erotic stimulation. In clinical studies, 70 to 80 percent of impotent men have gotten good results. But a single pill costs $10—and demand for the drug has been breathtaking. Before Viagra hit the market in early April, erection aids garnered perhaps 20,000 prescriptions a week. Now that relief comes in pill form, American doctors are writing six times that number. If even half of the estimated 30 million U.S. men with erectile difficulties started taking Viagra once a week, the cost would approach $8 billion a year. That's terrific news for Pfizer—even a $1 billion drug is considered a blockbuster—but a big burden for the health-care system.

To control costs, health plans generally cover medical necessities, while eschewing treatments they deem experimental or purely cosmetic. Cancer surgery gets covered; nose jobs don't. And if a drug has more than one use, a health plan may exclude some while allowing others. Most plans cover Merck's Proscar as a treatment for benign prostate enlargement but not as a remedy for baldness. Likewise, your HMO may supply you with Retin-A for acne (a medical condition) but not for wrinkles (a normal sign of age). Viagra is hard to classify one way or the other. Impotence is undeniably a medical disorder, but completely impotent men are not the only ones clamoring for Viagra.

Where should insurers draw the line? Not surprisingly, Pfizer and some patient advocates favor complete coverage. "Managed-care plans cover conditions like arthritis and allergies because they threaten people's quality of life," says Pfizer spokeswoman Mariann Caprino. "That's exactly what we're talking about here."

Laurel Flynn, executive director of the National Alliance for the Mentally Ill, takes the same line, saying medical decisions shouldn't be "screened through a financial filter." But covering a drug like Viagra can have as many consequences as rejecting it. "Do you pay for Viagra or do you pay for prenatal care?" asks one managed-care executive. "There's not an unlimited number of dollars here. We get a fixed premium, not one that adjusts because we have Viagra."

Insurers aren't likely to nix the drug altogether; dose for dose, it's actually cheaper than the injections and suppositories they already cover. The challenge is to deal with Viagra's overwhelming popularity. For the time being, Cigna Healthcare is limiting coverage to six pills a month, based on estimates of an average couple's needs. And to qualify for that ration, you have to have "a pre-existing, documented condition of organic impotence, which is currently being treated by other medical means." Even if they're more expensive, other insurers will likely demand a diagnosis of "erectile dysfunction" before covering a prescription. But "dysfunction" is a relative term. "There's no blood test, no objective parameter," says Dr. Irwin Gold-

stein, a urologist at the Boston University Medical Center. "It's entirely subjective." In short, anyone who's dissatisfied could qualify as dysfunctional.

At the moment, some men are stretching the definition to absurd lengths. In New York, nightclub kids talk of using Viagra to trump the erection-quashing effects of disco drugs such as Ecstacy and crystal meth. Fortunately, the new pill won't fulfill such fantasies. Handy as it is for treating chronic impotence, there is no evidence that Viagra can boost a healthy man's sexual performance. As thrill seekers learn that lesson, demand may wane a bit. But for millions of men with erectile problems, Viagra seems sure to become a way of life—with or without insurance coverage. "Jack," a 28-year-old Brooklynite, has been partially impotent for six years due to a bike-seat injury. Viagra has restored his sexuality—and he hasn't taken a minute of flak from a health plan because he doesn't have one. "I have a friend who's a pharmacist," he says. "I pay $7 a pill." He considers it a steal.

With THEODORE GIDEONSE *and*
ELLYN E. SPRAGINS

SEX
(American Style)

If we spiced our lives with more sexuality, we might make public life more sensuous and the gutters classier.

By Thomas Moore

AS I'VE BEEN WRITING A BOOK ABOUT SEX IN RECENT months, I've had the *Kama Sutra,* the Indian guide to personal sexual culture, on my desk, and occasionally I've consulted the Internet to track down relevant books and articles. On the Internet, I've noticed, as soon as you venture in the direction of sex you quickly come upon crude, unadorned images of stark sexual union. Apparently we have finally found a public place where we can show our private parts and secret fantasies, free of the repressive eyes of the government agencies that serve our culture's dominant Puritan philosophies. But here there is no love, little sentimentality and almost nothing that could be called foreplay in any innocent sense of the word.

In contrast, the *Kama Sutra* discusses a wide range of sexual matters, from the general comportment of one's life (*dharma*) to the establishment of personal economic security (*artha*) and the cultivation of the arts of love (*kama*). The *Kama Sutra,* graphic and open-minded in its own way, places sex within the context of a refined, humane life, while the Internet focuses on organs and acts. I'm reminded of the beautiful erotic figures carved into the Indian temples of Kharujaho and Konarak more than 1,000 years ago, images that depict every imaginable sex act within a context of worship and prayer, and I wonder why the Indians put their sexual fantasies on temples while we give ours over to pornography. This is one of those questions that I believe, if we could answer it, would pinpoint exactly what's wrong with our culture.

Although I'm convinced we're all moralists at heart, I'm not interested in making any judgments here about the ethics of appropriateness of the *Kama Sutra,* the temple sex couples, or the Internet, but I am interested in the

sexual life of the community in which I live. We seem to be obsessed with sex and embarrassed by it. Sex sells, I'm told by almost everyone who hears I'm writing about the theme. Some insinuate that I must be writing about sex for the royalties alone, cashing in on our mass compulsion, but I wonder if I'll lose readers, because you aren't supposed to be interested in both spirituality and sex—unless you're writing about sacred sex (whatever that is), or offering suitably cantankerous health or moral cautions.

Medieval monks spent hours copying the Bible, while in the margins, called gutters, they would occasionally doodle obscene images and phrases. We do something similar when we create an efficient, clean world of speedy highways and no-nonsense office buildings, while our extravagant sexual images—our dirty thoughts—are funneled into red-light districts, a 42nd Street or a Hollywood and Vine, or into an unregulated highway called the Internet. We divide sex from ordinary life and then wonder why it enjoys emotional autonomy in our lives.

History shows that sex has always had its selected areas of tolerance—usually far from the center of daily commerce, except perhaps in ancient Pompeii, Greece, Rome, or Sodom and Gomorrah. I'm not arguing for a democratization of sexual images; it is appropriate to be as careful about sex in public as a parent might be about it at home. But I do question the sharpness of the line drawn between public life and the gutter. I wonder why we demand that

---

Thomas Moore is the author of the best-selling Care of the Soul *and, more recently,* The Re-Enchantment of Everyday Life. *His latest book,* The Soul of Sex, *was published by HarperCollins (1998).*

Reprinted with permission from *Mother Jones,* September/October 1997, pp. 56-63. © 1997 by the Foundation for National Progress.

> **Office buildings are the most sexless places in public life. Our vision of work translates into cold granite.**

our political leaders be without sexual fault—I discovered while practicing psychotherapy that everyone, including our most upright fellow citizens, has skeletons in the closet or lurid dreams and fantasies.

Maybe if we spiced our daily lives with qualities associated with sex, we might make public life more sensuous and the gutters classier. People used to build beautiful, sexy bridges, for instance, but now we build them for cost-efficiency. People used to build roads that you'd want to drive on for a Sunday outing, but today we just want to get from one place to another as quickly as possible— no foreplay. In some parts of the world they still make life itself sexy with their sensuous movies, their extravagant cuisines, and their seductive streets. In, say a piazza in Rome or a plaza in Mexico, cafés fill the square with chairs and tables decked out with food that makes you salivate as you pass by. We have our oases of public sensuality (Bourbon Street in New Orleans and maybe the casinos of Las Vegas) but usually they are so removed from the culture at large that they quickly become outrageous and tinged with unsavory—a telling word—associations.

When I'm out in public spaces, I look in vain for a good chair. Most have no place to sit down, or if they do, the seats appear to be designed for something other than the human body. Sitting on a concrete slab doesn't do much for my sexuality. My body would also like to see some nourishing color in place of the ubiquitous metallic glass; an abundance of flowers and trees instead of an architect's skimpy afterthought—the token juniper and the de rigueur marigolds; and sensuous flowing water that isn't hidden behind warehouses and bridge supports. I hope it's obvious that food, flowers, seats, colors, and water have something to do with sex.

Office buildings are the most sexless places in public life. Our vision of work translates into hard marble, cold granite, pale walls, authorless art, green-only vegetation, scarce windows, white light, modular desks, thin carpets, and disembodied background music. No wonder Eros ignites the office affair as often as possible; it's his only refuge. Here I find a rule that has broad application: Take sex out of the world we live in daily, and it will become a giant, unsettling force in our personal lives.

Religion has a powerful influence on sex in America, but the religious institutions merely reflect an attitude deep in the American psyche. Spiritually we are virtually all believers in transcendence, imagining our values, inspiration, and faith all coming from above the clouds, off the earth, out of our bodies, far from sex. We believe in the mind, and we don't trust the body. We are profoundly unsettled when we hear about a priest, preacher, or guru caught in some sexual scandal—our outrage comes from the old theological idea that humanity is contrary to divinity. We are working up a fever making new laws against touching, and we're more scandalized by a photograph or painting showing a nipple or a penis than by the image of a starving child on a dry, dusty road.

The body is our central embarrassment—merely having one, making love with one, or indulging in the human fascination for the sexual body. To all appearances, we'd like to be bodiless, and most of our recent inventions point toward that goal; they encourage us to sit in front of a screen and work, play, shop, and meet with old friends electronically. But after a lifetime of avoiding the body we meet it face to face in illness, where, not coincidentally, we also discover our souls. Illness teaches us lessons our high-tech education has overlooked: We are mortal, we have a body, to be human is to have sensation, and we would discover what is really important by paying attention to the body's reactions. I suspect we could learn all these lessons more pleasurably by living every day less mentally and more sexually.

> **Where is graphic sexual imagery today? Religious erotic art shows us how profound sex is in the nature of things.**

The repression of the body and its main work, sex, wounds the soul immeasurably and deprives us of our humanity. Often we refer to sex as "physical love," the work of a soulless body, and then we try to justify this biological act morally by making sure that it's in the service of affection. But the bifurcation of body and soul can't be healed so easily. We have yet to discover that sex is not physical love but the love of souls. You don't have to spiritualize sex to make it valuable, because by its very nature sex is a deep act of the interior life and always brings with it a wealth of emotional and spiritual meaning.

Mircea Eliade, the religion scholar, remarked that the sacred sometimes lies camouflaged in the mundane. As a student of world religions myself, I notice that the positions and organs on the Web's erotic pages are identical to those on Indian temples, on Greek pottery, in ancient ritual, and in religious legend and lore. Oddly, pornography may, at its root, be an unconscious attempt to preserve the sacredness of sex. Where do you find graphic sexual imagery today? In pornography, in religious ritual and statutory, and in dreams. If we assume that dreams portray the soul's interests in pure form, untainted by conscious manipulation, then they tell of the psyche's necessities and of what role erotic feeling and fantasies play in the economy of the heart. Religious erotic art shows us how profound sex is in the nature of things, and how much like religious ecstasy is the pleasing oblivion it grants. Pornography plays the role of providing a symptomatic presentation of the erotic realities that we've excluded from our canons of propriety.

We have lost religion, not as an institution or as a set of beliefs, but as a way of living in touch with the raw roots of desire and meaning. With religion absent, sex, historically wedded to religious practice, falls into the gutter, as much outside of life as religion. Now shaded in darkness, potent sexual imagery, removed from public life, appears only in graffiti and in taboo magazines and movies. Artists, always intimate with religion, intuitively perceive the relation between sex and religion and try to give Eros a prominent place in their work, but since art, too, has become marginalized, we misjudge sexual imagery in art as irreligious and pornographic.

Sex is trying to break through and out of our secularism, but we misread the signs, thinking we're beholding the work of the devil instead of the angels. Pornography is the return of the repressed, the religious nature of sex presenting itself in dark instead of bright colors. Every time we think of sex as biological, every time we teach sex education as a secular study, we are setting ourselves up for more pornography. But mercifully, for all its stupidity, lack of taste, and outrageousness, pornography keeps sex from becoming the heartless preserve of the medical establishment and the social scientist.

Sex is the ritual recovery of vitality and life. It makes marriages, creates families, and sustains love. It takes us momentarily out of our minds and into our souls. In sex we "come"—come back to ourselves in unmediated sensation, come back into our world from our mental outposts. It's no wonder we're obsessed with sex, since it is the very epitome of vitality, and yet, because it is full of vibrancy, we're also deathly afraid of it. Unlike many other cultures, we don't appreciate orgy, even within strict ritual limits. We leave it to pornography, where it is either indulged compulsively in the way of a spectator or moralized against, or both simultaneously.

The most common story I heard from people in psychotherapy dealt with a happy marriage in which one or both partners felt compelled to engage in an extramarital affair. The parties involved couldn't understand the reason for the overwhelming allure of another carnal liaison. They assumed something must be wrong in the marriage or in their own past. They never considered that there might be some deep need for orgy, for sex without the weight of moralism, or for enough and varied sex to offset the bodi-less, passionless life that modern work and family values insist upon.

In many cases, the affair looks to me like the office flirtation and the pornographic photo—it's symptomatic of a failure to give sex enough prominence in daily life and in the privacy of a marriage. I don't advocate affairs, but I can understand their allure in an age of incessant labor, anxious leisure, compulsive entertainment, uprooted ethics, and a public life built on efficiency and machinery. In this cool, gray world, we're starved for friendship, excitement, and intimate conversation. One sought-after reward of an affair might be a forgetting of responsibilities, as the participants risk their reputations, marriages, and, in some cases, their livelihoods for a few wicked hours of carnal delight.

Some, of course, would say that affairs are the result of a breakdown in traditional morality. Whatever the merits of this analysis, it is generally presented in a self-righteous, paternalistic, and uncompassionate tone—indicating discomfort with sex and with the moral complexity it may bring into the lives of ordinary people. It's difficult to trust an approach to life's most fascinating and challenging mystery that demonizes sex or deals with sexual problems without showing heart.

One solution to our obsession/repression pattern would be to align sex with intelligence, civility, spiritual values, and all the other aspects of our daily lives. In the realm of the psyche, it seems that the segregation of any element leads to trouble. If the only thing in life is your depression, then you may have little chance of being liberated from it. If money is the aim of your life, then it will probably reveal its emptiness in due time. Sex makes important demands for privacy and secrecy, but if we cut it off from the fabric of life's totality, it may begin to show itself as odd and even monstrous.

It isn't enough to make easy intellectual deals—"I'm willing to understand that sexual feelings are basically good and normal, if you, Sex, are willing to leave me alone and let me live my life according to my plans." A more substantive weaving of sex into life may be accomplished by softening the barriers between ordinary living and sexuality.

We might temper our moralistic approaches to food. If you want to feel guilty these days, eat a sumptuous dinner with friends or boldly buy some food that someone in a lab coat has determined is bad for you. Few things in life are closer to sex than food, and yet we have gone too far in surrendering this ordinary pleasure to the medicine-haunted guardians of kitchen virtue.

Or, in a culture that frowns on idleness, give yourself some completely unproductive time. Excessive productivity is incompatible with an erotically interesting life because the senses get distracted by busyness. Not spending your time profitably might be the best thing you can do for your sex life.

We might give serious attention to qualities associated with sex, such as pleasure, desire, intimacy, and sensuality,

> **Eat a sumptuous dinner or boldly buy food that someone in a lab coat has determined is bad for you.**

and give these very qualities a place in all aspects of daily life. We might take the body's needs into consideration as we build and arrange our world. Sex finds its way by means of desire, and it follows that if we were to live in tune with our sexuality, we would give desire its proper place. Some would object that responding to our appetites is narcissistic and irresponsible, but taking desire into account is not the same as doing whatever we feel like. We are not sophisticated about desire, and so tend to reduce discussion of it to absurd, simplistic, and obviously objectionable terms.

Every day desires spring up from the pool that is the human soul and source of life. Some are strong, some weak. Some often contradict others. Some are impossible to satisfy, some we can deal with in a few minutes. The point is, desire serves vitality and ushers in life. We can't act on all desires. If that were possible, at this moment I'd be living in several states and countries. Some desires stay with us for years—late in life we may find a desire fulfilled after many years of containment. Being loyal to desire, giving certain desires time to show themselves more fully and reveal how they might make their way into life, is a form of sexual living. Broadly speaking, it is an erotic way of life.

We could learn from sex to live all of life more intimately. There's something sexual, again in a broad sense of the word, in a warm neighborhood community. I will never forget the afternoon, shortly before we moved from Massachusetts, when our family gathered our neighbors together for a goodbye ritual. We created a small, spontaneous ceremony in which we all said something from the heart about our history in the neighborhood and about the loss we were all feeling. This moment reflected an intimate way of living there. We could have kept our thoughts and feelings to ourselves, but the closeness of that moment represented the Eros, the sexuality, of living among good friends.

In the area of sex, our society can hardly be called compassionate. We quickly judge celebrities whose private sexual difficulties become public. We dispose of politicians and military personnel who miss the mark of our anxiously protected norms. Because sex is so full of life, it is rarely neatly arranged or easy to deal with. In general, if we want to live a soulful life we have to allow some latitude for the unexpected in ourselves and others, but this is especially true of sex. It is the nature of sex, maybe its purpose, to blast some holes in our thinking, our planning, and our moralisms—sex is life in all its boldness.

Read the biographies of the men and women who have made extraordinary contributions to humanity. List their achievements in one column and their sexual idiosyncrasies in another. Notice the direct proportion between sexual individuality and creative output, between desire heeded and compassion acted upon. Then reflect long on your moral attitudes: Are they suitably deep, humane, compassionate, and complex?

Every day we could choose to be intimate rather than distant, acting bodily rather than mentally, responding thoughtfully from desire instead of from discipline, seeking deep pleasures rather than superficial entertainments, getting in touch with the world rather than analyzing it at a distance, making a culture that gives us pleasure rather than one that merely works, allowing plenty of room in our own and in others' lives for the eccentricities of sexual desire—generally taking the role of lovers rather than doers and judges.

Once there were only two: male and female. Men, mostly, were the big ones, with deep voices and sturdy shoes, sitting with legs splayed. Women, mostly, were the smaller ones, with dainty high heels, legs crossed tightly at the ankle, and painted mouths. It was easy to tell them apart. These days, it's not so easy. Men wear makeup and women smoke cigars; male figure skaters are macho—but Dennis Rodman wears a dress. We can be one gender on the Internet and another in bed. Even science, bastion of the rational, can't prove valid the lines that used to separate and define us. Although researching the biology of gender has answered some old questions, it has also raised important new one. The consensus? Gender is more fluid than we ever thought. Queer theorists call gender a social construct, saying that when we engage in traditional behaviors and sexual practices, we are nothing but actors playing ancient, empty roles. Others suggest that gender is performance, a collection of masks we can take on and off at will. So are we witnessing the birth of thrilling new freedoms, or the disintegration of the values and behaviors that bind us together? Will we encounter new opportunities for self-realization, or hopeless confusion? Whatever the answers, agreeing that our destinies aren't preordained will launch a search that will profoundly affect society, and will eventually engage us all.   —*The Editors*

By Deborah Blum

The Gender Blur

where does biology end and society take over

I was raised in one of those university-based, liberal elite families that politicians like to ridicule. In my childhood, every human being—regardless of gender—was exactly alike under the skin, and I mean exactly, barring his or her different opportunities. My parents wasted no opportunity to bring this point home. One Christmas, I received a Barbie doll and a softball glove. Another brought a green enamel stove, which baked tiny cakes by the heat of a lightbulb, and also a set of steel-tipped darts and competition-quality dart-board. Did I mention the year of the chemistry set and the ballerina doll?

It wasn't until I became a parent—I should say, a parent of two boys—that I realized I had been fed a line and swallowed it like a sucker (barring the part about opportunities, which I still believe). This dawned on me during my older son's dinosaur phase, which began when he was about 2 ½. Oh, he

loved dinosaurs, all right, but only the blood-swilling carnivores. Plant-eaters were wimps and losers, and he refused to wear a T-shirt marred by a picture of a stegosaur. I looked down at him one day, as he was snarling around my feet and doing his toddler best to gnaw off my right leg, and I thought: This goes a lot deeper then culture.

Raising children tends to bring on this kind of politically-incorrect reaction. Another friend came to the same conclusion watching a son determinedly bite his breakfast toast into the shape of a pistol he hoped would blow away—or at least terrify—his younger brother. Once you get past the guilt part—Did I do this? Should I have bought him that plastic allosaur with the oversized teeth?—such revelations can lead you to consider the far more interesting field of gender biology, where the questions take a different shape: Does love of carnage begin in culture or genetics, and which

drives which? Do the gender roles of our culture reflect an underlying biology, and, in turn, does the way we behave influence that biology?

The point I'm leading up to—through the example of my son's innocent love of predatory dinosaurs—is actually one of the most straightforward in this debate. One of the reasons we're so fascinated by childhood behaviors is that, as the old saying goes, the child becomes the man (or woman, of course.) Most girls don't spend their preschool years snarling around the house and pretending to chew off their companion's legs. And they—mostly—don't grow up to be as aggressive as men. Do the ways that we amplify those early differences in childhood shape the adults we become? Absolutely. But it's worth exploring the starting place—the faint signal that somehow gets amplified.

"There's plenty of room in society to influence sex differences," says Marc

From *Utne Reader*, September/October 1998, pp. 44-48. Reprinted by permission of International Creative Management, Inc. © 1998 by Deborah Blum.

Breedlove, a behavioral endocrinologist at the University of California at Berkeley and a pioneer in defining how hormones can help build sexually different nervous systems. "Yes, we're born with predispositions, but it's society that amplifies them, exaggerates them. I believe that—except for the sex differences in aggression. Those [differences] are too massive to be explained simply by society."

Aggression does allow a straightforward look at the issue. Consider the following statistics: Crime reports in both the United States and Europe record between 10 and 15 robberies committed by men for every one by a woman. At one point, people argued that this was explained by size difference. Women weren't big enough to intimidate, but that would change, they predicted, with the availability of compact weapons. But just as little girls don't routinely make weapons out of toast, women—even criminal ones—

sexual encounters, more offspring, more genetic future. For the female—especially in a species like ours, with time for just one successful pregnancy a year—what's the genetic advantage in brawling?

Thus the issue becomes not whether there is a biologically influenced sex difference in aggression—the answer being a solid, technical "You betcha"—but rather how rigid that difference is. The best science, in my opinion, tends to align with basic common sense. We all know that there are extraordinarily gentle men and murderous women. Sex differences are always generalizations: They refer to a behavior, with some evolutionary rationale behind it. They never define, entirely, an individual. And that fact alone should tell us that there's always—even in the most biologically dominated traits—some flexibility, an instinctive ability to respond, for better and worse, to the world around us.

mal matches. One is that even with this apparently precise system, there's nothing precise—or guaranteed—about the physical construction of male and female. The other point makes that possible. It appears that sex doesn't matter in the early states of embryonic development. We are unisex at the point of conception.

If you examine an embryo at about six weeks, you see that it has the ability to develop in either direction. The fledgling embryo has two sets of ducts—Wolffian for male, Muellerian for female—an either/or structure, held in readiness for further development. If testosterone and other androgens are released by hormone-producing cells, then the Wolffian ducts develop into the channel that connects penis to testes, and the female ducts wither away.

Without testosterone, the embryo takes on a female form; the male ducts vanish and the Muellerian ducts expand into oviducts, uterus, and vagina. In other words, in humans, anyway (the opposite is true in birds), the female is the default sex. Back in the 1950s, the famed biologist Alfred Jost showed that if you castrate a male rabbit fetus, choking off testosterone, you produce a completely feminized rabbit.

We don't do these experiments in humans—for obvious reasons—but there are naturally occurring instances that prove the same point. For instance: In the fetal testes are a group of cells, called Leydig cells, that make testosterone. In rare cases, the fetus doesn't make enough of these cells (a defect known as Leydig cell hypoplasia). In this circumstance we see the limited power of the XY chromosome. These boys have the right chromosomes and the right genes to be boys; they just don't grow a penis. Obstetricians and parents often think they see a baby girl, and these children are routinely raised as daughters. Usually, the "mistake" is caught about the time of puberty, when menstruation doesn't start. A doctor's examination shows the child to be internally male; there are usually small testes, often tucked within the abdomen. As the researchers put it, if the condition had been known from the beginning, "the sisters would have been born as brothers."

Just to emphasize how tricky all this body-building can get, there's a peculiar genetic defect that seems to be clustered by heredity in a small group of villages in the Dominican Republic. The result of the defect is a failure to produce an enzyme that concentrates testosterone, specifically for building

will that wonderful, unpredictable, flexible biology that we have been given allow a shift, so that one day, we will literally be far more alike?

don't seem drawn to weaponry in the same way that men are. Almost twice as many male thieves and robbers use guns as their female counterparts do.

Or you can look at more personal crimes: domestic partner murders. Three-fourths of men use guns in those killings; 50 percent of women do. Here's more from the domestic front: In conflicts in which a woman killed a man, he tended to be the one who had started the fight—in 51.8 percent of the cases, to be exact. When the man was the killer, he again was the likely first aggressor, and by an even more dramatic margin. In fights in which women died, they had started the argument only 12.5 percent of the time.

Enough. You can parade endless similar statistics but the point is this: Males are more aggressive, not just among humans but among almost all species on earth. Male chimpanzees, for instance, declare war on neighboring troops, and one of their strategies is a warning strike: They kill females and infants to terrorize and intimidate. In terms of simple, reproductive genetics, it's an advantage of males to be aggressive: You can muscle your way into dominance, winning more

This is true even with physical characteristics that we've often assumed are nailed down by genetics. Scientists now believe height, for instance, is only about 90 percent heritable. A person's genes might code for a six-foot-tall body, but malnutrition could literally cut that short. And there's also some evidence, in girls anyway, that children with stressful childhoods tend to become shorter adults. So while some factors are predetermined, there's evidence that the prototypical male/female body design can be readily altered.

It's a given that humans, like most other species—bananas, spiders, sharks, ducks, any rabbit you pull out of a hat—rely on two sexes for reproduction. So basic is that requirement that we have chromosomes whose primary purpose is to deliver the genes that order up a male or a female. All other chromosomes are numbered, but we label the sex chromosomes with the letters X and Y. We get one each from our mother and our father, and the basic combinations are these: XX makes female, XY makes male.

There are two important—and little known—points about these chromoso-

the genitals. One obscure little enzyme only, but here's what happens without it: You get a boy with undescended testes and a penis so short and stubby that is resembles an oversized clitoris.

In the mountain villages of this Caribbean nation, people are used to it. The children are usually raised as "conditional" girls. At puberty, the secondary tide of androgens rises and is apparently enough to finish the construction project. The scrotum suddenly descends, the phallus grows, and the child develops a distinctly male body—narrow hips, muscular build, and even slight beard growth. At that point, the family shifts the child over from daughter to son. The dresses are thrown out. He begins to wear male clothes and starts dating girls. People in the Dominican Republic are so familiar with this condition that there's a colloquial name for it: *guevedoces*, meaning "eggs (or testes) at 12."

stances, behave differently than if the individual was a female."

Do the ways that we amplify physical and behavioral differences in childhood shape who we become as adults? Absolutely. But to understand that, you have to understand the differences themselves—their beginning and the very real biochemistry that may lie behind them.

Here is a good place to focus on testosterone—a hormone that is both well-studied and generally underrated. First, however, I want to acknowledge that there are many other hormones and neurotransmitters that appear to influence behavior. Preliminary work shows that fetal boys are a little more active than fetal girls. It's pretty difficult to argue socialization at that point. There's a strong suspicion that testosterone may create the difference.

And there are a couple of relevant animal models to emphasize the point.

consensus seems to be that full-blown "I'm a girl" or "I'm a boy" instincts arrive between the ages of 2 and 3. Research shows that if a family operates in a very traditional, Beaver Cleaver kind of environment, filled with awareness of and association with "proper" gender behaviors, the "boys do trucks, girls do dolls" attitude seems to come very early. If a child grows up in a less traditional family, with an emphasis on partnership and sharing—"We all do the dishes, Joshua"—children maintain a more flexible sense of gender roles until about age 6.

In this period, too, relationships between boys and girls tend to fall into remarkably strict lines. Interviews with children find that 3-year-olds say that about half their friendships are with the opposite sex. By the age of 5, that drops to 20 percent. By 7, almost no boys or girls have, or will admit to having, best friends of the opposite sex. They still hang out on the same playground, play on the same soccer teams. They may be friendly, but the real friendships tend to be boy-to-boy or girl-to-girl.

There's some interesting science that suggests that the space between boys and girls is a normal part of development; there are periods during which children may thrive and learn from hanging out with peers of the same sex. Do we, as parents, as a culture at large, reinforce such separation? Is the pope Catholic? One of my favorite studies looked at little boys who asked for toys. If they asked for a heavily armed action figure, they got the soldier about 70 percent of the time. If they asked for a "girl" toy, like a baby doll or a Barbie, their parents purchased it maybe 40 percent of the time. Name a child who won't figure out how to work *that* system.

How does all this fit together—toys and testosterone, biology and behavior, the development of the child into the adult, the way that men and women relate to one another?

Let me make a cautious statement about testosterone: It not only has some body-building functions, it influences some behaviors as well. Let's make that a little less cautious: These behaviors include rowdy play, sex drive, competitiveness, and an in-your-face attitude. Males tend to have a higher baseline of testosterone than females—in our species, about seven to ten times as much—and therefore you would predict (correctly, I think) that all of those behaviors would be more generally found in men than in women.

do the ways that we amplify differences in childhood shape who we become as adults?

It's the comfort level with this slip-slide of sexual identity that's so remarkable and, I imagine, so comforting to the children involved. I'm positive that the sexual transition of these children is less traumatic than the abrupt awareness of the "sisters who would have been brothers." There's a message of tolerance there, well worth repeating, and there are some other key lessons too.

These defects are rare and don't alter the basic male-female division of our species. They do emphasize how fragile those divisions can be. Biology allows flexibility, room to change, to vary and grow. With that comes room for error as well. That it's possible to live with these genetic defects, that they don't merely kill us off, is a reminder that we, male and female alike, exist on a continuum of biological possibilities that can overlap and sustain either sex.

Marc Breedlove points out that the most difficult task may be separating how the brain responds to hormones from how the brain responds to the *results* of hormones. Which brings us back, briefly, below the belt: In this context, the penis is just a result, the product of androgens at work before birth. "And after birth," says Breedlove, "virtually everyone who interacts with that individual will note that he has a penis, and will, in many in-

Back in the 1960s, Robert Goy, a psychologist at the University of Wisconsin at Madison, first documented that young male monkeys play much more roughly than young females. Goy went on to show that if you manipulate testosterone level—raising it in females, damping it down in males—you can reverse those effects, creating sweet little male monkeys and rowdy young females.

Is testosterone the only factor at work here? I don't think so. But clearly we can argue a strong influence, and, interestingly, studies have found that girls with congenital adrenal hypoplasia—who run high in testosterone—tend to be far more fascinated by trucks and toy weaponry than most little girls are. They lean toward rough-and-tumble play, too. As it turns out, the strongest influence on this "abnormal" behavior is not parental disapproval, but the company of other little girls, who tone them down and direct them toward more routine girl games.

And that reinforces an early point: If there is indeed a biology to sex differences, we amplify it. At some point—when it is still up for debate—we gain a sense of our gender, and with it a sense of "gender-appropriate" behavior.

Some scientists argue for some evidence of gender awareness in infancy, perhaps by the age of 12 months. The

But testosterone is also one of my favorite examples of how responsive biology is, how attuned it is to the way we live our lives. Testosterone, it turns out, rises in response to competition and threat. In the days of our ancestors, this might have been hand-to-hand combat or high-risk hunting endeavors. Today, scientists have measured testosterone rise in athletes preparing for a game, in chess players awaiting a match, in spectators following a soccer competition.

If a person—or even just a person's favored team—wins, testosterone continues to rise. It falls with a loss. (This also makes sense in an evolutionary perspective. If one was being clobbered with a club, it would be extremely unhelpful to have a hormone [under] one to battle on.) Testosterone also rises in the competitive world of dating, settles down with a stable and supportive relationship, climbs again if the relationship starts to falter.

It's been known for years that men in high-stress professions—say, police work or corporate law—have higher testosterone levels than men in the ministry. It turns out that women in the same kind of strong-attitude professions have higher testosterone than women who choose to stay home. What I like about this is the chicken-or-egg aspect. If you argue that testosterone influenced the behavior of those women, which came first? Did they have high testosterone and choose the law? Or did they choose the law, and the competitive environment ratcheted them up on the androgen scale? Or could both be at work?

And, returning to children for a moment, there's an ongoing study by Pennsylvania researchers, tracking that question in adolescent girls, who are being encouraged by their parents to engage in competitive activities that were once for boys only. As they do so, the researchers are monitoring, regularly, two hormones: testosterone and cortisol, a stress hormone. Will these hormones rise in response to this new, more traditionally male environment?

What if more girls choose the competitive path; more boys choose the other? Will female testosterone levels rise, male levels fall? Will that wonderful, unpredictable, flexible biology that we've been given allow a shift, so that one day, we will literally be far more alike?

We may not have answers to all those questions, but we can ask them, and we can expect that the answers will come someday, because science clearly shows us that such possibilities exist. In this most important sense, sex differences offer us a paradox. It is only through exploring and understanding what makes us different that we can begin to understand what binds us together.

Deborah Blum is a Pulitzer Prize-winning science writer, a professor of journalism at the University of Wisconsin-Madison, and author of Sex on the Brain: The Biological Differences Between Men and Women (*Penguin, 1997*).

Sex in the Future:
Virtuous and Virtual?

By Kenneth Maxwell

Sex will flourish in the twenty-first century as growing openness about sexual matters and new technologies pave the way to new sexual experiences, including virtual sex.

Equated with sin since the encounter of Adam and Eve, sexuality is now emerging torturously from the dark shadows of secret shame. Ancient shibboleths and taboos are already yielding to a rapidly spreading mantle of enlightenment over a broad spectrum of humanity.

The most spectacular development in the near future will be a flourishing of openness and frankness in discussing sex and sexuality, comparable to the ease with which people have always discussed other facets of human behavior—food and drink, clothing, children, recreation, work, religion, physical ailments, appendectomies, and spats with the spouse.

Physicians, who in the past received little or no training in sexual matters except for highly specialized problems, will be carried along with the tide. Conditioned from childhood to view sex as sinful or secret, or both, old-fashioned general practitioners will be replaced by physicians who will see sexual problems and practices as major health problems important to the welfare of their patients. Conservative medical schools will reluctantly expand their curricula to include instruction in sex, sex problems, and their treatment, and this will be followed by certified board specialties.

Sex therapy will have an expanding role as part of the physician's arsenal, creating a new category of

highly trained medical assistants, both male and female. It may find a place in premarital instruction in ensuring at least an auspicious start along the rocky road of marital bliss. However, the need for premarital instruction, and in fact the need for all sex therapy, will be minimized by an enlightened view and acceptance of nudity as normal and innocuous behavior.

Modern pharmacology has already embarked on a new generation of sex drugs, but the main thrust is not for developing aphrodisiacs, but for drugs to correct sexual dysfunctions, especially to overcome impotence, problems that are more common than most people realize. So-called sex toys are of limited therapeutic value, but will have increasing use for sexual gratification. Now available in a small number of unobtrusive shops or by mail order, sex toys will come to be openly available in mall shops and will be a topic of open discussion as prudery fades.

The inevitable decline of prudery will contribute to sexual relationships that enable man and woman to see each other as equals with differences in desires and needs openly shared. Bed roles will evolve with an awakening to the fact that knowledge of intimate sexual matters is something to share and that individuals differ in their desires and needs.

Videotapes will be used increasingly for instruction as well as for erotic stimulation and entertainment. Many people view erotic movies and tapes as pornographic trash, but the fact that at least a third of erotic videos now sold are used and enjoyed by married couples suggests that an increase in demand will lead to improved quality and variety. Erotic interactive CD-ROMs are now used almost exclusively by voyeurs for entertainment, but the technology offers possibilities for educational material of a wide variety.

Gay Marriage and Legal Prostitution

The legal status of same-sex relationships is in a state of flux. The action of the state of Hawaii in authorizing same-sex marriages gave encouragement to gays and lesbians, who anticipated the protection of a federal law that recognizes marriage in any state as being valid in all states. Several states had already passed laws banning same-sex marriages, and additional states had such legislation under consideration.

It remains unpredictable to what extent several thousand years of tradition that "marriage" is solely a union of man and woman will influence justices' decisions. But even if same-sex marriages in general are denied legal standing, there will remain a strong trend toward granting specific legal rights to same-sex couples, such as hospital visitation, inheritance of assets, health insurance, and pensions. The same privileges will be granted to committed unmarried heterosexual couples.

Prostitution, a traditional human activity since at least the beginning of historical memory, will continue to flourish worldwide. In parts of the world, such as most parts of the United States, where prostitution is a criminal offense, it will be gradually decriminalized. This will come about less through a moral awakening and sense of justice and fairness than through fear of uncontrollable disease epidemics, especially if the heterosexual AIDS epidemic materializes as widely predicted. Decriminalization will open the way to licensing prostitutes, accompanied by mandatory weekly health examinations and collection of fees and taxes, which, in turn, will create funds for public prevention and treatment of venereal diseases.

Eros on the Internet

Dissemination of erotic material on the Internet is worrisome to many people, especially if they have children with access to a computer and an online service. The 1996 Communications Decency Act made it a federal crime in the United States to transmit "indecent" material over the Internet without ensuring that children cannot see it. The law also required software services to establish a rating system for use by parents who want to block objectionable programs. The American Civil Liberties Union, along with several communication businesses, immediately challenged the constitutionality of the Decency Act, and they took it to the Supreme Court. If the Act is upheld, what is "indecent" will be argued interminably.

A rating standard agreed upon by a consortium of 39 software and computer companies implemented a variety of privately developed rating systems. For example, one based on the Platform for Internet Content Selection (PICS) has a scale of nine rankings from "subtle innuendo" to "explicitly for adults," with one level reserved for technical references to sex, such as medical information. The company that offers this system ranked, at last count, 30,000 of the half million or so sites on the World Wide Web alone.

It's clear that something new and portentous has happened to eroticism, pornography, and obscenity. These time-honored forms of art and literature now wing their way on cyberspace to all parts of the world in dissemination of all levels of erotica from benign to violent, with the added feature of children being both participants and victims.

A battle of gigantic proportions is looming between the champions of free speech and the defenders of privacy. It's a battle with no end in sight. The mass of cyberporn backed up by an insatiable appetite and a free-speech commitment pitted against the anger of desperation and determination to defend the honor of home and family is a no-win crusade for either side. There will be compromises in which there will be something for everyone but not enough for anyone. Users will be permitted to use the Internet for almost anything they wish, but there will be a requirement that their identity and interests will be clearly stated and available.

Attempts to censor the Internet are futile because the information is available from so many sources. Even if a computer genius comes up with a practical way of doing it, protection of privacy and defense against objectionable intrusion will not be perfect. Hackers and clever adults will continue to find ways to gain access to and transmit unauthorized material. And children will, as always, find ways to outwit their parents.

Sex with a Computer?

A new form of erotic adventure, *virtual sex*, may soon be developed. The technique, now called virtual reality, is envisioned as a way to enhance the pleasure of viewing a scene or action. It is not merely watching actors perform as on stage or in a movie. In virtual sex, for example, the voyeuristic pleasure of watching people engage in coital capers, or whatever, is replaced by providing the realism of the user participating in the action. The user puts on a helmet or gets into a large box, and the experience happens in the privacy of the space provided.

For a long time, we've been able to transmit sound electronically, including the intense emotions of music in its various forms. And we can supplement and intensify the feelings with visual imagery. Sensations still untapped electronically are odors, tastes, touch, pressure, and kinesthetic sensations.

In the case of odors, we can expect that research will unravel the presently unsolved mystery of human sex pheromones (body odors and flavors). Sex pheromones—mainly aphrodisiacs—are so common throughout the animal world, including the higher primates, that it is almost certain that they have a subliminal role in human sexuality, even though they escape our conscious awareness. Our clumsy effort to find the answer through a multi-billion-dollar perfume industry will be replaced by a breakthrough in biotechnology that will find one of its benefits in virtual sex. The human nose has 10 million olfactory receptors, and with training, the nose can discriminate between about 10,000 odors. There is already available an "electronic nose," called the Aroma-Scanner, that visualizes odors in 3-D, and the odors can be precisely identified with an instrument called a gas chromatograph.

Instruments of this kind will lead to the identification of human sex pheromones and their action as a prelude to how their effects can be duplicated and intensified electronically. Similar determinations will be made of the senses of touch, taste, pressure, and kinesthesia in studies of how to intensify or modify them. Virtual sex will greatly enhance normal sensations and will add some never before experienced.

Virtual-sex programs for solo use will be available, but the more popular programs will be those in which the viewer can choose one or more partners from a wide selection of choices. The choices can be, but will not have to be, those offered by a programmer. A man or woman will be able to choose his or her spouse or lover.

Sex from Afar

The most advanced techniques will make it possible for a couple to join in virtual sex even though separated. An e-mail message to set an agreed upon time will enable a traveling man or woman to enjoy the

Sex and Reproduction

Science and technology have drastically affected human sexuality for many years, most notably in their effect on fertility through the use of the contraceptive pill.

Infertile couples who want babies will increasingly seek and receive help from science. Artificial insemination in the future will differ greatly from the early slipshod practice of collecting sperm with minimum attention to genetic and health suitability. Much more attention will be given to sperm donors' characteristics other than health and physical appearance, especially mental achievements and other outstanding qualities.

Other methods of overcoming infertility, including in vitro fertilization and embryo transfer, will become increasingly available. Assisted reproductive technology, along with its variations, and surrogate motherhood are currently so expensive that availability is limited to moderately affluent couples. While improved success rates will reduce the cost, the methods will still not be cheap.

Techniques for producing and handling human embryos have suggested the possibility of using excess embryos for scientific and medical research. But ethical questions are so serious that most such research will be delayed indefinitely. Some procedures are clearly out of bounds even if possible, such as implantations of human embryos into other species and hybridizing humans with other species. Cloning human embryos for a limited purpose such as determining genetic characteristics will encounter objections.

The greatest potential for benefits from work with human embryos is the determination of genetic characteristics and correction of deficiencies. Close ethical monitoring is predictable, but gestating human embryos to term *in vitro* (outside the womb) is so far from present capability that even consideration of the ethical impact is in the distant future.

—*Kenneth Maxwell*

comforts of home. The availability of virtual sex will not eliminate prostitution, but for the first time, it will allow completely safe prostitution, as well as safe sex generally. People may be able to pick out a good-looking virtual partner from an electronic catalog and engage in a completely safe and fulfilling encounter.

Areas near military bases are notorious for having a plethora of cafes, bars, dance halls, dives of various kinds, B-girls, and prostitutes. Standards of health and safety will improve dramatically when virtual sex parlors are established in competition with the usual places of entertainment. Sexually transmitted diseases, including AIDS, will decline dramatically. Military commanders have the authority to declare places of entertainment off-limits if they pose a threat to the health and welfare of military personnel. Commanders will be more inclined to declare the sleazier joints off-limits if wholesome recreation becomes attractive.

Virtual sex will not necessarily be confined to establishment sex parlors. If history is a guide, technical development will bring about miniaturization. The bulge you see in a traveler's briefcase may not be a weighty report but a two-way virtual-sex unit with a built-in modem that will make a business trip as much pleasure as staying at home.

No one has produced virtual sex, and there is no certainty that it can be done with any degree of perfection. Still, the idea will continue to challenge electronic entrepreneurs. Part of the appeal will be the privacy and safety of virtual sex in a society that is becoming increasingly aware of the threat of AIDS and other STDs. Virtual sex will be preferred by many men and women to surreptitious affairs, cocktail bar pickups, or the currently criminal patronage of prostitutes. Besides, virtual sex, as envisioned, will provide more intense sensations than actual sex, as well as sensations that are nonex-

istent in natural sex. Sensations will be more than addictive, they will be synergistic—a system whereby the input of one sensation enhances another, or several other sensations, rather than merely adding to them. Virtual sex will have special appeal to couples, who will be able to enhance the sensations of their own style and preferences.

Advances in Stimulation

The more advanced devices will be able to stimulate the specific pleasure centers of the brain to enhance sensations beyond anything experienced naturally. Laboratory experiments with animals have established the fact that when a sex hormone (testosterone) is injected into a certain area of the hypothalamus, the animal is stimulated into female behavior regardless of its sex. And when the hormone is injected into another nearby area of the hypothalamus, the animal is stimulated into behaving as a male.

The animals were unable to communicate what their sensations were like, but it is well known that the hypothalamus, which is both part of the brain and an organ of internal secretion, is the emotional switchboard of the brain, standing in command of sexual development, performance, and emotions. The hypothalamus has connections to the eye nerves (hence its ability to reset the circadian rhythm) and to the amygdala, where at least some of the emotion signals originate. Imaging machines, more sensitive than those now used for medical diagnosis, will make it possible to map the brain in detail and to pinpoint areas of emotions and sensations.

People would not want needles, even as small as hypodermics, stuck into their brains to get their kicks. Although chemicals taken by mouth are capable of reaching the brain, the most effective way to activate the pleasure centers without side effects will be a noninvasive probe, possibly with a low-energy colored laser.

People will choose between enhanced male sensations or enhanced female sensations, or both at the same time. Because of the intensity of the sensations, the sessions might have to be limited in duration, say no more than a few minutes at a time, to avoid overloading the brain circuits. But they could be repeated as frequently as the nerve cells regenerate their functional capacity.

Conclusion: The Future of Sex

The modern world's view of sex ranges from restraint to tolerance to "the more the better," especially if the result is more children. Still, the sex scene is on the verge of new developments in the Western world. In some places and in some societies there will be little observable change in the immediate future, but a strong undercurrent of change will have global effects.

Change will be brought about by the control or manipulation of sex-related developments and activities, especially population control and care of pregnant women and children. Some things may get worse before they get better, and changes will be accompanied by acrimonious debate and prolonged disputes. But the long-term trend will be a vast improvement in the quality of life.

The world of sex is at the threshold of trends amounting to a twenty-first-century revolution, bringing about the most dramatic changes in sexual relationships, habits, health, pleasures, pains, and living standards the world has ever seen.

About the Author
Kenneth Maxwell is the author of *A Sexual Odyssey: From Forbidden Fruit to Cybersex*, from which this article is adapted with permission of Plenum Press. The book is available from the Futurist Bookstore for $25.95 ($23.95 for Society members), cat. no. B-2025.

He is an emeritus professor of biology at California State University–Long Beach. His address is P.O. Box 3217, Idyllwild, California 92549

Abnormal: Anything considered not to be normal, i.e., not conforming to the subjective standards a social group has established as the norm.

Abortifacients: Substances that cause termination of pregnancy.

Abortion: The termination of a pregnancy.

Acquaintance (date) rape: A sexual encounter forced by someone who is known to the victim.

Acquired immunodeficiency syndrome (AIDS): Fatal disease caused by a virus that is transmitted through the exchange of bodily fluids, primarily in sexual activity and intravenous drug use.

Activating effect: The direct influence some hormones can have on activating or deactivating sexual behavior.

Actual use failure rate: A measure of how often a birth control method can be expected to fail when human error and technical failure are considered.

Adolescence: Period of emotional, social, and physical transition from childhood to adulthood.

Adultery: Extramarital sex.

Adultery toleration: Marriage partners extending the freedom to each other to have sex with others.

Affectional: Relating to feelings or emotions, such as romantic attachments.

Agenesis (absence) of the penis (ae-JEN-a-ses): A congenital condition in which the penis is undersized and nonfunctional.

AIDS: Acquired immunodeficiency syndrome.

Ambisexual: Alternate term for bisexual.

Amniocentesis: A process whereby medical problems with a fetus can be determined while it is still in the womb; a needle is inserted into the amniotic sac, amniotic fluid is withdrawn, and fetal cells are examined.

Anal intercourse: Insertion of the penis into the rectum of a partner.

Androgen: A male hormone, such as testosterone, that affects physical development, sexual desire, and behavior.

Androgynous: Possessing high frequencies of both masculine and feminine behaviors and traits.

Anejaculation: Lack of ejaculation at the time of orgasm.

Apgar test: An exam that determines the overall health of a newborn by testing his or her color, appearance, heart rate, reflex ability, and respiration.

Aphrodisiacs (af-ro-DEE-si-aks): Foods or chemicals purported to foster sexual arousal; they are believed to be more myth than fact.

Apoptosis: Programmed cell death that occurs naturally in living tissues. HIV may induce abnormal apoptosis in immune cells.

Apotemnophilia: A rare condition characterized by the desire to function sexually after having a leg amputated.

Areola (a-REE-a-la): Darkened, circular area of skin surrounding the nipple of the breast.

Artificial insemination: Injection of the sperm cells of a male into a woman's vagina, with the intention of conceiving a child.

Asceticism (a-SET-a-siz-um): Usually characterized by celibacy, this philosophy emphasizes spiritual purity through self-denial and self-discipline.

Asexuality: A condition characterized by a low interest in sex.

Autoerotic asphyxiation: Accidental death from pressure placed around the neck during masturbatory behavior.

Autofellatio (fe-LAY-she-o): A male providing oral stimulation to his own penis, an act most males do not have the physical agility to perform.

Autogynephilia: The tendency of some males to become sexually aroused by the thought or image of themselves with female attributes.

Bartholin's glands (BAR-tha-lenz): Small glands located in the minor lips that produce some secretion during sexual arousal.

Behavior therapy: Therapy that uses techniques to change patterns of behavior; often employed in sex therapy.

Berdache (bare-DAHSH): Anthropological term for cross-dressing in other cultures.

Bestiality (beest-ee-AL-i-tee): A human being having sexual contact with an animal.

Biological essentialists: Those who believe that sexual orientation is an inborn trait, resulting from biological factors during development.

Biphobia: Prejudice, negative attitudes, and misconceptions relating to bisexual people and their lifestyles.

Bisexual: Refers to some degree of sexual activity with or attraction to members of both sexes.

Bond: The emotional link between parent and child created by cuddling, cooing, and physical and eye contact early in a newborn's life.

Bondage: Tying, restraining, or applying pressure to body parts as part of sexual arousal.

Brachioproctic activity (brake-ee-o-PRAHK-tik): Known in slang as "fisting"; a hand is inserted into the rectum of a partner.

Brothel: House of prostitution.

Bulbourethral glands: Also called Cowper's glands.

Call boys: Highly paid male prostitutes.

Call girls: Highly paid female prostitutes.

Case study: An in-depth analysis of a particular individual and how he or she might have been helped to solve a sexual or other problem.

Catharsis theory: A suggestion that viewing pornography will provide a release for sexual tension, thus preventing antisocial behavior.

Celibacy (SELL-a-ba-see): Choosing not to share sexual activity with others.

Cervical cap: A contraceptive device that is shaped like a large thimble and fits over the cervix and blocks sperm from entering the uterus.

Cervical intraepithelial neoplasia (CIN): Abnormal, precancerous cells sometimes identified in a Pap smear.

Cervix (SERV-ix): Lower "neck" of the uterus that extends into the back part of the vagina.

Cesarean section: A surgical method of childbirth in which delivery occurs through an incision in the abdominal wall and uterus.

Chancroid (SHAN-kroyd): An STD caused by the bacterium *Hemophilus ducreyi* and characterized by sores on the genitals, which, if left untreated, could result in pain and rupture of the sores.

Child molesting: Sexual abuse of a child by an adult.

Chlamydia (klu-MID-ee-uh): Now known to be a common STD, this organism is a major cause of urethritis in males; in females it often presents no symptoms.

Circumcision: Of the clitoris—surgical procedure that cuts the prepuce, exposing the clitoral shaft; in the male, surgical removal of the foreskin from the penis.

Climacteric: Mid-life period experienced by both men and women when there is greater emotional stress than usual and sometimes physical symptoms.

Climax: Another term for orgasm.

Clinical research: The study of the cause, treatment, or prevention of a disease or condition by testing large numbers of people.

Clitoridectomy: Surgical removal of the clitoris; practiced routinely in some cultures.

Clitoris (KLIT-a-rus): Sexually sensitive organ found in the female vulva; it becomes engorged with blood during arousal.

Clone: The genetic-duplicate organism produced by the cloning process.

Cloning: A process involving the transfer of a full complement of chromosomes from a body cell of an organism into an ovum from which the chromosomal material has been removed; if allowed to develop into a new organism, it is an exact genetic duplicate of the one from which the original body cell was taken; the process is not yet used for humans, but it has been performed in lower animal species.

Cohabitation: Living together and sharing sex without marrying.

Coitus (ko-EET-us *or* KO-ut-us): Heterosexual, penis-in-vagina intercourse.

Coitus interruptus: A method of birth control in which the penis is withdrawn from the vagina prior to ejaculation.

Comarital sex: One couple swapping sexual partners with another couple; also called mate swapping.

Combining of chromosomes: The process by which a sperm unites with an egg, normally joining 23 pairs of chromosomes to establish the genetic "blueprint" for a new individual. The sex chromosomes establish its sex: XX for female and XY for male.

Coming out: To acknowledge to oneself and others that one is a lesbian, a gay male, or bisexual.

Condom: A sheath worn over the penis during intercourse to collect semen and prevent conception or venereal disease.

Consensual adultery: Permission given to at least one partner within the marital relationship to participate in extramarital sexual activity.

Controlled experiment: Research in which the investigator examines what is happening to one variable while all other variables are kept constant.

Coprophilia: Sexual arousal connected with feces.

Core gender identity: A child's early inner sense of its maleness, femaleness, or ambivalence, established prior to puberty.

Corona: The ridge around the penile glans.

Corpus luteum: Cell cluster of the follicle that remains after the ovum is released, secreting hormones that help regulate the menstrual cycle.

Cowper's glands: Two small glands in the male that secrete an alkaline fluid into the urethra during sexual arousal.

Cross-genderists: Transgenderists.

219

Cryptorchidism (krip-TOR-ka-diz-um): Condition in which the testes have not descended into the scrotum prior to birth.

Cunnilingus (kun-a-LEAN-gus): Oral stimulation of the clitoris, vaginal opening, or other parts of the vulva.

Cystitis (sis-TITE-us): A nonsexually transmitted infection of the urinary bladder.

Deoxyribonucleic acid (DNA): The chemical in each cell that carries the genetic code.

Depo-Provera: An injectable form of progestin that can prevent pregnancy for 3 months; it was approved for use in the United States in 1992.

Deprivation homosexuality: Can occur when members of the opposite sex are unavailable.

Desire phase: Sex researcher and therapist Helen Singer Kaplan's term for the psychological interest in sex that precedes a physiological, sexual arousal.

Deviation: Term applied to behaviors or orientations that do not conform to a society's accepted norms; it often has negative connotations.

Diaphragm (DY-a-fram): A latex rubber cup, filled with spermicide, that is fitted to the cervix by a clinician; the woman must learn to insert it properly for full contraceptive effectiveness.

Diethylstilbestrol (DES): Synthetic estrogen compound once given to mothers whose pregnancies were at high risk of miscarrying.

Dilation: The gradual opening of the cervical opening of the uterus prior to and during labor.

Direct sperm injection: A technique involving the injection of a single sperm cell directly into an ovum. It is useful in cases where the male has a low sperm count.

Discrimination: The process by which an individual extinguishes a response to one stimulus while preserving it for other stimuli.

Dysfunction: Condition in which the body does not function as expected or desired during sex.

Dysmenorrhea (dis-men-a-REE-a): Painful menstruation.

Dyspareunia: Recurrent or persistent genital pain related to sexual activity.

E. coli *(Escherichia coli)*: Bacteria naturally living in the human colon, which often cause urinary tract infection.

Ectopic pregnancy (ek-TOP-ik): The implantation of a blastocyst somewhere other than in the uterus (usually in the fallopian tube).

Ejaculation: Muscular expulsion of semen from the penis.

Ejaculatory inevitability: The sensation in the male that ejaculation is imminent.

ELISA (enzyme-linked immunosorbent assay): The primary test used to determine the presence of HIV in humans.

Embryo (EM-bree-o): The term applied to the developing cells when, about a week after fertilization, the blastocyst implants itself in the uterine wall.

Endometrial hyperplasia (hy-per-PLAY-zhee-a): Excessive growth of the inner lining of the uterus (endometrium).

Endometriosis (en-doe-mee-tree-O-sus): Growth of the endometrium out of the uterus into surrounding organs.

Endometrium: Interior lining of the uterus, innermost of three layers.

Endorphins: A chemical produced by the brain in response to physical intimacy and sexual satisfaction.

Epidemiology (e-pe-dee-mee-A-la-jee): The branch of medical science that deals with the incidence, distribution, and control of disease in a population.

Epididymis (ep-a-DID-a-mus): Tubular structure on each testis in which sperm cells mature.

Epididymitis (ep-a-did-a-MITE-us): Inflammation of the epididymis of the testis.

Episiotomy (ee-piz-ee-OTT-a-mee): A surgical incision in the vaginal opening made by the clinician or obstetrician to prevent the baby from tearing the opening in the process of being born.

Epispadias (ep-a-SPADE-ee-as): Birth defect in which the urinary bladder empties through an abdominal opening and the urethra is malformed.

Erectile dysfunction: Difficulty achieving or maintaining penile erection (impotence).

Erection: Enlargement and stiffening of the penis as internal muscles relax and blood engorges the columns of spongy tissue.

Erogenous zone (a-RAJ-a-nus): Any area of the body that is sensitive to sexual arousal.

Erotica: Artistic representations of nudity or sexual activity.

Erotomania: A very rare form of mental illness characterized by a highly compulsive need for sex.

Erotophilia: Consistent positive responding to sexual cues.

Erotophobia: Consistent negative responding to sexual cues.

Estrogen (ES-tro-jen): Hormone produced abundantly by the ovaries; it plays an important role in the menstrual cycle.

Estrogen replacement therapy (ERT): Controversial treatment of the physical changes of menopause by administering dosages of the hormone estrogen.

Ethnocentricity: The tendency of the members of one culture to assume that their values and norms of behavior are the "right" ones in comparison to other cultures.

Ethnography: The anthropological study of other cultures.

Ethnosexual: Referring to data concerning the sexual beliefs and customs of other cultures.

Excitement: The arousal phase of sex researchers William Masters and Virginia Johnson's four-phase model of the sexual response cycle.

Exhibitionism: Exposing the genitals to others for sexual pleasure.

External values: The belief systems available from one's society and culture.

Extramarital sex: Married person having sexual intercourse with someone other than her or his spouse; adultery.

Fallopian tubes: Structures that are connected to the uterus and lead the ovum from an ovary to the inner cavity of the uterus.

Fellatio: Oral stimulation of the penis.

Female condom: A lubricated polyurethane pouch that is inserted into the vagina for intercourse to collect semen and to help prevent disease transmission and pregnancy.

Female sexual arousal disorder: Difficulty for a woman in achieving sexual arousal.

Fetal alcohol syndrome (FAS): A condition in a fetus characterized by abnormal growth, neurological damage, and facial distortion caused by the mother's heavy alcohol consumption.

Fetishism (FET-a-shizm): Sexual arousal triggered by objects or materials not usually considered to be sexual.

Fetus: The term given to the embryo after 2 months of development in the womb.

Fibrous hymen: Condition in which the hymen is composed of unnaturally thick, tough tissue.

Follicles: Capsules of cells in which an ovum matures.

Follicle-stimulating hormone (FSH): Pituitary hormone that stimulates the ovaries or testes.

Foreplay: Sexual activities shared in early stages of sexual arousal, with the term implying that they are leading to a more intense, orgasm-oriented form of activity such as intercourse.

Foreskin: Fold of skin covering the penile glans; also called prepuce.

Frenulum (FREN-yu-lum): Thin, tightly-drawn fold of skin on the underside of the penile glans; it is highly sensitive.

Frotteurism: Gaining sexual gratification from anonymously pressing or rubbing one's genitals against others, usually in crowded settings.

G Spot: A vaginal area that some researchers feel is particularly sensitive to sexual stimulation.

Gamete intra-fallopian transfer (GIFT): Direct placement of ovum and concentrated sperm cells into the woman's fallopian tube to increase the chances of fertilization.

Gay: Refers to persons who have a predominantly same-gender sexual orientation and identity. More often applied to males.

Gender dysphoria (dis-FOR-ee-a): Some degree of discomfort with one's identity as male or female, and/or nonconformity to the norms considered appropriate for one's physical sex.

Gender identity: A person's inner experience of gender feelings of maleness, femaleness, or some ambivalent position between the two.

Gender identity disorder: The expression of gender identity in a way that is socially inconsistent with one's anatomical gender; may also be described as gender dysphoria.

Gender transportation: Gender dysphoria.

Gene therapy: Treatment of genetically caused disorders by substitution of healthy genes.

General sexual dysfunction: Difficulty for a woman in achieving sexual arousal.

Generalization: Application of specific learned responses to other, similar situations or experiences.

Genetic engineering: The modification of the gene structure of cells to change cellular functioning.

Genital herpes (HER-peez): Viral STD characterized by painful sores on the sex organs.

Genital warts: Small lesions on genital skin caused by papilloma virus; this STD increases later risks of certain malignancies.

Glans: Sensitive head of the female clitoris, visible between the upper folds of the minor lips; in the male, the sensitive head of the penis.

Gonadotropin releasing hormone (GnRH) (go-nad-a-TRO-pen): Hormone from the hypothalamus that stimulates the release of FSH and LH by the pituitary.

Gonads: Sex and reproductive glands, either testes or ovaries, that produce hormones and, eventually, reproductive cells (sperm or eggs).

Gonorrhea (gon-uh-REE-uh): Bacterial STD causing urethral pain and discharge in males; often no initial symptoms in females.

Granuloma inguinale (gran-ya-LOW-ma in-gwa-NAL-ee or NALE): STD characterized by ulcerations and granulations beginning in the groin and spreading to the buttocks and genitals.

Group marriage: Three or more people in a committed relationship who share sex with one another.

Hard-core pornography: Pornography that makes use of highly explicit depictions of sexual activity or shows lengthy scenes of genitals.

Hedonists: People who believe that pleasure is the highest good.

Hemophiliac (hee-mo-FIL-ee-ak): Someone with the hereditary blood defect hemophilia, primarily affecting males and characterized by difficulty in clotting.

Hepatitis B: Liver infection caused by a sexually transmitted virus (HBV).

Heterosexism: The assumption that people are, or should be, attracted to members of the other gender.

Heterosexual: Attractions or activities between males and females.

HIV: Human immunodeficiency virus.

Homophobia (ho-mo-PHO-bee-a): Strongly held negative attitudes and irrational fears relating to gay men and/or lesbians and their life-styles.

Homosexual: The term that is traditionally applied to romantic and sexual attractions and activities between members of the same gender.

Hookers: Street name for female prostitutes.

Hormone implants: Contraceptive method in which hormone-releasing plastic containers are surgically inserted under the skin.

Hormone pumping: A fertility-enhancing technique involving the injection of progesterone into a woman's system.

Hormone replacement therapy (HRT): Treatment of the physical changes of menopause by administering dosages of the hormones estrogen and progesterone.

Hot flash: A flushed, sweaty feeling in the skin caused by dilated blood vessels, often associated with menopause.

Human chorionic gonadotropin (HCG): A hormone detectable in the urine of a pregnant woman. Most home pregnancy tests work by detecting its presence in woman's urine.

Human immunodeficiency virus: The virus that initially attacks the human immune system, eventually causing AIDS.

Hustlers: Male street prostitutes.

H-Y antigen: A biochemical produced in an embryo when the Y chromosome is present; it causes fetal gonads to develop into testes.

Hymen: Membranous tissue that can cover part of the vaginal opening.

Hyperfemininity: A tendency to exaggerate characteristics typically associated with femininity.

Hypermasculinity: A tendency on the part of someone to exaggerate manly behaviors, sometimes called machismo.

Hypersexuality: Unusually high level of interest in and drive for sex.

Hypoactive sexual desire (HSD) disorder: Loss of interest and pleasure in what were formerly arousing sexual stimuli.

Hyposexuality: An especially low level of sexual interest and drive.

Hypospadias (hye-pa-SPADE-ee-as): Birth defect caused by incomplete closure of the urethra during fetal development.

Imperforate hymen: Lack of any openings in the hymen.

Impotence (IM-pa-tens): Difficulty achieving or maintaining erection of the penis.

In vitro fertilization (IVF): A process whereby the union of the sperm and egg occurs outside the mother's body.

Incest (IN-sest): Sexual activity between closely related family members.

Incest taboo: Cultural prohibitions against incest, typical of most societies.

Infertility: The inability to produce offspring.

Infibulation: Surgical procedure, performed in some cultures, that nearly seals the opening of the genitals.

Informed consent: The consent given by research subjects, indicating their willingness to participate in a study, after they are informed about the purpose of the study and how they will be asked to participate.

Inhibited sexual desire (ISD): Loss of interest and pleasure in formerly arousing sexual stimuli.

Internal values: Intrinsic values.

Intersexuality: A combination of female and male anatomical structures, so that the individual cannot be clearly defined as male or female.

Interstitial-cell-stimulating hormone (ICSH): Pituitary hormone that stimulates the testes to secrete testosterone; known as luteinizing hormone (LH) in females.

Intrauterine devices (IUDs): Birth control method involving the insertion of a small plastic device into the uterus.

Intrinsic values: The individualized beliefs and attitudes that a person develops by sorting through external values and personal needs.

Introitus (in-TROID-us): The outer opening of the vagina.

Kiddie porn: Term used to describe the distribution and sale of photographs and films of children or young teenagers engaging in some form of sexual activity.

Kleptomania: Extreme form of fetishism in which sexual arousal is generated by stealing.

Labor: Uterine contractions in a pregnant woman; an indication that the birth process is beginning.

Lactation: Production of milk by the milk glands of the breasts.

Lamaze method (la-MAHZ): A birthing process based on relaxation techniques practiced by the expectant mother; her partner coaches her throughout the birth.

Laparoscopy: Simpler procedure for tubal ligation, involving the insertion of a small fiber optic scope into the abdomen, through which the surgeon can see the fallopian tubes and close them off.

Laparotomy: Operation to perform a tubal ligation, or female sterilization, involving an abdominal incision.

Latency period: A stage in human development characterized, in Freud's theory, by little interest in or awareness of sexual feelings; recent research tends to suggest that latency does not exist.

Lesbian (LEZ-bee-un): Refers to females who have a predominantly same-gender sexual orientation and identity.

Libido (la-BEED-o or LIB-a-do): A term first used by Freud to define human sexual longing or sex drive.

Lumpectomy: Surgical removal of a breast lump, along with a small amount of surrounding tissue.

Luteinizing hormone (LH): Pituitary hormone that triggers ovulation in the ovaries and stimulates sperm production in the testes.

Lymphogranuloma venereum (LGV) (lim-foe-gran-yu-LOW-ma-va-NEAR-ee-um): Contagious STD caused by several strains of Chlamydia and marked by swelling and ulceration of lymph nodes in the groin.

Major lips: Two outer folds of skin covering the minor lips, clitoris, urethral opening, and vaginal opening.

Male condom: A sheath worn over the penis during intercourse that collects semen and helps prevent disease transmission and conception.

Male erectile disorder: Difficulty achieving or maintaining penile erection (impotence).

Mammography: Sensitive X-ray technique used to discover small breast tumors.

Marital rape: A woman being forced by her husband to have sex.

Masochist: The individual in a sadomasochistic sexual relationship who takes the submissive role.

Massage parlors: A business that provides massage treatment; places where women can be hired to perform sexual acts in addition to or in lieu of a massage.

Mastectomy: Surgical removal of all or part of a breast.

Ménage à trois (may-NAZH-ah-TRWAH): See Troilism.

Menarche (MEN-are-kee): Onset of menstruation at puberty.

Menopause (MEN-a-poz): Time in mid-life when menstruation ceases.

Menstrual cycle: The hormonal interactions that prepare a woman's body for possible pregnancy at roughly monthly intervals.

Menstruation (men-stru-AY-shun): Phase of menstrual cycle in which the inner uterine lining breaks down and sloughs off; the tissue, along with some blood, flows out through the vagina; also called the period.

Midwives: Medical professionals, both women and men, trained to assist with the birthing process.

Minor lips: Two inner folds of skin that join above the clitoris and extend along the sides of the vaginal and urethral openings.

Miscarriage: A natural termination of pregnancy.

Modeling theory: Suggests that people will copy behavior they view in pornography.

Molluscum contagiosum (ma-LUS-kum kan-taje-ee-O-sum): A skin disease transmitted by direct bodily contact, not necessarily sexual, that is characterized by eruptions on the skin that appear similar to whiteheads, with a hard seed-like core.

Monogamous: Sharing sexual relations with only one person.

Monorchidism (ma-NOR-ka-dizm): Presence of only one testis in the scrotum.

Mons: Cushion of fatty tissue located over the female's pubic bone.

Moral values: Beliefs associated with ethical issues, or rights and wrongs; they are often a part of sexual decision making.

Müllerian ducts (myul-EAR-ee-an): Embryonic structures that develop into female sexual and reproductive organs unless inhibited by male hormones.

Müllerian inhibiting substance: Hormone produced by fetal testes that prevents further development of female structures from the Müllerian ducts.

Multiplier effect: When biological and socioenvironmental factors build on one another more and more in the process of human development.

National Birth Control League: An organization founded in 1914 by Margaret Sanger to promote use of contraceptives.

Natural childbirth: A birthing process that encourages the mother to take control, thus minimizing medical intervention.

Necrophilia (nek-ro-FILL-ee-a): Having sexual activity with a dead body.

Nongonococcal urethritis (NGU) (non-gon-uh-KOK-ul yur-i-THRYT-us): Urethral infection or irritation in the male urethra caused by bacteria or local irritants.

Nonspecific uethritis (NSU) (yur-i-THRYT-us): Infection or irritation in the male urethra caused by bacteria or local irritants.

Normal: A subjective term used to describe sexual behaviors and orientations. Standards of normalcy are determined by social, cultural, and historical standards.

Normal asexuality: An absence or low level of sexual desire, considered normal for a particular person.

Normalization: Integration of mentally retarded persons into the social mainstream as much as possible.

Norplant implants: Contraceptive method in which hormone-releasing rubber cylinders are surgically inserted under the skin.

Nymphomania (nim-fa-MANE-ee-a): A term sometimes used to describe erotomania in women.

Obscenity: Depiction of sexual activity in a repulsive or disgusting manner.

Onanism (O-na-niz-um): A term sometimes used to describe masturbation, it comes from the biblical story of Onan, who practiced coitus interruptus and "spilled his seed on the ground."

Open-ended marriage: Marriage in which each partner in the primary relationship grants the other freedom to have emotional and sexual relationships with others.

Opportunistic infection: A disease resulting from lowered resistance of a weakened immune system.

Organizing effect: Manner in which hormones control patterns of early development in the body.

Orgasm (OR-gaz-em): A rush of pleasurable physical sensations and series of contractions associated with the release of sexual tension; usually accompanied by ejaculation in men.

Orgasmic release: Reversal of the vasocongestion and muscular tension of sexual arousal, triggered by orgasm.

Orgy (OR-jee): Group sex.

Osteoporosis (ah-stee-o-po-ROW-sus): Disease caused by loss of calcium from the bones in postmenopausal women, leading to brittle bones and stooped posture.

Ova: Egg cells produced in the ovary. One cell is an ovum; in reproduction, it is fertilized by a sperm cell.

Ovaries: Pair of female gonads, located in the abdominal cavity, that produce ova and female hormones.

Ovulation: Release of a mature ovum through the wall of an ovary.

Ovum donation: Use of an egg from another woman for conception, with the fertilized ovum then being implanted in the uterus of the woman wanting to become pregnant.

Oxytocin: Pituitary hormone that plays a role in lactation and in uterine contractions; brain secretions that act as natural tranquilizers and pain relievers.

Pansexual: Lacking highly specific sexual orientations or preferences; open to a range of sexual activities.

Pap smear: Medical test that examines a smear of cervical cells to detect any cellular abnormalities.

Paraphilia (pair-a-FIL-ee-a): A newer term used to describe sexual orientations and behaviors that vary from the norm; it means "a love beside."

Paraphiliac: A person who is drawn to one or more of the paraphilias.

Partial zona dissection (PZD): A technique used to increase the chances of fertilization by making a microscopic incision in the zona pellucida of an ovum. This creates a passageway through which sperm may enter the egg more easily.

Pedophilia (peed-a-FIL-ee-a): Another term for child sexual abuse.

Pelvic inflammatory disease (PID): A chronic internal infection associated with certain types of IUDs.

Penile strain gauge: A device placed on the penis to measure even subtle changes in its size due to sexual arousal.

Penis: Male sexual organ that can become erect when stimulated; it leads urine and sperm to the outside of the body.

Perimetrium: Outer covering of the uterus.

Perinatal: A term used to describe things related to pregnancy, birth, or the period immediately following the birth.

Perineal area (pair-a-NEE-al): The sensitive skin between the genitals and the anus.

Peyronie's disease (pay-ra-NEEZ): Development of fibrous tissue in spongy erectile columns within the penis.

Phimosis (fye-MOE-sus): A condition in which an abnormally long, tight foreskin on the penis does not retract easily.

Pimps: Men who have female prostitutes working for them.

Placenta (pla-SENT-a): The organ that unites the fetus to the mother by bringing their blood vessels closer together; it provides nourishment for and removes waste from the developing baby.

Plateau phase: The stable, leveled-off phase of sex researchers William Masters and Virginia Johnson's four-phase model of the sexual response cycle.

Plethysmograph: A laboratory measuring device that charts physiological changes over time. Attached to a penile strain gauge, it can chart changes in penis size. This is called penile plethysmography.

Polygamy: The practice, in some cultures, of being married to more than one spouse.

Pornography: Photographs, films, or literature intended to be sexually arousing through explicit depictions of sexual activity.

Potentiation: Establishment of stimuli early in life that form ranges of response for later in life.

Premature birth: A birth that takes place prior to the 36th week of pregnancy.

Premature ejaculation: Difficulty that some men experience in controlling the ejaculatory reflex, which results in rapid ejaculation.

Premenstrual syndrome (PMS): Symptoms of physical discomfort, moodiness, and emotional tensions that occur in some women for a few days prior to menstruation.

Preorgasmic: A term often applied to women who have not yet been able to reach orgasm during sexual response.

Prepuce (PREE-peus): In the female, tissue of the upper vulva that covers the clitoral shaft.

Priapism (pry-AE-pizm): Continual, undesired, and painful erection of the penis.

Primary dysfunction: A difficulty with sexual functioning that has always existed for a particular person.

Progesterone (pro-JES-ter-one): Ovarian hormone that causes the uterine lining to thicken.

Prolapse of the uterus: Weakening of the supportive ligaments of the uterus, causing it to protrude into the vagina.

Promiscuity (prah-mis-KIU-i-tee): Sharing casual sexual activity with many different partners.

Prostaglandin: Hormone-like chemical whose concentrations increase in a woman's body just prior to menstruation.

Prostaglandin- or saline-induced abortion: Used in the 16th–24th weeks of pregnancy, prostaglandins, salt solutions, or urea are injected into the amniotic sac, administered intravenously, or inserted into the vagina in suppository form to induce contractions and fetal delivery.

Prostate: Gland located beneath the urinary bladder in the male; it produces some of the secretions in semen.

Prostatitis (pras-tuh-TITE-us): Inflammation of the prostate gland.

Pseudohermaphrodite: A person who possesses either testes or ovaries in combination with some external genitals of the other sex.

Pseudonecrophilia: A fantasy about having sex with the dead.

Psychosexual development: Complex interaction of factors that form a person's sexual feelings, orientations, and patterns of behavior.

Psychosocial development: The cultural and social influences that help shape human sexual identity.

Puberty: Time of life when reproductive capacity develops and secondary sex characteristics appear.

Pubic lice: Small insects that can infect skin in the pubic area, causing a rash and severe itching.

Pubococcygeus (PC) muscle (pyub-o-kox-a-JEE-us): Part of the supporting musculature of the vagina that is involved in orgasmic response and over which a woman can exert some control.

Pyromania: Sexual arousal generated by setting fires.

Random sample: A representative group of the larger population that is the focus of a scientific poll or study in which care is taken to select participants without a pattern that might sway research results.

Rape trauma syndrome: The predictable sequence of reactions that a victim experiences following a rape.

Recreational adultery: Extramarital sex with a low level of emotional commitment and performed for fun and variety.

Recreational marriage: Recreational adultery.

Refractory period: Time following orgasm during which a man cannot be restimulated to orgasm.

Reinforcement: In conditioning theory, any influence that helps shape future behavior as a punishment or reward stimulus.

Resolution phase: The term for the return of a body to its unexcited state following orgasm.

Retarded ejaculation: A male who has never been able to reach an orgasm.

Retrograde ejaculation: Abnormal passage of semen into the urinary bladder at the time of ejaculation.

Retrovirus (RE-tro-vi-rus): A class of viruses that reproduces with the aid of the enzyme reverse transcriptase, which allows the virus to integrate its genetic code into that of the host cell, thus establishing permanent infection.

Rh factor: A blood-clotting protein agent whose presence or absence in the blood signals an Rh+ or Rh- person.

Rh incompatibility: Condition in which a blood protein of the infant is not the same as the mother's; antibodies formed in the mother can destroy red blood cells in the fetus.

Rho GAM: Medication administered to a mother to prevent formation of antibodies when the baby is Rh positive and its mother Rh negative.

Rhythm method: A natural method of birth control that depends on an awareness of the woman's menstrual/fertility cycle.

RU 486: A French abortion drug; a progesterone antagonist used as a postcoital contraceptive.

Rubber dam: Small square sheet of latex, such as that used in dental work, placed over the vulva, vagina, or anus to help prevent transmission of HIV during sexual activity.

Sadist: The individual in a sadomasochistic sexual relationship who takes the dominant role.

Sadomasochism (sade-o-MASS-o-kiz-um): Refers to sexual themes or activities involving bondage, pain, domination, or humiliation of one partner by the other.

Sample: A representative group of a population that is the focus of a scientific poll or study.

Satyriasis (sate-a-RYE-a-sus): A term sometimes used to describe erotomania in men.

Scabies (SKAY-beez): A skin disease caused by a mite that burrows under the skin to lay its eggs, causing redness and itching; transmitted by bodily contact that may or may not be sexual.

Scrotum (SKROTE-um): Pouch of skin in which the testes are contained.

Secondary dysfunction: A difficulty with sexual functioning that develops after some period of normal sexual functioning.

Selective reduction: The use of abortion techniques to reduce the number of fetuses when there are more than three in a pregnancy, thus increasing the chances of survival for the remaining fetuses.

Self-gratification: Giving oneself pleasure, as in masturbation; a term typically used today instead of more negative descriptors.

Self-pleasuring: Self-gratification; masturbation.

Semen (SEE-men): Mixture of fluids and sperm cells that is ejaculated through the penis.

Seminal vesicle (SEM-un-al): Gland at the end of each vas deferens that secretes a chemical that helps sperm to become mobile.

Seminiferous tubules (sem-a-NIF-a-rus): Tightly coiled tubules in the testes in which sperm cells are formed.

Sensate focus: Early phase of sex therapy treatment, in which the partners pleasure each other without employing direct stimulation of sex organs.

Sex addiction: Inability to regulate sexual behavior.

Sex therapist: Professional trained in the treatment of sexual dysfunctions.

Sexual aversion disorder: Avoidance of or exaggerated fears toward forms of sexual expression (sexual phobia).

Sexual differentiation: The developmental processes—biological, social, and psychological—that lead to different sexes or genders.

Sexual dysfunctions: Difficulties people have in achieving sexual arousal and in other stages of sexual response.

Sexual harassment: Unwanted sexual advances or coercion that can occur in the workplace or academic settings.

Sexual individuality: The unique set of sexual needs, orientations, fantasies, feelings, and activities that develops in each human being.

Sexual orientation: A person's erotic and emotional attraction toward and interest in members of one or both genders.

Sexual revolution: The changes in thinking about sexuality and sexual behavior in society that occurred in the 1960s and 1970s.

Sexual surrogates: Paid partners used during sex therapy with clients lacking their own partners; only rarely used today.

Sexually transmitted diseases (STDs): Various diseases transmitted by direct sexual contact.

Shaft: In the female, the longer body of the clitoris, containing erectile tissue; in the male, cylindrical base of penis that contains three columns of spongy tissue: two corpora cavernosa and a corpus spongiosum.

Shunga: Ancient scrolls used in Japan to instruct couples in sexual practices through the use of paintings.

Situational homosexuality: Deprivation homosexuality.

Skene's glands: Secretory cells located inside the female urethra.

Smegma: Thick, oily substance that may accumulate under the prepuce of the clitoris or penis.

Social constructionists: Those who believe that same-gender sexual orientation is at least partly the result of social and environmental factors.

Social learning theory: Suggests that human learning is influenced by observation of and identification with other people.

Social scripts: A complex set of learned responses to a particular situation that is formed by social influences.

Sodomy laws: Laws that, in some states, prohibit a variety of sexual behaviors, often described as deviate sexual intercourse. These laws are often enforced discriminatorily against particular groups, such as gay males.

Sonograms: Ultrasonic rays used to project a picture of internal structures such as the fetus; often used in conjunction with amniocentesis or fetal surgery.

Spectatoring: Term used by sex researchers William Masters and Virginia Johnson to describe self-consciousness and self-observation during sex.

Sperm: Reproductive cells produced in the testes; in fertilization, one sperm unites with an ovum.

Sperm banks: Centers that store frozen sperm for the purpose of artificial insemination.

Spermatocytes (sper-MAT-o-sites): Cells lining the seminiferous tubules from which sperm cells are produced.

Spermicidal jelly (cream): Sperm-killing chemical in a gel base or cream, used with other contraceptives such as diaphragms.

Spermicides: Chemicals that kill sperm; available as foams, creams, jellies, or implants in sponges or suppositories.

Sponge: A thick polyurethane disk that holds a spermicide and fits over the cervix to prevent conception.

Spontaneous abortion: Another term for miscarriage.

Staphylococcus aureus (staf-a-low-KAK-us): The bacteria that can cause toxic shock syndrome.

Statutory rape: A legal term used to indicate sexual activity when one partner is under the age of consent; in most states that age is 18.

STDs: Sexually transmitted diseases.

Sterilization: Rendering a person permanently incapable of conceiving, usually by interrupting passage of the egg or sperm.

Straight: Slang term for heterosexual.

Streetwalkers: Female prostitutes who work on the streets.

Suppositories: Contraceptive devices designed to distribute their spermicide by melting or foaming in the vagina.

Syndrome (SIN-drome): A group of signs or symptoms that occur together and characterize a given condition.

Syphilis (SIF-uh-lus): Sexually transmitted disease (STD) characterized by four stages, beginning with the appearance of a chancre.

Systematic desensitization: Step-by-step approaches to unlearning tension-producing behaviors and developing new behavior patterns.

Testes (TEST-ees): Pair of male gonads that produce sperm and male hormones.

Testicular cancer: Malignancy in the testis that may be detected by testicular self-examination.

Testicular failure: Lack of sperm and/or hormone production by the testes.

Testosterone (tes-TAS-ter-one): Major male hormone produced by the testes; it helps to produce male secondary sex characteristics.

Testosterone replacement therapy: Administering testosterone injections to increase sexual interest or potency in older men; not considered safe for routine use.

Theoretical failure rate: A measure of how often a birth control method can be expected to fail when used without error or technical problems.

Thrush: A disease caused by a fungus and characterized by white patches in the oral cavity.

Toucherism: Gaining sexual gratification from the touching of an unknown person's body, such as on the buttocks or breasts.

Toxic shock syndrome (TSS): An acute disease characterized by fever and sore throat, and caused by normal bacteria in the vagina that are activated if tampons or contraceptive devices such as diaphragms or sponges are left in for long periods of time.

Transgenderists: People who live in clothing and roles considered appropriate for the opposite sex for sustained periods of time.

Transsexuals: People who feel as though they should have the body of the opposite sex.

Transvestism: Dressing in clothes considered appropriate for the other gender.

Transvestite: An individual who dresses in clothing and adopts mannerisms considered appropriate for the opposite sex.

Trichomoniasis (trik-uh-ma-NEE-uh-sis): A vaginal infection caused by the *Trichomonas* organism.

Troilism (TROY-i-lizm): Sexual activity shared by three people.

True hermaphrodite: A person who has one testis and one ovary. External appearance may vary.

Tubal ligation: A surgical cutting and tying of the fallopian tubes to induce permanent female sterilization.

Umbilical cord: The tubelike tissues and blood vessels originating at the embryo's navel that connect it to the placenta.

Urethra (yu-REE-thrah): Tube that passes from the urinary bladder to the outside of the body.

Urethral opening: Opening through which urine passes to the outside of the body.

Urophilia: Sexual arousal connected with urine or urination.

Uterus (YUTE-a-rus): Muscular organ of the female reproductive system; a fertilized egg implants itself within the uterus.

Vacuum curettage (kyur-a-TAZH): A method of induced abortion performed with a suction pump.

Vagina (vu-JI-na): Muscular canal in the female that is responsive to sexual arousal; it receives semen during heterosexual intercourse for reproduction.

Vaginal atresia (a-TREE-zha): Birth defect in which the vagina is absent or closed.

Vaginal atrophy: Shrinking and deterioration of vaginal lining, usually the result of low estrogen levels during aging.

Vaginal fistulae (FISH-cha-lee or -lie): Abnormal channels that can develop between the vagina and other internal organs.

Vaginismus (vaj-uh-NIZ-mus): Involuntary spasm of the outer vaginal musculature, making penetration of the vagina difficult or impossible.

Vaginitis (vaj-uh-NITE-us): General term for inflammation of the vagina.

Values: System of beliefs with which people view life and make decisions, including their sexual decisions.

Variation: A less pejorative term to describe nonconformity to accepted norms.

Varicose veins: Overexpanded blood vessels; can occur in veins surrounding the vagina.

Vas deferens: Tube that leads sperm upward from each testis to the seminal vesicles.

Vasa efferentia: Larger tubes within the testes, into which sperm move after being produced in the seminiferous tubules.

Vasectomy (va-SEK-ta-mee or vay-ZEK-ta-mee): A surgical cutting and tying of the vas deferens to induce permanent male sterilization.

Villi: Fingerlike projections of the chorion; they form a major part of the placenta.

Viral hepatitis: Inflammation of the liver caused by a virus.

Voyeurism (VOYE-yu-rizm): Sexual gratification from viewing others who are nude or who are engaging in sexual activities.

Vulva: External sex organs of the female, including the mons, major and minor lips, clitoris, and opening of the vagina.

Vulvovaginitis: General term for inflammation of the vulva and/or vagina.

Western blot: The test used to verify the presence of HIV antibodies already detected by the ELISA.

Wolffian ducts (WOOL-fee-an): Embryonic structures that develop into male sexual and reproductive organs if male hormones are present.

Yeast infection: A type of vaginitis caused by an overgrowth of a fungus normally found in an inactive state in the vagina.

Zero population growth: The point at which the world's population would stabilize, and there would be no further increase in the number of people on Earth. Birthrate and death rate become essentially equal.

Zona pellucida (ZO-nah pe-LOO-sa-da): The transparent, outer membrane of an ovum.

Zoophilia (zoo-a-FILL-ee-a): Bestiality.

Zygote: An ovum that has been fertilized by a sperm.

SOURCES

Sexuality Today: The Human Perspective, Kelly, Gary F., Fifth Edition, 1995. Dushkin/McGraw-Hill, Guilford, CT 06437.

Pregnancy, Childbirth, and Parenting (Wellness), 1992. Dushkin/McGraw-Hill, Guilford, CT 06437.

mothers and, 67–70; myths about, 158; nature vs. nurture and, 67–70, 73–75
hostile environment sexual harassment, 183
human papilloma virus (HPV), 55, 57
hypothalamus, 218
hysterectomies, loss of sexual desire and, 64–66

I

ICSI (intracytoplasmic sperm injection), 189
implantable progestins, 115
implantation, abortion and, 203–204
impotence, 166; in India, 47–50; Viagra and, 47, 50, 51–54
in vitro fertilization. *See* IVF
India, 18; impotency and, 47–50
Infergen, 61
infertility, assisted reproductive technology and, 187–197
inhibitions, 165
injections, penile, and erectile dysfunction, 47, 50
interferon, 61
Internet, 216–217
intimacy, 103, 106; sex differences in use of language and, 89
intrauterine devices (IUDs), 115, 117
isolation, emotional, of gay and lesbian adolescents, 152, 154
IVF (in vitro fertilization), 187, 189, 192

K

Kama Sutra, 207
Kinesthesia, 217
Klindera, Kent, 58

L

language, sex differences in use of, and brain, 89–93
Larson, Reed, 133, 134, 136
Lasch, Christopher, 88
Lebed, Alexander, 13
lesbians, 151–160; gestational surrogacy and, 193–194. *See also* homosexuality
Leydig cell hypoplasia, 212
life expectancy, sex differences in, in Russia, 11
love, 41
Loveline, 144
Lucent Technologies, 72
Lyons, Henry J., 177, 179

M

mafiya, Russian, and sexual slavery, 174–176

marriage, 216; ending, and therapists, 97–102; gays and, 198; same-sex, 216
marriage counselors, 99
massage, 166
masturbation, 165, 166
McBeal, Ally, 29
McIlhaney, Joe, 56, 57, 58
medical schools, in future, 215
men, 32–35; education of, against rape, 172; improving, 94–96; pregnancy and, 128–130; in Russia, 8–13
Menninger, Karl, 98
menopause, loss of sexual desire and, 65
Meritor Savings Bank v. Vinson, 183
Messenger of God (MOG) model, of manhood, 34
methotrexate, 203
middle school, teachers and bisexual and homosexual issues in, 151–160
mind-blowing sex, 162–163
minipills, 114, 117
ministers, adultery and, 177–180
monasticism, celibacy and, 107–108
monogamy, 120
Montemayor, Roland, 133, 134, 136
"morning after" pill, 114, 200–202
Morning After, The (Roiphe), 30
mothers, homosexuality and, 67–70
multifetal pregnancy reduction, assisted reproductive technology and, 190–191

N

NARTH (National Association for Research and Therapy of Homosexuality), 74–75
National Middle School Association, 157
natural family planning, 115
nature vs. nurture: gender and, 211–214; homosexuality and, 67–70, 73–75
Nelson, Mariah Burton, 34
neocortex, 90
Nicolosi, Joseph, 74–75
no-dating policies, sexual harassment and, 181, 182–183
nonjudgmental atmosphere: about homosexuality, 158; about nudity, 145–147
nudity, children and, 145–147

O

odors, electronic enhancement of perception of, 217
oral contraceptives, 114, 117
oral sex, 120
orgasm, 166
Oskowitz, Selwyn, 187, 193, 195
ovum freezing, 196–197
oysters, 39

P

Paglia, Camille, 29, 54
Palac, Lisa, 29
parents, adolescents and, 131–137
Partner and Leader (PAL) model, of manhood, 34–35
Pauker, Susan, 190, 192, 195
peer support, for gay and lesbian youth, 159
pelvic inflammatory disease (PID), 57
penile implants, erectile dysfunction and, 47
pensions, same-sex couples and, 216
perimenopause, loss of sexual desire and, 65
periodic abstinence. *See* natural family planning
Peru, sterilization program in, 14–15
pharmacology, 216
pheromones, 217
phosphodiesterase type 5 (PDE5), 53
Pillard, Richard, 68
Pinsky, Drew, 144
Pittman, Frank, 99
Platform for Internet Content Selection (PICS), 216
pornography, 208–209
preachers, adultery and, 177–180
pregnancy, 166; fear of fatness and, 83; in lesbian adolescents, 153; men and, 128–130; sex during, 126–127, 129
premature ejaculation, 166
pressure, sense of, electronically intensified, 217
primary impotence, 48
privacy, 146, 147, 148–149, 216
progesterone, 105
Promiscuities (Wolf), 30
promiscuity, STDs and, 55–57, 59
prostitution: decriminalization of, 216; homosexual adolescents and, 153; sexual slavery and, 174–176

Q

quickies, 161–162
quid pro quo sexual harassment, 182

R

rape: control and, 171; male, 171–172
rapport talk, 91, 92–93
refugees, sexuality education and, 19–22
religion: adultery by ministers and, 177–180; sex and 207, 208–209
report talk, 91
reproductive policy, Catholic hospital systems and, 200, 202
reproductive technologies, 187–197
"residual trust," 101
Resurgent Angry Macho Man (RAMM), 34
Riot Grrrl movement; 30–31

role models, lack of, for gay and lesbian youth, 154
Roman Catholic Church: assistive reproductive technology and, 195; celibacy and, 108; hospital policies about birth control and, 200, 202
Russia, men in, 8–13
Russian *mafiya*, sexual slavery and, 174–176
Ryan, Kenneth, 193, 194–195

S

Sanger, Carol, 182–183, 185, 186
schools: gays and, 198–199; sexual harassment in, 184–185
secondary impotence, 48
self-defense, 173
self-esteem, low, 152
self-worth, teaching of, to children, 172
sensational sex, 162–163
Sensitive New Age Guy (SNAG), 34
sex, 40; fatigue and, 165; midlife, 164–167; myths about, 104–105; pregnancy and, 126–127, 129; religion and morality and, 207–210; three kinds of, 161–163
sex differences: gender and, 211–214; in use of language and brain, 89–93
sex therapy, 215–216
sex-reassignment surgery, 71
sexual abuse, 79, 85
sexual desire, 64–66, 103, 104, 166, 216
sexual dysfunction, 166, 216
sexual harassment, 181–186; hostile environment, 182; quid pro quo, 182
Sexual Personae (Paglia), 29
sexual slavery, Russian *mafiya* and, 174–176
sexuality education: conservative view of, 56–57, 58–59; liberal view of, 57–58, 59; refugees and, 19–22; STDs and, 56–59
sexuality transmitted diseases (STDs), 18, 55–59, 113, 116, 120, 153, 157, 191, 218
Shanken, Marvin, 33
sharing, 216

Smith, Shepherd, 55–56, 57
Sollee, Diane, 98, 99
sperm counts, 191
splenium, 90
sponge, contraceptive, 113–114, 116
sports, men and, 33–34
SRY, 90
Steinberg, Laurence, 132, 133, 134
sterilization, 116, 117; in Peru, 14–15
stress: impotence and, 49; loss of sexual desire and, 65
substance abuse: in homosexual youth, 153; sexually transmitted diseases and, 61
suicide, 152–153
syphilis, 55, 57

T

taboos, 171, 217
Talese, Gay, 54
Tannen, Deborah, 91–93
taste, sense of, electronically intensified, 217
Tavris, Carol, 90
teachers, bisexual and homosexual issue in middle school and, 151–160
teenagers. *See* adolescents
testosterone, 90, 218; gender differences and, 213–214
therapists, ending romantic relationships and, 97–102
Title VII, of Civil Rights Act of 1964, 182
To Be Real (Walker), 30
tobacco, 41
touch, sense of, electronically intensified, 217
touching: of self, in children, 145, 149; pleasures of, 105, 148
toxic shock syndrome, 113, 114
training, of middle school teachers about homosexual and bisexual issues, 151–160
Transformation Ministries, 73
transgenders, 71–72
trichomoniasis, 55, 57
trustworthiness, 101
tubal ligations, in Peru, 14–15

urethritis, 57

vacuum devices, erectile dysfunction and, 47
Vagina Monologues, The (Ensler), 26
vesico-vaginal fistulae (VVF), 21
Viagra, 47, 50, 51–54; health insurance and, 205–206
vibrators, 165
videotapes: for erotic instruction and entertainment, 216; sex, 165
virtual sex, 215–218
voyeurism, 216
vulvar self-exam, 43

W

Wagers, Tina, 131
Walker, Rebecca, 30
Webb, Susan, 183
Westheimer, Ruth, 54
Whitman, Walt, 159
wild yams, 39
Williams v. Saxbe, 182
withdrawal, 115
Wolf, Naomi, 30
Working Girl Can't Win, A (Garrison), 30
workplace, sexual harassment and, 181–186
Wurtzel, Elizabeth, 30

Y

yams, 39
yohimbe, 39
You Just Don't Understand: Women and Men in Conversation (Tannen), 91–93

Z

ZIFT (zygote intrafallopian transfer), 189

AE Article Review Form

We encourage you to photocopy and use this page as a tool to assess how the articles in **Annual Editions** expand on the information in your textbook. By reflecting on the articles you will gain enhanced text information. You can also access this useful form on a product's book support Web site at **http://www.dushkin.com/online/.**

NAME: _____ DATE: _____

TITLE AND NUMBER OF ARTICLE: _____

BRIEFLY STATE THE MAIN IDEA OF THIS ARTICLE: _____

LIST THREE IMPORTANT FACTS THAT THE AUTHOR USES TO SUPPORT THE MAIN IDEA:

WHAT INFORMATION OR IDEAS DISCUSSED IN THIS ARTICLE ARE ALSO DISCUSSED IN YOUR TEXTBOOK OR OTHER READINGS THAT YOU HAVE DONE? LIST THE TEXTBOOK CHAPTERS AND PAGE NUMBERS:

LIST ANY EXAMPLES OF BIAS OR FAULTY REASONING THAT YOU FOUND IN THE ARTICLE:

LIST ANY NEW TERMS/CONCEPTS THAT WERE DISCUSSED IN THE ARTICLE, AND WRITE A SHORT DEFINITION:

ANNUAL EDITIONS revisions depend on two major opinion sources: one is our Advisory Board, listed in the front of this volume, which works with us in scanning the thousands of articles published in the public press each year; the other is you—the person actually using the book. Please help us and the users of the next edition by completing the prepaid article rating form on this page and returning it to us. Thank you for your help!

ANNUAL EDITIONS: Human Sexuality 99/00

ARTICLE RATING FORM

Here is an opportunity for you to have direct input into the next revision of this volume. We would like you to rate each of the 46 articles listed below, using the following scale:

1. **Excellent: should definitely be retained**
2. **Above average: should probably be retained**
3. **Below average: should probably be deleted**
4. **Poor: should definitely be deleted**

Your ratings will play a vital part in the next revision. So please mail this prepaid form to us just as soon as you complete it. Thanks for your help!

RATING · ARTICLE

1. In Search of Russia's "Strong Sex"
2. Secrets and Lies
3. Another Planet
4. Where There Is No Village: Teaching about Sexuality in Crisis Situations
5. The World Made Flesh
6. Feminism: It's All about Me!
7. Men in Crisis
8. Recipes for Lust
9. Your Sexual Landscape
10. Impotency: Growing Malaise
11. The Viagra Craze
12. America: Awash in STDs
13. Hepatitis C: A Silent Killer
14. Not Tonight, Baby
15. What Made Troy Gay?
16. Trans across America
17. Can Gays 'Convert'?
18. The 1997 Body Image Survey Results
19. Brain Sex and the Language of Love
20. Men for Sale
21. Should You Leave?
22. 'It' Doesn't Just Happen: A Lifetime Prescription for Sizzling Sex
23. Celibate Passion: The Hidden Rewards of Quitting Sex
24. Protecting against Unintended Pregnancy: A Guide to Contraceptive Choices

RATING · ARTICLE

25. How Reliable Are Condoms?
26. Pregnant Pleasures
27. Six Dads Dish
28. The Cost of Children
29. Where'd You Learn That?
30. Age-by-Age Guide to Nudity
31. Raising Sexually Healthy Kids
32. Breaking through the Wall of Silence: Gay, Lesbian, and Bisexual Issues for Middle Level Educators
33. The 3 Kinds of Sex Happy Couples Need
34. The Joy of Midlife Sex
35. Healing the Scars
36. These Women Uncovered Sexual Slavery in America
37. When Preachers Prey
38. Sex @ Work: What Are the Rules?
39. The New Fertility
40. Battling Backlash
41. Blocking Women's Health Care
42. The Last Abortion: How Science Could Silence the Debate
43. Is Sex a Necessity?
44. Sex (American Style)
45. The Gender Blur
46. Sex in the Future: Virtuous and Virtual?

We Want Your Advice

(Continued on next page)

NO POSTAGE
NECESSARY
IF MAILED
IN THE
UNITED STATE

BUSINESS REPLY MAIL
FIRST-CLASS MAIL PERMIT NO. 84 GUILFORD CT

POSTAGE WILL BE PAID BY ADDRESSEE

Dushkin/McGraw-Hill
Sluice Dock
Guilford, CT 06437-9989

ABOUT YOU

Name   Date
_____   _____

Are you a teacher? ☐ A student? ☐
Your school's name
_____

Department
_____

Address   City   State   Zip
_____

School telephone #
_____

YOUR COMMENTS ARE IMPORTANT TO US !

Please fill in the following information:
For which course did you use this book?
_____

Did you use a text with this *ANNUAL EDITION*? ☐ yes ☐ no
What was the title of the text?
_____

What are your general reactions to the *Annual Editions* concept?
_____

Have you read any particular articles recently that you think should be included in the next edition?
_____

Are there any articles you feel should be replaced in the next edition? Why?
_____

Are there any World Wide Web sites you feel should be included in the next edition? Please annotate.
_____

May we contact you for editorial input? ☐ yes ☐ no
May we quote your comments? ☐ yes ☐ no